Johannes von Gumpach

The treaty-rights of the foreign merchant, and the transit-system, in China supported throughout by official documents, partly unpublished

Johannes von Gumpach

The treaty-rights of the foreign merchant, and the transit-system, in China supported throughout by official documents, partly unpublished

ISBN/EAN: 9783337208189

Printed in Europe, USA, Canada, Australia, Japan

Cover: Foto ©Suzi / pixelio.de

More available books at **www.hansebooks.com**

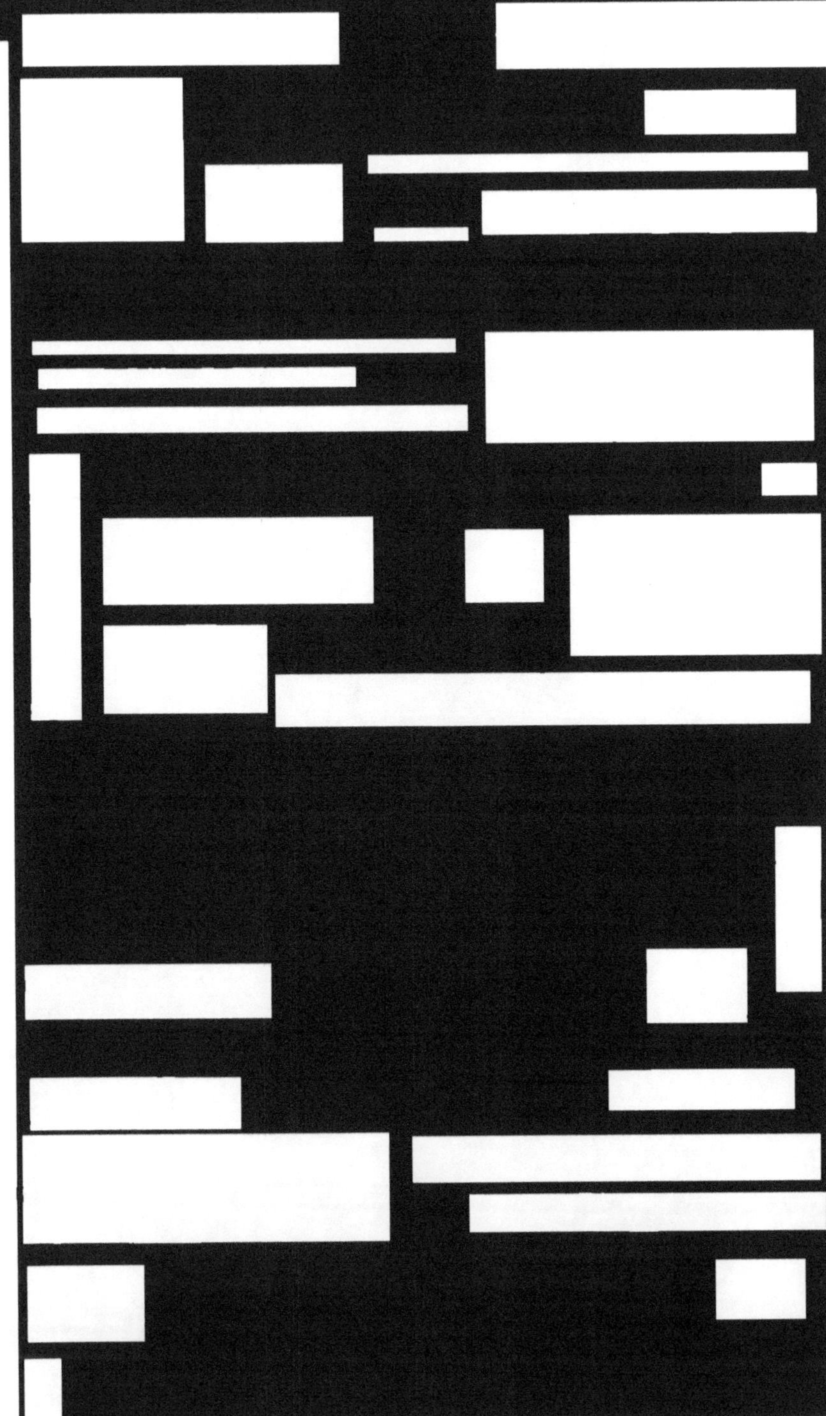

CONTENTS:

PREFACE .... p. ix.

I.

INTRODUCTORY REMARKS.

Political bearing of the Subject under discussion—Non-observance of Treaty-stipulations by the Chinese Government—Sir Frederick Bruce's protestations and warnings—Prince Kung's recriminations—Sarcastic and offensive tone of the Tsung-li Ya-mên's despatches—The Hon. J. Ross Browne and Dr. Williams on Chinese obstructiveness—Mr. Wade on the disregard of ART. xxviii of the Treaty of Tientsin—The *le-kin*—Apologists for Chinese "poverty" and "feebleness"—True position of the Tsung-li Ya-mên—Provincial Authorities and "the Central Government"—Tatar policy of political and commercial isolation .... p. 3.

II.

THE TRANSIT-QUESTION.

Vital Importance of the Transit-question—Public attention recalled to it by a "communicated" article in the *North-China Herald*—Motives for the appearance of the paper—Its author—The paper reproduced—Mr. Wade's Memorandum of December, 1868—His views relative to the Transit-question transcribed—Their adoption by Her Majesty's Government—The Board of Trade to the Foreign Office—Stand-point taken up by the Tsung-li Ya-mên at the Revision of the Treaty of Tientsin—New Regulations proposed by the Ya-men—Concurrence of authorities in favour of the "*in transitu*" theory—Differing views of the Merchants—Latest opinion of Sir Rutherford Alcock .... p. 14.

III.

PRELIMINARY INQUIRIES.

What is to be understood by the "Transit-System" in China?—Usual charges leviable on inland traffic in China—Peculiarities of the

Chinese system of financial Administration—The Sacred Edict on the payment of duties—Practice and theory—Fiscal corruption in China—Chinese sources of revenue—Effects of the first English war and the Tai-ping rebellion—Introduction of the *le-kin* as a war-tax—Rapid extension of the new impost—Barriers and Custom-houses—Chinese "squeezing"—The Peking Board of Revenue and the *le-kin*—The *chow-fang* tax—Historical sketch of its introduction—Objects for which the *le-kin* was professedly imposed—Those objects have ceased to exist—Abolition of the tax proposed to the Tsung-li Ya-mên and declined—Causes of the failure of the English Revision of the Treaty of Tientsin—Sir Rutherford Alcock's diplomatic incapacity—Real purposes, to which the *le-kin* is devoted .... p. 47.

IV.

TREATY RIGHTS OF THE BRITISH MERCHANT.

The English Treaties of Nanking and Tientsin—Main object of the war of 1812—ART. x of the Treaty of Nanking—The Hongkong Declaration—The Supplementary Treaty of Hoomun-Chae—Commercial advantages secured by the Treaty of Nanking—ART. ix, xiii, xxiv, xxviii, and LIV of the English Treaty of Tientsin—RULES v, vii, and viii of the Supplementary Agreement of Shanghai—ART. viii of the English Convention of Peking—ART. xxiii and xxvii of the French Treaty of Tientsin—ART. iii and iv of the Russian Treaty of Tientsin—ART. iv, v and vii of the Russian Convention of Peking—Main object of the war of 1859-60—The principle of free transit through China upheld in the English Treaty of Tientsin, but swerved from in the subsequent Trade Rules—Errors committed in framing the Trade Rules—Summary of the Provisions of the Treaty of Tientsin relative to Trade—Real meaning of the terms "transit-certificate" and "transit-dues"—Lord Elgin on the commuted Transit-dues tax—The optional clause of ART. xxviii of the Treaty of Tientsin abrogated by RULE vii of the Shanghai Agreement—Confusion of views on the subject—Commutation-tax includes *le-kin* and all other inland charges whatsoever—No taxes on Foreign Commerce lawfully leviable in China, save those agreed upon by Treaty—Illegal system of taxation resorted to by the Chinese Government—Liability of the Chinese Government to

British demands for compensation, and of Chinese Customs-officials to judicial punishment—Payment of Commutation-tax exempts *merchandize*, on which it is paid, irrespective of ownership—Conclusive evidence adduced to this effect—Testimony of Lord Elgin, the Tsung-li Ya-mên, and the highest native Provincial Authorities—Perfidy of the Chinese Government..............................p. 72.

V.

EXAMINATION OF AUTHORITATIVE VIEWS.

Position of the Foreign Inspector-General in the Chinese Customs' Service—Value to be attached to his opinions—Obstructive tendency of his views illustrated—The "cream" of the Transit-System—The Inspector-General's mis-statements, duplicity of sight, and logical inconsistency—Prince Kung's "sincerity"—The Tsung-li Ya-mên's newly proposed Regulations discussed—Sir R. Alcock's opinions in 1868 and 1870 contrasted—His ill-judgment and bad taste—A novel doctrine—What gives validity to Chinese State-papers—The Great Imperial Seal and the Stamp, by the Tsung-li Ya-mên attached to International Treaties—"The Emperor's gem" and Mr. Wade—Mr. Wade's errors of translation—Unsatisfactory diplomatic state of our Treaty-relations with China—Sir R. Alcock's ignorance of Chinese State affairs—Mr. Wade's Memorandum of 1868 characterised—His inaccuracies and self-contradictions—Mr. Wade, the *le-kin* tax, and the Foreign Customs—His pro-Chinese bias and warm apology for the *le-kin*—His two-sided exaggerations—Amount of Chinese Revenue—"The Central Government" wanting, not in the power, but in the will to abrogate the *le-kin*—Prince Kung's "timidity"—His Imperial Highness in disgrace—Mr. Wade's strange fiscal notions—Untenable character of the "*in transitu*" theory demonstrated—Its first originator—The theory refuted—Pernicious doctrines involved in Mr. Wade's views—The Lords of the Committee of the Privy Council for Trade misled by Mr. Wade—Mr. Wade's impressions and Lord Elgin's written statements—Alleged right of the Chinese Government to tax *ad libitum* foreign merchandize, which has paid the Commutation-dues, after passing into Chinese possession—Confusion of ideas on the subject—Sir Frederick Bruce's views—Mr. Wade's key-note to the whole question—Its false and discordant sound—The real nature of

the problem stated—Justice *versus* Expediency—Two unholy wars against China—Sinful policy of Lord Palmerston and atoning policy of the Right Hon. W. E. Gladstone .... p. 113.

VI.

Practical Working of the Transit-System.

Alleged abuse of Treaty-provisions on the part of Foreign merchants—Sale of Transit-certificates, in 1866, at Ningpo—The Commissioner of Customs' unfair statement of the case—The Foreign Custom-house responsible for the practice of open infringement of Customs' rules—What became of a sum, exceeding £5,000, paid, in 1866, by way of Commutation-dues at Ningpo?—What of a sum total of about £70,000 of similar origin?—Faulty arithmetic of the Inspector-General—Errors in Customs' Returns—Fines and Confiscations—State of the Wusung Bar—The Chinese Customs, Mr. Wade, and the British Merchant—Mr. Wade's groundless alarm—Tendency of British Representatives in Peking to favour the Chinese—History of the confiscation-case of Messrs. Bower & Hanbury—Illegality of the confiscation proved—How the British Merchant in China is protected by the British Minister—The Sun-yang claims of Messrs. Jardine, Matheson & Co.—Disadvantages, under which foreign merchants are placed touching the payment of *le-kin*—The Tsung-li Ya-mên's "own Hart"—First-fruits of Mr. Hart's appointment—The Ya-mên proposes new regulations respecting trade on the river Yangtsze, the Transit-System, and the Coast-Trade—Sir Frederick Bruce's Notification of his "Revised Provisional Regulations for British Trade in the Yangtsze River," and "Regulations (sanctioned by Mr. Bruce) regarding Transit-Dues, Exemption Certificates, and Coast-Trade Duties"—Promulgation of corresponding documents by the Tsung-li Ya-mên—Offensive style of the latter—Sir Frederick Bruce represented as in the Service of China—Translation of the Ya-mên's proposed "Five Regulations respecting War-Taxes payable at inland stations, Coast-Trade Duties, and Exemption Certificates" apparently withheld from the knowledge of Her Majesty's Government—Essential discrepancies between the English text of Sir Frederick Bruce's "Regulations regarding Transit-Dues," etc., and Mr. Wade's Chinese version, as officially published by the Tsung-li Ya-mên—The latter grants to China the unrestricted im-

position of *le-kin*—Both the English text and the Chinese version violate Treaty-provisions and mislead the mercantile community—Who is responsible?—Imperative necessity for an explanation on Mr. Wade's part—"T'u's five Rules"—Attempt, made by the Native Intendant, and Foreign Commissioner, of Customs at Shanghai, to place the Transit-System on a new basis—Tsêng Kwo-fan's despatch of Nov. 5, 1868, to the Shanghai Customs Authorities ignored, and his instructions disobeyed—Responsibility incurred by the Inspector-General and the Shanghai Commissioner of Customs —"A new and valuable Chinese Concession"—The Transit-dues question and the local Press...p. 224.

VII.

Illegal Taxation.

Tabular view of the amount of illegal taxation and total amount of imposts, levied on Foreign Trade, during the year 1870, by the Chinese Government—Complementary "Stationary" trade taxes—Produce taxes—Comparison of the Tabular view with the similar Table, published in 1869, by the Shanghai Commissioner of Customs, Mr. Dick—The latter, including only a portion of the native charges known to be levied, designed to mislead—Taxes on Opium and Cotton Goods—Principle of Chinese illegal Taxation—Taxes on Woollen Goods, Metals and sundry articles of importation—Taxes on Silk, Tea, and sundry articles of exportation—General remarks—The Commissioner of Customs at Kiukiang on *le-kin*—Unreliability of his special data—Examination of details, on which Mr. Dick's Table is based—His Table officially admitted to be restricted to inland charges, collected at, or near, the ports—Its arithmetical errors and incongruities—Object of its publication—Alleged "loss to Chinese Revenue by Hongkong being a free port" —Mr. Dick's "Hongkong Claims"—Smuggling in Opium—Inefficiency of the Foreign and Native Customs-Service—Corruption of Chinese officials—India *versus* China—The British Possession of Victoria a thorn in Mr. Dick's side—His "Hongkong Claims" examined—They vanish into air—Mr. Dick defeats his own arguments—The Chinese Customs-tariff compared with the tariffs of some other countries—Opium not taxed more heavily in China, than are imports generally—Defence of the Opium trade—Opium,

as a stimulant, peculiarly adapted to the physical constitution of the Chinese—Its use and abuse—Deceptive and hypocritical character of the Tsung-li Ya-mên's Opium Memorial—The Memorial essentially the composition of a foreigner—Its leading motive—The growth of the poppy in India a legitimate branch of agricultural industry—Duty of Her Majesty's Government to protect it—Annual amount of illegal taxation to which Foreign Trade is subject in China—The Tonnage-dues—The Inspector-General's anticipated Memorandum on the subject—Systematic fabrication of Chinese public accounts—Differential Coast-trade duties—They constitute an indirect tax, imposed contrary to Treaty and justice, on foreign shipping—Mr. Dick's threatened "Withdrawal of the Department from its connection with the Home trade"—Amount of imposts, inclusive of coast-trade dues and excess of export duties, by the Chinese Government annually levied on Foreign Trade in open and systematic violation of Treaty-stipulations—Share (at the present time exceeding £3,000,000 a year) falling upon British Trade—Estimate of the accumulated debt, thus surreptitiously contracted by China towards England since the Treaty of Nanking......p. 306.

VIII.

CONCLUSION.

Law, Morality, and Expediency—The principle of "Free Transit through China" shown to rest on both human law and divine—War a necessary factor of Progress, Development, and Civilisation in the economy of native and human destiny—The morality of the Opium trade, and the justice of the stipulations of the Treaty of Tientsin vindicated—Politico-social state of England—Conflict between Labour and Capital—Necessity of finding wider employment for home Labour—Obstructive policy of the Tsung-li Ya-mên—Expansibility of the China Trade—Actual state of affairs—Warning to the Manchu Government..............................p. 401.

INDEX..p. 1.

NOTE.

THE following work was commenced by the Baron VON GUMPACH some two or three years ago, and came into my hands for publication last March. For some months it was printed under the personal supervision of the author himself; but his sudden death on the 31st July left the completion of his task to me, and I have no choice but to fulfil the responsibility thus devolving upon my shoulders. I wish however most distinctly to state that my connection with the present volume is of a purely commercial nature. In accepting the position of editor, I entirely repudiate that of sponsor; I commit myself to no single theory or statement put forward by the writer; nor do I in any way endorse the spirit of insinuation which underlies the whole. It is undeniable that the Baron VON GUMPACH was not only a man of brilliant parts, but endowed with a capacity for labour and research that was truly marvellous. Heterodox to the verge of monomania on many scientific theories of universal acceptation, the works he has left behind him all bear the impress of an unusually powerful but badly-balanced mind. Untrammelled by the slightest fear of ridicule or retaliation,—higher considerations being quite beside the mark—his attacks on existing institutions were fearless and virulent, and might have led to real enquiry and reform had they not been so highly coloured with individual bias. The present work however deals with facts, and facts the importance of which it would be impolitic to ignore. It is of the highest moment that the position of British subjects in China should be clearly defined, and the trading rights and privileges secured to them by Treaty placed in a clear and proper light. Had the spirit of our Treaties been enforced by our Ministers with the same energy and determination with which the letter of them was dictated by the Plenipotentiaries who drew them up, no uncertainty and indecision would ever have prevailed; the Chinese officials would have submitted, as none can do better, to a *force majeure*, the people would have known and felt the hand of the foreigner whose arms they had learnt to respect, the clear understanding arrived at upon the conclusion of peace at Tientsin would have been maintained, and foreign goods and foreign enterprise would have penetrated from one end of the Empire to the other. Instead however of this clear enforcement of our prerogatives, our Ministers have tacitly allowed the Chinese authorities to annul the spirit and even to encroach upon the letter of our hard-earned Treaty rights. The events of the past few months, too, have exposed much misapprehension on the part of foreigners as to the true import of many of the provisions contained in the Treaty of Tientsin; misapprehensions which have arisen partly from sheer apathy on the part of those most interested, and partly from the loose and uncertain phraseology employed in the Treaty itself. Moreover, the present moment is eminently opportune for the free and unbiassed discussion of every point bearing upon our rights in China. We are now passing through a period in the history of our relations with the Middle Kingdom which has attracted unusual attention from all quarters, fraught with results which cannot fail to exercise a powerful influence upon those relations in the future; and the position of affairs in the North is at present both anomalous and critical. We are in a transition-state. The first Chinese Ambassador to England has recently been appointed; the relative position of the two Empires has received a severe shock, and the shock has been immediately followed by an apparent, strong reaction. The time is rapidly approaching when China will, by force of circumstances, emerge from the cloud of exclusiveness and conservatism under which she has been so long obscured, and which has been so stern a barrier in her path of progress; the oldest people upon the face of the Earth will be at last compelled to take their place in what is euphemistically called the comity of nations, and to participate in, and contribute to, the universal weal. In view therefore of the growing importance of all questions bearing upon our Treaty rights in China, I feel less reluctance than I otherwise should, in discharging my present function. The Baron VON GUMPACH'S latest book *may* furnish some quota, in the way of suggestion, to the general enlightenment; I therefore publish it as it stands, upon its merits.

FREDERIC H. BALFOUR.

Office of the *Celestial Empire*,
Shanghai, October, 1875.

significance. Actual experience shows, that the trade in our staple-manufactures alone is susceptible of an expansion to the annual value of from sixty to eighty million pounds sterling, provided that the principle of free transit through the Interior be honestly carried out, and the mineral resources of the country be sufficiently developed to keep the balance of trade in a state of due equilibrium. The great expectations, in this sense entertained at the conclusion of the last war, were disappointed, not because they rested on an erroneous foundation, but solely because their realisation has been frustrated by the obstructive policy of the Manchu Government, more or less countenanced by the Representatives of England in Peking, and actively supported by the foreign *employés* of the Tsung-li Ya-mên.

The proofs to this effect will, no doubt, be accepted without surprise by many. Few readers will be prepared to learn that the amount of illegal taxation, with which, in open and systematic defiance of existing Treaties, British trade is, and for years past has been, burdened in China, now reaches a yearly total of six million pounds sterling; that the major portion of this amount is expended by the Chinese Government,—seemingly more than ever bent, not only on a return to the old system of political and commercial isolation, but on the expulsion of "the outer barbarian" from "the bayonet-ploughed soil of Cathay," as China has been designated—for purposes of military armaments, or is being accumulated, as a reserve fund; and that the aggregate sum, which thus gradually and at a progressive rate has been levied by China upon British trade since the conclusion of the Treaty at Nanking, may be estimated at some thirty million pounds sterling.

In connection with these facts, the author would call attention to certain remarkable discrepancies, which there exist in that important document, the "Regulations sanctioned by Mr. (subsequently Sir Frederick) Bruce (then Her Majesty's Minister Plenipotentiary and Chief Superintendent of British Trade in China) regarding Transit Dues, Exemption Certificates, and Coast-Trade Duties," between the official English text, and its official Chinese version made, it has to be concluded, by the then Chinese Secretary to the British Legation in Peking. In the English text, which was, in 1861, transmitted by the British Minister to Her Majesty's Government and publicly notified, at Shanghai, to the British mercantile community in China for their guidance, there occurs no mention of *li-kin* or war-taxes. In the Chinese version, which, at the same time, was by the Tsung-li Ya-mên communicated to the Chinese Provincial Authorities for their guidançe, the unrestricted right of levying such *li-kin* or war-taxes upon British trade, is in explicit terms conceded to the Chinese Government,—apparently without the cognizance and sanction of Her Majesty's Government. But it is by means of these very imposts, that the Chinese Government has inflicted, and continues to inflict, on the Commerce of England that onerous amount of illegal taxation, just referred to.

An apology for, and a discourse in support of the maintenance of, this taxation, both as remarkable as the discrepancy, on the sole ground of which the impost rests,—which were submitted to the consideration of Her Majesty's Government by His Excellency the present Representative of England at Peking, Thos. Francis Wade, Esq., C.B., in an official Memorandum, dated December, 1868, add much to the gravity of a question, which seems to the author so deeply to affect both the interests of British commerce and the character of British diplomacy, as to present a case of positive necessity for Parliamentary inquiry.

It is not that the Chinese Government, being unaware of the true state of matters, had on its own part acted in good faith respecting the *li-kin* clause. Proofs will be found below, that the Tsung-li Ya-mên and the highest Provincial Authorities from first to last distinctly admit the "war-tax" to be imposed on foreign commerce in violation of existing Treaty-provisions. Nor is it the case, as is generally asserted and believed, that this impost weighs equally heavy on the native trade. Comparatively speaking, it hardly touches any branch of Chinese inland traffic, save those branches which are carried on in foreign imports, and native produce destined for exportation to foreign parts. The *li-kin,* in fact, was introduced, at the termination of the war of 1842, on the Chinese principle of paying the outer barbarian with his own money, and for the purpose of obstructing foreign trade to the utmost by taxing it to the utmost.

Notice may here also be directed to a document bearing upon the same subject, and which originated almost simultaneously with the Memorandum referred to. It was printed, a year later, in December, 1869, by order of the Foreign Inspectorate-General of Chinese Maritime Customs, at the Shanghai Customs' Press; but has become little known in "Far Cathay." This official pamphlet, calculated to mislead the European reader, served as the basis for another official essay, published by the same authority in the same year, with the object of showing, that the annual total "Excess of taxes collected by the Chinese Authorities over Treaty-rates" amounted, in reality and considering a yearly loss of Taels 300,000, which, it is asserted, the Chinese Government experiences owing to Hongkong a free port, to barely half a million pounds sterling, and the aggregate of the imposts, to which foreign commerce is subject in China, to twelve per cent. *ad valorem* only. In the sequel, positive proof will be offered, that the former now amounts annually to twenty-two and a half per cent., the latter to thirty per cent., *ad valorem*.

In unison with this system of overburdensome inland taxation, the author would invite further attention to the new Regulations touching Foreign trade with the Interior of China, by the Tsung-li Ya-mên in December, 1872, submitted to the Representatives of Foreign Powers in Peking, and of which a translation, from an authentic copy of the Chinese text, is here for the first time presented to the public. The document, held a diplomatic secret by the Foreign Ministers, is an important one, inasmuch as it deliberately proposes, by means of Chinese Rules of Trade to place the commercial relations of England with this country, as established by the Treaties of Nanking and Tientsin, on a different basis; whilst it, at the same time, forcibly shows, not only that the commercial obstructiveness of the Chinese Government rests on a principle of policy, but that the settled aim of that policy is to close the inland marts of the Ta-Ching Empire against all direct foreign trade and, so far as present circumstances will permit, against foreign trade generally. The Regulations, under instructions from the Tsung-li Yamen, were framed conjointly by the Foreign Inspector-General, and the Tautai of Shanghai as native Commissioner, of Chinese Maritime Customs; and one of the objects being to legalise both the illegal inland taxes themselves, and, by stealth, their amount: it thus came to pass that this amount, in the form of "ten times the half-duty," was introduced into the document in question, placing upon the evidence as to the height to which, from one-tenth per cent in 1844, the *le-kin* tax has been gradually raised, evidence, previously and independently collected by the author, the conclusive official seal.

That Her Majesty's Chief Superintendent of British Trade in

China should, under such circumstances, have deemed it his duty to withhold from the mercantile community in China a well considered and matured plan of the Chinese Government, so vitally affecting, in the future even more than in the present, the vast interests of British merchants, trading with this country on their faith in existing Treaties, appears almost a contradiction in terms, and is well calculated to suggest matter for grave consideration to those whose fortunes are at stake.

There is, amidst a variety of more or less important subjects touched upon in the following pages, only one more point, to which the author desires to advert in this place. The foreign and commercial policy of the late Administration of the Right Hon. W. E. Gladstone, and the action of the Representatives of England in Peking, have at the same time imperilled our trade, and brought the country to the verge of another war with China. Whether it be still possible to avoid such a war by the adoption of a different policy, the display of a strong naval force in Chinese waters, the insisting on the strict fulfilment of Treaty-obligations, and the firm pressure of the right of free transit through the length and breadth of the Ta-Ching Dominions, in connection with the immediate abrogation of the *le-kin* tax upon foreign trade, may be a question open to a difference of opinion. The experiment, more especially in view of the actual political state of Europe appears not undeserving of a trial. Under any circumstances, Her Majesty's present Administration, unless they be prepared either to carry on a costly and inefficacious armed contest with China every decennium, or else to allow the Manchu Government to gradually repulse British trade, British merchants, and British subjects from the soil of Cathay, will have to contemplate the early contingency of a new war with that Government,—a war which, once that it is actually forced upon England, should be undertaken and carried through with the clearly defined object of precluding the necessity for further wars, and of regulating the future of China accordingly.

SHANGHAI, May, 1875.

I.

INTRODUCTORY REMARKS.

Political bearing of the subject under discussion—Non-observance of Treaty-stipulations by the Chinese Government—Sir Frederick Bruce's protestations and warnings—Prince Kung's recriminations—Sarcastic and offensive tone of the Tsung-li Ya-mên's despatches—The Hon. J. Ross Browne and Dr. Williams on Chinese obstructiveness—Mr. Wade on the diregard of ART. xxviii of the Treaty of Tientsin—The *le-kin*—Apologists for Chinese "poverty" and "feebleness"—The position of the Tsung-li Ya-mên—Provincial Authorities and "the Central Government"—Tatar policy of political and commercial isolation.

THERE are few subjects, not excluding the Audience question,* of greater moment to the best interests of China and the maintenance of friendly relations between the Peking Government and Western Powers, than is a satisfactory settlement of the so-called *Transit-system*, involving, as it does, the effective opening up of the Ta-Ching dominions to foreign commerce, in accordance with existing treaties. More than once Sir Frederick Bruce, who represented the British Government at Peking from 1860 to 1865, had to call the attention of the Tsung-li Ya-mên to a violation of

* The audience question is commonly understood to have been finally solved, and in a very satisfactory manner, too, by the so-called "audience" which, on Sunday, the 29th June, 1873, was "granted to the Foreign Ministers resident in Peking, by the Emperor of China." Such, however is far from being the case. The character, import, and tendency of that singular formality have been entirely misrepresented to the Western public. It constitutes a complete triumph of Chinese, over European, diplomacy: and, in my humble opinion, the Representatives of Foreign Powers, in acceding to the terms of studied insult and political dependence, on which they were permitted to appear in the distant presence of "the One Vice-gerent of Heaven and Autocrator of the Earth," have on this occasion betrayed the first duty they owed to their Sovereigns and their Countries, and incurred a grave responsibility.

the transit-provisions of those treaties as a matter of the highest importance to "the peace of the Empire in its external relations," and the necessity of doing away with a system of deliberate obstruction, which might ultimately force the British Government to adopt proceedings "inconsistent with amicable relations, and which had proved the source of disaster to China before;" and in his despatch to Prince Kung, as President of the Tsung-li Ya-mên, of November 9th, 1868, Sir Rutherford Alcock, Sir Frederick Bruce's successor as British Minister at "the Northern Capital," expressed himself in these terms:—"I still hope Your Imperial Highness and the Ministers of the Ya-mên collectively, will see that the time has arrived for removing all just cause of complaint and placing the trading-relations of British subjects in the Interior on a footing of security and immunity from illegal taxation and obstruction, without which the Treaty itself becomes a dead letter. This day eight years ago Lord Elgin and the army that accompanied him left the gates of Peking, after having secured the ratification of the Treaty of Tientsin, and, in negotiation with Your Imperial Highness, a further convention that, in the terms of Your proclamation then issued, 'Hereafter the weapons of war may for ever be laid aside, and all should join together in the work of promoting peace,' ....† and I will not allow myself to think that there can be any ultimate failure, whatever difficulties may have been ex-

† Sir R. Alcock appears not to have been aware that the passage, marked by Prince Kung, was repeated from the proclamation of the notorious Yeh, Governor-General of the Two Kuang, on the occasion of the signing of the Supplementary Treaty of Hoomun-Chae, informing the Chinese of the conclusion of the Treaty of *perpetual* Peace and Friendship of Nanking. His Imperial Highness, in promulgating, a few years subsequently, the notification of another Treaty of *perpetual* Peace and Friendship, indulges in a humor, which takes delight in intensifying the "solemnity" of proclaiming such a peace with "the outer barbarian," by an admixture of that broad and cynical sarcasm peculiar to him.

perienced hitherto in coming to a mutual understanding on the important subjects under consideration".

Indeed, ever since the conclusion of the Treaty of Tientsin, signed on the 26th June, 1858, and ratified at Peking‡ on the 24th October, 1860, and the attempts made, on the part chiefly of British subjects, to carry its provisions relative to trade with the Interior of China into practical effect, those provisions have proved little more than an abundant source of correspondence to diplomatists and statesmen; of annoyance, vexation, and disappointment to foreign merchants; of "squeezes" and extortion to native officials and their underlings; and of practice in duplicity and evasion to the Tsung-li Ya-mên. Thus, Sir Frederick Bruce, than whom a more easy-going Representative of the interests of his country and one more favorably and indulgently disposed towards the Chinese the Ya-mên could hardly have wished to deal with, found himself under the necessity of writing to Prince Kung, on June 16th, 1863:—

Your Imperial Highness will have received the note I had the honor to address you on the 9th instant, inclosing a memorandum of the substance of certain observations I had felt it my duty to make when I met Your Imperial Highness on the 7th instant. As regards the first of the two important subjects to which my observations related, the foreign policy of China, I shall add nothing to what I have already said, upon the danger which the Empire will incur, should its Government fail promptly and completely to satisfy the Representatives of other States,

‡ The Capital of China, 北京 *Peking, i.e.* "the Northern Capital,"—as distinguished from 南京, *Nan-king, i.e.* "the Southern Capital,"—is so designated by foreigners only. The Chinese call it simply 京, *King,* (in the north pronounced *Tjing*), "*the* Capital," namely, of the Ching Empire Universal. The real name of the City is 順天府, Shên T'iên Fu, and so, of course, it should be styled in all official documents. The use of *Peking* by foreign diplomatists implies, on their part, an acknowledgement of the contended- for Chinese autocracy of the world. The proper name of "the (former) Southern Capital", *Nanking,* is 江寧府, Kiang Ning Fu.

who are awaiting its action. My present business is with the claim of my own Government. I put first on the list the forcible exclusion of Her Majesty's Consul from Chao-Chow-Foo, and the refusal of the Authorities at Ningpo and Shanghai to refund transit-duties surcharged to British subjects. I place these foremost because Your Imperial Highness has fully admitted the justice of my representations regarding these, and has more than once promised that the wrong done should be set right. But complaints are incessant from almost every port, of entire indifference, on the part of the authorities, to the provisions of the Treaties affecting transit duties passports, the free employment of Chinese, the acquisition of building-sites, and the recovery of debts. Your Imperial Highness assured me that a circular of instructions, which you communicated to me, would obtain the desired end (of persuading the local Authorities of the fact that the Treaties form part of the law of the land, and that neglect or violation of their provisions will be denounced and published as breaches of the law), and as I was indifferent to the form, I insisted no further. But it is not too much to affirm that up to the present time the circular has produced no effect whatever. The grievances then unredressed remain unredressed still, and fresh grievances are constantly occurring. At Hankow, the Authorities deliberately violate the Treaties in the matter of transit-duties, and at Swatow they refuse to issue passports unless the words "for purposes of trade" be excluded, alleging that this departure from the letter of the Treaty is in obedience to the express command of the Tsung-li Ya-mên (Foreign Board). Under these circumstances, I am driven to one of two conclusions. Either the Imperial Government is unwilling to use its influence to cause the Treaty to be fairly carried out, or it has not the power to cause its orders to be obeyed. It then becomes my duty to bring these facts under the consideration of Her Majesty's Government as soon as possible, in order that it may decide on the propriety of discontinuing the moral and material aid hitherto afforded to the Chinese Government, and confine its efforts to the protection of its own interests in China.

In the Tsung-li Ya-mên's answer, dated June 19th 1863, we read :—

The Prince was considering a reply to the British Minister's note of the 9th, when His Excellency's despatch arrived. With reference to the proposition on which it insists, that the Treaty should rank with the law, the Prince has to observe that the principle that the Treaty is identical with the laws of the Imperial Government, and that breach of Treaty is the same thing as violation of the law, is the principle on which the Government of China proceeds, and that its only desire is that foreign nations should regard the Treaty in the same light, as there would then, to the end of time, be peace between the native and the foreigner. As regards the cases still undetermined in the provinces, the Prince hopes that the British Minister will refer to the record and inform him, case by case, of the particulars of each, and the Ya-mên will at once write to the Provincial Governments concerned, to hurry them with the cases enumerated. The Ya-mên will on its part, supply the British Minister with a list of the cases still undecided by British Authorities, and will request His Excellency to send them orders to use equal expedition. Under these conditions neither side will have a pretext for complaint.

To this communication, the sarcastic and offensive tone of which characterises but too many of the despatches, addressed by the Tsung-li Ya-mên to the Representatives of Foreign Powers, and which, in official translations like those here quoted from, usually assume a very mild and subdued form, Sir Frederick Bruce replied, on July 3, 1863, as follows :—

I have received the reply of Your Imperial Highness to my despatch of the 16th of June. Your Imperial Highness states in explicit terms that the Government of China recognizes the Treaties as the law of the Empire in its relations with foreigners, and that breaches of Treaty are considered as violations of those laws. But the despatch of Your Imperial Highness contains nothing to show that this principle will be carried out in practice. I stated instances at Hankow and Swatow in which the Authorities, in spite of the remonstrances of Her Majesty's Consuls, have deliberately set aside the letter of the Treaty for no other object than to curtail the privileges of Her Majesty's subjects. Your Imperial Highness in your reply does not allude to these cases, nor do you inform me that any steps have been taken to remedy these grievances, or to prevent a repetition of such conduct. I am simply requested to send in a list of the grievances complained of, and I am informed that the local Authorities will be urged to settle them with speed. Such a proposal is entirely unsatisfactory, for, what reason have I to suppose that the instructions now to be sent by Your Imperial Highness will be obeyed, when those for the redress of outrages, such as that committed on Her Majesty's Consul at Chao-chow-foo, and for the repayment of surcharges at Shanghai and Hankow have been disobeyed? Moreover, I do not complain of particular acts only; I complain of the disregard generally shown to Treaty obligations by the local Authorities, and to the constant complaints I receive from the ports of the levy of excessive duties, and of the refusal to repay surcharges improperly levied, &c. . . . With respect to the deliberate breach of Treaty stipulations, of which I gave instances both at Hankow and Swatow, I have simply to observe that, as long as the Imperial Government refuses to proceed in the usual Chinese form against local officers against these breaches of law, the Government becomes itself responsible for these acts by the impunity it accords to its subordinate agents. I feel convinced that, if Your Imperial Highness had obtained a decree in the terms I suggested eighteen months ago, and the provincial authorities had seen that it would be really enforced, the subsequent acts complained of would not have been committed.

At about the same period, the United States' Minister, "Mr. Burlingame,"—his successor, the Hon. J. Ross Browne, observes in his strictures upon Mr. Hart's "Note on Chinese Matters," in 1868,—"made similar complaints, and said that the tergiversations of the officers, who administered the Government, rendered it difficult to hold relations with them without a sacrifice of personal dignity. Dr. Williams, in 1866, (then American Chargé d'Affaires), stated that "the effects of the lesson, taught by the war of 1860, were passing away and the Rulers were becoming more obstructive and impracticable than ever."

The Hon. J. Ross Browne himself writes:—

The whole diplomatic corps at Peking up to the present time (1866) have, during the entire term of their residence at the Capital, been chiefly engaged in making protests and remonstrances against the *vis inertiæ* and shuffling evasions of the Imperial Government. The merchants at the Treaty-ports, through their Chambers of Commerce, have filled the archives of the Legations with proofs of the persistent manner, in which trade has been obstructed and Treaty-rights violated; in fact there is no difference of opinion on the subject among foreigners in China. Is this universal testimony to be disregarded? To whom are we to look for the truth, if not to our own Representatives, and to all classes who hold intercourse with the Chinese?

The present British Minister in Peking, Thomas Francis Wade, Esq., in his "Memorandum respecting the Revision of the Treaty of Tientsin," written in December, 1868, states:—

It is on the injury inflicted on their business by the non-observance of Art. xxviii. that the Merchants, one and all, most loudly complain; and that the burden that has fallen upon their trade is indeed hard to bear, no one will attempt to deny......... The more serious drawback on the development of foreign trade is occasioned by the fitful and irregular incidence of local taxation upon the trade of the native community .... Even in time of peace a very slight plea of local necessity will enable a Provincial Governor to increase the amount of the dues to be collected, or to impose provisionally a tax upon trade, if I may use the expression, *in situ*......... Though ostensibly a voluntary contribution, the *le-kin* is in reality a tax of great elasticity upon all trade, and one which, in course of time, becomes as grievous in the arbitrariness of its imposition as the 'benevolence' of our Kings of old......... Through the native trade, undoubtedly, the *le-kin* hits our own trade hard, and for more reasons than one we are justified in crying out......... I have said that Art. xxviii. (of the Treaty of Tien-tsin) has been ill observed. Whenever a Chinese authority has refused to issue a transit-duty certificate, or has disregarded the certificate presented, a breach of Treaty has been committed, and I regret to say that of the latter offence more particularly there are instances enough on record, and that the claims of applicants for reimbursement of the dues levied in excess, have been left, after much argument and correspondence, unsatisfied. I shall presently have to explain what it is that has tempted the Provincial Governments to these acts of undoubted illegality, and why it is that the Central Government has been so slow to redress the wrong when appealed to.

The various official testimonies, here adduced, can, quite independently of those of the foreign merchants themselves and a reference to special cases, leave no manner of doubt as to the broad fact, that, owing to the obstructiveness of native officials, the treaties, concluded between China and Western Powers at Tientsin in 1858 and 1861, have, so far as regards their provisions for the opening up of the Interior of the Tatar Empire to foreign commerce, virtually remained, and remain, " a dead letter." Apologists, however, as the concluding words of our quotation from Mr. Wade's memorandum show, are not wanting, who would fain relieve the Chinese Government of its responsibility for this grave state of matters, and transfer it to the shoulders of the Provincial Authorities. The British Minister, in continuance of the observations just cited, goes on to say :—" It is the poverty of the exchequer and the feebleness of the Central Government which explain, though they do not excuse, the disregard of the transit duty clauses. The Provincial Governors, knowing that their general necessity is beyond dispute, have overtaxed the native, and, when they could reach him, the foreigner ; not, as I believe, at the instance, very probably often in defiance, of the Central Government ; and the Central Government, though not powerless, would it but exert itself, has been scared by the bug-bear of war expenditure from interference in provincial finance. The Central Government will not, of course, avow such feebleness when defending itself."—I am unable to agree in these views with his Excellency, who, indeed, so far as the alleged feebleness of the Chinese Government is concerned, falls into such palpable self-contraditions as to cause his argument to defeat itself. Constitutionally and practically the Chinese Government is, for all purposes of internal administration, the strongest Government in the world. Mr. Wade manifestly confounds it here with the "Tsung-li Ya-mên,"—as its official title designates, a mere temporary "Imperially-appointed Commission for the General Control of the (Commercial) Affairs of the Individual (Tributary) States of the Ta-Ching Empire," —(such as England, the United States, France, Russia, and Germany,)—under the Presidency of Prince Kung.|| Certain members of this, of itself powerless Commission, including His Imperial Highness, are also members of the Chinese Government in the wider acceptation of the term, *i. e.* of the Emperor's Privy Council and State Secretariate; but the Foreign Ministers at Peking, unless we exclude the Representative of Russia,§ come only in contact with them in their former capacity.

In that capacity Prince Kung delights in the British Minister's theory of the feebleness of the Central Government, because this imagined feebleness constitutes the Tsung-li Ya-mên's strength. Occasionally, it is true, when the Ya-mên is by the Representative of England charged with having expressly commanded the Provincial Authorities "to depart from the letter of the Treaties," *i. e.* to set the treaty-provisions systematically at naught, the Prince, as we have seen, does not even trouble himself to deny the charge. Upon other occasions, however, when His Imperial Highness may have found it more expedient, as President of the Tsung-li Ya-mên, to assure the British Minister that instructions

|| The origin and position of the Tsung-li Ya-mên, usually, but in our sense erroneously, rendered "the (Chinese) Foreign Office," will be fully explained in another place.

§ By Art. ii. of the Russian Treaty of Tientsin, of June 1/13, 1858, the Russian Foreign Office and the Russian Minister at Peking have the right of correspondence, and the latter that of personal communication, with the oldest member of the Privy Council, or the First Minister at Peking (le membre ainé du Conseil d'Etat ou le premier Ministre à Pékin),—that is to say, according to the Russian-French version. The Chinese text reads very differently.

for the redress of a certain grievance have actually been sent to the Provincial Governors, and, perchance, to communicate to him a copy of the very despatch conveying them, whilst, as a Member of the Privy Council, the Prince submits to the Chinese Government the propriety of ordering those instructions to be rescinded, which is done accordingly: what could, in subsequent explanation of the fact that "it is not too much to say that the circular of His Imperial Highness has produced no effect whatever," be more acceptable to Prince Kung than, despite of a life-time's experience of Chinese duplicity, the British Minister's persistent belief in the Ya-mên's good faith and "the feebleness of the Central Government?" What more grateful, than Mr. Wade's plea in favor of that "poor, feeble" Government, which finds millions to waste upon military armaments against the West and, in the consciousness of its imagined strength, challenges to mortal combat the whole civilized world by conniving at, and exultingly accepting the responsibility of, the Tientsin Massacre, that, in the matter of commercial treaty-violations, it is the financial necessity of Provincial Governors, which forces them to act "in defiance" of the Imperial commands?

If, then, in combination with the broad and unquestionable fact, pointed out in a preceding paragraph, we consider that the policy of the Chinese Government has ever been one of commercial and political isolation; that a departure from that policy has only been forced upon it at the cannon's mouth; and that, of late years, its tendency, not to say its determination, to return to a state of hereditary seclusion, has assumed a form and expression, increasing in energy and boldness with its increasing strength, since 1841-42 so greatly impaired by foreign invasion and internal rebellion: it appears to me difficult for any unbiassed and soberly thinking person to avoid the conclusion, that the systematic violation and evasion of the provisions of the Treaties of Tientsin respecting trade with the Interior of China, on the part of native officials, has not only been sanctioned and supported by, but has been, and is being, carried out at the instance of, the Imperial Government itself. The positive proof to this effect will be furnished in the sequel.

II.

THE TRANSIT-QUESTION.

Vital importance of the Transit-question—Public attention recalled to it by a "communicated" article in the *North-China Herald*—Motives for the appearance of the paper—Its author—The paper reproduced —Mr. Wade's Memorandum of December, 1868—His views relative to the Transit-question transcribed—Their adoption by the British Government—The Board of Trade to the Foreign Office—Stand-point taken up by the Tsung-li Ya-mên at the Revision of the Treaty of Tientsin—New regulations proposed by the Ya-mên —Concurrence of authorities in favor of the "*in transitu*" theory —Differing views of the Merchants—Latest opinion of Sir Rutherford Alcock.

It is quite recently only that, although occasionally commented on in the local papers, public attention has been more generally directed to the subject introduced in the preceding section, notwithstanding that it is one of such vital importance both to China and the West. I am alluding to a "communicated" article on "The Transit-system," which appeared in the *North-China Herald* of the 1st November, 1871, and the reputed author of which is the Inspector-General of Chinese Maritime Customs, Mr. Robert Hart. Some six months previously an attempt had been made by Mr. T'u, the then Tau-tai and native Intendant,—in concert with Mr. Dick, the then foreign Commissioner,—of Customs in Shanghai, to place the transit-system, so far at least as this port was concerned, on a new basis. It led to an energetic counter-action on the part of the General Chamber of Commerce, and the whole Consular Body; and the matter was referred to Peking. Awaiting the result of this appeal, at a meeting of the Treaty Consuls on October 16th, 1871, "The Senior Consul"—I quote from the Minutes of the Meeting—"said, that he had asked Mr. Hart to state the action which had been taken at Peking and had been told that the first intimation received at Peking that a new interpretation had been placed upon the Transit Dues stipulations at Shanghai, had come up in the newspapers. Mr. Hart at once brought the subject before the Foreign Office [as the Tsung-li Ya-mên is here erroneously styled], and asked that clear instructions should be sent to the ports. He at the same time reminded the Board that the subject had been discussed in 1868, and the point then decided that passes might be taken out by Chinese or by foreigners. He understood that the Ya-mên at once assented to his statement and recommendation, and had sent orders accordingly to the ports."—Under these circumstances, the Inspector-General is supposed to have "communicated" to the Press the memorandum alluded to, with the view of setting himself right at the same time with the Tsung-li Ya-mên, the Consular Body of Shanghai, and the public. Hence, also, we find the anonymous writer to speak as one having authority and equally enjoying the confidence, if not of the Chinese Government, certainly of the Ya-mên alluded to, the Foreign Representatives at Peking, and the Inspector General of Chinese Maritime Customs.

In order to avoid any misunderstanding as to the exact import and bearing of the article itself, I will here reproduce it *in extenso*:—

THE TRANSIT SYSTEM.

[*Communicated.*]

The treaty of Nankin stipulated for the conveyance of foreign merchandise, that is merchandise of foreign origin, into the interior by

Chinese under a transit system; and the treaty of Tientsin arranged the procedure and fixed the amount of the Transit Dues, and it further provided for what the treaty of Nankin had left untouched—the conveyance of native, or Chinese, produce, intended for shipment foreign, from the interior to a treaty port under a Transit system.

In discussing Transit questions, it must be kept in mind that there are two kinds of transit, viz., outward and inward, and that each has its own peculiarities.

When the ratifications of the Tientsin Treaty were exchanged in 1860, the Transit system stood thus: (outward) *Foreign merchants* were authorised to go inland, purchase and convey to a treaty port native produce intended for shipment foreign, and (inward) Foreign *and Chinese* merchants were authorised to convey foreign merchandise from a treaty port *to a specified mart* in the interior; and, in each case, exemption from taxation *en route* was to be procured by the payment of a single tax—the treaty or tariff Transit Due. The first question that came up under the Transit system as established in 1860, was the following:—Must the Foreigner *in person* be with his merchandise *en route*, entering or leaving the interior? The Authorities at Peking took a common sense view of the matter; and at once decided, in 1861, that the Foreigner need not accompany his goods; he may employ any agents for their conveyance, but Agent, Goods and Certificate must travel in company, to secure exemption.

It was not till 1868 that any other question was referred to Peking. Meanwhile, however, the Transit stipulation *outward* was abused, and the double malpractice which constituted the abuse of the transit privilege or treaty right, induced inland officials to object to the Transit system as a whole. The malpractice was of this kind: whereas it was only for native produce *intended for shipment foreign* that the Transit system outward was devised, there were now Foreign merchants who brought from the interior native produce owned by themselves but intended for other ports of China, and who protected such produce from ordinary inland taxation by carrying it under the Transit system and as though intended for *boná fide export*; and there were other foreign merchants who brought down native produce from the interior in the same way,—produce, which was not their own but *Chinese property*, and in respect of which the Chinese owners paid the Foreign merchant a more or less remunerative fee for the assistance which enabled the produce to evade local taxation inland. Chinese officials naturally objected to this abuse; and, while they allowed foreigners in charge of goods to pass on without difficulty, they carried their opposition to the abuse, so far as to make it almost impossible for the native agent of the foreigner to bring down native produce really entitled to transit privileges. In some places, less experienced officials began to suppose that even foreign merchandise going inland, if under Chinese protection, was evading taxation, and therefore subject to confiscation. From 1861 to 1868 the Provincial Officials were constantly complaining at the Ya-mên of the abuse of the Transit system; and the abuse of the system as intended for Produce Outward, added to the neglect to distinguish clearly between Transit Inward and Transit Outward, threatened to make the whole system inoperative.

In 1868, the question which came up was this. The Taotai at Ningpo had seized some goods of foreign origin which a Chinese merchant was carrying under a Transit Pass into the interior; the goods were Chinese property: had the Chinese merchant a right to the Transit privilege? The Taotai at Ningpo, on receipt of a note from the Consul questioning the propriety of the seizure, referred the matter to the Imperial Commissioner, Tsêng-kwo-fan, who in turn referred it to the Ya-mên. The Ya-mên at once wrote back to say, that the Taotai's desire to guard against evasion of inland taxes had blinded him to his duties under foreign treaties, and ruled that, putting the stipulations of the Nańkin and Tientsin Treaties side by side, their meaning clearly is that merchandise of foreign origin, no matter to whom belonging, may be taken into the interior by either foreigner or native, and participate in all the advantages of the Transit system, if provided with *and accompanied by* a Transit certificate (*shui tan.*) The Imperial Commissioner was instructed by the Ya-mên to acquaint the various Custom-houses with the reply sent to the question that had arisen at Ningpo, for their guidance. The despatch is in the archives of each Custom-house, and a former Taotai at Shanghai printed and published it in a volume of regulations, as an authoritative interpretation of a treaty point that had been misunderstood.

The question as to the rights of foreign merchandise purchased by Chinese, had not come up for discussion before 1868, and when Sir Rutherford Alcock was in communication with the Ya-mên on the point, *à propos* of revision, the Ya-mên held that, under the Tientsin Treaty, *taken by itself* foreign merchandise could only claim the Transit right while belonging to Foreign merchants. Sir Rutherford Alcock pointed out that, under the Nankin Treaty, renewed by that of Tientsin, *origin* and *not ownership* was the condition; the Ya-mên replied that it had no copy of the Nankin Treaty (the original copy having been carried away from either the Imperial Commissioner Yeh's Ya-mên or the Yuan-Ming-Yuan); a copy was thereon procured, and Sir Rutherford Alcock's interpretation was held to be correct. It was just at this time that the Ningpo question came forward, and the Ya-mên's instructions were issued, in reply to it, without any foreign pressure or suggestion. When it was thus authoritatively stated that Chinese as well as Foreigners might be the owners of goods of Foreign origin entering the interior in transit, it naturally followed that, for such goods, Chinese as well as Foreigners might apply for Transit Passes. And as the Ya-mên's action in 1868 was the issuing, for Chinese guidance, of what was merely a clearer statement of a rule already made public by the notification of Treaties, it was not thought in any way necessary to communicate the despatch to Foreign officials.

Some months back, the newspapers stated that the Shanghai Customs required Foreign merchants to declare that they themselves owned the merchandise for which they applied for Transit Passes. The moment this was known at Peking, the Ya-mên directed the Imperial Commissioner, Tsêng-kwo-fan, to inform the Taotai that merchandise of foreign origin can be taken into the interior in transit as well by Chinese as by Foreigners, and that consequently his action, which might lead to a repetition of the mistake made at Ningpo in 1868, ought to be discontinued. Since the receipt of those orders, the Transit Pass for goods of foreign origin about to be sent inland, and which are the property of Chinese, has been issued to Chinese on application. The Ya-mên's instructions were issued before the Consuls addressed the Taotai on the subject, and were neither more nor less than a repetition, addressed specially to Shanghai, of instructions issued for the information of all the Ports in 1868.

The instructions lately received by the Taotai at Shanghai have not been sent to the Taotai at Ningpo; and the proclamation recently translated as published at Ningpo refers to a distinct and separate question.

The position in which transit business now stands, as understood by the Ya-mên and Foreign Representatives at Peking, is as follows:—

1. Inward Transit.—Goods of foreign origin, no matter whether owned by natives or foreigners, may be carried inland, from a port to

the mart named in the certificate, in transit, and the certificate may be applied for by native or foreigner without distinction. The certificate lapses on arrival at the place specified, and thereafter the goods, having once entered the stream of general Chinese trade, are liable to the incidence of local taxation. The certificate is simply a *Transit* certificate; *it protects from a port to a place.*

2. OUTWARD TRANSIT.—Native Produce purchased by Foreigners or by Natives the agents of Foreigners, if intended for exportation, that is for shipment to a foreign country, may be brought from the interior to a Treaty Port in transit by Foreigners or their agents. Produce not intended for shipment foreign is *not* entitled to the Transit privilege, even should it be the *bonâ fide* property of Foreigners. Produce which is the property of Chinese is not permitted to be covered by Transit certificates: Chinese applicants are not allowed to take out such native produce certificates, and Foreigners who lend their names to Chinese to procure such certificates, are abusing a Treaty right and assisting natives to evade the authorised taxes of the interior.

As regards *Inward Transit*, it has been supposed that Sir Rutherford Alcock at one time upheld the broad interpretation which allows Chinese to take foreign merchandise inland in transit, and that at a late period both H. E. himself and the British Government withdrew from that interpretation. Such is not the case, however; from first to last, Sir Rutherford Alcock maintained that *origin and not ownership* was the condition, but, at one time, H. E. went further than the British Government could authorise: he maintained that a transit due once paid, frees merchandise from all other taxation, and in that view he was wrong, for the only taxation which the payment of a transit due frees from is *taxation en route from a Treaty Port to a specified place*, no matter how distant from the port that place may be. Sir Rutherford Alcock did not make use of such exact language as should make his meaning unmistakeable, but if the reader will remark the difference between Inward and Outward Transit, and will also recollect that, in respect of Inward Transit, foreign merchandise may be viewed in three distinct stages, H. E.'s remarks will be quite intelligible. There is a time, first of all, during which Inward certificates can be obtained, and that time is while the goods are still at the Treaty Port; there is, secondly, a time during which such Inward certificates are valid and to be respected, and that time is while the goods are travelling from the Treaty

Port to a specified place, accompanied by that certificate; and there is, lastly, a time after which certificates cannot be obtained, or after which certificates previously obtained are no longer of any value, and that time is when, in the vicinity of the port, goods that have not taken out Transit certificates mingle in the stream of Chinese traffic, or when, in the interior, goods which have been protected by a certificate have arrived at the place specified or cease to be accompanied by the certificate. What Sir Rutherford Alcock's remarks meant was that, during the first period and at a port, Transit Certificates ought to be issued to foreign merchandise irrespective of ownership,—that, during the second period, *en route* from a port to a place, Inward Certificates ought to protect Foreign Goods, no matter by whom owned or conveyed, from taxation,—and that, during the third period, after arrival at the place specified, not even the fact of a transit due having been paid in the first instance nor continued foreign ownership could protect from taxation Foreign Goods unaccompanied by a valid certificate.

In issuing its instructions in 1868, and in repeating them to the Shanghai Customs in 1871, the Ya-mên has made no new concession in respect of *Inward Transit*, but has merely honestly ordered subordinate offices to give full and proper effect to a previously existing right. In 1870, however, and in respect of *Outward Transit*, the Ya-mên did make a concession: in the Revised Treaty, rejected at the prayer of the Mercantile Communities, the Ya-mên had agreed to regard *destination and not ownership* as the condition of the title of *Native Produce* to the Transit privilege.

Similar views regarding the treaty-provisions relative to trade with the Interior are entertained by the British Representative in Peking, Mr. Wade. They may be gathered from his "Memorandum respecting the Revision of the Treaty of Tientsin," to which reference has been already made, and which was submitted by him, when on leave of absence in England, in December 1858, to his Government. In this memorandum we read:—

What we are, in my opinion, by Treaty, really entitled to, will be best shown by a brief review of the antecedent history of the transit-duty question. When the Treaty of 1842 opened the trade at Canton, till then the close monopoly of a privileged association, it was stipulated that there should be established at the five ports, at which we were now authorised to trade, a fair Tariff of import and export customs, and that the Tariff duty once paid at any open port, our imports should be conveyed by Chinese to any province or city in the interior, on a payment of a further amount as transit duty. This was not to exceed a certain per-centage upon their Tariff values, the amount of which percentage was to be presently declared.

A fair Tariff was published in 1843, but the promised declaration, by which the inland transit duty was to have been regulated, never appeared*; and before many years elapsed, it was seen that the foreign merchants' business in imports, and in exports no less, was affected, at a rate annually increasing, by what his broker or his native constituents represented to be charges imposed by the local or provincial authorities upon merchandise *in transitu*. In normal times, that is to say, when the country is undisturbed, the transit dues are leviable only at certain fixed points or barriers, a list of which is published in the Code of the Board of Revenue. It was, doubtless, of the rates to be charged at these barriers, that the declaration required by Sir Henry Pottinger, in 1842, was demanded. The provincial governments do not, legally, possess the right to multiply these collectorates without reference to the Board of Revenue; nor can their number be added to by the Board itself, without the sanction of an Imperial Decree.........

Through the native trade, undoubtedly, the *le-kin* hits our own trade hard, and for more reasons than one we are justified in crying out; but again we must be careful to remember what the tax really is. Its nature appears to me to be singularly misunderstood. Since the last payment of our indemnity in 1865, only, has the central government caused two-fifths of the customs receipts (the amount that the French and ourselves drew annually from 1860 to 1865) to be remitted to Peking†. The remaining three-fifths are applied to the expenditure of the Provinces. So they were throughout the whole five years of indemnity payments; and, except the Canton quota, which, up to a certain date, had always gone to the purse of the Imperial household, so, for the last fifteen years of trouble, have the whole of the maritime duties, collected on foreign trade, been applied. The "squeezes" of the local authorities, that is, I

* This, as will be seen hereafter, rests on an erroneous impression on Mr. Wade's part.

† The amount is understood to have been even somewhat less, viz. two-sevenths.

presume, the *le-kin* or war-tax, of the abuses connected with which I shall have enough to say, owe their existence and evil growth to the same demand for supplies, not to any action taken by or through the Customs Inspectorate. In some form or degree the impost is of far older birth than the Inspectorate, and must be at this moment a chief resóurce of the government in regions far beyond the influence of that institution.

In the earlier years of the open trade, it is true, from 1843 to 1850, it is much to be doubted, that the tolls of the Provincial governments hindered circulation of our imports to anything like the extent that the native intermediary was pleased to allege. The foreigner, restricted by Treaty to the five ports open, was powerless to test the truth of assertions that it might suit interested natives to make touching either the conditions of the markets or the proceedings of the authorities inland, and it is not to be supposed that his Chinese broker would not turn this ignorance to account. So lately as 1858, when direct communication between Shanghae and Hankow had been more or less interrupted by the presence of the Taeping insurgents in the valley of the Great River for upwards of five years, Lord Elgin found British imports selling in Hankow at rates that by no means bore out the statements of the Chinese at Shanghai regarding the onerousness of the transit duties. From the outbreak of the Taeping insurrection in 1852, no doubt, the patriotic contribution was very freely exacted, but whether in the proportions affirmed we were not as yet in a position to ascertain. On the other part we do now know that until the insurrection of 1853 began to tell on the tea duties, the port of Foo-chow was closed to that trade by Imperial authority. Teas were diverted by the government from Foo-chow up to the year 1854. Whatever the truth, however, all trade suffered severely; and in 1858, the inland charges upon tea coming from Hankow to Shanghae amounted, according to the native brokers, to nearly cent per cent upon its value: in some ten years they had about trebled themselves.

By Art. ix of the Treaty of Tientsin, Lord Elgin obtained for the British merchant the right to travel with a passport, on business or for pleasure, to any part of the Empire. This gave him personal access to the markets whether as buyer or seller, and secured him, at all events, against false information.‡ By Art. xxviii it was agreed that within

‡ This was hardly the case. Mr. Wade overlooks that few, if any, of the foreign mer-

four months from the signature of the Treaty, there should be published at every port, on application of the Consul to the Superintendent of Customs, a notification of the amount of duties to be levied on produce passing from the place of production to the port of the Consul applying, and on imports from the same port to the inland markets named by the Consul; or that it should be at the option of the merchant to clear his goods, inland or portwards, by one single payment to be fixed as near as possible at 2½ per cent upon their Tariff value. This stipulation, like that in the Treaty of Nanking, had reference to the barriers that had been sanctioned by the Board of Revenue.|| The new Tariff was negotiated at Shanghae within four months after the signature of the Treaty; but it was found that in the then conditions of the interior, and especially of the valley of the Great River, the required notification, if producible at all, could not be looked for without very considerable delay. By the 7th of the Rules appended to the Tariff, therefore, the inland duty on all imports and exports therein enumerated was limited to a sum equal to 2½ per cent upon value; exemption from any additional impost *in transitu* being secured by certificate.

There is this difference, then, between the transit duty clauses of the two Treaties of 1842 and 1858. The earlier claimed to clear imports alone, carried inland in Chinese hands; the later, to clear both imports and exports, if certificated, whether carried by a Chinese or a foreigner. I am not in a position to state whether Sir Henry Pottinger supposed that the single payment by which he stipulated the Chinese merchant was to compound for his barrier dues, would exempt the goods he carried inland from all farther taxation. I suspect that he did; and the mercantile community, though, with reason, not sanguine that the promised scale of inland duties would ever be published at all, were, I think, under the same impression as to the sense of the Treaty stipulation. Lord Elgin, I am certain, did not look for more than the protection, *in transitu*, of certificated goods.

chants possess a sufficient knowledge of the Chinese language and its numerous dialects, to converse directly with the natives. I apprehend, the distinguished sinologue himself would make but an indifferent and not very reliable interpreter between his countrymen and the tea- and silk-worm- farmers of China.

|| Mr. Wade seems to be so little acquainted with the subject, that he constantly confounds the Custom-houses, 關, "sanctioned by the Board of Revenue", with the newly added barriers, 卡. The Treaty of Nan-king refers to the former only, because the latter had then not as yet been invented. The Treaty of Tientsin refers to *both*, *i. e.* to toll, octroi, and any impost whatever, levied inland.

So far as Art. ix of the treaty of Tientsin is concerned, it is my impression that the privilege it guarantees has been fairly enjoyed. The Article accords us the right to travel inland for business or for pleasure. It does not accord us, nor, as I have argued elsewhere, does any other Article accord, the right of residing otherwise than a tourist or mercantile traveller may reside, in any part of China but the Consular ports. The personal access which it does authorize to whatever places the foreigner desires to visit, has been, with rare exceptions at all events, conceded him. As an exporter he may not have benefited by the exercise of his right to the extent anticipated; but that is not the fault of the Treaty provision or of the Chinese government. At Shanghae, notwithstanding our power of visiting the producing districts, tea and silk are procurable on as good terms at the port as up the country, if not on better, but this because the native community have the wit to combine. The foreign community invariably compete. The combination of the tea-growers proves, I fancy, too much even for the native brokers.

The anticipations founded on Art. xxviii regarding our trade, and particularly our import trade, have been no less disappointed; but again admitting that its conditions have been in some, indeed in many, instances ill observed, I must, on the other part, contend that much, though not all, of the disappointment which is set down to the non-fulfilment of these conditions is due to the fact, that a far greater measure of freedom has been expected of them than the framers of the Treaty contemplated their providing. The Article promises exemption from all charges *in transitu* over and above those specified in the Treaty on imports passing from a port to an inland market, or on produce from an inland market to a port of shipment, provided always, as Sir Frederick Bruce read the Treaty, that such imports or produce, being *bonâ fide* British-owned, were accompanied by a certificate. Lord Elgin did hope that imports so certificated might not only be carried by travellers from one centre of traffic to another, but disposed of in parcels along the line, an order of proceeding not impossible in quieter times; but I remember his Lordship expressly stating that he did not see his way to the farther protection of imports against taxation once they had passed into the hands of a Chinese purchaser. They must then, said he, take their chance.

I do not pretend that, in 1858, Lord Elgin, any more than any one else, contemplated as possible such a weight of taxation as now indirectly oppresses our trade. Neither at Shanghae nor elsewhere had the *le-kin* attained the dimensions to which, since 1860, it has swollen in those provinces where trade is likely to feel it most. But, could the rebel-movement of 1860-1865, to which we owe the great rise of war-taxes throughout the valley of the Great River, have been predicted, no Treaty provision could, in my belief, have been devised that would have afforded imports the protection that our merchants conceive they are entitled to. The protection of imports, and of exports no less, *in transitu*, is a different matter, and we were entitled to hope§ that the terms of Art. xxviii, as interpreted by the Tariff rule, would have been respected; for the charge of 2½ per cent, therein agreed to, was believed, on good authority, to exceed the sum of the barrier dues heretofore levied on goods carried by the native trader, at all events between Shanghae and its natural markets, and it was not unreasonable to argue from this to other lines of communication.

Now I have said that this Article has been ill observed.........The great weight, however, pressing upon the import and export trade of the British merchant, is the weight of the *le-kin* contribution as distinct from the transit-dues. But this import, although in its excessive degree objectionable, is not in its nature more open to objection than our own income-tax, nor, indeed, than any extraordinary tax by which a state, short of money, may recruit its finances.........

I hold that the transit duty, defined by Treaty, once paid, the certificate thereon granted should clear the foreign payer's imports of transit dues to any inland market he may choose, or his exports, purchased inland, to any open port. Refusal to issue a certificate is a breach of Treaty; so is the levy of any due in excess of the payment for which the certificate is, in fact, a receipt. But the certificate will not except the goods, cleared under it, from the *le-kin*, or from any other tax once they have become Chinese property. The merchants hold that it should; and more, conceiving that transit dues and *le-kin* are identical, they contend that to levy the *le-kin* on duty-paid goods in the port-town at which they are sold, or in the country between the port-town and the transit-duty collectorates surrounding it, on ground, that is, that has to be traversed before a transit-duty can become leviable, is a violation of the

§ It is characteristic of Mr. Wade's manner of viewing things, that he considers positive Treaty stipulations to merely *entitle to the hope* of their being observed on the part of China.

treaty...... I have laboured at great length to show that the *le-kin* and the transit dues are, so far as we are concerned, imposts of a totally different character; that we may fight any augmentation of the latter by Treaty, but that the treaty will not help us against the *le-kin*. On the suggestions, therefore, that it should be wholly, or even partially, suppressed, I shall offer but this additional remark, that, if we could drive the Chinese to admit that the present mode of levying the war tax is in breach of Treaty, there is, in my belief, nothing to prevent them turning our flank by a change in its denomination. A house-tax, shop-tax, or corporation tax, would effect the same object, and press almost, if not quite, as grievously as the *le-kin* on our trade.

What greatly adds to the importance of these views is their having been adopted by the British Government. We learn this from a letter, addressed by the Secretary of the Board of Trade to the Hon. J. Hammond, then Permanent Under-Secretary of the Foreign Office, and dated "Office of Committee of Privy Council for Trade," May 19th, 1869. I extract from it what relates to our subject, besides its interesting and suggestive introduction:—

In reply to your letter of the 4th March. I am directed by the Lords of the Committee of Privy Council for Trade to request that you will inform the Earl of Clarendon, that they have carefully considered the various questions raised in the correspondence transmitted to them by his Lordship on the subject of the commercial relations between this country and China, more especially in connection with the proposed revision of the Treaty of Tientsin.

Two distinct and conflicting lines of policy are presented for the consideration of Her Majesty's Government on the occasion of a revision of our Treaty relations with China:—

1. To insist not only upon the effectual execution of existing engagements, but also upon new and important concessions with a view to what is called "opening up," China to foreign trade, and introducing Western civilisation into the Empire.

2. To confine the present negotiations to the assertion of admitted Treaty rights essential to the gradual progress of foreign trade, to the removal of such defects in the Chinese Administration affecting foreign

trade, as the Chinese Government is willing and able to undertake to remedy, and to the acceptance of some spontaneous concessions.

It appears to my Lords, after reading this correspondence, that if any doubt at any time existed as to the impossibility of obtaining at the present time, except by force, the larger concessions which are called for by the mercantile body in China, such as the right of residence in the interior and of working mines, the introduction of railroads and telegraphs, and inland steam-navigation,—such doubts can no longer be entertained.

Sir R. Alcock, who at some stages of the transactions under review, especially at the date of his despatch of the 10th November, 1868, seems to have been to a certain extent under the influence of his more sanguine, and less responsible, diplomatic colleagues,¶ and of the order of ideas inspired by the display of force at Yang-chow, arrives, at the close of the correspondence, at the conclusion that the results of the labours of the Mixed Commission,* reported in his despatch of the 6th December, 1868, are all that can be obtained by negotiation at the present time; and that, unless Her Majesty's Government is prepared to resort to other means than those which he has felt authorised to employ, and with a clear contingency of war for the attainment of the main points insisted on by the merchants and by his colleagues generally as alone important and essential to all effective progress, they must be content with much less, and with the somewhat vague hope of gradual progress.

My Lords believe that this view is, moreover, shared by Mr. Wade, by whom, in accordance with Lord Clarendon's suggestion, they have conferred upon this subject, and many other persons, whose opinion is deserving of great consideration.

It is true, that the Memorials, which have been addressed to Her Majesty's Government and to Sir R. Alcock by the British mercantile body in China, are generally in favor of what is termed a more vigorous policy, and that the language of the foreign Representatives at the Court of Peking,† and especially that of the United States' Minister, Mr. Ross

¶ I have good reason to doubt the correctness of this statement. So far as personal knowledge entitles me to speak, I may affirm that rather the reverse was the case.

* "The Mixed Commission", in the sense in which it is here used, was virtually a misnomer. The one feeble English element, which entered into its composition, was the then senior second Secretary of Legation, Mr. Hugh Fraser.

† "At the Court of Peking". Were their Lordships unaware of the humiliating fact, that the Representatives of Western Powers were then, and are as yet, only suffered "a temporary shelter" in the Capital of "the One Autocrator of the Earth", and that they are excluded from the very threshold of his Palace?

Brown (although even that gentleman himself admits in his letter to Sir R. Alcock of 17th December, 1868, that "all has been accomplished which can at present be achieved by diplomatic means"), lead to the inference that they incline to the same view.

It is unnecessary for my Lords to observe, that they have every disposition to give due weight to the representations of those who are more directly interested than any other class of Her Majesty's subjects in the question under discussion, but they cannot forget (as is stated in Sir R. Alcock's despatch of 23rd December last) that "our position in China has been created by force—naked physical force; that any intelligent attempt to improve or maintain that position must still look to force in some form, latent or expressed, for the results"; and the responsibilities and sacrifices involved in the exercise of force must fall upon the British nation, and not upon that section of its people which is engaged in the trade with China.

The same remark applies with scarcely less weight to the case of the Representatives of other countries at Peking. Any policy which led to the interruption of peaceful relations with China would be attended with far greater danger to British interests than to those of other nations, and in advocating a course liable to such contingencies both merchants and Ministers are urging on a policy in the fruits of which, if successful, they would largely share, and in which the consequences of failure would fall chiefly upon other interests than those which they represent.

The course, therefore, which my Lords would recommend for the consideration of Her Majesty's Government under existing circumstances is as follows:—

1. To endeavour to arrive at an understanding with the Government of China by which the formal revision of the Treaty of Tientsin may be deferred until the majority of the Emperor, which Sir R. Alcock states will take place in 1872 or 1873. Such a postponement of the revision is in my Lords' opinion desirable for three reasons: *(a.)* There will then be a "personal and tangible" power with whom to deal. *(b.)* It may be hoped that in five years there may exist a greater disposition to extend foreign trade and relations than at present. *(c.)* The claim for revision will then coincide in point of time with that of the last Treaty power entitled to prefer it, and it may be hoped that the simultaneous action and co-operation of all those Powers may then be secured.

2. That in the meantime, and pending such general revision, Sir R.

Alcock should be instructed to obtain, if possible, the consent of the Chinese Government to such arrangements as they have already expressed their willingness to adopt in view of an immediate revision, such arrangements to be effected either by a short Convention, if this be necessary, or by independent action.

These arrangements are stated in Sir R. Alcock's despatch of the 6th December, and are the result of the negotiations conducted by the Mixed Commission, which was appointed at his request to arrive at a preliminary understanding as to the basis of revision.

My Lords will enumerate them in order, and whenever necessary make such remarks upon them as occur to them in connection with the questions to which they respectively refer:—

TRANSIT DUES.

This proposal is nothing more than a literal fulfilment of existing stipulations in the Treaty of Tientsin, and involves no new concessions whatever.

The question of transit dues is stated by all the authorities on this subject to be the next important point in connection with the present negotiations. A considerable difference of opinion exists in different quarters as to the precise nature of the claims which, in virtue of the 7th Supplementary Treaty rule, in execution of Art. xxviii. of the Treaty of Tientsin, Her Majesty's Government is equitably entitled to assert.

My Lords entertain no doubt that the view expressed in some of the Memorials, and even at one time by Sir R. Alcock himself, viz., that the payment of the transit dues ought to be held to exempt the goods upon which it has been paid from all subsequent internal taxation, and to insure the sale of the goods to their ultimate consumer with no enhancement of cost derived from taxation, save that represented by the import and transit duties, is a view which cannot be entertained by Her Majesty's Government. There is nothing in the terms of the Treaty which appears to my Lords to justify such a sweeping demand, and in view of the internal taxation to which native goods are subject in China, it would be in their opinion both unjust and inexpedient to enforce such a demand, even if it were warranted by the terms of Treaty stipulations.

All that Her Majesty's Government can claim in this respect, appears to my Lords to be, that in the Treaty ports the importer shall have the right to sell his goods in the market, after payment of Customs duties stipulated, and that he shall have the right to send goods to any internal market which he may select, free from any other charge than the Customs duty on importation, and the stipulated transit duty; but that both at the port, and at the internal market, when once the goods have passed out of his hands they must take their chance in common with native goods, and bear whatever impositions the rapacity or necessities of Chinese administration may inflict.

It must also be remembered, that the imperfect execution of the Treaty of Tientsin in this particular, is due not alone to the weakness or inaction of the Chinese Government, but also to the fraudulent evasion by British merchants of the obligations and conditions which it imposes.

My Lords refer to the sale of transit certificates to the Chinese, by which malpractice the difficulties in the way of a just administration were greatly increased. A stricter execution of the stipulation on the English side should be, if possible, enforced, as well as on the part of China.

Under these circumstances my Lords are of opinion that the arrangement which, after much discussion and correspondence, appears to have been considered satisfactory by Sir R. Alcock may be approved by Her Majesty's Government. The terms accepted by the Yamên seem in themselves perfectly equitable, and entirely in accordance with what my Lords believe to have been the intention of the stipulation to which it relates. It is to be hoped that the renewed adhesion of the Chinese Government to the principle therein asserted, and the measures which they propose to take with a view of making known and enforcing the provisions of the stipulation will operate in diminishing and restraining, if not in removing, the obstructions caused to the circulation of foreign-owned goods in the interior by the exactions of the Provincial Government.

The general character and principles of this arrangement are as follows:—"1. To allow all foreign goods to circulate freely on payment of import duty and transit duty together. 2. To enable all Chinese produce to get to foreign markets, after payment of transit duty and export duty simply. 3. To place native produce, with the exception of Government monopolies, such as salt, to be traded in, in China, on the same footing as it is when traded in, in China, by Chinese."

These general principles appear to my Lords to have been observed in the arrangements ultimately proposed by the Chinese Government, and they think they should receive the approval of Her Majesty's Government subject to any modifications of the details, which further experience may have led Sir R. Alcock to deem desirable.

The most favorable aspect, under which the Transit-question was regarded by the Tsung-li Ya-mên, and we have therefore to conclude, by the Chinese Government, in 1869, may be inferred from the repudiated "Supplementary Convention of Peking, of October 2nd, 1869," the provisions of which relative to inland trade had been framed to the following effect:—

Art. iii.—It is agreed that articles of the following classes and denominations, namely, Cottons, Linens, Woollens and Cotton Mixtures, &c., imported by British merchants, shall pay both Import Duties and Transit Dues simultaneously at the time of importation; on the other hand China agrees that the above mentioned commodities imported by British merchants and having paid Import Duties and Transit Dues simultaneously at the time of importation, shall be exempt from all other taxes and charges whatever, in treaty port provinces.

Art. iv.—It is agreed that Native Produce purchased in the interior by British merchants furnished with the documents prescribed by the Supplementary Regulations shall pay all inland dues and charges on its way to the treaty Ports; on the other part China agrees that any such native produce, having paid all inland dues and charges on the way to the port from the place of purchase, shall be entitled to the return of any amount that may have been thus paid over and above the treaty Transit Due (half Export Duty) provided the exportation by British merchants to foreign ports takes place within twelve months. It is further agreed that native produce shipped to other treaty Ports shall not be entitled to such refund.

Art. v.—It is agreed that Chinese produce shipped from Hongkong to a Treaty Port, shall not be carried inland under the Transit Rule, but shall pay dues, duty and inland charges with all other native produce at all barriers passed; on the other part, China agrees to issue to native produce shipped by British merchants, from Treaty Ports to Hongkong, the ordinary duty proofs, and to collect on such produce on their arrival at the second Treaty Port, the ordinary Coast Trade (half import) duty....

SUPPLEMENTARY RULES AND TARIFF.

Whereas it is expedient that Supplementary Regulations should be drawn up for the better explanation of the Articles of this Convention, the plenipotentiaries do hereby agree that the appended Tariff and Rules, the latter being in ten Articles following, shall be equally binding on the Governments and subjects of both countries with the Convention itself. In witness whereof they thereto affix their seals and signatures.

Rule i.—The Convention permits certain specified commodities of foreign origin to circulate freely in Treaty-Port provinces, without further liability to inland dues or charges, on payment simultaneously of Import Duty and Transit Dues at the time of Importation—when taken inland by British merchants in person or by Chinese, the Agents of British merchants, or by Chinese purchasers, while the British merchant will be required, as provided by the Treaty of Tientsin, to travel provided with the usual passport, the commodities aforesaid may be conveyed unaccompanied by any Transit certificate and may be sold freely and at pleasure along the road without being in any place called on to pay further dues and duties or inland charges. The various Customs' stations passed by such commodities will, however, make such examination as is usual, in order to provide against fraudulent substitution and the transport of prohibited articles.

(2.) With the exception of those classes of commodities which are to pay Import Duty and Transit Dues simultaneously, all other foreign Merchandize, carried inland will continue to be exempt from all Dues and charges *en route*, provided, having paid full Import Duty on Importation and the Tariff Transit Due when leaving the port to enter the interior, it is found to be accompanied by the ordinary próof of payment of Transit Dues, namely a Transit Certificate. Such goods will be liable to all Dues, Duties and Charges, whenever found inland unaccompanied by Transit Certificates; both British and Chinese merchants will be treated in accordance with the provisions herein set forth.

Since that period, however, the views of the Tsung-li Ya-mên have entered into a still more retrogressive phase. For, already in a circular despatch, dated March 23rd, 1872, the Ya-mên submitted to the Foreign Ministers in Peking, in reference to Drawbacks, Exemption-Certificates, and Transit-Dues, the following New Regulations, framed by the

Foreign Inspector-General, in concert with the Tau-tai as the Native Intendant of Customs at Shanghai, and which, with a view to the sequel, I will mark "Regulations A." The translation of these documents is reproduced from the *North-China Herald.*

The Tsung-li Ya-mên's Circular Despatch of March 23, 1872.

Prince Kung and the Ministers whose cards are enclosed make the following communication:—

In the 7th moon of last year (August 1871) the Prince and the Ministers instructed Mr. Hart, Inspector-General of Customs‡ to proceed to Shanghai, and, in concert with the Intendant Tautai, who is Superintendent of Customs at that port, to prepare rules for the satisfactory regulation of drawbacks, transit-certificates inwards and transit-certificates outwards.

In the 11th moon (December-January) the Inspector-General submitted the Rules framed in consultation as above for the consideration (of the Prince and Ministers by whom) they have been again and again discussed, the desideration being that, while trade should not be inconvenienced, no loss should either be sustained by the Customs revenue; that not only wrong doing on the part of foreign merchants should be guarded against, but that various mal-practices of Chinese merchants, such as misrepresentation and collusion (with the former) should also be put a stop to.

Upon the rules relating to the drawback and to transit-certificates inwards, the Ya-mên has come to a decision, but it will be necessary to forward them to the Ministers Superintendent of Trade for the Northern and Southern ports, who will instruct the Intendants being Superintendents of Customs to examine them most carefully.

The Chinese Government has the right at every port to adopt the means best calculated to secure the revenue against fraud and smuggling; (this is not only the spirit but) the plain language of the Treaty. The Intendants appointed to the Custom-houses at the ports being the officers (whose business it is) and consequently the persons best informed in all particulars respecting this, it is of course right that they should be directed to (look into what is proposed) with very great care,

‡ I reproduce here an official translation with all its imperfections, and inaccuracies, as published in the *North-China Herald* of April 27, 1862.

that so, when they shall have thoroughly digested these regulations, regulations may then be so framed as to leave them without occasion for pretending that they are inconvenient, and that they are consequently unable faithfully to abide by arrangements to which the Chinese (Authorities or Government) have agreed.

When the two Ministers Superintendents shall have replied, (the Prince and Ministers) will, after due deliberation, address an official communication to the American Minister and the Ministers of other Powers, in order that they may instruct their subordinates accordingly. Meanwhile they forward, in this note, the drafts of the regulations affecting drawbacks and transit-certificates inwards, which have been considered with the Inspector-General, for the information of the American Minister to whom they will be obliged for an early reply.

As to the rule to affect the memorandum and transit-certificate for produce, the Ya-mên has not yet satisfied itself. As, however, in accordance with the spirit of the Treaty, no produce but produce destined for a foreign port can be allowed to come within the scope of the Transit-Regulations, and merchants will be of necessity obliged to pay Barrier-duties at the Barriers, and *le-kin* duties at the lekin stations|| on all produce not destined to be carried to another Treaty-port, (the writers) will be obliged to the American Minister to issue instructions to the foreign merchants at the ports in this sense.

As regards drawbacks at Shanghae, the Ya-mên is writing to the Minister Superintendent of Trade in the Southern Ports to instruct the Intendant to issue drawbacks in all cases occurring before the end of the 10th foreign month of the 17th year of Tung Chih (31st October, 1871), where it is ascertained that drawbacks have been applied for and refused. From the above date forward merchants applying will of course have to conform to the new regulations. Such is the object of this note.

Compliments, 2nd moon, 11th day (23rd March, 1872).

(REGULATIONS A.)

DRAWBACKS AND EXEMPTION CERTIFICATES.

RULE I.—If a merchant desires to re-export Imports that have paid Tariff duty to a foreign country, it will be his business to give notice to the Customs, and the officer deputed by the Superintendent having as-

|| The translator has misapprehended the text from his unacquaintance with the true distinctive meaning of 關 and 卡.

certained by inspection that the goods are the original goods imported, and in the original package, and that none have been withdrawn or exchanged, the issue of a drawback to the applicant will be authorised, provided that the application shall have been made in thirty months from the day the Imports entered the port. (If the time the goods have been in port) exceed this term (the importer) will not be authorised to take out (*lit.* apply for and receive) a drawback; and if the goods be found to be other than the goods they are stated to be, the drawback will be refused, and the goods will farther be confiscated, in accordance with the Treaty.

Rule ii.—Merchants sending Imports that have paid the full duty at one port, to any other of the Northern or Southern ports, excepting always the ports on the Yang-tze at which no Import-duty is collected, are free to apply either for an exemption-certificate or a drawback, as it may suit their convenience. The drawback can only be claimed, as in the case of Imports re-exported to a foreign port, within the limit of thirty months, and in all particulars affecting it the provisions of Rule i. must be abided by; but the exemption-certificate will have to be dealt with as the Treaty farther prescribes.

Rule iii.—If the merchant, applying for drawback or exemption-certificate, be other than the original importer, the application must bear not only his own signature, but also the signature of the original importer.

If the establishment of the latter shall have been closed, it will be simply necessary that the goods be identified by inspection, and the signature of the original importer can be dispensed with.

Rule iv.—Application for drawback or exemption-certificates on Imports re-exported must be made before the ship's port clearance is issued, and the document applied for will be issued, if the Customs find that the goods concerned are the original goods unchanged. When a ship's accounts are closed and her clearance is issued, inasmuch as examination and identification of goods, for which a drawback or certificate is claimed, is no longer possible, the Customs cannot in such a case entertain the application.

TRANSIT DUES.

Rule i.—Application for Transit-passes, under which to carry Imports inland, must be made by the merchant who originally imported the goods. He must state the denomination and quantity of the goods; the name of the ship in which they were imported, and the date of her arrival; the place to which they are to be carried and the name of the person who is to carry them.

Rule ii.—If the applicant be not the original importer, in addition to the information required by the foregoing rule, to which he will sign his own name, he must state who the original importer was, and he must cause the original importer to certify that it was he who imported the goods, on the face of his application. Should the firm of the original importer have been closed, he need not require the original importer to sign the application.

Rule iii.—The information required by the two foregoing rules having been furnished under signature, the certificate (or pass) will be issued on payment of the half-duty, and the goods can then be carried inland covered by this certificate, whether the trader carrying be Chinese or foreign. To enable traders, Chinese or foreign, however, to carry goods inland under cover of the certificate, it is essential that the goods be really foreign imports.

Rule iv.—The certificate obtained as above, for the carriage of the foreign goods inland, must be exhibited at every barrier or duty-station along the line of transit, and any such office having ascertained by inspection that the goods are really the goods certificated, and are not carried by any other than the route by which they should be carried, will then stamp the certificate and allow the goods to proceed without payment of *lekin* charges. If it be found, on inspection of the certificate, that the goods are not on the line on which they ought to be, or that they are other than the goods for which the certificate was taken out, these being acts of departure from the proper route and smuggling, the whole will be confiscated, as provided by Rule vii. of those appended to the Tariff.

The certificate (or pass) here spoken of is available only as security against taxation in addition (to the duties already paid on goods) *en route* from port to inland destination. On the arrival of the goods it covers at the place of destination specified in it, it ceases to have any value, and should be immediately presented to the nearest authority, who will enter upon it the date on which the merchant specified arrived with the goods specified, and will affix his seal to it, and hand it back to the merchant presenting it, to serve as his guarantee against levy of *le-kin* or other tax in the place, to which the goods have been carried, so long as they remain unsold.

If, on arrival of the goods at their point of destination, the certificate be not presented as above, an additional half tariff-duty will be levied upon them as a fine. When they shall have been sold, the local government will of course levy the *le-kin* of the buyer, and with this levy the dealer who brought up the goods will have no concern.

Rule v.—Whenever a certificate (or pass) is applied for for the carriage of Imports inland, a term will be fixed for its reproduction, the number of days being calculated according to the distance between the port where the application is made, and the place of destination as declared by the applicant, and so many days being allowed for every 100 *li*; and a note will accordingly be made upon the certificate, that it was issued on such a date by the Custom-house specified to the merchant specified, and that he is to surrender it in so many days to the Ya-mên or inland duty station specified. The certificate will be stamped with the official seal (of the Superintendent), and on issuing it, he will advise the proper authority at the place entered as the place to which the imports are to be carried, who, at any time before the expiry of the transit-term, will put his *visa* on the certificate. On the sale of the goods he will call in the certificate and will forward it to the Custom-house which issued it, to be cancelled.

(Original note). The Superintendent of Customs and the Inspector-General will settle together the number of days to be allowed with reference to such or such a distance, as the term within which the certificate is to be surrendered.

Rule vi.—Imports carried inland under certificate must be accompanied by the certificate. Where a trader is carrying foreign imports not enumerated in his certificate, or goods without any certificate at all, if he be *bonâ fide* prepared to pay the barrier duties and *le-kin* charges at the different stations he passes, it will be his duty as he arrives at the barriers and stations, to give notice that his goods are uncertificated, in order that these duties and charges may be levied thereon. If he does not give such notice, his goods will be dealt with as contraband.

If the goods carried be other goods than those particularised on the certificate; or if they exceed the quantity specified in it; the barrier or station detecting (the irregularities) is authorised to detain the goods, and to make a written report to the Custom-house which issued the certificate, and which, in accordance with the Treaty, will investigate the case and (if necessary) confiscate the goods.

These Regulations (A.) were communicated to the Shanghai General Chamber of Commerce, and published at the time, eliciting from the Chamber a letter to the British Chief Superintendent of Trade in China, dated June 21st, 1872, which will be placed before the reader, and animadverted upon, further on.

Apparently in consequence of its contents, or of certain points of its contents, the Tsung-li Ya-mên instructed the Inspector-General, Mr. Hart, in communion with the Tao-tai of Shanghai to revise the Regulations (A.) in question, which, together with the new Regulations, relative to the transit of Chinese exports, framed by the same officials, were thereupon, in a circular despatch of December 25th, 1872, by the Tsung-li Ya-mên transmitted to the Foreign Ministers. The last-named documents, which I will mark "Regulations B," and "Regulations C," respectively, have been, and still are, kept a diplomatic secret. An authentic copy of the Chinese text, however, is now lying before me; and I am thus in a position to subjoin a translation of both papers. The former Rules concerning Drawbacks and Exemption Certificates, having undergone no essential modifications, are not here repeated.

(REGULATIONS B.)

Rules relative to the Transit of Foreign Goods to the Interior.

RULE I.—1. As regards all foreign goods Chinese as well as foreign merchants may apply to the Customs for a duty-certificate (or "transit-pass") for the purpose of conveying such goods into the Interior, and there shall, according to Treaty, no fresh taxes be levied on them. But they must be really goods imported from abroad, for which a duty-certificate is to be granted. Native goods, resembling foreign, which have been imported in foreign ships from another port and have paid duty as foreign goods at the Custom-house, are not included in these Regulations.

2. Whenever a merchant desires to apply for a certificate, he must hand in a written statement, in which he truly declares the denomination and the quantity of the goods, as well as the name of the place to which they are to be conveyed, and sign that declaration with his own hand. Whereupon the Custom-house office will cause to be ascertained, whether the goods are truly foreign goods and whether the declaration has been correctly made; after which it may issue the duty-certificate.

3. Whenever in the certificate one province shall have been designated, and the merchant goes with the goods to another province, the certificate shall be no longer of use, and the customary duties will be levied.

4. The duty-certificate is nothing more than a token to show that no further duties are to be levied on the road (*i. e. in transitu*). When once the goods shall have arrived at their place of destination, the certificate, even though the stipulated term have not yet expired, must be taken to the local Custom-house or barrier offices for the purpose of examination; and should the place have neither Custom-house nor Barrier, the merchant has to take the certificate to the local Magistrate.

5. So soon as the goods shall have been landed or stored, the merchant, without waiting till he has deposited the certificate, is bound to pay all the customary taxes levied at the place; only that he may not be charged, in addition to them, any further transit-(or road)-duties.

Rule II.—1. All persons, conveying goods into the Interior without a duty-certificate, must pay duties at every Custom-house and Barrier they pass. When, however, they have taken out a certificate for a place previously designated, they must follow the direct road to it. If, without an understanding, they take a bye-road, they will have to pay the usual charges at all the Custom-houses and Barriers which they pass, notwithstanding their being furnished with a duty-certificate.

2. The duty-certificate and the goods conveyed under its protection, must always travel and remain together. If the certificate be sent on before and the goods follow, or *vice versâ*, the goods, which are accompanied by no certificate, shall pay the usual duties.

3. If Chinese merchants, under cover of such a certificate, convey foreign goods into the Interior, they shall in no case be permitted to use foreign letters or devices and flags; and if they act in opposition to this, the whole of the goods shall be confiscated.

Rule III.—1. Those, who convey goods, under cover of the said certificate, into the Interior, must stop at each Custom-house and Barrier, and display them for examination.

2. Each Custom-house or Barrier office, having ascertained that the goods agree with the certificate, that they are in reality foreign goods, and that no bye-road has been taken in conveying them, shall thereupon affix its stamp and let the goods pass without further payment of duties.

3. In case of goods being conveyed besides those declared in the duty-certificate, information must be given beforehand at the Custom-houses and Barriers, as to what portion of the goods are not included in the certificate, in order that the usual duties may be levied thereon. If no information of this is given beforehand, all such goods shall be confiscated.

4. If certain goods are named in the duty-certificate and the merchant, under cover of the latter, should convey other goods, or if he should declare native goods to be foreign goods, then, so soon as this is discovered, all such goods shall be confiscated, and information given to the Custom-house which has issued the duty-certificate, in order that inquiry may be instituted.

Rule IV.—1. Whenever a Custom-house grants a duty-certificate, it shall, in accordance with the merchant's declaration of the place for which the goods are destined, always and beforehand fix a term, within which the duty-certificate must be again delivered up. For the same province this term shall be fifty days; for an adjoining province one hundred days; and for a more distant province two-hundred days.

2. If, within such an ample term a merchant should twice convey goods under cover of the same certificate, the Custom-house or Barrier-offices on discovering this, shall, although the term have not expired, confiscate all the goods and record the name of the merchant, to whom no duty-certificate shall ever be granted again.

3. If any term should be allowed to expire without the duty-certificate being delivered up to the Magistrate of the place for which the goods are destined, or if the certificate be retained and not given up at all, the Custom-house or Barrier-officials, or the local Authorities shall, after inquiry, give information thereof to the Custom-house of the sea-port, in order that it may register the name of the merchant, and never again allow him to apply for a certificate.

4. The term must be fixed at the same time that the duty-certificate is granted, and information be given of it at once to the local Autho-

rities and the Custom-house and Barrier-offices of the place for which the goods are destined, in order that they, after the merchant shall have arrived with his goods and delivered up his duty-certificate, the same may be returned for cancelling to the sea-port Custom-house, by which the certificate was originally issued.

(REGULATIONS C.)

Regulations concerning the purchasing of native produce in the Interior, and the conveying it to a treaty-port for exportation abroad by foreign merchants.

RULE I.—1. When a foreign merchant desires to proceed to the Interior and buy produce of the soil for exportation abroad, he may apply at the Custom-house for a "direction" (照) or a "directing" pass in three parts.

2. In his application he must distinctly state that the goods, which he intends to buy, shall be really exported abroad, and, if this be not done, that he is willing to pay the prescribed fine, in proof of which he must affix his own signature to the application. He must further state therein the name of the province, the district, and the place he is going to; what articles he wants to purchase; and whether he will go himself, or send a person or (persons) of his household (內 人).

3. This being clearly explained by the Custom-house, a pass may be granted in three parts, two of which shall contain the application, and one be left in blank for tha transit, the whole of the three parts forming one sheet.

4. The application, duly signed, is handed over to an official, appointed for the purpose, to be kept by him and entered in a register, so that matters connected with it may be investigated at any time and treated according to these regulations.

RULE II.—1. When a foreign merchant, provided with such a tripartite pass for the purchasing of native produce, shall have arrived in the prefecture, district, and village or mart stated, and producing the things named by him in his application, and bought such goods, he has to enter the name of the person charged with their conveyance, the name of his firm, and the number of packages and weight of the goods in the two first parts of the pass, containing the application.

2. At the first Custom-house or Barrier on the way back to the port, the tripartite pass has to be presented for inspection. The Custom-house or Barrier officials, after ascertaining that the goods agree with the

declaration, cut off and keep the two first parts of the pass, while they fill up with its different items the transit-pass until then left in blank; adding the date and the stamp of the Custom-house or Barrier.

3. The transit-pass is hereupon handed to the merchant, who may now proceed with his goods; but must, according to Treaty-stipulations, at every Custom-house and Barrier on his way present the pass for examination and stamping.

4. If the goods agree with the pass, the Custom-house and Barrier affixes to it a stamp, to the effect that the goods have been examined and passed without paying duty; and the merchant is allowed to proceed without delay.

5. If there are goods found, not mentioned in the pass and conveyed secretly by the merchant, or if the goods fall short of the quantity declared in the pass, which shows that they have been secretly sold on the way, the Custom-house or Barrier Office shall seize the whole of the goods and confiscate them by way of punishment; giving information to the Custom-house which has granted the pass.

6. On the merchants' arrival at the last Custom-house or Barrier before the sea-port, he must deliver up the transit-pass and pay the half-duty; and the official of the sea-port Custom-house, appointed to this charge, shall issue a certificate to the effect that the half-duty has been paid, and allow the merchant to pass the Barrier; and he shall likewise enter the list of the goods declared in the pass and the date of their arrival at the port in the register containing the application, so that the details may at any time be referred to.

7. If any one passes a Barrier on the road without subjecting to inspection, or if he pass the last Custom-house or Barrier without first paying the half-duty: all the goods that have passed the Barrier shall be confiscated.

8. Native produce, not covered by a transit-pass, must pay duties at every Custom-house and *le-kin* at every Barrier on the road; but native produce, not covered by such a pass, shall not be brought for inspection to any Custom-house or Barrier simultaneously with goods covered by a pass. If this be not attended to, the Custom-house or Barrier shall confiscate all the goods.

Rule III.—1. When the foreign merchant has brought native produce down to the sea-port and paid the half-duty, he must go to the Custom-house and pay the export-duty thereon. A term of twelve months is granted to him for exporting the goods. If, at the expiration of this term he has not effected their exportation, on his stating true and good reasons for it, the term may be prolonged for one month. But if, at the end of thirteen months, the goods are still not exported to a foreign country, or have been sold at the port, this shall be ascertained by officials appointed for the purpose by the Commissioner of Customs, and the merchant, who has made the original application shall be fined ten times the half duty, in order to compensate for the duties and the *le-kin*, the payment of which he has avoided on the road.

2. Native produce, which has been conveyed to a port under cover of a transit-pass, must be exported to a foreign country, and if the merchant attempt to ship them to another Chinese port, no matter whether within thirteen months or otherwise, he shall not only be fined in the payment of ten times the half-duty; but he shall moreover pay the export-duty at the first port, and at the other the half-duty for reimportation: after which he will be free to sell the goods.

3. If a merchant should state that goods have been exported abroad, and he should subsequently ship them to another Chinese port, the whole of such goods shall be confiscated.

Rule iv.—1. In all cases, in which a foreign merchant applies for a tripartite transit-pass, the following limits shall be fixed, reckoned from the day that the pass is delivered by the Custom-house up to the day that the pass is again presented, *viz.*, for places in the same province a hundred days; for adjoining provinces two-hundred days; and for other provinces four hundred days.

2.—If, at the expiration of these terms respectively, the transit-pass shall not have been presented again, the name of the merchant shall be registered, and he shall never again be permitted to apply for such a pass.

3. The time of the expiration of the pass shall be stated on it by the Custom-house, which shall also send information to the local Authorities of the Custom-house and Barrier at the place where the goods are to be purchased, in order to enable them to act in concert.

4. If the pass, which is brought back, should be found not to bear the stamps of all the Custom-houses and Barriers passed on the way, it shall fall under the provisions of Rule ii. (§ 7.) "If any one passes a Barrier," etc., and the goods shall be confiscated.

5. After the first Custom-house or Barrier has cut off and retained two parts of the tripartite pass, one of those parts shall be kept in the

archives of the said Custom-house or Barrier, and the other be sent to the Custom-house, which has issued the pass; and when the merchants shall have returned to the ports with their goods and again delivered up up the transit-pass, the second parts of the passes alluded to, shall be sent monthly to the Tsung-li Ya-mên for inspection.

The one important point, then, referred to in these documents and upon which the British Board of Trade and the Representative of England in Peking, Mr. Wade,—supported by the latest opinion of Sir R. Alcock, Mr. Wade's predecessor,—are found to agree with the Tsung-li Ya-mên and the Foreign Inspector-General of Chinese Maritime Customs, is this: that the provisions of the existing Treaties between Western Powers and China exempt, by the payment of the stipulated "transit"-duty, foreign merchandise destined for consumption in the Interior, and native produce destined for exportation to foreign ports, from certain inland "barrier" dues *in transitu* only, and not, as the merchants hold, from war-and all other taxes, to which such goods may by Chinese Officials be subjected in the Interior, to the detriment of trade.

The latest known view of the late versatile Representative of England at Peking, Sir Rutherford Alcock, to which reference has been made, was expressed by him in an official "Memorandum on Further Memorials respecting the China Treaty Convention", dated May 3, 1870, in these terms:—

The assertions contained in the first part of the Resolution [of the East India and China Association, transmitted to Lord Clarendon] that the proposed distinction between Treaty and non-Treaty provinces is contrary to the interests of commerce, retrograde in policy, and entails the forfeiture of former Treaty privileges, rest upon a total misapprehension of what those privileges are. The merchants have persistently maintained both in regard to the Art. xxviii of the Treaty of Tientsin and Rule 7, an interpretation distinctly and authoritatively repudiated by the only competent authorities in such a matter—the two High Contracting Parties, the British and Chinese Government. Neither the opinion of the Law Officers of the Crown as to the legal and proper interpretation of these Articles, nor the equally clear testimony of the late Sir F. Bruce and Mr. Wade, both engaged as the Secretaries of Lord Elgin in drawing up the several clauses of the Treaty, as to the true meaning and intent of those Articles in his Lordship's conception, have availed to deter the merchants from reiterating a fallacy, and insisting upon an interpretation, which rests upon no better foundation than their own opinion against all evidence and authority.

But Treaties are not of private interpretation, according to the interests or caprice of individuals trading under their stipulations. What the Treaty of Tientsin does grant in this matter of transit both Governments are agreed, and their joint decision is without appeal. By that Treaty, the importer of foreign goods has the right to sell them at the port without liability, while they remain his property, to any other duty than the import duty, or to send them to any internal market he may select, free from any other charge than the Customs dues on importation and the stipulated Treaty duty of 2½ per cent. But both at the port and at the internal Market, when once the goods have passed out of his hands, they are liable to bear whatever taxes or duties the Chinese administration may see fit to levy on them in common with similar goods of Chinese origin. This is the authoritative reading of the article in question, accepted by Her Majesty's Government.

At present, under the Treaty of Tientsin, the British merchant is entitled by a payment of a half duty rate of 2½ per cent. to have all his imports protected while in transit to any place in the interior from further charge if they continue his own property, not otherwise; and any Chinese produce he may have purchased in the interior is in like manner protected by a transit certificate to the port of shipment......

That the merchants contend for a different interpretation of the rights secured by Art. xxviii of the Treaty of Tientsin and Rule 7, appended to the same, has already been shown. But these are the conditions of trade, as determined by the only authoritative reading of existing Treaties. There are foreign merchants, it is true, in China, British and others, who contend nevertheless, that both foreign goods and Chinese produce, *not foreign owned*, are entitled to the protection of transit-certificates, besides insisting upon that protection extending to exemption from all inland taxation whatever, and have acted accordingly by selling certificates for Chinese owned goods and produce [destined for exportation to foreign ports]; but that does not prove that the Treaty gives any such rights.

The opinion here expressed by Sir Rutherford Alcock is in diametrical opposition to the opinion so warmly maintained by him in the summer of 1868, as will be presently seen. Still, the array of authorities against the view taken by the body of foreign merchants in China is a formidable one. Before, however, proceeding to its examination, it will be necessary, for a clear apprehension of the case, to enter upon one or two preliminary inquiries.

III.

PRELIMINARY INQUIRIES.

What is to be understood by "the Transit-System" in China?—Usual charges leviable on inland traffic in China—Peculiarities of the Chinese system of financial Administration—The Sacred Edict on the payment of duties—Practice and theory—Fiscal corruption in China—Chinese sources of revenue—Effects of the first English war and the Tai-ping rebellion—Introduction of the *le-kin* as a war-tax—Rapid extension of the new impost—Barriers and Custom-houses—Chinese "squeezing"—The Peking Board of Revenue and the *le-kin*—The *chow-fang* tax—Historical sketch of its introduction—Objects for which the *le-kin* was professedly imposed—Those have ceased to exist—Abolition of the tax proposed to the Tsung-li Ya-mên and declined—Causes of the failure of the English Revision of the Treaty of Tientsin—Sir Rutherford Alcock's diplomatic incapacity—Real purposes, to which the *le-kin* is devoted.

The first question, which our subject suggests, is:—What are we to understand by a "Transit-System" and "Transit-Dues" in China? In Europe, when there are two independent States separated by a third independent State, and merchandise is for local consumption or sale conveyed from either of the former into the other through the territory of the latter, this third independent State, in consideration of the merchandise being permitted thus to pass through its independent territory, used to levy upon such merchandise a certain tax, as a source of revenue to the public exchequer, in the shape of transit-dues. Invariably small in comparison with the corresponding import duty, these Dues have now altogether ceased to be imposed by England,

Germany, Austria, and other European States, even by Turkey. In China no conditions similar to those referred to exist. Irrespective of the claim of "the Son of Heaven" to Universal Supremacy, his dominions constitute an absolute monarchy. No Chinese province possesses the right to prohibit or interdict the conveyance of merchandise, through its territory, from one adjoining province into another one; and, consequently, on the frontiers of no Chinese province or dependency does a system of levying Transit-Dues obtain. Nor does such a system obtain at any place in the Interior of the country relative to merchandise conveyed thither from any Chinese port.

Hence, the Transit-Duty system in China cannot be understood in the European sense. It must necessarily be construed to refer to certain inland taxes, to which all merchandise generally, whether of foreign or home origin, is subject in the Interior of the Empire; and that such is indeed the case is positively proved by the fact, that the Chinese themselves know nothing of a "transit-system," nor even of "transit"-duties, and that in the Chinese Treaty-texts the latter are correctly designated as 內地稅, *néi-ti-shúi*, literally: "inland taxes" or "inland duties;" and the "transit-certificate" as 稅單, *shúi-tan*, "a receipt for duties paid." Without, however, stopping to draw, for the present, any conclusion from this fact, our next inquiry will have to be: What is the nature and approximate amount of those taxes?

The constitution of the Chinese Government presents a remarkable blending of divine absolutism and modern centralisation with profane democracy and ancient feudalism. Its power is of the nature of the former, its mode of administration partakes of that of the latter, element. Taxes, in China, are imposed by the Imperial Government, while their collection, and to some small extent their appropriation, is left to the Provincial Authorities; a certain proportion only, both in money and kind, being transmitted to the Capital for general purposes. The fourteenth apothegm of the Sacred Edict of the Emperor Shêng Tsu Jên (*K'ang-hsi*, 1662-1723) instructs the people :—" Be punctual in the payment of taxes, and you will avoid the collector's importunities." In amplification of which maxim, the Emperor Shih Tsung Hsién; (*Yung-Chêng*, 1723-1736) states :— " From the highest antiquity the country has been divided into shires, and taxes have been paid in proportion to the productiveness of the land........Since the establishment of Our Dynasty, the rates of revenue have been fixed by an universally approved statute, all unjust impositions being completely done away with, and not a farthing in excess required from the people." The purposes to which the taxes are applicable, we find described by Wang Yu-Po, in his paraphrase of the Sacred Edict, thus :—

You people, being without understanding, fancy that the Emperor requires the whole for the support of his own household, and do not consider the numerous ends to which these taxes are applied. Are not the salaries of the officials paid out of the revenue? They are bestowed on them in order that, possessing adequate means of support, they may be able to attend the more carefully to the regulation of your affairs. The pay of the army, also, is taken from the revenue, and given for the support of the soldiers, that you may have protection against robbers and thieves. It is out of the revenue, moreover, that grain is bought for storage in the granaries, to prevent, in years of famine, your dying of hunger. Besides these, there are numberless other purposes for which the taxes are made to serve, such as the repair of cities; the dredging of the beds of rivers,§ and the preservation of their embankments; the fit-

§ The Rev. Mr. Milne (The Sacred Edict, Shanghai, 1870. 8° p. 168) translates : "clearing out the bottoms of rivers." The text has simply : 修河, " to clear out " or " dredge

ting out of ships for the conveyance of the taxes paid in kind; the purchase of copper for the coinage; the repair of public buildings. All this is done with your money; and all this money is expended on your own behalf.

Practice and theory are wont to differ widely. Nowhere more so than in China. The great stumbling-block of her fiscal system is, that the uninterrupted tenure of office of the mandarins is always more or less uncertain; that the class of candidates for office far exceeds the requirements of the State; that most of the officials in actual service are underpaid; and that their numerous "expectant" inferiors and underlings are not paid at all. Hence, in combination with other causes, has arisen an unparalleled state of fiscal corruption and extortion—or "squeezing," as the process is technically called in China,—which has gradually, in different forms, permeated all classes of society, and constitutes one of the most characteristic features of the every-day intercourse of the whole people. The mandarin in office, "making hay while the sun shines," strives to provide for the future or to amass wealth within the shortest possible period; and the crowd of subordinates attached to his ya-mên have to gain, as best they may, at least the means of existence: the Government shutting its eye to evils which its own policy has originated, and extending the utmost clemency to individual delinquents, in cases of more flagrant corruption or extortion brought under its special notice, *so long as the taxes themselves are forthcoming and the public peace is not disturbed.* From these circumstances it will be readily inferred that, although taxation in China be nominally light, it is by no means so in reality.

---

the rivers;" but the meaning is plain, and how His Highness Prince Kung and the Tsung-li Yâ-mên are able to reconcile their opposition to the dredging of the Wusung bar with the sacred injunctions of the Emperors Shêng Tsu Jên and Shih Tsung Hsién, twice a month to be publicly explained to the people, is not readily intelligible.

The main source of revenue to the Chinese Government is a land-tax, varying according to the nature and quality of the soil, and in the mean equal to about one shilling and six-pence or more probably two shillings per acre, payable partly in silver, partly in kind. It yields more than eight-tenths of the entire public income; the remainder being derived from the salt-monopoly, the Customs, house- and shop-taxes, licenses, river- and road-tolls, etc. The latter tax forms an insignificant item. In ordinary times the revenue amply suffices for the wants of the Empire, and twice during the prosperous reign of Káo Tsung Shun ¶ *(Chien-lung,* 1736-1796*)*, the entire land-tax was remitted by that munificent and conquering Monarch to his subjects. It is in times of national disaster that the Government finds it difficult to meet the exigencies of the State by extraordinary taxation. The fiscal system, deranged in consequence of the English war with China in 1841–1842, and disastrous inundations of the Yellow River and the Yang-tze, had scarcely returned to something like its normal condition, when, in 1850, the Tai-ping rebellion broke out, and an incapable and corrupt sovereign, the Emperor Wên Tsung Hsién *(Hsien-fêng* 1851-1862*)*, succeeded to the throne. The rebellion soon assumed large proportions. Its leader, formerly a poor student of Christianity, in 1853 established his rule in the "Southern Capital," Nanking, under the title of *T'ien Wang*, "Heaven's

¶ The Emperors of China, during their life time, are simply designated as "*the* Emperor," namely, according to Chinese ideas, of 天下, literally "all there is under Heaven" *i. e.* the Earth. It is only after their death, that a historical or Temple-name is given to them. Their milk-name, so long as they occupy the throne, no Chinaman is permitted either to write or to pronounce. In the case of the present Ruler and his two predecessors only, this rule has been restricted to the second element of the name. What is, in the West, mistaken for the Chinese Sovereign's name, such as Chien Lung, Sien Fêng, Tung Chih, is a motto or epithet of good augury, by which it is desired and hoped that *the period of the reign* may be distinguished. It is, therefore, as inappropriate to speak *f. i.* of Kào Tsung Shun as "His Majesty the Emperor *Chien Lung*", as it would be to speak *f. i.* of George IV of England as "His Majesty King *Anno Domini* 1820-30."

Monarch." Yet, in 1859 the Chinese Government felt strong enough to provoke the English-French war of 1859-1860. The Tai-pings, profiting by the opportunity, marched to the capture of Suchow, and committed the error of attacking Shanghai. Thereupon the Treaty of Tientsin was ratified, and Western support given to the Manchu Government, then carried on by an Imperial Council in the name of the Boy-Emperor Tsai-Chun, who succeeded his father in August, 1861, against the rebellion. It was crushed in 1864; and followed by the Mahometan rising in Shen-si and Kansu, and the Nien-fei troubles in Chih-li and Shan-tung. In 1868, the Empire relapsed into its wonted state of ruffled stagnation, with a largely increased amount of corruption, ruin, and devastation, but only the usual extent of chronic insurrection in one or two of the provinces, and a settled determination, on the part of the anti-foreign Tatar Government, to "wipe out China's shame," which, already in 1870, led to the Plot of the Summer-Solstice, its partial carrying into effect by the successful massacre of foreigners at Tientsin, and those vigorous efforts for its devoutly desired consummation, to which all the energies and resources of the present administration continue to be directed.

Under these circumstances and at an early period of the Tai-ping rebellion, the Chinese Government, in order to provide for the financial necessities of the State, resolved on having recourse to, among other measures, that of collecting a war-tax, under the peaceful name of *le-kin*, at a rate of about $\frac{1}{10}$ per cent.,—on an extended scale upon the inland commerce of the country, by the multiplied machinery of the old established river- and road-custom- and toll-houses. It was only, however, after the ratification of the British Treaty of Tientsin, and *with the special view of paralysing, as far as practicable, its provisions relative to foreign inland trade and, whilst burdening that trade to the utmost, to benefit the public Exchequer to a corresponding extent*, that the scheme was fully organized. "Now, with regard to war-taxes"; a Memorandum addressed by the Tsung-li Ya-mên to the British Minister on June 28th, 1868, observes, "the fundamental revenue of China is the land tax, the system of national loans being unknown. But during the rebellion His Majesty has, out of compassion for the sufferings of his people," as the Memorandum naïvely has it, "remitted the land tax, wholly or partly, *in the disturbed districts;* and, as a temporary measure, consequently, the national necessities must be supplied by these extraordinary levies." And in the official Minute of the Proceedings, March 3rd, 1868, of the Mixed Commission on the Revision of the Treaty of Tientsin, we read: "Mr. Tsai accounted for the origin of the war-tax by stating, that, as some of the richest cities in China, particularising Nanking, Suchow (taken in May 1860, re-taken in December 1863) and Hang-chow, had been destroyed by the Tai-pings, and numbers of what had been wealthy districts so devastated that it was impossible to levy the accustomed land-tax, the Government had no choice but to invent such a tax as the *le-kin.* He said, a system of loans, prevalent in Western countries, would not work in China, where there are few great capitalists, and fewer still who would be willing to lend money to the State."

"The Provincial Governments," Mr. Wade states in his memorandum of 1868, "do not, legally, possess the right to multiply the collectorates or barriers, a list of which is published in the Code of the Board of Revenue, without reference to that Board; nor can their number be added to by the Board itself without the sanction of an Imperial

Decree." But his Excellency, lest, perchance, he should compromise the "Provincial Governments" * omits to inform his own, whether such a multiplication of "barriers" has taken place, and, if so, whether with or without the sanction of an Imperial Edict. I am not aware of the existence of such an Edict; whereas the multiplication of barriers is simply a fact. Indeed, the old inland Custom-houses, levying their accustomed duties, continue in operation independently of the subsequently established offices or "barriers" for the collection of the 釐金, *le-kin*,—or what might not inappropriately be termed, "Peter's pence"† namely: 釐捐總局, *li-tjüen-tsung-tjü*, "Chief Offices of the Cash-Contribution," one for each Province, and 釐捐分局. *li-tjüen-fën-tjü*, "Branch Offices of the Cash-Contribution", with their sub-branches, multiplied throughout the country according to circumstances, both on roads and rivers; burdening the inland traffic generally, but the foreign inland trade especially, with onerous taxes and exactions. "Should the special tax-barriers," the Tsung-li Ya-mên states in a memorandum of August 1st, 1868, addressed to the British Minister, "be hereafter abolished, and the old custom-houses alone be retained in the Interior and along the Yang-tze, we might arrange these matters afresh. Meanwhile we have to repeat with regard to these special taxes and con-

* The diplomatists at Pe-king, more particularly since the introduction of the co-operative policy, now defunct, have contracted the habit of designating the Chinese Government as "the Central Government" in contradistinction to "the Provincial Governments," a habit, which leads and can lead to nothing but misconceptions and erroneous impressions. There exist no provincial "governments" in China, but only provincial "Administrations," and at the head of which there are placed no "Vice-Roys," as they are usually styled, but only *Tsung-tu*, *i. e.* "Head Directors" or "Governors," and *Fu-tai*, *i. e.* "Lieutenant-Governors," subordinate to the former when Governors of two (or three) Provinces united. Strictly speaking, as has been already observed, the Chinese Government is the Emperor, and, in diplomatic language, it would be as correct to speak of "the Central Emperor," as of "the Central Government", of China.

† The character 釐 *le*, also written simply 厘, designates a small brass or copper-coin of China known to foreigners by the English name of "a cash." The meaning of 金, *tjin*, or *kin*, is "metal".

tributions, *that they spring from the military necessities of the country*. So long as the Custom-houses in the Interior cannot be re-opened on the former basis, the Government must needs place the burden on the trading communities: hence, the more or less numerous inland barriers; and hence, again, the heavier or lighter contributions demanded."

The *le-kin* tax is not collected at a uniform rate, but at rates differing in different provinces and at different times, though hitherto only upon an increasing scale. In China there is no Chancellor of the Exchequer, save the wants of the Government. The annual or periodical sum required is by the Board of Revenue apportioned among the various Provinces, and an Imperial Edict orders each Province to furnish its quota. To see to this, and to provide for the similar Provincial necessities, is the business of the Governor and the Treasurer of the Province. The Imperial and Provincial sum-total is by the Treasurer again apportioned among the various circuits, and the Governor orders each Circuit to furnish *its* quota. To see to this, and, in addition, to provide for the similar local necessities, is the business of the Tau-tai or other specially appointed official, under whose immediate supervision the collectorates of his district are placed. The latter have wants of their own. Every official, high and low, connected with the *le-kin* tax, looks upon it as an institution for "squeezing" to the utmost degree of his individual power, and the underlings, attached to the collectorates, have no other means of subsistence. The trader, and ultimately the consumer, has to pay for all this in the aggregate. Hence, the taxes, actually levied in each province, depend on the sum apportioned to it by the Chinese Government, the amount added to that sum for Provincial necessities, the further amount added to the latter for local purposes, the rapacity of officials, and the degree of extortion practicable. It is difficult, therefore, to arrive at the details of the rates imposed on inland trade in the shape of *le-kin*, and a variety of minor taxes of a similar nature. For this purpose it would be necessary to possess the lists of charges, in use, throughout China, at each collectorate, toll-house, and other fiscal office.

In certain parts of the province of Kuan-tung, probably in order to obstruct foreign trade with the provinces of Kuang-si, Kwei-chow, Yün-nan, and Sze-Chuen, and in the province of Fu-kien, those charges are raised, always with the cognizance, or at the instance, of the Chinese Government, to prohibitive rates; whilst in the northern provinces they used to be so moderate that, in Tientsin, transit-passes were rarely taken out. Yet, in contradiction to this fact, reported as such in 1867 by the then Foreign Commissioner of Customs at the port in question, Mr. Dick, the imposts levied already in 1871, upon a quantity of native sugar, sent by a Chinese merchant from Tientsin to Peking, a distance of about 80 English miles, amounted to nearly 20 per cent. on its value. At present they are the same in the northern Provinces, as they are in other parts, of China. On foreign goods, sent, without a certificate, by water from Shanghai to Su-chow, a distance of little more than eighty miles, there are collected, besides minor tolls and "squeezes," the following taxes, *viz.*, at Shanghai: import duty about 5 per cent.;‡ *chow-fang* about 2½ per cent.; *le-kin* about 2½ per cent; *en route* at the first collectorate: *le-kin* about

‡ The Tariff import- and export-duties were calculated on the basis of 5 per cent. *ad valorem* in the mean, and articles not enumerated in the Tariff are actually taxed at that rate. In reality, however, the mean amount of import- and export-duties levied is very nearly 6 per cent., as will be seen further on.

1½ per cent.; at a second collectorate: *le-kin* about 1½ per cent.; at Su-chow: *le-kin* about 2½ per cent.:—in all, from fifteen to sixteen per cent *ad valorem.* Between Chin-kiang and Wu-hu, a distance of about 100 miles, at no less than four Custom-houses duties have to be paid independently of war-taxes, the various charges amounting in the aggregate to something like twenty-five per cent. *ad valorem.* Supposing the goods to be accompanied by a transit-pass, they would then up to their place of destination be subject only to import-duty about 5°/₀, *chow-fang* about 2½°/₀, transit-duty about 2½°/₀, in all about ten per cent. *ad valorem*, besides "squeezes"; but, although the Tsung-li Ya-mên insists that the foreign merchant has thus a considerable advantage over the native trader, the Chinese officials find means, on the arrival of the goods at the inland market,—which, for this reason, has to be specified in the transit-pass taken out at the port,—to make up for the difference; and by the time that the foreign merchandise passes into the possession of the native consumer, it may be safely calculated, that it has paid to the Chinese Government a tax of twenty-five per cent. *ad valorem*, as already stated. In other words, the "*le-kin*" *per se* since its first imposition in 1843 or 1844, has been increased to *one hundred and fifty times its original rate*, and now, including *chow-fang*, is equal to twice the tariff import- and transit-duties on foreign merchandise taken together. It is true, that to some extent its payment may be avoided by unscrupulous traders, in unison with more unscrupulous collectorate-officials, to the detriment of the honorable merchant; that excessive impositions,—excessive as compared with a tax of 15°/₀ or 18°/₀, such as would be payable *f. i.* between Shanghai and Hankow by water,—were frequently avoided by shipment of the goods to Ningpo and a long round-about land-journey; and that in some parts of the northern provinces the *le-kin* levied does possibly not as yet reach the full amount per cent.: but, so far as the materials at my disposal permit of a deliberate and well-considered judgment, I am of opinion, that twenty-five per cent. *ad valorem*, as the *mean* amount of taxation, to which all foreign goods imported into China and consumed at the ports or conveyed for sale into the Interior, as well as all native articles of produce exported abroad, are at present subject, is a moderate estimate.||

The *chow-fang* contribution, 籌防捐, at first named '*Húi-fang Yüen*, 會防捐, became known to foreigners under the name of "defence tax," when, after the Tai-pings had taken Suchow in May, 1860, it was imposed, in the shape of a "voluntary" capitation tax for the recovery of that famous city. "Heaven," a Chinese proverb says, "has its paradise; the Earth its Su and 'Hang" (Su-chow and 'Hang-chow). As has been already remarked, the city was re-captured by the Imperialists in December, 1863; but the tax for its re-capture was continued under the altered name of "*chow-fang* contribution," changed into a tax upon inland trade, and extended to other ports. On the outset the Tau-tai of Shanghai had some little difficulty in introducing this new exaction into *the Foreign Settlement*. Thanks, however, to the complaisance of Sir Frederick Bruce and Lord John Russell, then English Secretary of State for Foreign Affairs, the astute Chinese official, introducing, moreover, the salt-monopoly into his arguments and killing two birds with one stone, carried his insidious design. The correspondence on the subject, transcribed from the Blue-Book "China, No. 3, 1864," is deserving of a place here:—

|| This was written before the information fully and literally confirming the above statement had reached me.

The Taoutae Woo to Consul Medhurst.

(Translation). Shanghae, July 1, 1861.

I write in consequence of a letter received from one Wang, expectant Taoutae and Superintendent of the Tai-shan Salt Contributions, that the number of people living in the foreign settlement at Shanghae must needs consume a large quantity of salt; that the officer Yu had accordingly hired a number of men to sell it, but a very small quantity had been disposed of; that it is evident therefore that it is smuggled; that having received orders to supervise the salt trade, it behoved him to devise some means of regulating it, that the taxes might be paid and the salt contractors not lose; that he had assembled the head men to discuss the subject, and proposed to establish the Le-tai-seng salt-shop in the French Concession, and the Chang-cheang-shun salt shop in the English Concession to supply the two settlements, the permits hitherto issued being withdrawn. But as it was to be feared that bad characters would take advantage of the foreign character of the place, and induce the police to throw obstacles in the way, it was necessary that the English and French Consuls should be written to that they might direct the police to arrest any smugglers, by which means the Government sales would increase and the legal trade flourish. That he had directed therefore the two shops to open, and begged me to write to the two Consuls to give the necessary orders.

I have therefore written to the French Consul, and do also to you to beg you will direct the police to assist in arresting any illicit traders.

The Taoutae Woo to Consul Medhurst.

(Translation.) Shanghae, July 5, 1862.

I write to ask your co-operation in a matter by which I may remedy the insufficiency of the taxes to meet the large and most necessary expenditures.

At the end of the last year I established a committee which when your countrymen and the French assisted us against the rebels were called upon to pay for rent, coolies, roads, batteries, the destruction of houses, boats, rice, firewood, artillery, lascars, &c., &c., to the amount of 50,000 or 60,000 taels a month, besides 200,000 odd for the troops brought down from Nyanching, to meet which they were only able to collect some 100,000 taels in all, a sum quite insufficient.

The above claims, moreover, are for the protection of Shanghae and must be paid. While the Treasury and contribution receipt being insufficient for the purpose to which they are devoted, the pay of the troops, it is absolutely necessary to lay on some new taxes to procure the funds so urgently required.

I therefore on the 15th of the 4th moon wrote you with reference to three taxes I proposed imposing, they being in accordance with Treaty, to wit, a tax on native produce, an increased tax on opium, and a capitation tax, subsequently writing further letters on the subject.

With reference to the two first taxes, you have already written me that you have referred them to Her Majesty's Minister for consideration, and that it behoveth to await his decision; but the capitation tax is entirely Chinese and does not affect foreigners at all, and I see no reason therefore why the Chinese residents should not pay it.

Again, the great majority of Chinese residents on the French and English settlements are Che-chiang and Keang-si refugees who have not paid their proper taxes, and who have fled there since the great collection of the allied troops, and who carry on their business solely by their protection; and as unless the troops are maintained the people cannot continue to enjoy security, as they are innumerable, I have proposed to divide them into three classes, the first paying five dollars, the second one dollar, the third half a dollar per head, children and women being exempted, and one collection being final.

In registering them for the tax, moreover, one will be able to discover any bad characters that may be here.

This cannot be considered squeezing, and a double advantage will result from it. It appears, moreover, in accordance with foreign laws, and has already been put in practice as far as the city and suburbs are concerned; but I have to request you will appoint some one to take cognizance of the natives, whether householders or in foreign employ, in the British settlement, as I am at my wit's end to obtain the enormous sums required for the defence of the place, and this is the only way open to me to meet them.

As the matter concerns us both I trust you will co-operate with me without delay.

Consul Medhurst to the Taoutae Woo.

Shanghae, July 16, 1862.

Sir,—I have had the honour to receive your two letters dated the 1st and 5th instant, the one asking me to co-operate with you in imposing a capitation tax on all Chinese residents within the British limits, the other announcing the establishment of licensed salt-dealers in the British and French Concessions, whose right of monopoly you wish to have protected.

The local authorities are no doubt entitled to impose on their own subjects any tax or monopoly which does not interfere with foreign Treaty rights; but as regards those natives who reside within these limits, I am not in a position to recognize such a right, as it has been a matter of understanding for years past between the local authorities and this Consulate that the jurisdiction of the former over their own subjects living within these limits shall only be exercised through and with the consent of the British Consul, and with the large Chinese population now depending on our protection and sharing our interests, it would be inexpedient to allow of any departure from this rule.

I shall send copies of your letters and this reply to the Hon. Mr. Bruce.

I have, &c.

(Signed) W. H. Medhurst.

Mr. Bruce to Consul Medhurst.

Peking, November 5, 1862.

Sir,—In reply to your despatch of the 14th August last, requesting my advice as to the proposals made by the Taoutae for the taxation of Chinese subjects within the limits of the so-called British Concession, I have to observe that there is nothing in the Treaties which warrants me in interfering in any way in such questions. The Taoutae is entitled to levy taxes as he pleases; and as long as he merely seeks to impose taxes on persons resident in the Concession, which are paid by those living in the city and suburb, I see no reason for objecting to it at a time when it is our interest as well as that of the Chinese that the Government shall not be deprived of its resources.

A heavy responsibility will rest on the Consul of any port should his action in such matters lead to the disbanding or mutiny of the highly-paid force under foreign officers which the Chinese have embodied by our advice.

I am, &c.,

(Signed) Frederick W. A. Bruce.

Earl Russell to Sir F. Bruce.

Foreign Office, April 8, 1863.

Sir,—I have to state to you that Her Majesty's Government entirely concur in your views and approve the instructions which you have addressed to Her Majesty's Consul at Shanghae, as reported in your despatch of the 5th November last, with regard to the proposals made by the Taoutae for taxing Chinese subjects who reside within the limits of so-called British Concessions.

The lands situated within the limits of the British Settlement are without doubt Chinese territory, and it cannot reasonably be held that the mere fact of a residence within those limits exempts Chinese subjects from fulfilling their natural obligations.

I am, &c.,

(Signed) Russell.

I shall take some future occasion to revert to the important principle involved in this question, and content myself, in this place, to point out that Sir Frederick Bruce himself makes his decision to rest solely on the ground of *temporary expediency*, whilst Lord Russell's doctrine, that it is one of the "natural obligations" of John Chinaman to be "squeezed"§

---

§ The Tautai Wu, in observing relative to the tax proposed by him, that "this cannot be considered squeezing", was manifestly not aware of the Western saying: "*Qui s'excuse, s'accuse.*"

To illustrate the manner in which the *chow-fang* tax is now levied at Shanghai, in the very British Settlement and even on articles of small value intended for local consumption, the following case may serve, which some time ago came before the Mixed Court. A highly respectable German firm sent by one of their coolies a sample-piece of habit-cloth to a shop situated, like their own *hong*, in the English Settlement. The coolie was stopped by a Chinaman, who claimed a tax of Tl. 0.16 (about 2*s*. 9*d*. British money) on the parcel. In vain he was told that it contained foreign property. *He demanded proofs to that effect, and meanwhile seized the cloth*, and deposited it in another shop. The firm referred to very properly had the case at once submitted to the Mixed Court. The value of the piece of cloth and illegally taxed at the will and pleasure of any Tau-tai, presents one of those transparent fallacies, for which his Lordship is so noted; and further that a tax imposed upon the inland trade of China, injuriously affecting the interests and the Treaty-rights of the foreign merchant, and a capitation-tax laid on Chinese subjects, are two utterly different things.

We have seen from statements of the Tsung-li Ya-mên, that the *le-kin* was imposed,—*1*, with the view of making up the deficiency in the land-tax, caused by the Tai-ping rebellion and the Nien-fei troubles; *2*, for military purposes alone; and *3*, as a mere temporary measure. But the Tai-ping rebellion came to an end a dozen years ago; the Nien-fei troubles, which a regiment or two of European Light Cavalry would have suppressed within six months, have been forgotten these eight years past; the State is less disturbed by rebellion than it chronically is; the Army perhaps more numerous but no better paid, than habitually; China has, now for years, been at peace with all the Outer World; and the land-tax, it is credibly reported, yields once more fully its medium amount of revenue to the public Exchequer.

Already at the meetings of the Mixed Commission for the Revision of the Treaty of Tientsin, the abolition of the *le-kin* dues was more than once brought up for discussion. From the Minute of Proceedings on March 3rd, 1868, it appears that Mr. Tsai stated:—"It had been the intention of the Tsung-li Ya-mên"—the war in the south-east of China being then at an end—"to suggest that the tax should be abolished,

---

was Tls. 21 (about £6.6.0); the legal Tariff import-duty, which had been paid upon it, Tl. 0.89 (about 5s. 4d.); the chow-fang Tl. 0.4.4.5, and the "squeeze" of the tax-gatherer Tl. 0.0.1.5, or rather more than 50 per cent of the former, *levied within one hundred yards of the Foreign Custom-House.* The Chinese Magistrate Chên decided, that "the man had committed a serious offence in asking for the impost on the public road and on goods not a Chinaman's, but *in itself the tax was perfectly right*; only its collection should be gone about privately and quietly."

but that the sudden appearance of Nien-fei in Chih-li, entailing great expense, had rendered this impossible for the present; but, as soon as the high officers now commanding armies in Chih-li had quelled the rebellion and returned to their several jurisdictions,¶ the Ya-mên would take measures to induce them to memorialize the Throne, and to pray for the abolition of the war-tax. The Ya-mên could not do this itself, the question being one not lying in its province." At the meeting of the Commission on June 27th, 1868, the Chinese Members again declared that, "the *le-kin* tax being the principal source from which were drawn the means of maintaining troops for the pacification of the provinces, and the ports being the most important preserves of such taxes, it is not possible, so long as the country continues to be disturbed by rebels in arms, to order the provincial authorities to desist from levying them; but that it might be relied on that they would be removed as soon as such pacification should be accomplished."

In his Memorandum relative to this negative resolution on the part of the Chinese Government, the British Minister, (Sir Rutherford Alcock), says:—

The non-abolition of *le-king** taxes at the ports demands further consideration...... It has been plainly stated before that one of the chief objects he had in view in suggesting a Commission, was, 1stly, to correct some great abuses in the collection of duties to the injury of trade (of which the worst is the *le-king*); and 2ndly, to supply compensation for past losses entailed by those abuses, and thus forestal large claims for indemnity, otherwise likely to be preferred. Both these important ends will be missed by the maintenance of the *le-king* taxation on foreign goods

¶ In China armies are commanded by civilians. The military profession is altogether held in contempt.

* Sir Rutherford Alcock and the British Commissioner spell; "*le-king*", as though they had associated the idea of *leaking* or *leeching* with the Chinese term. Mr. Wade, whose ear does not catch the difference of sound between *tjin* and *chin*, pronounces 金 "*chin*." The southern pronunciation is *kin*. I have followed the accustomed mode of writing *le-kin*.

more especially, and the main object of the Commission defeated. The non-consent to do away with all surcharges and objectionable taxes on foreign trade in the vicinity of the Treaty ports, as soon as the tranquillity of the country is assured and demands for special military expenditure have ceased, must be considered as a negation of any present relief from taxation which is imposed contrary to Treaty; and the period fixed for its cessation much too uncertain, if not distant, to be satisfactory. China, like most other countries, by entering into Commercial Treaties with Foreign States,† has, in consideration of a fixed payment of maritime and transit duties, foregone all further right of taxation on whatever can be shown to constitute the foreign trade, import, or export. Otherwise, of what use could be the provisions of the Treaties so carefully fixing and limiting the Tariff rates, import, export, and transit? If the Territorial Government retained the right to surcharge these at pleasure, the whole trade could at any moment be stopped, or more gradually dwarfed and finally ruined by burdens it is unable to bear, or prohibitive duties. To say that the Chinese Government has urgent need of funds is not a reason that can be accepted by a Treaty Power for a plain violation of so essential an Article in all the Treaties, affecting the prosperity and very existence of the trade...... The *le-king* taxes are eminently variable, uncertain in amount from year to year, arbitrary in their exaction, and otherwise constituting a violation of Treaty-rights. The only portion of the *le-king* taxes, which are not in this sense illegal and contrary to Treaty, are those levied on Opium. *On that one article alone* the Chinese Government reserved its absolute right of taxation without limitation by Treaty, except as regarded the maritime duty...... The difficulties of the Tsung-li Yamên and the necessities of the country have been fully recognized by the British Minister, and there is every desire on his part to avoid embarrassing discussions, or pressing for impracticable measures, either beyond or within the limits of existing Treaties. But this one question of an assumed right of the Chinese Government to tax foreign trade *ad libitum* is one of principle, and of such vital moment to the interests of commerce that a British Minister

† It should be remembered, that the Chinese do not acknowledge the existence of Foreign States in our sense, *i. e.* as *independent* States. They term Great Britain, Russia, France, Germany, the United States, &c., "Outer" States, holding them to be subject to the One Emperor of the Earth,—whom we "barbarians" are in the habit of calling the Emperor of *China*,—and forming integral portions of the Ching Empire Universal. In the Chinese texts or translations of every official despatch and diplomatic document, the Western Powers are represented as vassals of China.

can have no discretionary power in protesting against it as a violation of Treaty.

Consequently, the subject was once more discussed at the following meeting of the Revision-Commission on July 14th, 1868.‡ The Minute of the Proceedings of that meeting says:—

Of the demands, altogether negatived, it was necessary to press one: the abolition of *le-kin* taxes and local dues upon articles of foreign commerce. It was represented that the xth Article of the Treaty of Nanking provides that, even in Chinese hands, articles of British commerce should only pay such rates as are provided by Tariff, and that the Treaty thus protecting the actual staples of British trade, in whatever hands, it could not be but an infraction to subject them, once out of the foreign merchant's possession, at the ports and in the Interior, to capricious and arbitrary levies. To this representation, however, the Chinese members were prepared with an answer. The Tsung-li Ya-mên had not been acquainted with the Treaty of Nanking, their copy having been carried away from Yuen-ming-yuen; they acknowledged fully the obligations it imposed, and recognized their application to the point in question; but they hoped that the British Minister would not press this point; urging, in support, the many concessions already made to foreign commerce, the absolute necessity for raising funds to meet the enormous military expenditure called for by the disturbances in the provinces, the impossibility of raising these elsewhere than at the ports and upon articles affecting foreign commerce; saying that, as these necessities disappeared, measures would be taken into consideration for the protection of foreign trade in the future.

At the last meeting of the Revision-Commission, on July 16, 1868, "the Chinese were informed that Sir Rutherford Alcock adhered to his decision, that the thirty-

‡ The Minute of the meeting states:—"Present:—Hsia, Tsai, Sun I, Sun II, Kao, Mr. Hart, and *the British Members.*" This is, as regards the latter, only said to make a show. The solitary British Member of the Commission was Mr. Hugh Fraser, Second Secretary of Legation, a diplomatist of the mildest character, who would appear to have occasionally misunderstood the very memoranda of his chief. He was assisted by Mr. Thomas Adkins as *Interpreter.* Mr. Hart attended in his capacity of a Chinese mandarin. Of the thirteen meetings of the Commission, a few were held at the Tsung-li Ya-mên, a few at the British Legation and the majority at Mr. Hart's residence.

li radius was the most practical mode of dealing with the *le-kin* difficulty. The reply made was, that the Ya-mên cannot see that the collection of the *le-kin*, which is a special tax for local wants and military purposes, constitutes any breach of Treaty. But they are willing to admit, that foreign goods *in transit* should be treated alike, whether in the hands of Chinese or foreign merchants, as prescribed by Tariff, Rule 7, *while under transit certificate;* the attempt to pass goods otherwise than under such certificate rendering them liable to be treated as native goods. The thirty-*li* radius shall be conceded so soon as the state of the country will permit, a modification in the collection of the opium tax being accepted as a partial equivalent........The Ya-mên allows the application of the provisions of the Treaty of Nanking only so far as to concede that Chinese merchants, as well as foreign merchants, may convey foreign goods free under transit-certificate."

The sudden and important change in the views of the Tsung-li Ya-mên, here indicated, fully coinciding as it does with the corresponding views of the Inspector-General Mr. Hart: are we not justified in concluding, that the latter were suggested to the Ya-mên by its confidential adviser? Be this as it may: the final reply of the Tsung-li Yamên to the two principal propositions of the British Minister is thus stated by the Commission:—

1. Repayment in full of exactions on foreign trade in the Interior.—*Answer:* A proclamation will be issued by the Ya-mên requiring the Barrier Officials to act in accordance with Treaty, thus avoiding illegal levies in future. Previous claims will be treated as they are found to be acts of extortion by Officials, or the result of the separation of the goods from the transit-passes.

2. No levy of *le-kin* to be made on produce for export or on foreign imported goods within a radius of thirty *li*, to be measured from the

Custom-house at each port.—*Answer:* The war expenses of foreign countries are met by loans negotiated with the merchants. Having no such resource, China is compelled to resort to the *le-kin*. The impost is on the native and not on the foreigner. Endless confusions and evasions would result from the adoption of this suggestion to do away with the *le-kin* within the thirty *li*. The military supplies, too, would be interfered with. This, after all, is a matter for the consideration of China herself. With the disbanding of her armies and the restoration of tranquillity, alterations may be made in her fiscal arrangements and, out of consideration for the merchants, the *le-kin* will be abolished.

Thus "the main object of the Commission," to use Sir Rutherford Alcock's own words, "was defeated." The failure of the Revision itself, however, had from the commencement been insured by the late British Minister, in selecting Mr. Hugh Fraser as the only British Member of the Mixed Commission for discussing the preliminaries, and his consenting to the Foreign Inspector-General of Maritime Customs and Confidential Adviser of the Tsung-li Ya-mên representing, in association with several native members, Chinese interests.|| As to his "thirty *li* radius" scheme, which so gravely compromised, if it did not virtually abandon, the very principle at issue: it was simply a crotchet, furnishing but another proof of that want of judgment, inconsistency, and diplomatic incapacity, which have almost invariably paralyzed the natural abilities Sir Rutherford Alcock is endowed with, and altogether frustrated the usefulness of his public career.

What in this place alone interests us is, that the arguments adduced in 1868, by the then British Minister in support of the abolition of the *le-kin* tax, apply to it at

|| "When, at the time of the attempted revising of the Treaty of Tientsin, Sir Rutherford Alcock was directed by the then Government to place himself in communication with the Tsung-li Ya-mên, we have his own words for the fact, that Mr. Hart, Inspector-General of Foreign Marine Customs having *offered* his services as an intermediary, those services were accepted."—The *North-China Daily News*, May 30, 1875.

the present time with tenfold force. For, as has been already observed, the public revenue of China from the land-tax and other ordinary sources has, some years since, returned to its normal state of productiveness, amply sufficient for the common wants of the State; the country continues unusually quiet; for the reconquest of Yün-nan, now accomplished, and the suppression of a chronic outbreak in Kan-su, the Government had, and has, adopted no measures involving an excess of usual expenditure; no internal improvements are attempted; and, certainly, no symptoms of an aggressive or hostile spirit, on the part of any of his "loyal Principalities"§ in the West, can have tended to disturb the slumbers of "the Son of Heaven." Under these circumstances two further preliminary questions present themselves to us, namely: Whether the actual continuance of the *le-kin* tax is legal of itself? and: What are the military purposes, for which the large surplus of revenue, which that tax is now yielding, and for the last ten years past has yielded, to the Chinese Exchequer, is applied? I should have no difficulty in showing that, according to the constitutional laws and usages of China, the native trading community has, and for several years past has had, a just claim to relief from a burden imposed on it under exceptional circumstances, which have ceased to exist; but, on the one hand, the will of the Emperor is, in China, after all the source of Chinese law; and, on the other hand, the question is a purely Chinese one, which directly concerns no foreigner. It would be out of place, therefore, here to discuss it; although it has no unimportant bearing on the so-called "sale of transit-passes by foreigners," *i.e.* Chinese merchants availing them-

§ Thus the United States, Great Britain, France, Germany, Russia, and other European countries were officially designated in the late Mr. Burlingame's Letters of Credence.

selves of foreign aid to avoid, in accordance with their constitutional rights, taxes unlawfully and arbitrarily imposed upon them.¶

The second question presents a different aspect. It is acknowledged by the Tsung-li Ya-mên that the *le-kin* tax continues to be levied almost solely for military purposes; and it is certain, that the internal condition of China no longer warrants an extraordinary impost for such purposes. Are we then to conclude, that the military object, with a view to which the Chinese Government refuses to abolish the war-tax, has reference to the "Outer" relations of China? It is a notorious fact, that the foreign policy of the Imperial Government has resumed a strongly retrogressive tendency; that the Plot of the Summer-Solstice, in 1870, for the expulsion or massacre of Foreigners, and a partial success of which was attained in Tientsin, had been designed with the full cognizance and concurrence of the Government; that the Government had then, and has ever since, been making preparations for a foreign war; that a large army, covering Tientsin, is kept on a war-footing in the tranquil province of Chih-li; that another and larger army has been formed, and is kept in reserve, in Kan-su; that the Taku forts are being continually strengthened, new forts erected and rifle-pits dug for the defence of the Capital, the coast, the Yang-tze and the Wu-sung; that fresh encampments are being formed in the vicinity of the ports; that the arsenals, navy-yards, and powder manufactories are being extended, and kept in full activity; that immense quantities of foreign arms and munitions of war are imported from every quarter; and that not only is this vast expenditure defrayed, in part out of the foreign Maritime Customs revenue, in part out of the *le-kin*

¶ Compare also the following note *.

tax, but that from both sources, more especially from the latter, large sums, if I am well informed, have, during the last five or six years, been sent up to Peking and allowed to accumulate,* with the view of placing the Chinese Government in a financial position to meet the exigencies of another contest with Foreign Powers. Combining, then, all the various and striking circumstances, here alluded to, we are simply forced to arrive at the conclusion, that the *le-kin* taxes continue to be levied by the Chinese Government, unconstitutionally, upon the inland trade, and more especially upon the foreign inland trade of China, *for the twofold purpose of obstructing that trade to the utmost extent practicable, and at the same time deriving from it the ways and means for carrying on a new and more formidable war, either offensive or defensive as circumstances may determine, against the West, Western Commerce, and Western ideas of Development, Progress, and Civilisation.*

---

* This is incidentally confirmed by a memorial of Liu Kuo-kuang, Superintending Censor of Fu-kien, against a proposed increase of the Emperor's Civil List, which appeared in the "Peking Gazette" for Oct. 22, 1871. "A short time ago," the plain spoken memorialist states, "the department for controlling the affairs of the Imperial Household applied for an additional annual grant, *payable out of the surplus Customs dues*, and His Majesty was pleased to refer the application to a Committee of Inquiry. But such an application is, considering the distress of the people around Tientsin, very much out of place at the present time, and diametrically opposed to the economy inculcated in recent edicts. True, it may be said by way of excuse, that the Department only asks for a grant from "*the surplus* of the Customs dues, and does not contemplate any increase in the dues themselves. But it must be borne in mind that, *of late years, the Customs underlings*"—this is prettily put by the Censor—"*have practised so much extortion, that merchants stand in dread of these Customs altogether*; and, let the application for an allowance *out of the surplus funds* of the Customs be acceded to, that these underlings will make it a handle for wholesale squeezing."—For these and other reasons, Mr. Liu prays that the appointment of the Committee referred to may be cancelled, and that the Department in question be directed to practice the economy so much inculcated, to regulate its expenditure according to the income, and to furnish truthful returns of that expenditure.

The principal points in this memorial, deserving of attention, are, that the native merchants themselves had already then become impatient of the extortionate taxation, with which the inland trade of China continues to be burdened; and that the *surplus revenue*, derived by the Government from this source, must have accumulated in Peking to so large a sum, as to induce and warrant the Court to demand its share of it.

IV.

TREATY RIGHTS OF THE FOREIGN MERCHANT.

The English Treaties of Nanking and Tientsin—Main object of the war of 1842—Art. x of the Treaty of Nanking—The Hongkong Declaration—The Supplementary Treaty of Hoomun-Chae—Commercial advantages secured by the Treaty of Nanking—Art. ix, xiii, xxiv, xxviii, and liv of the English Treaty of Tientsin—Rules v, vii, and viii of the Supplementary Agreement of Shanghai—Art. viii of the English Convention of Peking—Art. xxiii and xxvii of the French Treaty of Tientsin—Art. iii and iv of the Russian Treaty of Tientsin—Art. iv, v, and vii of the Russian Convention of Peking—Main object of the war of 1859-60—The principle of free transit through China upheld in the English Treaty of Tientsin, but swerved from in the subsequent Trade Rules—Errors committed in framing the Trade Rules—Summary of the Provisions of the Treaty of Tientsin relative to Trade—Real meaning of the terms "transit-certificate" and "transit-dues"—Lord Elgin on the commuted Transit-dues tax—The optional clause of Art. xxviii of the Treaty of Tientsin abrogated by Rule vii of the Shanghai Agreement—Confusion of views on the subject—Commutation-tax includes *le-kin* and all other inland charges whatsoever—No taxes on Foreign Commerce lawfully leviable in China, save those agreed upon by Treaty—Illegal system of taxation resorted to by the Chinese Government—Liability of the Chinese Government to demands for compensation, and of Chinese Customs-officials to judicial punishment—Payment of Commutation-tax exempts *merchandize*, on which it is paid, irrespective of ownership—Conclusive evidence adduced to this effect—Testimony of Lord Elgin, the Tsung-li Ya-mên, and the highest native Provincial Authorities—Perfidy of the Chinese Government.

We may now proceed to a consideration of the treaties themselves, so far as they relate to our subject; premising that, by the British Treaty of Tientsin:—*1.* "Art. i. The Treaty of Peace and Amity between the two nations (England and China), signed at Nanking on the 29th August, 1842, is renewed and confirmed (excepting the Supplementary

Treaty and General Regulations of Trade, abrogated). *2.* Art. liv. The British Government and its subjects are confirmed in all privileges, immunities, and advantages conferred on them by previous Treaties; and it is expressly stipulated, that the British Government and its subjects will be allowed free and equal participation in all privileges, immunities, and advantages that may have been, or may be hereafter, granted by His Majesty the Emperor of China to the Government or subjects of any other nation. *3.* Art. l. All official communications, addressed by the Diplomatic and Consular Agents of Her Majesty the Queen to the Chinese Authorities, shall, henceforth, be written in English. They will for the present be accompanied by a Chinese version, but it is understood that, in the event of there being any difference of meaning between the English and Chinese texts, the English Government will hold the sense as expressed in the English text to be the correct sense. This provision is to apply to the Treaty now negotiated, the Chinese text of which has been carefully corrected by the English original."

The Treaty of Nanking was concluded by the British Plenipotentiary, Sir Henry Pottinger, at the head of a victorious and resistless force, and ended a war, which had been mainly undertaken with the aim of opening up China to foreign commerce in general and to British commerce in particular. Art. x. of this Treaty, relative to "Import- and Export-Duties," reads thus:—

His Imperial Majesty the Emperor of China agrees to establish at all the ports, which are, by the Second Article of this Treaty, to be thrown open for the resort of British merchants, a fair and regular Tariff of export- and import-customs and other dues, which Tariff shall be publickly notified and promulgated for general information; and the Emperor further engages that, when British merchandise shall have once paid at any of the said ports the regulated customs and dues, agreeable to the Tariff to be hereafter fixed, such merchandise may be conveyed by Chinese merchants to any province or city in the Interior of the Empire of China, on paying a further amount as transit duties, which shall not exceed — per cent. on the tariff value of such goods.

The amount, here left open, was notified in a "Declaration respecting Transit Duties," dated Hongkong, the 26th June, 1843, and affixed to the Treaty on the exchange of Ratifications; when it had been agreed and was declared "that the further amount of duty to be levied on British merchandise, as transit duty, shall not exceed the present rates, which are upon a moderate scale; and the Ratifications of the said Treaty are exchanged subject to the express declaration and stipulation herein contained."

However unsatisfactory the wording of this clause, chiefly on account of the inappropriate term "*Transit-Duties*," used in it, may now appear: there can exist no doubt as to its meaning on the part of Sir Henry Pottinger. His one great object was to open up the Empire of China to British trade. He had accomplished this object by obtaining for the merchant full liberty to carry on a free commerce with the Chinese people at large, directly at five Chinese sea-ports as a basis of operations, and through native traders with any province or city in the Interior of the Empire, on the payment to the Chinese Government of certain fair and regular export- and import-customs and other dues, as fixed by a Tariff to be publickly notified and promulgated for general information. Such was the main agreement, concluded by Sir Henry Pottinger between England and China. But, on the circumstance being pressed upon his consideration that certain *inland taxes* were habitually levied by the Chinese Government on native trade: the British Plenipotentiary finally consented to the British merchant also paying the same taxes on British merchandise sent through, or by, Chinese traders for sale to an inland market; *with a proviso that they should in future not exceed the rates then actually leviable*,—those rates being upon a moderate scale. It is true, that the actual scale, at that period in use, was not appended to the Declaration; but, as will be presently seen, the scale, referred to, was the one fixed by the Chinese Board of Revenue and published in its official manual: 欽定戶部則列; and, no *le-kin* or *chow-fang* taxes being imposed upon trade at the time, it follows, that no *le-kin*, *chow-fang*, or any extraordinary taxes, were and are, by the Treaty of Nanking, legally leviable on British merchandise within the limits of the Chinese Empire.

On reading the "Supplementary Treaty made at Hoomun-Chae on the 8th October, 1843, it might appear even dubious, whether the payment of the ordinary inland taxes on trade, by Sir Henry Pottinger agreed to, under the designation of "Transit-Duties," in the Treaty of Nanking, had not been again abrogated. Such, however, is not the case; as we find from the following, subsequently published documents:—

Sir Henry Pottinger to the Earl of Aberdeen.

Government House, Victoria, Hongkong.
February 27, 1844.

My Lord,—I have the honor to forward to your Lordship a statement of Transit or Inland Duties, levied in the Chinese Empire. I have, &c.

Government Notification.

The annexed translated Extract regarding the Transit or Inland Duties of the Chinese Empire is published for general information.

By order of his Excellency, the Superintendent of Trade, &c., in China,
(Signed) Richard Woosnam.

Government House, Victoria, Hongkong, February 20, 1844.

True Extract, (Signed) Charles Gützlaff,
Chinese Secretary.

"*Transit Duties paid at the Custom-houses of Kan, Taeping and Pihsin, on goods that are going down to Canton, or thence transported to the Northern Provinces.*

(Extracted from the "Hoopootsihle," 30th and 31st vols., a work on the revenues, published by Imperial authority.)

EXPORT.

	Kankwan.	Taepingkwan.	Pihsinkwan.
	T. m. c. c.	T. m. c. c.	T. m. c. c.
Alum, per 100 catties	0 0 0 8 3-10	0 0 2 7 6-10	0 0 0 8
Aniseed star, ditto	0 0 4 2	0 0 4 2	0 0 4 0
Arsenic, ditto	0 0 2 6 3-10	0 0 2 7 6-10	0 0 4 0
Bamboo screens and bamboo ware of all kinds, ditto	—	0 0 4 0	0 0 4 0
Camphor, ditto	0 1 0 5	0 3 6 4	0 1 4 0
Capoor catchery, ditto	—	0 0 2 8 1-5	—
Cassia, ditto	0 0 3 5½	—	—
China root, ditto	0 0 3 5 1-5	0 0 2 7 6-10	0 0 4 0
Copper ware, pewter ditto, &c. ditto	0 0 9 1 9-10	0 1 5 0	0 6 0 0
Cubebs, ditto..	0 1 8 7 7-10	—	0 4 0 0
Galingal ditto	0 0 1 7 6-10	0 0 2 7 6-10	0 0 4 0
Gamboge, ditto	0 0 3 5½	0 3 3 8 4-10	0 0 1 3 6-10
Grass cloth, all kinds, per piece ..	0 0 5 9 1-10	0 0 0 7 8-10	0 0 0 2½
Hartall, per 100 catties	0 4 5 9 6-10	0 2 5 6	0 1 0 0
Lead (white lead), ditto	—	—	0 1 3 6
Mats (straw, rattan, bamboo, &c.) ditto	0 0 2 6 3-10	0 1 1 7	—
Musk, per catty	0 9 1 9 1-10	3 1 4 2	1 3 6 0
Nankeen and cotton cloth, of all kinds, per 100 catties	0 0 5 2½	0 4 5 5	0 0 2 5 6-10
Rhubarb, ditto	0 0 2 3½	0 0 2 7 6-10	0 0 4 0
Silk, raw, first quality, ditto ..	1 0 0 0	1 4 3 2	0 8 5 7 3-5
Coarse, or refuse silk, ditto.. ..	0 4 5 9 6-10	0 3 6 4	0 6 4 0
Silk, piece goods, ribands, thread, &c.	0 9 1 9 1-10	3 1 4 2	1 4 7 2
Middling raw silk, ditto	—	0 7 2 4	0 6 8 0
Silk and cotton mixtures, silk and woollen mixtures, and goods of such classes, per piece	—	0 7 2 4	0 0 1 2
Soy, per 100 catties	0 2 6 2 6-10	0 0 2 7 6-10	0 0 4 0
Tea, coarse, ditto	0 0 7 8 8-10	0 0 4 2	0 0 4 2
	per 10 baskts.	per 100 catts.	per 100 catts.
Tea, fine, ditto	0 0 3 9 4-10	0 0 7 6	—
		Chekeang Teas.	
Vermillion, per 100 catties	0 5 2 5 2-10	1 4 4 6	1 3 6 0

IMPORTS.

	Kankwan.	Taepingkwan.	Pihsinkwan.
	T. m. c. c.	T. m. c. c.	T. m. c. c.
Assafœtida, per 100 catties	1 7 5 9½	1 4 4 6	0 4 0 0
Beeswax, ditto	0 3 9 3 9-10	—	—
Betelnut, ditto	0 0 1 7 6-10	0 0 4 2	0 0 4 0
Bicho de Mar, ditto	0 0 3 5 2-10	0 1 1 7	0 4 0 0
Birds' nests, ditto	1 1 7 2 7-10	1 1 1 6	1 3 6 0
Camphor (Malay), per catty ..	0 9 2 0	3 1 4 2	1 3 6 0
Cloves, per 100 catties	0 2 3 4 6-10	0 6 1 7	0 2 0 0
Carnelian beads, ditto	0 0 5 0	—	—
Cotton, ditto	—	—	0 0 8 0
Cotton manufactures of all kinds, whether coarse or fine, per 10 pieces	0 1 0 0	0 1 4 8	0 0 5 5 1-5
Cow bezoar, per catty	1 1 7 2 7-10	1 1 1 6	2 4 0 0
Cutch, per 100 catties	0 1 4 0 4-5	0 1 8 3 4-5	0 2 0 0
Elephants' teeth, ditto	0 2 3 4 3-5	1 4 4 6	1 0 0 0
Gold and silver thread, per catty ..	0 2 6 2 3-5	0 1 5 0	0 0 2 4 4-5
Gum Benjamin, per 100 catties ..	0 1 4 8	0 3 6 7	0 2 0 0
Olibanum, ditto	—	0 3 6 7	—
Myrrh, ditto	0 2 3 4 3-5	0 6 8 4	0 2 0 0
Horns, unicorns' or rhinoceros, per 100 catties	1 7 5 0	1 4 4 6	1 3 6 0
Quicksilver, ditto	0 2 3 4 3-5	1 4 4 4	1 3 6 0
Nutmegs, ditto	0 1 0 0	0 1 8 3 3-5	0 2 3 4 3-5
Pepper, ditto	0 3 5 1 9-10	0 2 5 9	0 2 0 0
Putchuck, ditto	0 2 3 4 3-5	0 3 6 6	0 2 0 0
Rattans, ditto	0 0 4 9 9-10	0 0 4 2	0 0 1 6
Rose maloes, ditto	0 9 3 8 4-10	0 8 3 4	—
Sharks' fins ditto	0 0 5 8 7-10	0 1 1 7	0 4 0 0
Smalts, ditto	0 6 5 6½	1 4 4 6	—
Ebony, ditto	0 0 9 3 4-5	—	0 2 0 0
Sandalwood, ditto	0 5 8 6½	0 2 5 9	0 2 0 0
Sapanwood, ditto	0 1 4 0 2-5	0 0 4 2	0 2 0 0
Woollen manufactures, per piece ..	0 2 0 0	0 2 0 0	0 1 1 0 2-5 per 1 chang.
Narrow woollens, per chang 141 inches	0 1 0 0	0 1 0 0	0 1 1 0 6-5
Dutch camlets, ditto	0 2 0 0	—	0 1 1 0 2-5
Camlets, ditto	0 2 0 0	—	0 1 1 0 2-5
Woollen yarn, per 100 catties ..	3 1 4 2	3 1 4 2	0 2 0 4 4-5

What, then, the Treaty of Nanking accomplished for Commerce, may be stated in a few concise words, thus:—It threw open the whole of the dominions of the Emperor of China to British and Foreign Trade on the following conditions, viz., *Firstly*, that the merchants confine their direct trade to the ports of Canton, Amoy, Fuchow, Ningpo, and Shanghai; at which ports full liberty was given of residence and transacting business in the way of importing, for sale and consumption throughout China, British and foreign merchandise on payment to the Chinese Government of certain import-duties, fixed by Tariff, and exporting Chinese or native merchandise from all parts of the Empire on payment to the Imperial Government of certain export-duties, fixed by Tariff, upon such merchandise, and on the further payment of certain tonnage-dues on British and foreign vessels entering the five treaty-ports. *Secondly*, that the foreign merchants personally abstain from entering the Interior of the country for purposes of trade, but have full and complete liberty to carry on business with the Chinese people at large in, and to convey British and foreign merchandise for sale and consumption to, any part, province, or city of China, and *freely to circulate such merchandise within the Chinese dominions*, through the agency of native traders, and on payment to the Chinese Government of such moderate INLAND TAXES *as were at that period levied on the home trade, and with the proviso that the then customary rates of those taxes were not to be exceeded in future.* When, therefore, the Inspector-General, Mr. Hart, states that "the Treaty of Nankin stipulated for the conveyance of foreign merchandise into the interior by Chinese *under a transit system*," he is in error and has no authority for his assertion. It would be about as reasonable to say that the road-tolls and similar taxes, which used to be, or still continue to be, levied in England, were levied under a "transit-system," as it is to say that the inland barrier-charges, to which the home trade of China was subject in 1842, were levied under such a system.

Turning now to the British Treaty of Tientsin and other Treaties,—for we have to bear in mind the tenour of Art. liv. of the former contract previously quoted,—we find the principal provisions, bearing on our subject, to be the following:—

British Treaty of Tientsin, signed June 26, 1858, ratified October 24, 1860.

Art. ix.—British subjects are hereby authorised to travel, for their pleasure or for purposes of trade, to all parts of the interior, under passports.... No opposition shall be offered to his (the bearer of a passport not irregular) hiring persons or hiring vessels for the carriage of his baggage or merchandise....

Art. xiii.—The Chinese Government will place no restrictions whatever upon the employment, by British subjects, of Chinese subjects in any lawful capacity.

Art. xiv.—British subjects may hire whatever boats they please for the transport of goods or passengers.... The number of these boats shall not be limited, nor shall a monopoly in respect either of the boats, or of the porters or coolies engaged in carrying the goods, be granted to any parties.

Art. xxiv.—It is agreed that British subjects shall pay, on all merchandise imported or exported by them, the duties prescribed by the Tariff; but in no case shall they be called upon to pay other or higher duties than are required of the subjects of any other foreign nation.

Art. xxviii.—Whereas it was agreed in Article x. of the Treaty of Nanking that British imports, having paid the tariff duties, should be conveyed into the interior free of all further charges, except a transit duty, the amount whereof was not to exceed a certain per-centage on tariff value; and whereas no accurate information having been furnished of the amount of such duty, British merchants have constantly complained that charges are suddenly and and arbitrarily imposed by the provincial authorities as transit duties upon produce on its way to the foreign market, and on imports on their way into the interior, to the detriment of trade; it is agreed that within four months from the signing of this Treaty, at all ports now open to British trade, and within a similar period at all ports that may hereafter be opened, the authority appointed to superintend the collection of duties shall be obliged, upon application to the Consul, to declare the amount of duties leviable on produce between the places of production and the port of shipment, and upon imports between the Consular port in the question and the inland market named by the Consul; and that a notification thereof shall be published in English and Chinese for general information.

But it shall be at the option of any British subject desiring to convey produce purchased inland to a port, or to convey imports from a port to an inland market, to clear his goods of all transit duties, by payment of a single charge. The amount of this charge shall be leviable on exports at the first barrier they may have to pass, or, on imports, at the port at which they are landed; and on payment thereof, a certificate shall be issued, which shall exempt the goods from all further inland charges whatsoever.

It is further agreed that the amount of this charge shall be calculated, as nearly as possible, at the rate of two and-a-half per cent. *ad valorem*, and that it shall be fixed for each article at the conference to be held at Shanghae for the revision of the tariff.

It is distinctly understood that the payment of transit dues, by commutation or otherwise, shall in no way affect the tariff duties on imports, or exports, which will continue to be levied separately and in full.

Agreement in Pursuance of Art. xxvi. and xxviii. of the Treaty of Tientsin signed at Shanghae, November 8, 1858.

Rule 5.—*Regarding certain Commodities heretofore Contraband.*—The restrictions affecting trade in opium, cash, grain, pulse, sulphur, brimstone, saltpetre, and spelter, are relaxed, under the following conditions:

I. Opium will henceforth pay thirty taels per picul import duty. The importer will sell it only at the port. It will be carried into the interior by Chinese only, and only as Chinese property: the foreign trader will not be allowed to accompany it. The provisions of Article ix of the Treaty of Tientsin, by which British subjects are authorized to proceed into the interior with passports to trade, will not extend to it, nor will those of Article xxviii of the same treaty, by which the transit-dues are regulated. The transit-dues on it will be arranged as the Chinese Government see fit; nor is in future revisions of the Tariff the same rule of revision to be applied to opium as to other goods.

RULE 7.—*Transit Dues.*—It is agreed that Article XXVIII of the Treaty of Tientsin shall be interpreted to declare the amounts of transit-dues legally leviable upon merchandise imported or exported by British subjects, to be one-half of the tariff duties, except in the case of the duty-free goods liable to a transit-duty of 2½ per cent. *ad valorem*, as provided in Article II of these Rules. Merchandise shall be cleared of its transit dues under the following conditions:—

In the case of Imports.—Notice being given at the port of entry, from which the Imports are to be forwarded inland, of the nature and quantity of the goods, the ship from which they have been landed, and the place inland to which they are bound, with all other necessary particulars, the Collector of Customs will, on due inspection made, and on receipt of the transit-duty due, issue a transit-duty certificate. This must be produced at every barrier station, and *viséd*. No further duty will be leviable upon imports so certificated, no matter how distant the place of their destination.

In the case of Exports.—Produce purchased by a British subject in the interior will be inspected, and taken account of, at the first barrier it passes on its way to the port of shipment. A memorandum showing the amount of the produce and the port at which it is to be shipped, will be deposited there by the person in charge of the produce; he will then receive a certificate, which must be exhibited and *viséd* at every barrier, on his way to the port of shipment. On the arrival of the produce at the barrier nearest the port, and the transit-dues due thereon being paid, it will be passed. On exportation the produce will pay the tariff-duty.

Any attempt to pass goods inwards or outwards, otherwise than in compliance with the rule here laid down, will render them liable to confiscation.

Unauthorised sale, *in transitu*, of goods that have been entered as above for a port, will render them liable to confiscation. Any attempt to pass goods in excess of the quantity specified in the certificate will render all the goods of the same denomination, named in the certificate, liable to confiscation. Permission to export produce, which cannot be proved to have paid its transit-dues, will be refused by the Customs until the transit-dues shall have been paid. The above being the arrangement agreed to regarding the transit-dues, which will thus be levied once and for all, the notification required under Article XXVIII of the Treaty of Tientsin, for the information of British and Chinese subjects, is hereby dispensed with.

RULE 8.—*Foreign Trade under Passport.*—It is agreed that Article IX. of the Treaty of Tientsin shall not be interpreted as authorising British subjects to enter the capital city of Peking, for the purposes of trade.

BRITISH CONVENTION OF PEACE, SIGNED AT PEKING, OCTOBER 24, 1860.

ART. VIII.—It is agreed that, as soon as the ratifications of the Treaty of the year one thousand eight hundred and fifty-eight shall have been exchanged, His Imperial Majesty the Emperor of China shall, by decree, command the high authorities in the capital, and in the provinces, to print and publish the aforesaid Treaty and the present Convention, for general information.

FRENCH TREATY OF TIENTSIN, SIGNED JUNE 27, 1858.

ART XXIII.—All French merchandise, after having paid at one of the ports of China the Customs duties prescribed by the Tariff, may be conveyed into the Interior, without being subjected to any other additional charge besides the payment of transit dues according to the moderate rates actually agreed upon, and which transit-dues shall be liable to no further augmentation in future.

If Chinese Customs-officials, contrary to the tenour of the present Treaty, were to exact illegal taxes, or to levy higher rates of duties, they are to be punished in accordance with the laws of the Empire.

ART. XXVII.—In consideration of the payment of these duties (import and export duties as fixed by Tariff), the amount of which it is expressly prohibited to increase, and which shall be enhanceable by no kind of charge or additional tax whatsoever, French subjects will be at liberty to import into China for any destination, all merchandise which, at the date of the signing of the present Treaty and according to the classification of the annexed Tariff, is not the object of a formal prohibition or a special monopoly.

"RÈGLEMENTS COMMERCIAUX," ATTACHED TO THE FRENCH TREATY OF TIENTSIN.

RULE VII.—It is agreed that the transit dues, referred to in ART. XXIV. of the Treaty, shall be one half of the duties fixed by Tariff, excepting the duty-free goods, mentioned in Rule ii., which shall only pay a transit duty of 2½ per cent. *ad valorem.*†

AMERICAN SUPPLEMENTARY TREATY OF SHANGHAI,
SIGNED NOVEMBER 8, 1858.

RULE VII.—*Transit Dues.*—It is agreed that the transit dues upon goods imported or exported shall be one half of the tariff duties, except in the case of the duty-free goods liable to a transit duty of 2½ per cent. *ad valorem* .... It being allowed by this rule that the transit dues on merchandise shall be levied once for all, no others shall be demanded after they have been paid.

RUSSIAN TREATY OF TIENTSIN, SIGNED JUNE 1/13, 1858.

ART. III.—Henceforth the Commerce between Russia and China shall not be restricted to the places fixed upon at the frontiers, but shall be free also by sea....

ART. IV.—As regards the Commerce by sea and all details relative to it.... Russian subjects shall conform themselves to the general regulations of foreign trade, in force at the ports of China....

CONVENTION OF PEKING, SIGNED NOVEMBER 14/26, 1860, AND AFFIXED TO THE RUSSIAN TREATY OF TIENTSIN.

ART. IV.—At all places, along the frontiers agreed upon in the first Article of this Convention, Russian and Chinese subjects may hold free intercourse. There shall no duties be levied in any case; and all officials, stationed on the frontiers, shall afford protection to merchants who quietly carry on trade.

ART. V.—... Russian merchants, visiting the Chinese marts, shall be under no restrictions either as to the time at which they may visit such places or the duration of their stay; but the number of merchants at any one place shall not exceed two hundred.

ATT. VII.—The merchants of both countries may trade as they please at the various marts, and shall not be subjected to any obstructions on the part of the officials; they may as they think proper frequent the shops and markets for trade and barter, and they may there make ready money payments or, if they trust each other, open credit accounts; and as to the length of time, that the merchants of the one country may sojourn

† The provisions of the North-German Treaty of Tientsin, signed September 2, 1861, and ratified January 14, 1863, at Shanghai, are identical with those of the French Treaty.

in the other country, the only limit shall be the merchants' own pleasure and convenience.‡

I need not remind the reader that, consequent on the British Treaty of Tientsin and the subsequent Convention, in addition to the five Chinese ports already open, Swatow, Takow, Taiwan, Tamsui, Kelung, Chinkiang, Kiukiang, Hankow, Chefu, Tientsin, and Nuchuang were rendered effectually accessible to foreign trade; that the ratification of the Treaty had to be enforced by the war of 1859–1860; and that the Convention of Peace, which concluded that war, was signed, after the destruction of the Emperor's Summer-Palace, under the very walls of the Capital of China.

The main object of the second Chinese war was identical with that of the first one, namely, the more efficient opening up of the Interior of the country to foreign commerce in general, and British commerce in particular. Yet, strange to say, from the wording of Art. xxviii. of the Treaty of Tientsin it would appear that Lord Elgin, who conducted the whole of the negotiations, had been acquainted with neither the Hongkong Declaration nor the Supplementary Treaty of "Hoomun-Chae." It is true, that the Treaty of Tientsin secures great additional advantages to the merchant, and, so far as the text itself goes, fully upholds and further carries out the principle of *unrestricted free trade in and with the Interior of China on the sole condition of the payment of certain fixed duties to the Chinese Government*; but unhappily, this principle was swerved from or relaxed, when practically applied in the Rules of Trade, appended to the Tariff.

In framing these Rules, three grave errors were committed. The first is, that, as has been just observed, a

‡ There exists a later Convention between Russia and China, the text of which I have not before me.

material restriction was by Rule vii. placed on the free circulation, in the Interior, of goods which had paid the prescribed duties, by agreeing that, on sending from the open ports foreign merchandise inland, *a given place of destination* had to be specified and declared, and that the accompanying "transit-duty certificate" had to be produced and *viséd at every intervening barrier.* The second error committed is, that, contrary to the provisions of both the Treaties of Nanking and Tientsin, the capital city of Peking was, for purposes of trade, by Rule viii. excluded from the operations of the latter Treaty. The third error consists in this, that the inland taxes, to the additional payment of which Lord Elgin consented, were designated as "*transit* dues," and the protective certificate, to be issued in consequence of such payment, as a "*transit*-duty certificate;" and that it was stated in Rule vii., that "no further duty will be leviable upon imports so certificated, no matter *how distant* the place of their *destination.*" I shall have to revert to these topics. All I desire to point out in this place is, that,—although in the "Agreement *in pursuance of* Articles xxvi. and xxviii. of the Treaty of Tientsin, signed at Shanghai, Nov. 8, 1858," it is stated that "the said (Tariff and) Rules shall be equally binding on the Governments and subjects of both countries with the Treaty itself," yet,—when there exist difficulties of interpretation, whether real or apparent, between the Treaty and the Rules, *the Rules are to be construed in conformity with the Treaty, and not the Treaty in conformity with the Rules.*

Now, on an analysis of the Treaty of Tientsin, so far as it relates to British and foreign commerce, it will, taken in connection with the Treaty of Nanking and other Treaties and Conventions (Art. i. and liv.), be found to provide:—

I. *Generally.*—That the whole of the dominions of the Emperor of China, with the sole exception of the capital city of Peking (Rule viii.), are thrown open to British and other foreign trade against the payment to the Chinese Government of certain *fixed* duties, import-, export-, "transit"-, and tonnage-dues; such trade, subject to certain rules relative to inland traffic (Art. ix., Rule vii.), to be unrestrictedly carried on from certain specified ports with any part of the Empire—the capital alone excepted,—in the way of purchasing, selling, or bartering foreign and native merchandise, whether by or through British and foreign merchants and agents (Art. ix.) or through Chinese agents and traders (Art. xiii.), and with the fullest liberty, on the part of British and other foreign subjects, to transact business and to stay at any mart or place in the Interior of the country, (so long at it may suit their own pleasure or convenience Art. ix.; *Russ. Con.* Art. v., vii.).

II. *As to Imports.*—1. That British and other foreign subjects, residing whether permanently or temporarily, at one of the Chinese ports open to foreign trade, shall be at liberty to import, from foreign parts—including the British possession of Hongkong—into such Chinese ports any kind of British or foreign merchandise; and after having paid to the Chinese Government the stipulated import-duty, if any, on the goods imported, that they shall be further at liberty to dispose of, sell, or barter the same, *in loco*, to foreigners or natives, either for re-sale and trade *in loco* or inland, or for individual use and consumption, *without such goods, be they in the possession of natives or foreigners, being liable, on the part of the Chinese Government or of Chinese officials, to any additional taxation or charges whatsoever.*

2. That British and other foreign subjects, resident at

one of the open ports, shall be at liberty to convey or to have conveyed by foreigners or natives to any given destination, place, or mart within the dominions of the Emperor of China,—Peking alone excepted,—for barter or sale to Chinese subjects, and whether for re-sale and trade further inland, or individual use and consumption *in loco* or otherwise, any British or foreign merchandise imported into the said port, after having paid to the Chinese Government upon such merchandise, the stipulated import-duty, if any, and, in lieu of all inland taxes and charges leviable or levied upon native trade, an inland duties commutation-tax of one half the import-duty fixed by Tariff, or of 2½ per cent. *ad valorem* on goods not subject to import-duty, *without such goods, whether the property, or in the possession, of Chinese, British or other foreign subjects, being liable, on the part of the Chinese Government or of Chinese officials, to any additional taxation or charges whatsoever.*

3. That, upon the payment to the Chinese Government of the stipulated import-duty, if any, and the stipulated inland charges commutation or "transit"-tax on any foreign merchandise whether the property intended for sale in the Interior, or in the possession of Foreigners or Chinese, a certificate of payment shall be given to accompany such merchandise, and which certificate shall exempt the same—*i. e. the foreign goods on which the stipulated import and inland exemption or commutation-tax has been paid, whether such goods be the property, or in the possession, of Chinese or Foreigners, from all further inland charges whatsoever.*

III. *As to Exports.*—1. That British and other foreign subjects, resident at one of the open ports, shall be at liberty to purchase or barter *in loco* any native produce or merchandise, and export the same to foreign parts, on paying to the Chinese Government upon such goods the export-duty, if any, stipulated by Tariff.

2. That British and other foreign subjects, resident at one of the open ports, shall be at liberty at any mart or place within the dominions of the Emperor of China, Peking alone excepted, to purchase or barter, directly or through agents whether foreigners or natives, and whether for immediate payment and delivery, or for payment and, or on, delivery at the port (*Russ. Conv.* Art. vii), any Chinese produce or merchandise for exportation to foreign parts; to convey the same or have the same conveyed, by foreigners or natives, to one of the open ports, on paying to the Chinese Government, at the last barrier or Custom-house between the place of barter or purchase and the specified port, an inland charges commutation or "transit"-tax of one-half the export-duty fixed by Tariff, or of 2½ per cent *ad valorem* on goods not subject to export-duty; and, after the arrival of such goods at the port, to export the same to foreign parts, on further paying upon them to the Chinese Government the export-duty, if any, stipulated by Tariff.

3. That, upon promise of payment to the Chinese Government of the stipulated inland charges commutation- or "transit"-tax on Chinese produce or merchandise, to be bought inland for exportation by British or other foreign subjects at one of the open ports, a certificate shall be given by the proper Chinese Authorities to accompany such goods, and which certificate shall exempt the same,—*i. e. the goods, on which the payment of the stipulated inland exemption- or "transit"- duty has been promised, whether these goods are by the native trader sold for immediate payment and delivery on the spot or for payment and, or on, delivery at the specified port,— from all further inland charges whatsoever.*

There are only three or four points included in this *résumé*, which require explanation or special proof. The first is, that, what has improperly been termed a *transit*-certificate and *transit*-dues, is in reality and should have been termed *an inland duty-exemption certificate* and *an inland charges commutation-tax*, respectively. I have previously shown that the term, taken in its accustomed English sense, is wholly inapplicable in China, and therefore could not but lead to misconceptions and false impressions, more especially in connection with the mistake, made by Lord Elgin, in consenting by Tariff-Rule vii. to a given mart or destination having to be specified at the port for all merchandise, intended for transmission into, and sale in, the Interior of the country. The broad principle, universally accepted, and clearly laid down in Art. xxviii. of the Treaty itself, is that, by the payment to the Chinese Government of a stipulated import- and "transit-," *i.e. an inland charges commutation-tax*, all merchandise, intended for sale in the Interior, acquires, and in that case should acquire, the right of *free and unrestricted circulation within the dominions of the Emperor of China.* Indeed, Lord Elgin himself, in his despatch to the Foreign Office of November 8, 1858, speaks of the commutation-tax in question as "a sum, *in name* of transit-duty, which will free goods, whether of export or import, to pass between the port of shipment or entry to or from any part of China, without further charge of toll, octroi, or tax of any description whatsoever." But there is something in a name, after all; and in the present instance, the ill-chosen *names* of *transit*-dues and a *transit*-certificate *have alone rendered possible that "Transit-System," founded on those names, which has enabled the Tsung-li Ya-mên and the Foreign Inspector-General of Chinese Maritime Customs to reduce the Treaty of Tientsin, so far as its provisions relate to inland trade by British and other foreign subjects, in practice to a dead letter.*

The second point, adverted to, is one respecting which there would appear to exist a good deal of misapprehension, inasmuch as it is held by the Tsung-li Ya-mên, the Inspectorate-General, and foreign merchants, that the Treaties leave it optional with the latter to commute the inland duties and taxes by the payment of the stipulated commutation tax, or to pay, if such be their choice, the various inland charges levied by native authorities. But, although an agreement to this effect had been at first concluded, as Art. xxviii. of the British Treaty shows: it was finally arranged, by Tariff Rule vii., that the option-clause should be abandoned, and the one single, legally leviable commutation-tax alone remain in force. Undoubtedly this was the true principle to adopt; and Lord Elgin, in his despatch of November 8, 1868, already quoted, observes very justly:—"I have always thought that the remedy (against the grievances complied of by the merchants) was to be sought in the substitution of *one fixed payment* for the present irregular and multiplied levies." This also explains the fact, that the declaration and public notification of "the amount of duties leviable on produce between the place of production and the port of shipment, and upon imports between the Consular port in question and the inland markets named by the Consul," of which Art. xxviii. of the Treaty of Tientsin speaks, was no longer insisted on in the Rules of the subsequent Agreement or ever carried into effect,—an omission, which otherwise would have been equally unintelligible and unpardonable. Sir Frederick Bruce finally took the same view of the case; for, in his despatch to the Foreign Office of December 2, 1862, he remarks:—"The object of Rule No. 7

was to substitute one unvarying charge for the arbitrary exactions of provincial authorities, where Her Majesty's subjects bought or sold goods, in the interior." It is true that, in palpable contradiction with himself, and after stating, that the merchant "is *bound* to cover produce by taking out a transit-duty certificate," he adds: "If on the other hand, he thinks it more for his interest to buy produce and bring it down uncertificated, it will not be entitled to any special protection as British property, but will be subject to such charges and regulations as the Chinese Authorities may choose to impose." But in his despatch of September 18, 1863, to Prince Kung, he again and more distinctly states:—"If a British subject takes goods into the Interior without a certificate, or if he attempts to bring produce past the nearest barrier without obtaining a certificate, he exposes his property to confiscation." In the same sense, but with even greater inconsistency, ambiguity of view, and inaccuracy, Mr. Wade, in his Memorandum respecting the Revision of the Treaty of Tientsin, expresses himself thus:—"The Customs are empowered by Rule vii. to refuse permission to export produce, which cannot be proved to have paid its transit dues, until these dues have been paid. Imports, again, being still foreign property, if passing inwards without a certificate, are liable to confiscation." The clause of Rule vii., which, no doubt, both his Excellency and Sir Frederick Bruce bore in mind, reading: "Any attempt to pass goods inwards or outwards, otherwise than in compliance with the rule here laid down, will render them liable to confiscation," refers and can refer to attempts at *smuggling* alone. Considering that the option allowed to the merchant by *Treaty* has not been formally rescinded, and only been done away with by "interpretation" in an appended Rule of Trade: confiscation, for an unintentional infraction of such a Rule from its vague and somewhat obscure wording, very generally misapprehended, is legally out of the question, and could occur only to the boldest advocates of Chinese rapacity.

Another point, to which allusion has been made, is, that produce or merchandise, purchased inland for exportation to foreign ports, and on which the commutation-tax has been paid, is exempt from all further inland charges, "whether the goods were by the native trader sold to British or other foreign subjects for immediate payment and delivery on the spot, or for payment and, or on, delivery at the specified port;" in other words, whether the goods are virtually, during the period of transit, foreign or native property, so long as they were *bonâ fide* sold, though conditionally, for exportation, *or simply bonâ fide destined for exportation abroad*, by, British or other foreign subjects. This follows necessarily from the nature of mercantile transactions and the customs of trade, in connection more especially with Rule vii. of the Russian Convention and Art. liv. of the British Treaty of Tientsin.

The last and most important point, concluded by me from the Treaties, and in accordance with the views always held by the merchants, is, that the tax of half the import- or export-duties, fixed by Tariff, or of 2½ per cent. *ad valorem* on merchandise not subject to those duties, respectively, by which the "transit"-duties leviable or levied by the Chinese Authorities on native inland trade were commuted, exempts *the goods* on which that commutation-tax, independently of import- or export-duty, has been paid, from further exactions in the Interior, and exempts such goods from *all and every description of further imposts*, including *le-kin* and any other extraordinary tax, to which the home commerce of China was, is, or may become, subject so long as the existing Treaties remain in force. The positive proof to this effect, which I shall be able to adduce, is based on facts and generally recognised principles; on the literal wording of the Treaties; and on the united testimony of Sir Henry Pottinger and Lord Elgin, who framed the British Treaties of Nanking and Tientsin, of Sir Frederick Bruce, of some of the highest Chinese Provincial Authorities, and of the Tsung-li Ya-mên itself.

A public Treaty between two Nations involves the same principles of law and justice, as does a private contract between two individual persons. Suppose, now, two large establishments, say a bakery and a brewery, inclosed within their own walls and with all the workmen, employed in them, residing on the premises. Suppose further the managers of these concerns to conclude a legal agreement or contract to the effect, that the bakery shall supply, or be free to supply, the brewery with bread and the brewery the bakery with beer, on this condition that, independently of the natural market price of the two articles of consumption, the manager of the bakery, on the bread passing through the gate of his establishment, shall levy on it a small impost at a *fixed* rate, to go towards meeting the expenditure of the management of the concern, and that the manager of the brewery, on the bread entering the gate of his establishment, shall, for a similar purpose, levy on it a similar impost at a *fixed* rate, both of which imposts the consumers in the brewery will have to pay in addititition to the natural market price of the bread. In the same manner it shall be agreed, that the manager of the brewery, on the beer passing through the gate of his establishment, levy on it a small impost at a *fixed* rate, and the manager of the bakery, on its entering the gate of his premises a similar impost at a *fixed* rate, both of which imposts the consumers in the bakery will have to pay in addition to the natural market price of the beer. Lastly, suppose one of the contracting parties, say the brewery, to faithfully keep to the terms of the agreement entered into; but not so the other party, the manager of the bakery putting up, within his establishment and surreptitiously, additional gate-ways, at each of which he levies fresh imposts, at an increasing rate, upon the beer supplied by the brewery, so that most of the workmen employed in the bakery are thereby induced to brew their own beer, to obtain it elsewhere, or to take to other beverages, to the detriment of the legitimate trade of the brewery. Suppose, I say, all this: would not the manager of the bakery have indisputably committed a breach of contract, and laid himself open to being, by the manager of the brewery, sued in a Court of Justice for damage?

The breach of public Treaty, committed by the Government of China in its relations with England and other Western countries, constitutes a far grosser and more flagrant case, than the breach of private contract just assumed. It is, or should be, a recognised international principle, that any rate of *import*-duty, agreed upon between two Governments, exempts the merchandise on which that duty has been paid, from all further inland charges within the limits of the importing country, except such *customary local* imposts of small amount, as may be levied for purposes of *local* improvement in which trade directly or indirectly participates, and *which were publicly known to be levied at the time of the conclusion of the Treaty.* Certainly, no additional tax of any kind the Government of the importing country is entitled to impose, for the benefit of *the public Exchequer*, upon merchandise which has paid the covenanted *import-*duty, without the previous knowledge and express consent of the Government of the exporting country, as the other contracting party. It may possibly be argued that, in the case of China and England, the contract is a one-sided one, and that China has never been consulted as to the duties upon exports to, and imports from, the Chinese Empire, levied in Western States. True. But it has to be remembered that, as regards England, the stipulations of the Treaty at present in force are the price, not of a friendly agreement, but of two costly wars, imposed upon her by China; that the conquered had, consequently, no right to expect from the conqueror such terms as a state of mutual amity might have commanded; that England has, nevertheless, treated China with an extreme degree of moderation and forbearance; that China has never taken exception to the English Tariff; and, above all, that England, so far from increasing her scale of customs-duties in general, and those upon the staple-articles of export to, and import from, China in particular, since the conclusion of the Treaties of Nanking and Tientsin, has voluntarily subjected it to essential reductions. If to other Powers, who next to England carry on the most extensive trade with China and have concluded Treaties with her under conditions of mutual friendship, she has granted the same terms, which were "exacted" from her by the Plenipotentiaries of England and France, supported by victorious armies: she has done so *of her own free will*, and thereby but furnished a signal proof of that moderation and forbearance on the part of England, to which I have just alluded.

It is clear, then, from what has thus been said, that, after the conclusion of the Treaty of Nanking, the Chinese

Government had no right to levy upon foreign merchandise, imported by British and other foreign subjects for sale in China, or upon goods bought in China by British and other foreign subjects for exportation to foreign ports, in addition to the stipulated import- or export-duties, any tax whatsoever for the benefit of the public Exchequer, nor any other local imposts, besides those local imposts, which it was legal and customary to levy upon inland trade *at the time of the conclusion of the Treaty*, and to the payment of which the formal consent of England was given. Until the Treaty of Tientsin this agreement remained in force, with the distinct proviso, as has been seen, that the rates of inland taxes levied in 1842, being upon a moderate scale, *should not thereafter be exceeded;* and the import- and export-duties having been fixed by Tariff, whilst no *le-kin* or any other imposts of the kind had as yet been introduced: there consequently were, at the time of the conclusion of the Treaty of Nanking, absolutely no other imposts either leviable or actually levied on British and Foreign trade within the dominions of the Emperor of China, *save those agreed upon by Treaty.*

Scarcely, however, had that Treaty been signed, when the Chinese Government "invented" and imposed on trade, at first upon a very moderate scale, a war-tax under the name of *le-kin*, unknown to England, and on the principle, —a principle, generally cherished and applied by the Chinese Government,—of paying the barbarian,—in this case for war-expenses according to Art. vi. and vii. of the Nanking Treaty,—with the barbarian's own money; and with the simultaneous view of keeping the inland trade of foreigners, then exclusively carried on through native agency, by means of an increasing taxation not only under complete control, but at its absolute mercy. The scheme had thus far succeeded so well and proved so profitable both to the public, and the provincial, Exchequer, as well as to individual interests, that, with so rich and pleasant a mine of almost inexhaustible income opened up on the one hand, and the Tai-ping rebellion pressing upon the resources of the country on the other, the Chinese Government, at the time of the Tientsin Treaty, judged it expedient and, under a system of progressive taxation, considered it safe, to extend for a while the facilities of foreign commerce, and even to allow inland trade, under certain restrictions, to be carried on by foreigners themselves. Hence, the special correspondent of "the Times" in China during the years 1857–58, the late Mr. G. Wingrove Cooke, already at that period had to warn the home public to remember, "that, since the outbreak of the rebellion, the Chinese mandarins had levied a tax of full £2,000,000 a year upon the people of England; that this tax consisted almost entirely of local unauthorised extortion; and that it was capable of indefinite increase." "The English people," he adds, "should teach a starling to cry: *Free Transit through China!* and should hang the bird up in Lord Elgin's cabin. Nothing short of this will do,—nothing short of this will prevent future wars. What more is required, I do not now discuss; but this is the first and most indispensable of all conditions of peace. We do not know enough of the country to take any substitute or to submit to any modification."

When, therefore, in 1858 the British Treaty of Tientsin was concluded, it not only was well known to the English Government and Lord Elgin, the British Plenipotentiary in China, but it was a matter of public notoriety and of constant complaint on the part of British merchants, "that charges were suddenly and arbitrarily imposed by the provincial authorities as 'transit-duties' upon produce on its way to the foreign market, and on imports on their way to the Interior, to the detriment of trade" (Art. xxviii. of Tientsin Treaty); whilst all thinking men in China shared the conviction of the Correspondent of "the Times," that *nothing short of free transit through China would prevent future wars.* Nay, at so early a date as the year 1847, the subject had engaged the special attention of the English House of Commons; as the following extracts from the evidence, taken before a Select Committee in the months of April and May of that year, will indicate :—

Viscount Jocelyn :—Do you believe, that there are any very heavy transit-duties levied upon our manufactures which go from this country? —J. Matheson, Esq. :—I have no correct information upon that point.

Dr. Bowring :—Can you form an estimate of the cost of duties which attach to the conveyance of woollens from the port to the northern district of consumption ?—John Gott, Esq. :—What the internal duties are, I do not know.

Viscount Jocelyn :—Do you know anything as regards the internal duties levied by the Chinese upon the transit of imported goods ?—J. Silverlock, Esq :—I do not. We are sometimes told, that they levy certain duties ; but by the treaty, I think, there are to be no transit duties.

Are you aware, whether there are duties levied upon the imports as they pass up the country ?—I believe there are certain fees given to the mandarins at different passes.

The Chairman :—Would it not be possible *by the establishment of heavy transit duties in the country to defeat the whole object of the treaty* (of Nanking), with reference to the duties fixed upon the first entry of the goods ?—T. A. Gibb, Esq. :—No doubt; it is a very material consideration.

What alone, even in 1858 and still later, the English Government and the foreign public remained in ignorance of, as they virtually do to this day, was, and is, the exact extent, the systematic character, and the precise nature of the "transit-duties" levied upon the inland trade in China, as also of the fact that those inland taxes *were and are levied by order of the Chinese Government itself, as a source of public revenue,*|| and, of late years at least, mainly for purposes hostile to the West. To assume, then, that, with the knowledge and information actually possessed by the British Plenipotentiary, Lord Elgin, in framing the Treaty of Tientsin, should not have meant to effectually protect, and by Treaty effectually have protected, British trade in China from inland duties, charges, and exactions, on the part of the Chinese Authorities, of *every* kind; by consenting to the payment of one fixed *commutation*-tax, and that he should have equally failed therein when, master of the Capital of China, he subsequently concluded the Convention of Peking, appears to me,—notwithstanding that the arguments of the illustrious defenders of *le-kin*, *chow-fang*, and other imposts of the kind, imply nothing less,—simply irrational. Nor shall we find the wording of the Treaty of Tientsin to belie our confidence in Lord Elgin.

By ART. LIV. of this Treaty, all privileges, immunities, and advantages of previous Treaties generally are insured, and by ART. I., the Treaty of Nanking in particular is renewed and confirmed. But by ART. X. of the latter Treaty and the Hongkong Declaration, the *only inland imposts* to be levied upon foreign merchandise sent for sale into the Interior, and by ART. XXVIII. of the Treaty of Tientsin, upon native merchandise intended for exportation to foreign parts,

|| It might possibly be argued that, after all, the Chinese Government receives but a small portion of this revenue. But such is by no means the case. With the exception of the "squeezes" of the officials, the whole amount goes to the public Exchequer: only that in China, the Government, instead of collecting the entire income of the State into the national Treasury and directly administrating the whole expenditure again from Peking, allows the Local and Provincial Authorities to retain, out of the taxes collected, certain portions, fixed by the Board of Revenue and instructs them to remit only the remainder for Imperial or general purposes to the Capital.

were the then customary, moderate imposts *by Treaty agreed to, and which were in no way to be increased or added to in future.* Now, those imposts, certainly not amounting to 2½ per cent. *ad valorem* in the aggregate, included neither *le-kin* nor *chow-fang*, and the like subsequently invented taxes. Consequently, by the provisions of the British Treaties of Nanking and Tientsin taken in combination, the Chinese Government has no right to levy upon foreign merchandise sent by British and other foreign subjects for sale into the Interior, and native merchandise sold to British and other foreign subjects for exportation to foreign parts, any duties or imposts *whatever*, save and except such import-, export-, and inland-duties, respectively, *as have been agreed upon by Treaty.*

Again, by Art. xxviii. of the Treaty of Tientsin and Rule vii. of the Agreement appended to it, the rates of inland imposts, as stipulated by the Treaty of Nanking, having been exceeded on the part, it was believed, of the Provincial Authorities alone; and *le-kin* being already then levied, and surreptitiously so, it was provided, in order to do away with ALL irregular and arbitrary inland charges or exactions, to *commute* the same by, and *substitute for* them, the payment of *one single fixed* impost of one half the Tariff import- and export-duty respectively, or of 2½ per cent *ad valorem* on merchandise by Treaty not subject to those duties,—which impost, it is stated in the most explicit terms, "*shall*—by certificate—*exempt the goods*—on which the one tax, thus fixed, shall have been paid—*from all further inland charges whatsoever.*" Consequently, also by the British Treaty of Tientsin taken by itself, the Chinese Government has no right to levy, under whatever name or pretence it be, upon *foreign merchandise* sent by Foreign subjects for sale and consumption to any part of the Interior of China, and *native merchandise* sold in any part of the Interior of China to Foreign subjects for exportation to foreign parts, *le-kin*, *chow-fang*, or any duties or imposts *whatsoever*, save and except only such import-, export- and inland- (also improperly called *transit*-) duties, respectively, *as have been agreed upon by Treaty*. And hence, not only are the inland-imposts, actually levied by the Chinese Government through its officials, whether under the name of *le-kin*, *chow-fang*, or any other name, *in amount over and above the rates fixed by Treaty and Tariff*, illegal, and entitle the British and other Foreign Governments to demand from the Chinese Government due repayment of, or full compensation for, the same to the aggregate extent, to which they have accumulated: but by Art. xxiii. of the French, and Art. liv.. of the British, Treaty of Tientsin, the Chinese Customs- and other officials, moreover, who, contrary to the provisions of that Treaty, have been engaged in exacting the illegal taxes in question, and levied higher rates of inland- (or as they are styled *transit*-) duties than have been agreed upon and fixed by Treaty, have rendered themselves liable to be punished in accordance with the laws of China.

No language could be clearer than the words of the Treaty, stipulating that the inland duty-exemption (or, as for brevity's sake it is inappropriately *called*, the *transit*) certificate, to be issued by the proper Chinese Authorities upon payment of the stipulated commutation-tax, and to accompany the goods, upon which such a tax has been paid, "shall exempt *such goods* from all further inland charges *whatsoever*." The Chinese version of the whole passage is, perhaps, not quite so satisfactory; without, however, leaving any doubt as to the fact, that by the one single stipulated tax, once paid, *all* inland duties, however numerous, were to be commuted, and *the goods*—whether in the possession of foreigners or natives,—upon which such a tax has been paid, to be exempted from any further inland charges *whatsoever.* Independently of which, it was distinctly agreed by Art. L. of the Tientsin Treaty, as we have seen, that not the Chinese, but the English, text is to be considered the standard text for determining the true sense of the Treaty.

The same view had already, I find, been taken by F. B. Johnson, Esq., in his able memorandum on "Transit-Dues," submitted by him on September 13, 1869, to the General Chamber of Commerce of Shanghai, and subsequently printed by the Chamber. In reference to Art. xxviii. of the Treaty of Tientsin and Art. x. of the Treaty of Nanking, Mr. Johnson insists:—"If language can be said to be capable of any definite meaning, the terms of this clause apply to *British merchandize, as such,* without reference to its immediate ownership; and no other supposition than that it was foreign trade generally, and not the individual foreign merchant particularly, which was intended to be protected, is reconcileable with the remonstrances which, from time to time, were directed by H. M. Consuls to the Chinese authorities on the subject of transit-dues, and the negotiations regarding them, which took place between the signature of the Treaty of Nanking and the proposed settlement of the question by Art. xxviii. of the Treaty of Tientsin."

As a further proof, if such a proof be still needed, for the correctness of this interpretation, there is the despatch of the framer of the Treaty of Tientsin himself, addressed by him to the Home Government on November 8, 1858, and in which, on transmitting the Agreement of the same date, together with the accompanying Tariff and Rules, Lord

Elgin explains the sense, which he attaches to the latter.

Rule vii. applies, his Lordship writes to the Foreign Office, and extends *the principle* respecting transit-duties, which is laid down by Art. xxviii of the Treaty. Henceforward, on payment of a sum *in name* of transit duty, which for simplicity's sake has been fixed at one-half of the tariff-rate of duty, goods, whether of export or import, will be free to pass between the port of shipment or entry to or from any part of China, without further charge of toll, octroi, or tax of any description whatsoever. I confess that I consider this to be a most important point gained in the future interest of foreign trade with China. In every representation on the general subject of trade, which I have received from mercantile bodies or individuals since I came to China, the system, or no system, under which transit-duties are now levied, has been pressed upon me as a grievance, and I have always thought *that the remedy was to be sought in the substitution of one fixed payment for the present irregular and multiplied levies.* At the same time, in a country where the duties of octroi are habitually resorted to as an expedient for supplying the wants both of the local and Imperial treasuries, it was obviously difficult to devise *a scheme for the commutation of transit* [*i. e.* inland] *duties, which,* without creating great financial disturbance, *should prove an effectual protection to the importing and exporting merchants.* The rule now under consideration has been carefully framed, and will, I trust, in practice, afford a reasonable security against both of the two classes of evils which I have indicated.

The considerations, which induced Lord Elgin to consent to the payment of so high an inland impost as from 2½ to 3 °/₀ *ad valorem*, in addition to the stipulated import- and export-duties, we learn from the Plenipotentiary's despatch of July 12, 1858, to Lord Malmesbury, then English Secretary of State for Foreign Affairs. In reference to "the settlement of the vexed question of the transit-duties," Lord Elgin observes :—"This subject presented considerable difficulty. As duties of octroi are levied universally in China, on native as well as foreign products, and as canals and roads are kept up at the expense of the Government, it seemed to be unreasonable to require that articles, whether of foreign or native production, by the simple process of passing into the hands of foreigners, should become entitled to the use of roads and canals toll-free; and should, moreover, be relieved *altogether* from charges to which they would be liable if the property of natives."

In reading these extracts, it has to be borne in mind, that, even at the conclusion of the Treaty of Tientsin, no other charges were as yet levied upon trade, whether native or foreign, in the Interior of China, except charges *levied on the road*, and hence, when Lord Elgin speaks of transit-charges, octroi, etc., that he speaks of, and intends to be understood, the *Inland duties*, levied or leviable by the Chinese Government, *generally and collectively*.

If the reader could retain any doubt in regard to this point, he is referred to the Government Notification of Sir Henry Pottinger of February 20, 1844, and his despatch to the English Foreign Office of the 27th of the same month, previously quoted, in which already by the framer of the Treaty of Nanking the taxes in question are distinctly designated as "Transit or *Inland Duties of the Chinese Empire*," and "the Transit or *Inland Duties, levied in the Chinese Empire*;" and that also Sir Frederick Bruce, who was present at the framing of the Treaty of Tientsin, understood them in the same sense, is proved by his despatch of December 2, 1862, wherein he states, that "the object of the [Trade-] Rule No. 7, [appended to the Treaty of Tientsin], was to *substitute one unvarying charge for* [the whole of] *the arbitrary exactions of provincial authorities, . . . in the Interior.*"

To complete the evidence in support of this view, I shall now have only further to show that, immediately after the ratification of the Treaty of Tientsin, the same view was taken of ART. XXVIII. and Rule vii. by at least some of the highest Chinese Officials and, what is still more to the point, by the Tsung-li Ya-mên itself. The following papers, presented, in 1864, to both Houses of Parliament by command of Her Majesty, will suffice for this purpose :—

The Prince of Kung to Mr. Bruce.

(Translation) Peking, October 18, 1862.

The Prince of Kung makes a communication.

In the regulations forwarded by His Excellency Kwanwen, Governor-General of Hu Kwang, for the general regulation of trade on the Yang-tze-kiang, there were three, namely, the 11th, 12th, and 13th, affecting the levy of transit duties, and which, as they slightly modify the present regulations of the Customs (or in force at the different Custom-houses), he has requested His Highness to submit to his Excellency the British Minister.

It becomes the Prince's duty to forward a copy of these three regulations as a supplement to the list already communicated, and His Highness will be obliged to the British Minister to inform him whether there be in them anything objectionable.

A necessary communication.

Précis of Three Articles to Regulate the Collection of Transit Duties up the Yang-tze Kiang.

(Translation.)

ART. XI.—Proposed that certificates of transit duties on goods passing through Hu-peh and Hu-nan should be issued only at the Kiang-han kwan (Hankow Customs), on goods in Kiang-si and An-hwui, only at Kin-kiang ; on goods in Kiang-su only at the Kiang-hai kwan (Shanghae Customs). These two additional articles to a certain extent, would modify (the Treaty condition) so as to facilitate its operation.

ART. XII.—Merchants desiring to carry imports either in their own custody or that of a foreign agent from the port of entry, have issued to them by the Customs of that port a certificate that the Customs have inspected the goods, as particularised in the application, and that they are bound for such a point. This certificate the merchant produces at the Customs Receiving Office, and having paid into it the half Tariff duty due on the goods, presents its receipt for the money to the Customs, who thereon issue to the applicant a note (or pass) which enables the merchant to carry his goods *free of war tax charges* (*le-kin*) to the point specified in his application, no matter how distant this may be from the port. But the merchant is not obliged to take out this certificate at all, and goods going into the country, if not covered by such a certificate, become liable, whether in charge of foreigner or native, to the operation of the (local) laws already in force *under which the war taxes are imposed.*

If, therefore, a foreign merchant, having already disposed of his goods to a native merchant, shall obtain a certificate by fraudulently representing the goods to be his own, the goods shall, on discovery of the fraud, be confiscated; and whereas, at the present moment, military requirements produce a pressing demand for funds, the Customs above enumerated have moved (his Excellency Kwanwen or His Highness the Prince) to notify that the following distinctions will be made between foreign and native goods:—broad cloth, camlets, clocks and watches, shirtings, foreign wood, such article being *bonâ fide* foreign, can be covered by transit certificate; but sea-weed and other articles which are produced in China, as well as abroad, shall, for the present, not be so covered.

Art. xiii.—Any foreign merchant desiring to bring down produce to an open port either in his own charge or in that of a foreign Agent, can apply through his Consul to the Customs for a certificate. The merchant states in his note where he is going and what produce he wants to buy, and the Customs, on receipt of the Consul's application, forward to him for the merchant a triplicate certificate and a blank pass. The merchant takes these to the interior, and having purchased his produce submits it to the inspection of the first barrier it has to pass, and deposits there one of the triplicate certificates, on the face of which is entered the quantity of produce purchased. The barrier enters on his pass the amount of his produce, seals it, and returns it to the merchant, who is then authorized to proceed. When he arrives at the barrier nearest his port he produces his pass, and the amount of his produce being found to correspond with the entry, he clears it of the transit duty at the Custom-house of his port, and then takes it past the barrier.

Should the produce be unaccompanied by a transit certificate, it must *pay the war tax charges (le-kin)* imposed by the rules already in force at every barrier it has to pass.

But whereas oil, grain, and timber are articles consumed by the poorer classes, and there would be consequently much embarrassment attending the transit of these, it is proposed to issue no passes for them, and to punish any Chinese and any linguist who may combine with him in demanding a pass for the same, besides confiscating the goods.

I need hardly remark that these propositions, the insidious design and tendency of which are too patent, were declined by Sir Frederick Bruce as "inconsistent with Treaty rights and leading to endless embarrassment." What here alone interests us, is the distinct admission, by both the Governor-General of 'Hu-kuang and the Tsung-li Ya-mên, that foreign merchandise for inland consumption and native merchandise for export to foreign ports, conveyed without a certificate, are, whether in the hands of foreigner or native, liable to pay all inland war-tax charges *(i.e. le-kin, chow-fang, &c.)*; but, that, accompanied by a certificate, they are,—whether in the hands of native or foreigner,—exempt from such charges; and, consequently, that *le-kin, chow-fang, &c., are included in the inland charges commutation-tax*—being half the Tariff import- and export-duties, respectively, or of 2½ per cent. *ad valorem* on merchandise not subject to those charges, as *stipulated by Treaty*. And *hence*, and because at that time no machinery—in the shape of "Stationary trade taxes," "Grower's tax," etc., of which I shall have to speak hereafter,—had been invented to levy, at the mart of destination or the locality of production, the *complementary* amount of illegal imposts, desired by the Chinese Government, and which the "transit-pass," would prevent the native officials from levying on the road, it was, that his Excellency Kuan Wên felt so anxious to establish the doctrine, that "the merchant is not obliged to take out a certificate at all," and the Tsung-li Ya-mên so readily supported the proposition of the Governor-General of 'Hu-Kuang.

Again, Tsêng Kuo Fan, the late Governor-General of the Two Keang, and Superintendent of Trade for the Southern Ports, in a despatch dated Nanking, Nov. 5, 1868,—at the instance, Mr. Hart states, of the Tsung-li Ya-mên,—instructed the Tau-tai of Shanghai as Intendant of Customs, to the effect that "foreign merchandise, entering the Interior, shall pay duty at the Custom-houses and *le-kin* at the Customs-barriers only when the merchant is unable to produce a certificate;" that "if he hold a certificate showing that the transit-duty has been paid, then no further duty or *le-kin* shall be demanded;" and that, if the foreign merchant be not inclined to pay, on imports, the half-duty at the sea-port, he must pay the transit-dues and *le-kin* at the inland stations, and, if he be not inclined to pay, on exports, the transit-dues and *le-kin* at the inland stations, he must pay the half-duty in advance, in which matter he may have his choice." Nay, he writes:—"It is imperative that the Treaty-stipulations be observed, and under no circumstances should the *le-kin* be made to *violate existing Treaties*, and provoke constant disputes with the Consuls."§

And lastly, even after the Tsung-li Ya-mên's sudden change of view on the subject, it had, through its Commissioners, by promising that a proclamation should be issued, requiring the barrier-officials to act in accordance with existing Treaties, in order to "avoid illegal levies *in future*," once more to admit that the imposts, actually levied at the barriers, *i.e.* the *le-kin* taxes, are being levied *illegally*.

But, what renders these levies illegal, and alone renders them so, is not that they are collected in particular localities or at particular collectorates, but that they are collected in

§ The despatch of Tsêng-Kuo-Fan, here quoted from, was printed by Ying,—a late Tau-tai of Shanghai, to whom it waf addressed,—in a volume, known as: 各國和約, "Treaty-Obligations of Individual (Tributary) States," for private distribution only.

defiance of positive Treaty-stipulations. It matters nothing to the foreign merchant, manufacturer, or consumer, whether, in the Interior of China, he has to pay duties, enhancing the cost of merchandise, at 關 or 卡, at Chinese ports or "*in transitu;*" but it does matter to him, whether or not he has to pay such duties at all. It concerns no Foreign Power, with what imposts the Chinese Government burdens its own subjects, and lays them on native merchandise for *native* consumption; but it does concern every Foreign Power in treaty-relations with China, with what imposts the Government of China, *in violation of positive international engagements,* burdens *its* subjects by illegally burdening the property of those subjects,—their *manufactures* and other *merchandise* destined for sale in the Interior of China, and Chinese produce, destined for consumption *at home.* The distinction, involving a simple problem of "mine" and "thine," *could,* in despite of the labours of the Foreign Inspector-General of Chinese Maritime Customs and the Chief Superintendent of British Trade in China to confuse the views of Her Britannic Majesty's Board of Trade on the subject, hardly escape the penetration of the Tsung-li Ya-mên.

Nor could, otherwise, the Chinese Authorities be reasonably expected to hold a different opinion in regard to our question, for this additional reason that, by Rule v. of the Agreement appended to the Treaty of Tientsin, it was expressly stipulated that to opium alone Art. xxviii. of the Treaty should not extend, and that in regard to opium alone the Chinese Government should be at liberty to arrange the (transit- i.e. the) inland duties as it might see fit. Consequently, on the principle that the exception constitutes the rule, the exception here once more and forcibly supports the sense which, I venture to think, the Treaty has now been fully proved to bear, namely, that on no article of British and Foreign Commerce, *opium only excepted*, has the Chinese Government the right to levy any taxes whatever over and above those *agreed upon by Treaty*.

The entire question, in fact, lies in a nutshell. It presents to Common Sense but two points for consideration. The minor one of these points is: the *special object* of the commutation of a multiplicity of payments for inland duties by one single payment of an aggregate sum *in lieu* thereof. No rational person can misinterpret or misapprehend that object. The second and principal point is: the *general object* of any international Commercial Treaty. Foreign commerce consists essentially in a mutual exchange of commodities, natural $\frac{\text{and}}{\text{or}}$ industrial, between different countries, each country endeavouring to insure what is termed the balance of trade in its own favor. When, therefore, the Governments of two countries to this combined end conclude a Commercial Treaty, the *sole* object of such a Treaty, of its very nature, is: *firstly*, to *fix* the pecuniary terms or "duties" to be paid by the trading subjects of either country to the Government of the other, in consideration of which the natural and industrial productions of either country shall have free and direct access for purchase, barter, use, or consumption to the subjects of the other country; and *secondly*, to determine the regulations, under which trade is to be carried on with this view. Hence it follows that the Government of no country, having concluded a Treaty of Commerce with the Government of another country, can, *so long as that Treaty remains in force*, legally levy upon the commerce between the two countries any higher or further imposts, save and except *such imposts or duties as have been agreed upon and fixed by Treaty*. If it were otherwise; if either country be at liberty, after having entered into a contract, at any moment to change the terms of that contract to its own advantage; if it could lawfully, after accepting to-day a *fixed* Tariff of duties, to-morrow raise that Tariff or at pleasure add further imposts to those agreed upon: it is manifest that the signing of international Treaties would become simply a farce, the exchange of their ratifications a mockery instead of a solemnity, and the Treaties themselves just so much waste paper, and worth less than waste paper.

China has systematically and perfidiously broken her international contracts with England and the West generally, relative to inland trade,—the only subject here under consideration. By the Treaty of Nanking the Imperial Government engaged to levy, upon British merchandise, no inland taxes whatever over and above the customary and legalized taxes then generally leviable upon inland trade; and immediately afterwards, the Chinese Government not only "invented" and surreptitiously imposed upon British trade an *additional* inland tax, under the name of *le-kin*, being a kind of "war-tax," but rapidly *increased the rate* of that new and illegal tax from a small impost to the scale of a grievous burden. By the Treaty of Tientsin, England protesting against the system of unlawful inland taxation thus initiated, once more the Chinese Government, having arranged to commute the whole of the inland charges then levied and thereafter to be levied upon British trade, for the payment of *one fixed tax*, namely, of one half the stipulated import- and export-duties, respectively, or of 2½ per cent. *ad valorem* upon duty-free goods, solemnly engaged to levy in future upon Foreign trade no inland imposts of any kind whatsoever in addition to, or in excess of, the one single commutation-tax thus by Treaty agreed upon. But no sooner had this agreement been concluded, than the Chinese Government, in violation and defiance of its public engagements and of national good faith, resorted to the surreptitious imposition of still further inland-trade taxes and a still further extension of those already introduced to such a degree, that the mean aggregate of inland imposts over and above those fixed by Treaty, and which are at the present time being *illegally* levied, and for several years past have been so levied, upon Foreign commerce with the Interior of China, amount, at a moderate computation, to *more than seven times the rate by Treaty stipulated*, that is to say, to an annual sum, as will be presently seen, of upwards of £5,000,000 sterling, independently of Coast-trade duties. Nor does this large sum of money represent any thing like the injury, which the Chinese Government is thus suffered to inflict upon the Foreign merchant and Foreign Commerce and Industry, by deliberately and systematically violating the provisions of a Treaty, secured to the people of England by the national sacrifices involved in two distant wars.

V.

EXAMINATION OF AUTHORITATIVE VIEWS.

Position of the Foreign Inspector-General in the Chinese Customs' Service—Value to be attached to his opinions—Obstructive tendency of his views illustrated—The Transit-System brought home—The Inspector-General's misapprehensions and duplicity of sight—Prince Kung's "sincerity"—The Tsung li Yamên's newly proposed Regulations discussed—Sir R. Alcock's opinions in 1868 and 1870 contrasted—A novel doctrine—What gives validity to Chinese State-papers—The Great Imperial Seal and the Seal, by the Tsung-li Yamên attached to International Treaties—Unsatisfactory diplomatic state of Western Treaty-relations with China—Sir R. Alcock's imperfect knowledge of Chinese State affairs—Mr. Wade's Memorandum of 1868 characterised—His inaccuracies and self-contradictions —Mr. Wade, the *le-kin* tax, and the Foreign Customs—His warm apology for the *le-kin* and two-sided exaggerations—Amount of Chinese Revenue—"The Central Government" wanting not in the power, but in the will to abrogate the *le-kin*—Prince Kung's "timidity"—His Imperial Highness in disgrace—Mr. Wade's strange fiscal notions—Untenable character of the "*in transitu*" theory demonstrated—Its first originator—Pernicious doctrines involved in Mr. Wade's views—Mr. Wade's impressions and Lord Elgin's written statements—Alleged right of the Chinese Government to tax *ad libitum* foreign merchandize which has paid the Commutation-dues, after passing into Chinese possession—Confusion of ideas on the subject—Sir Frederick Bruce's views—Mr. Wade's key-note to the whole question—Its false and discordant sound—The real nature of the problem stated—Justice versus Expediency—Two unholy wars against China—Sinful policy of Lord Palmerston and atoning policy of the Right Hon. W. E. Gladstone.

Having shown what are the real Treaty-stipulations, agreed upon between China and England as well as other foreign States relative to inland- (usually but improperly termed transit-) dues, leviable upon British and other foreign trade by the Chinese Government; to what an extent the Chinese

Government, in addition to the imposts fixed by Treaty, has burdened foreign trade with illegal taxation; and to what purposes the large surplus of revenue, which the Imperial Exchequer is deriving from this source, is applied: there now presents itself for our consideration the basis of those views, which both Chinese and British officials of high position, including the Lords of the Committee of Her Majesty's Privy Council for Trade, hold at variance with the positive results of our inquiry; together with the arguments, by which some of the Authorities alluded to have endeavoured to justify or to palliate the conduct of the Chinese Government. For the sake of greater lucidity, it will be desirable to reserve the general and more important points, until we shall have passed in review and estimated at their proper value such individual opinions, as partake of a secondary character, yet enter as essential elements into the question.

Considerable allowance has to be made for, and therefore a proportionately less value attached to, the views expressed upon Chinese matters by the foreign Inspector-General of Maritime Customs, Mr. Hart, on account of his peculiar position in the Celestial service,—highly lucrative on the one hand, anomalous and somewhat precarious, on the other. The Chinese Government, *i. e.* the Emperor, and his Privy Council and State Secretariate, 內閣衙門, have never officially recognised so much as the existence of the foreign element of the Customs-Service, although this branch of public administration, so far as it relates to foreign trade, is chiefly directed and partly performed by foreign *employés*, of whom *none*, however, are in direct communication with the Imperial Government. The latter, having committed the "General control of Individual (Tributary) States' Affairs" to a mere temporary Commission, presided over by Prince Kung, and by foreigners usually, but erroneously, styled "the (Chinese) Foreign Office" or "Board of Foreign Affairs," has consigned also the *foreign* department of Maritime Customs to the general charge of that Commission, and the special charge of native "Superintendents of Trade" and "Intendants of Customs," their subordinates. The native Intendants of Customs correspond with the native Superintends of Trade, and have under their orders the foreign "Commissioners of Customs,"—whose real title is 江海關稅務司, "River- and Sea-Customs Inspector,"—and who, on their part, correspond with their immediate superiors, the native Intendants of Customs and the foreign 總江海關稅務司, "Chief River- and Sea-Customs Inspector,"—commonly, but erroneously, styled "Inspector-General of (Chinese Imperial) Customs,"—in rank inferior even to the native Intendant of Customs. The foreign Chief- or Head-Inspector of Maritime Customs, at present Mr. Hart, is the immediate subordinate of the native Superintendents of Trade and corresponds with the latter and,—in as much as he has of late years been permitted to reside in Peking instead of Shanghai, his proper station,—with the Tsung-li Ya-mên. The native Superintendents of Trade and the native Tsung-li Ya-mên alone correspond with the Imperial Board of Revenue and the Imperial Government, *i. e.* the Emperor's Privy Council and State Secretariate.*

The circumstances, under which the present Inspector-General succeeded to his post, I shall have occasion to speak of in another place. Mr. Hart's appointment by the Tsung-

* In the official State-Directory of China, which is published quarterly under the title 大清搢紳全書, the names of the native Superintendents of Trade and Intendants of Customs will be found duly registered, but neither the Foreign "Inspector-General of (Chinese Imperial Maritime) Customs" or any other foreign Customs employé, *nor the Tsung-li Ya-mên itself.* The latter authorities are completely ignored.

li Ya-mên is dated November, 1863. The translation, published in the Blue-book "China, No. 2, 1864", contains the following paragraphs:—" The Prince of Kung [the Tsung-li Ya-mên] issues these important instructions to Mr. Hart, for his information and guidance. Mr. Lay has been dismissed from the post of Inspector-General of Customs, and has been instructed to proceed to Shanghai to wind up everything still unsettled by him, and We (knowing that) you, from the date of your entering the Customs to the present time, have at all times acted harmoniously and with success, hereby appoint you to the post of Inspector-General of Customs Affairs. You will reside and transact all business at Shanghai: and if any important question arise, you are authorised, as heretofore, to come to the capital as occasion requires, to report and deliberate thereupon. You will report, as it may be necessary, all matters of daily occurrence at the several ports both on the northern and southern sea-board, and on the Yang-tze, to their Excellencies Li or Chung, as the case may be, Ministers Superintendents of Trade, and will abide by their instructions. Your tact, and experience are known to all, both Chinese and foreign, and it will behove you to be still more careful and diligent, so as to justify your present appointment".

To Sir Frederick Bruce the Tsung-li Ya-mên, on November, 15, 1863, wrote:—" The Prince [the Tsung-li Ya-mên, *i. e.* the temporary 'Commission for the General Control of Individual (Tributary-) States' Affairs', of which Prince Kung is the Chairman] has now appointed Mr. Hart to the post of Inspector-General of all the Customs Affairs. Inclosed are copies of the letters (of dismissal) to Mr. Lay, and of the letter appointing Mr. Hart Inspector-General of Customs, the purport of which the Prince would request the

British Minister to communicate to the Consuls at the several ports." In his despatch of November 27, 1863, to Earl Russell, then Secretary of State for Foreign Affairs, the British Minister in Peking, Sir Frederick Bruce, observed;—"Mr. Hart is appointed in his (Mr. Lay's) place, and I trust that the change will make the Custom-house work more smoothly. He will reside on the coast, coming here when sent for on business. It is very desirable, with a view to the maintenance of the Custom-house administration, that the head of it should not be permanently at Peking, for if he is," Sir Frederick naïvely adds, "he is supposed to act as the adviser of the Chinese in matters not appertaining to his office, and thereby incurs the odium of the errors they commit." In the same sense the late Mr. Burlingame, then United States Minister in Peking, wrote to his Government in a despatch, dated July 5, 1864:—"After what had happened [the dismissal of Mr. Lay] we felt it to be our duty to urge upon the Tsung-li Ya-mên the expediency of not permitting the Inspector of Customs, or any other foreign employé to reside at Peking in a quasi-diplomatic capacity. In this view they most heartily concurred, and immediately appointed Robert Hart, Esq., in the place of Mr. Lay, with instructions to reside at Shanghai."

In reference to this appointment, I should still observe that the despatches of the Tsung-li Ya-mên are never written in the name of Prince Kung but invariably in that of "the Commission" in question, *and in the third person;* and that the above translation, presumedly Mr. Wade's, if correctly reproduced in the Blue-book, is undoubtedly an incorrect one. Had Prince Kung assumed the Imperial 朕, "We,"—by which the translator evidently means to convey the impression that Mr. Hart is Imperially appointed,—His Imperial Highness would simply have had to pay for that greatest of Chinese crimes with his head. For "and We (knowing that) you....have at all times acted harmoniously and with success, hereby appoint you to the post of Inspector-General of Customs Affairs," the translation should read: "and your conduct having at all times been in harmony (with our—the Tsung-li Ya-mên's—wishes) and attended with success, you are hereby appointed....," etc.; whilst in the despatch to Sir Frederick Bruce the rendering should be: "of Customs Affairs," for: "of all the Customs Affairs." And in further illustration of the subject, I may quote a despatch of the Tsung-li Ya-mên to Sir Frederick Bruce of October 24, 1862, in which we read:—"By Tariff-Rule x., the high (native) Official, charged with the superintendence of foreign trade is at liberty to engage British subjects to aid in the prevention of smuggling. Accordingly in January 1861 the Prince [*i. e.* the Tsung-li Ya-mên] addressed a despatch to Mr. Horatio N. Lay, expressly appointing him Inspector-General of Customs, and directing him to engage a number of Englishmen of good character to assist in various subordinate offices at the different ports. In the spring of 1861 Mr. Lay applied for leave to return to England for the benefit of his health, and the Prince in a second despatch instructed Mr. Fitzroy and Mr. Hart to administer the functions of Inspector-General together jointly, Mr. Fitzroy continuing to discharge the duties of Commissioner at Shanghai, his proper station. The high officer appointed by the Chinese Government to superintend foreign trade, will, accordingly, from time to time, either himself visit, or will send a deputy to visit the different ports. The said high officer will be at liberty, of his own choice, and independently of the suggestion or nomination of any British authority, to select any British subject he may see fit to aid him in the administration of the Customs revenue; in the prevention of smuggling; in the definition of port-boundaries; or in discharging the duties of harbour-master; also in the distribution of lights, buoys, beacons, and the like, the maintenance of which shall be provided for out of the tonnage-dues."

The Tsung-li Ya-mên has no power or authority to admit any person whomsoever, least of all an "outer barbarian," into the service of the Imperial Government; and no one can enter that service, unless he be appointed, or unless his appointment be sanctioned, by Imperial Rescript. Mr. Hart, therefore, no Imperial Edict having ever been issued to sanction his appointment, is not in the service of the Chinese Government; nor is he "Inspector-General of (Chinese) Customs". He is simply a subordinate *employé*, viz., the foreign Head-Inspector of that Branch of the Chinese Maritime Customs Establishment, which relates to trade carried on in foreign-built vessels, nominated to his post by the Tsüng-li Ya-mên, and positively subordinated to the native Superintendents of Trade, who alone are authorised to appoint other foreign subordinate employés, a right, never formally transferred by them to the Foreign "Head-Inspector." Hence, it would appear, to say the least, that all the appointments of foreigners, employed in the Chinese Customs service, are irregular; that, strictly speaking, Mr. Hart is not even in the service of the Tsung-li Ya-mên, but, as a foreign subordinate, in no manner or way connected with the Chinese Government, and simply appointed by the Tsung-li Ya-mên, in the personal service of the native Superintendents of Trade; and that the foreign subordinates of the Head-Inspector of Customs, in their turn, are in the personal service of Mr. Hart.

I have considered it necessary here to point out the true position of Mr. Hart in the Chinese Customs-Service, because, the Inspector-General, for certain reasons of expediency, having been allowed by the Foreign Ministers—*contrary, as they themselves state, to their duty*,—to take up his permanent residence at Peking in the additional capacity of confidential political adviser of the Tsung-li Ya-mên, the importance of his public position and the extent and tendency of his influence and authority† have been as greatly misrepresented abroad, as his ability has been exaggerated, by interested persons.

The communicated article, previously reproduced and now claiming our attention, like all prior and subsequent papers, which have thus far emanated from the pen of the Inspector-General and found their way into the press, is a feeble production,—superficial, illogical, unreliable, and betraying the writer to lend himself simply as an instrument to the Chinese policy.‡ "When the ratifications of the Tientsin Treaty," Mr. Hart, or rather our anonymous memorandist, states,

† The Inspector-General's "authority" has penetrated even into the Government-offices. Referring to certain views of Sir Rutherford Alcock, the Secretary to H.B.M. Board of Trade, in a letter dated May 19, 1869, writes to the Under-Secretary for Foreign Affairs, the Rt. Hon. J. Hammond :—"This view is expressed even more emphatically by Mr. Hart who, in his very able letter to Sir Rutherford Alcock of December 4, 1868, says : 'Of course, force will wrest anything from China ; but *wherever there is action there is a reaction* ; and as sure as natural laws continue to act, so sure it is that appeals to force in one age will give to the men of a later day *a heritage of vengeance*—the Europeans of some future day may wish that their forefathers had not sown the seeds of *hatred* in the bayonet-ploughed soil of Cathay' ". Now, for what I know, this may be truly Irish, and emphatically poetical : but soberly and historically speaking, it is the reverse of sense and truth.

‡ In the *latter* sense, Mr. Hart's first memorandum, addressed in 1865 to the Tsung-li Ya-mên, and at the close of 1871, in a highly colored translation by the late Commissioner of Customs, Mr. Bowra, published *without date*, may seem to form an exception. But, if the very object of that paper had been, to counteract the simultaneous memorandum of Mr. Wade, which it accompanied, and to set the Chinese Authorities *against* all Western ideas of progress and reform, it could hardly have accomplished its object in a more effective manner, than it did. I shall examine it elsewhere.

"were exchanged in 1860, the transit system stood thus: (outward) *Foreign merchants* were authorised to go inland, purchase and convey to a treaty port native produce intended for shipment foreign, and (inward) Foreign *and Chinese* merchants were authorised to convey foreign merchandise from a treaty port *to a specified mart* in the interior; and, in each case; exemption from taxation *en route* was to be procured by the payment of a single tax—the treaty or tariff Transit Due. The first question that came up under the Transit system as established in 1860, was the following:—Must the Foreigner *in person* be with his merchandise *en route*, entering or leaving the interior? The Authorities at Peking took a common sense view of the matter; and at once decided, in 1861, that the Foreigner need not accompany his goods: he may employ any agents|| for their conveyance, but Agent, Goods and Certificate must travel in company, to secure exemption."

Those, who are familiar with the reasoning tactics of the Jesuit fathers, are aware that the point, on which the entire argument hinges, is almost invariably introduced by them into their *premises* as an indifferent and universally accepted fact. Just so the memorandist proceeds here in regard to the *in transitu* theory. That theory—the *petitio principii*—he presents to his readers as an unimportant, well-known Treaty-stipulation, a recognised law of China, *omnibus notissima;* in order to go on to the discussion of what, according to him, is the first *important* point, *viz.:* "Must the Foreigner *in person* be with his merchandise *en route*, entering or leaving the Interior?" The mere fact, that *such* a question

|| The text, certainly, reads: "any agents"; but from the subsequent passage:—"Native Produce purchased by Foreigners or by Natives the agents of Foreigners, if intended for exportation, that is for shipment to a foreign country, may be brought from the Interior to a Treaty-Port in transit by Foreigners or their agents," it is clear, that the agents, who had been employed for the purchase, are meant.

could have come up at all and been referred to Peking, shows more forcibly, perhaps, than any language of mine could, the obstructive spirit in which the Treaty-provisions had been committed to the Chinese Provincial Authorities. Art. xiii. of the British Treaty of Tientsin is plain. There was absolutely no room for any view of its own or any decision to be taken by the Tsung-li Yamên on the point mooted: they had but to look at the Treaty to convince themselves of the preposterous nature of the case submitted to them. Yet, what, after all, was the hardly less preposterous decision, so highly lauded and approved of by the anonymous memorandist, the Ya-mên came to?

Let us imagine, under Chinese-British stipulations similar to those of the British-Chinese Treaty, Mr. Yik A-Kwok, a general merchant and cheese-monger, set up in business in London, requesting his native agents, say Messrs. Smith, Brown & Co. of Exeter, to forward to him by an ordinary train a hundred tins of Devonshire cream for exportation abroad; imagine further every tenth station between Exeter and London to be a Custom-house, and every remaining station a war-tax barrier; and Messrs. Smith, Brown & Co., after having purchased the English produce, paid thereon to the British Authorities in Exeter the inland duties commutation-tax stipulated by Treaty, and been furnished accordingly with an inland-duty-paid certificate, to have to accompany, personally, Mr. Yik A-Kwok's hundred tins of Devonshire cream, in order to obtain to the certificate in question the *visa* of the native Customs and War-tax officials at every station between Exeter and London, and at every station to afford to the the native agents, Messrs. Smith, Brown & Co. the opportunity of "tipping" the native tax-collectors and their underlings. For, if, instead of conforming to the time-honored custom, Messrs. Smith, Brown & Co. were, perchance, to insist on the "outer-barbarian's," i. e. the Chinese merchant's Treaty-rights: why, the native Custom-house and War-tax barrier officials, high and low, would—we are still to imagine that all this could take place in England—consider it their natural duty to impede and delay the progress of Mr. Yik A-Kwok's Devonshire cream from the inland mart to the port of exportation and the inland-duty-paid certificate notwithstanding, by every dodge at their command. The tins, of course, will have to be weighed, and inspected, and the contents duly examined to make sure that they really are what the certificate describes them to be; and whilst one official is certain to declare the cream to be cheese, another will as certainly declare it to be butter, both agreeing as to the case being a dubious confiscation-case, demanding reference to the Authorities in London; and if "the Agents, Goods and Certificate, who and which must travel in company to secure exemption," reach their destination at the end of a month, both Messrs. Smith, Brown & Co., and their principal, the Chinese general merchant,—who had his Devonshire cream purchased for exportation to Paris, probably for a special occasion,—may thank their stars that they succeeded in "securing exemption" at all. But what, if the goods had not been accompanied by the agents? In that case, we are told, they would, in despite of payment of "transit"-duty and "transit" -certificate, have enjoyed *no* "exemption from taxation *en route*," that is to say, they would, besides the "squeezes" of native officials, have had to pay all the exorbitant Custom-house and war-tax barrier imposts, here assumed to be illegally levied by the British Government.

My object in adducing this imaginary case, has been to

bring home to the English reader the irrationally obstructive tendency of the "Transit-System", as it is actually practised in China, at the same time that it affords a fair illustration of the "common sense" of both the Tsung-li Ya-mên in deciding, that the agent as well as the duty-paid Certificate has to accompany goods, purchased inland, in order to secure them from illegal taxation, and of the Foreign Inspector-General in endorsing that decision. The only thing militating against the latter is that it has, by Treaty, absolutely no foundation to rest either itself or its "common sense" upon. Art. xxviii. broadly provides, that any British subject desiring to have produce, purchased inland, conveyed to a port, may clear his goods of all inland charges by one single payment, that of the stipulated commutation-tax; and that thereupon, "a certificate shall be issued, which shall exempt the goods from all further inland charges whatsoever." Nothing can be more clear. It is the certificate, which is to clear the goods, and, once granted, unconditionally so. Since in China, however, no more than elsewhere, a bale of silk, or a chest of tea, can be ordered and made to proceed to such or such a port by its own locomotion and geographical knowledge, but, as the Treaty intimates, has to be conveyed to its destination, and consequently, to be placed in charge of some person, *viz.*, the carrier or barge-master engaged for the purpose; and since Rule vii of the Rules of Trade subjects the certificate in question to a *visa* at every barrier: the same Rule states that "the person in charge of the produce will receive a certificate, which must be exhibited and *viséd* at every barrier, on its way to the port of shipment." It is not even said that the certificate is to be exhibited by the person in charge of the produce. As in the case of foreign goods, conveyed for sale into the Interior, it has simply "to be produced." If it be the British merchant's pleasure or interest to send a coolie, or to instruct his agent or any other person, to accompany to the port any native merchandise he may have purchased inland: he, certainly, is at liberty to do so; but there exists no Treaty-stipulation, which so much as implies that, the inland commutation-tax having been paid and a "transit"-certificate obtained, his "*Agent*, goods and certificate must travel in company to secure exemption" from further illegal taxation.

The Inspector-General wrote manifestly in total ignorance, or else in wilful disregard, of the real state of the case. For, in his despatch of October 26, 1861, to Earl Russell, Sir Frederick Bruce, in explaining certain Notifications then issued, and of which I shall have to speak hereafter, states:—"The Chinese were *anxious* that the exemption should not be claimed except in cases where the goods were accompanied by the *foreign* agent. They stated that, already, Chinese representing themselves to be agents for foreigners claimed certificates for inland produce at the first barrier, but instead of bringing it to the port, sold it *in transitu*, thus defrauding the revenue of all duties. *I objected to the proposed limitation as* inconvenient, *not in accordance with Treaty*, and giving no real security to the Chinese revenue. But as it was fair that the Chinese should be protected against such frauds, I agreed that, where a *Chinese* agent is employed, he is to produce proof of his being employed by a foreigner, and that the foreigner, in whose name he acts, is to declare himself responsible for the duties on the produce certificated, whether brought to the port or not."

Our memorandist relates another case, which, so late as 1868, had "come up for discussion" at Peking, the Tau-tai of Ningpo having seized some foreign goods, under a "transit-" pass for the Interior purchased by a Chinese trader: had, under these circumstances, the native merchant a right to the "transit" privilege? That he did possess that right by Treaty, has been already shown; and accordingly the Tsung-li Ya-mên, our memorandist assures us, "*at once* wrote back to say, that the Tautai's desire to guard against evasion of inland taxes *had blinded him to his duties under foreign treaties.*" Now, remembering what at the same time, Sir Rutherford Alcock saw occasion to impress upon the Tsung-li Ya-mên, and Mr. Wade confessed to Her Britannic Majesty's Board of Trade,—not to speak of the earlier despatches, addressed to the Ya-mên by Sir Frederick Bruce—on the subject of the Ya-mên's utter disregard of the duties imposed by Treaty on Provincial Authorities, as recorded at the commencement of this essay: a genuine despatch from the Tsung-li Ya-mên to Tsêng Kuo Fan, written in such a tone as the anonymous memorandist depicts, would be a unique document, indeed, and I only abstain from calling upon the Inspector-General to produce it as a historical *objet de vertu*, lest I should appear to take his pleasantry *au sérieux*. It is, I fear, with the asserted tone of the Tsung-li Ya-mên on this occasion, as it is with its asserted alacrity. If the reader will refer to the "communicated" memorandum itself, he will find that it was not till the Ya-mên had exhausted every unfair argument and subterfuge, that it could be brought to admit the plain import of the Treaty of Tientsin upon the point in question, "without," as the Inspector-General naïvely adds "any foreign pressure or suggestion."

The principal trait, however, in connection with this subject, to which I would call attention in the memorandist's statement, consists in a palpable self-contradiction on his part, couched in these words:—

The Imperial Commissioner was instructed by the Ya-mên§ to acquaint the various Custom-houses with the reply sent to the question that had arisen at Ningpo, for their guidance. The despatch is in the archives of each Custom-house, and a former Tau-tai at Shanghai printed and published it.

As the Tsung-li Ya-mên's action was the issuing, for Chinese guidance, of what was merely a clearer statement of a rule already made public by the notification of Treaties, it was not thought in any way necessary to communicate the despatch to Foreign officials.

But for Mr. Ying's publication, Tsêng Kuo Fan's despatch would probably never have quitted the mysterious recesses of "the various Custom-houses." There are in China Chinese and Foreign Custom-houses. The latter alone can be meant by the Inspector-General; who knew perfectly well, that his Excellency Tsêng had the right to address, and addressed, only those within his own jurisdiction. He also knew, that "Custom-houses" as such are not instructed, and that each foreign Custom-house has its native Intendant of Customs,—recognised by the Chinese Government—and, the former's subordinate, a foreign Inspector, usually styled Commissioner, of Customs—not recognised by the Chinese Government,—to whom instructions are, and have to be, addressed. Moreover, he knew that it would have been altogether against Chinese official etiquette for Tsêng-Kuo Fan to have directly addressed the foreign Commissioner of Customs; his own immediate foreign subordinate and the foreign Commissioner's superior being the Head-

§ No "Imperial Commissioner" receives, or would accept, instructions from the Tsung-li Ya-mên. It was in his capacity of Superintendent of Trade (for the Southern Ports, Canton excepted, or "Acting Superintendent of Customs," as he is styled in the translation, which appeared in the *North-China Herald* for Augt. 18, 1871), that Tsêng Kuo Fan issued his Notification of November 10, 1868. And even in that capacity it does not appear that he received either "instructions," or simply a "communication" from the Ya-mên to the effect referred to. They corresponded, moreover, on terms of perfect equality.

Inspector or "Inspector-General of Customs." To whom, then in reality, were Tsêng Kuo Fan's instructions conveyed? "The despatch," our memorandist asserts, "is in the archives of each Custom-house." But, what the archives of the native Intendants of Customs contain, is altogether unknown to him. He only knows, what documents are preserved in the archives of the Foreign Head-Inspectorate at Peking, and of the foreign Custom-houses at the ports. Again, however, he states, that "it was not thought in any way necessary to communicate the despatch to foreign officials." Here, then, there is seen to exist a palpable self-contradiction in the memorandist's statement; and once more we have to inquire: to whom was the despatch of the Superintendent of Trade addressed? I shall have some observations to offer upon this subject under the following Section.

Meanwhile, recurring a second time to the case just commented on, the anonymous memorandist, holding up to the public his own candour and the Tsung-li Ya-mên's honesty of purpose, remarks:—"In issuing its instructions in 1868, and in repeating them to the Shanghai Customs in 1871, the Ya-mên has made no new concession in respect of *Inward Transit*, but has merely honestly ordered subordinate offices to give full and proper effect to a previously existing right." Now, considering that the Treaty of Tientsin was concluded in 1858, and ratified in 1861; and that, after having, for the space of ten long years, supported its Customs-subordinates in resisting an indubitable right to which the provisions of that Treaty entitle the merchant, as well as in levying upon foreign inland trade illegal taxes, in defiance of the concluded Treaty and in the very year of its ratification enforced by special Regulations, it was not till

1868 that, under the pressure of British and foreign diplomacy, the Tsung-li Ya-mên took a first totally ineffective, and, three years later, a second only partially effective, step to carry a clear, existing Treaty-right into practice: it seems to me that, under such circumstances, even to allude to the Ya-mên's "honesty of purpose," required a man with a bold front.

"In 1870, however," the memorandist continues, "and in respect of *Outward Transit*, the Ya-mên did make a concession: in the Revised Treaty, rejected"—he sarcastically adds—"at the prayer of the Mercantile Communities, the Ya-mên had agreed to regard *destination and not ownership* as the condition of the title of *Native Produce* to the Transit privilege." It has already been shown that, both according to the spirit and the letter of the Treaty of Tientsin, destination, *i.e. bonâ fide* intended exportation to foreign parts by British and other foreign subjects, of native merchandise to be conveyed for that purpose from the Interior to a port, does constitute the essential and only condition entitling it to a commutation of inland charges, and that ownership most assuredly does not. But what in this place alone claims our attention, is the startling disclosure of Tsung-li Ya-mên generosity, in the shape of "a concession" hitherto unsuspected, in the rejected Supplementary Convention of Peking of October 23, 1869. I can but state, that Sir Rutherford Alcock himself,—although in his notes on the Convention he attributes to every single Article whatever possible advantages, real and imaginary, he could think of,—remained in complete ignorance of the fact, "communicated" by the Inspector-General. The British Board of Trade also, in reference to the preliminary understanding arrived at as to the bases of revision by the Mixed Commission, is of opinion, that:—"The proposal (regarding Transit Dues) is nothing more than a literal fulfilment of existing stipulations in the Treaty of Tientsin, and involves no new concessions whatever;" and if the reader will refer to the text of the Convention, he will convince himself, on a closer inspection, that the very reverse of the Inspector-General's assertion is the case. What the Tsung-li Yamên, in a memorandum, dated August 1st, 1868, and addressed to the Mixed Committee of Revision, proposed was, "that native produce, brought from the interior under a transit pass by foreign merchants, on arrival at the barrier nearest the port, should then pay there both Treaty transit due and tariff export duty, and should, in addition, lodge a separate amount equal to the transit dues, as a temporary deposit." This additional tax of about 3 °/₀ *ad valorem* was to be returned, if the produce was exported to a foreign port within three months; it was to be forfeited, if the produce was shipped, within three months, to another Chinese port; and it was equally to be forfeited, if the produce, at the expiration of three months, had not been shipped at all, because, according to the Ya-mên's view, it might then "be safely inferred that it had been sold to Chinese at the port." So much for the memorandist's "concession" and the Tsung-li Ya-mên's generosity, which consisted in this, that, instead of illegally confiscating goods, brought from the Interior, not shipped within three months after arrival at the port and *assumed* to have been sold to Chinese, the Ya-mên was content to inflict only an illegal fine of 3°/₀ for "the (assumed) improper use made of the transit pass." And was all this unknown to our memorandist, when he communicated his statement to the Press? The Inspector-General was himself a member of the Mixed Commission referred to, and took a leading part in the Revision of the Treaty of Tientsin, throughout.

Next, our memorandist, with that duplicity of view and its accompanying logical inconsistency, which a prolonged sojourn in China and a more constant intercourse with the Tsung-li Ya-mên would seem to impart to not a few Europeans, undertakes the task of showing, firstly, that Sir Rutherford Alcock, in rightly considering that the inland charges commutation-tax, stipulated by Treaty, frees merchandise from all other taxation, went further than the British Government could authorise and, therefore, was wrong in that view; and secondly, that Sir Rutherford Alcock, having come round to the wrong side of the question, was right in his first opinion, because, if it be remarked that there is a difference between Inward and Outward Transit, and if, in respect of Inward Transit, foreign merchandise be divided into three different stages as to time, what His Excellency *meant to* say was what he *did not* say. The Inspector-General, it would seem, has to labour hard for his support.

On summing up his views as to "the position, in which transit business now stands," the memorandist adds: "as understood by the Ya-mên *and Foreign Representatives at Peking*." What authority he had for this statement, I ignore; but, considering that, on the one hand, the memorandist's views are utterly at variance with, and detrimental to, the rights secured to foreign merchants by the Treaty of Tientsin, and that, on the other hand, the memorandist is publicly known to be the present Inspector-General of Chinese Maritime Customs, Mr. Hart: it appears to me, that it concerns the Consular Body and the General Chamber of Commerce of Shanghai, to ascertain officially from the Foreign Ministers in Peking, whether the Inspector-General's assertion be, or be not, founded in truth.

Lastly, our anonymous memorandist, whilst dwelling with emphasis on asserted malpractices of Foreign merchants, remains positively mute in regard to the proven violation, ceaseless, flagrant, and systematic, of the Treaty-rights of the Foreign merchant on the part of the Chinese Government, the Chinese Tsung-li Ya-mên, and the Chinese Provincial Authorities, their tax- and "squeeze"- gathering employés and underlings,—as rapacious, exacting, and unscrupulous as their masters, but in the memorandist's estimation, simple innocents, who, if they now and then happen to unwarrantably confiscate foreign goods, do so from mere want of sufficient official experience,—and concludes thus:—"From 1861 to 1868 the Provincial Officials were constantly complaining at the Ya-mên of the abuse of the Transit system; and the abuse of the system as intended for Produce Outward, added to the neglect to distinguish clearly between Transit Inward and Transit Outward, threatened to make the whole system inoperative." In other words, the Inspector-General, putting the saddle on the wrong horse, lays the fact, that the Treaty of Tientsin, so far as its provisions respecting foreign trade with the Interior of China are concerned, has virtually remained and remains "a dead letter," to the charge of Foreign merchants in general and, considering the relative extent of that trade, of the British merchant in particular. I might in silence pass over a statement of this nature as one of those peculiar attempts at pleasantry, in which the Inspector-General occasionally indulges for the benefit of his native employers, were it not that also the Lords of the Committee of Her Britannic Majesty's Privy Council for Trade—I cannot help thinking, with undue severity—remark upon "the fraudulent evasion by British merchants of the obligations and conditions imposed by the Treaty of Tientsin." I shall, therefore, revert to this subject when, in the next section, the practical working of the Treaty will be discussed.

The line of conduct and argument, adopted by the Tsung-li Ya-mên, in reference to our subject, explain themselves from the circumstances under which the ratification of the Treaty of Tientsin was enforced, the reactionary policy of the Chinese Government, and the character of Chinese statesmen. There was a time, when His Imperial Highness Prince Kung took every opportunity of impressing upon Foreign Plenipotentiaries and Representatives, that "the Prince in his dealings with men is most sincere; whatever he says is the truth." Foreigners have gradually come to know so well how to estimate the value of such asseverations, that even the Tsung-li Ya-mên thinks it useless to repeat them any more. What, in reference to its newly proposed regulations touching Transit-Passes, &c., in the first place deserves notice is, that, as has been previously pointed out, the Ya-mên is *not* the Chinese "Foreign Office." It forms no part of the Government-machinery of China. It has no place in the official State-directory of the Empire. It possesses no constitutional authority of its own.¶ Its assumed power we find, on the plain grounds just adduced, openly repudiated by the very City-officials of the Capital.* The Ya-mên, as its title expresses, is simply a temporary "Commission, by Imperial command appointed for the general control of the (commercial) affairs of (those)

¶ Dr. Williams also, in an official despatch of January 25, 1868, to the American Government, remarks that the Ya-mên, "notwithstanding its great influence (?) and the high rank of its members, has hitherto no legal existence of itself."

* See the *Shanghai Budget and Weekly Courier* for April 4, 1872, p. 210.

individual States, (which compose the Ching Empire Universal)."† In matters relative to *Treaties concluded*, it has no warrant to initiate propositions for any new rules or regulations, unless especially authorised to that effect by Imperial Rescript. In the present case it had been invested with no such authority. But the commercial relations between China and Western Powers rest on the basis of existing Treaties and certain Trade Rules, framed by duly authorised Plenipotentiaries in the name of, and subsequently ratified by, the Governments concerned, and hence, in principle, framed by those Governments themselves. Such Treaties, therefore, even in China admitted to possess the temporary force of Statute Laws,‡ having been publicly promulgated for general observance and guidance, admit of no modification so long as they obtain; nor can the Trade Rules, posteriorly incorporated with them, be lawfully altered or multiplied, save by the Governments concerned, in strict conformity with Treaty provisions, with the concurrence of the Mercantile Communities interested, and on due premonitory notice being given to the latter of the *terminus à quo* for any new regulations thus agreed upon.

The proposed Regulations (A), moreover,—I quote here the view, taken by me of these regulations at the time of their appearance, from the *Shanghai Evening Courier*,—are, professedly, on the one hand incomplete, on the other conditional. They are incomplete, inasmuch as they do not extend to Chinese produce destined for exportation, *i.e.*, to the better part of the whole foreign trade carried on with China, respecting which "the Ya-mên has not yet satisfied itself." They are conditional, inasmuch as the Ya-mên's "decision" is rendered subject to the approval

---

† The full official designation of the so-called Tsung-li Ya-mên is:—

大清欽命總理各國事務,

followed by the names of the members of the Commission.

‡ See the Tsung-li Ya-mên's Despatch of June 19, 1863, and Sir Frederick Bruce's reply above, p. 5-6.

of the native Superintendents of Trade for the Northern and Southern Ports. For the Tsung-li Ya-mên to have submitted to the consideration of the Representatives of Foreign Powers propositions *thus* formulated, constitutes of itself an offence.

But the Ya-mên does not stop here. When those native Superintendents of Trade, it writes, shall have replied, the Ya-mên "will, after due deliberation, address an *official communication* ‖ to the American Minister and to the Ministers of other (tributary) States, § *in order that they may instruct their subordinates accordingly.*" In this passage, the Yamên, assuming—as it does in its correspondence with the Foreign Ministers throughout,—the Autocracy Universal of the Emperor of China, by implication maintains that, as the Foreign Consuls are the subordinates of the Foreign Ministers, so the Foreign Ministers are the subordinates of the Tsung-li Ya-mên (and of the native Superintendents of Trade), whose "official communications" they have but to read and obey. Is it irrational to conjecture that the *British* Minister at least,—His Excellency being one of the most distinguished of living sinologues,—may have returned the Ya-mên's note, and demanded an apology for its insulting terms? ¶

The note further reads:—"(The Ya-mên) will be obliged to *the American Minister to issue instructions to the foreign merchants at the ports*" in the sense of its "communication" regarding the payment of *li-kin*, or war-taxes. The United States Minister, (as each other Minister individually), is here requested to issue instructions (being the Ya-mên's instructions to himself,) to the body of foreign Merchants in China at large,—a request, which draws no distinction between foreigners (according to the Ya-mên, without distinction subjects of the Emperor of China), and conveys a second insult to the Representatives of Foreign Powers generally. I need hardly observe, that *no* Minister can, without a flagrant breach of diplomatic decorum and neglect of his public duty, accept from the Government to which he is accredited—and the same remark applies here to the Tsung-li Ya-mên,—even a *semi*-official communication, attributing or imputing to him authority over the subjects of other Powers.

‖ The Chinese term is: 照會, and conveys the commanding sense of an *instruction*.

§ The American version renders erroneously: "the Ministers of other *Powers*;" the text reading 各國大臣.

¶ This was written before Mr. Johnson's letter to His Excellency, of June 21, 1872, had appeared, indicating that the Ya-mên's note was *not* returned by Mr. Wade.

Lastly, the Ya-mên bases its proposed new Rules solely on Art. XLVI. of the British Treaty of Tientsin, stating that—"The Chinese authorities at each port shall adopt the means they may judge most proper to prevent the revenue suffering from fraud and smuggling." But the Ya-mên overlooks or disregards, that the Article in question applies exclusively to the prevention of smuggling *at the ports;* that it has, and can have, no bearing whatever on the rights of the foreign merchant to trade and barter in the Interior; that it is but one out of sixty-six Articles, which compose the Treaty; and that the means which, on the ground of it, *the local authorities at each port* may judge most proper to adopt, have to be in accordance with the Treaty's sixty-five remaining Articles.*

As regards the proposed Rules themselves, which are distinctly stated to have been framed by the Inspector-General Mr. Hart, in concert with the native Intendant of Customs at Shanghai: those touching "Drawbacks and Exemption-Certificates," (notably Rule ii.) are worded with a degree of inconsistency, looseness, confusion, and disregard of Treaty-obligations, which speaks ill for the present Administration of the Chinese Maritime Customs-Service. Drawbacks and Exemption-Certificates, moreover, which have nothing in common with each other, are mixed up together; and the latter again, not even mentioned in the Tientsin Treaty, are subjected to anonymous Treaty-provisions.

The recovery, by Drawback, of duties, paid upon the importation of foreign goods, on their re-exportation to *foreign parts or Hongkong*, was, without any limitation as to time,† secured to the British merchant by

* It is true, that the concluding sentence of Rule 10 of the Trade Rules, attached to the Treaty of Tientsin, reads somewhat vaguely:—"The Chinese Government will adopt what measures it shall find requisite to prevent smuggling upon the Yang-tse-kiang, when that river shall be opened to trade." But, as I have already had occasion to remark in a more general sense, the Rule here has to be construed in conformity with the Treaty, not *vice versâ*. Besides which, the opening sentence of this very Rule 10 states:—"It being, *by Treaty*, at the option of the Chinese Government to adopt what means appear to it best suited to protect its revenue accruing on British trade, it is agreed that one uniform system shall be enforced *at every port*."

† From Mr. Consul-General Seward's letter to the Chamber of Commerce of Feb. 24, 1871, it would appear, that there obtains some misapprehension on this point. The term for the re-exportation of *Chinese produce* was originally fixed at 3 months in Sir Frederick Bruce's Notification of October 12, 1861, and subsequently, by the Tsung-li Ya-mên's despatch of June 25, 1863, extended to 12 months, as was also the term for the recovery by drawback of the *coast-trade duty*. It was on the occasion of applying for this extension, that Sir Frederick Bruce remarks:—"I am informed that, to meet the exigencies of trade, a period of twelve months should be allowed, within which the benefit of the regulation should be extended to the re-exporting merchant." It was no doubt this arrangement, which Prince Kung bore in mind, when "stating to the United States Minister at Peking,

Art. xlv of the Treaty of Tientsin. Art. v. of Sir Frederick Bruce's Notification of October 12, 1861, published in Shanghai on October 30, 1861, entitles him to Exemption-Certificates, "protecting duty-paid foreign imports, on being re-exported to *any port in China*, against all further exaction of duty by the Maritime Customs."

Rule i. proposes to violate Art. xlv. of the British Treaty of Tientsin in regard to two essential points, *viz;* the unlimited time open to applications for Drawbacks, which it is now unreasonably desired to limit to a period of thirty months from the date of importation; and the conditions, under which the Drawback-Certificate is to be granted, or the goods are to be seized. The Treaty-conditions, and the conditions of the proposed Rule, respectively, are :—

Treaty-Conditions.

In order to prevent fraud on the revenue, the (native) Intendant of Customs‡ shall cause examination to be made by *suitable officers*, to see that the *duties* paid on such goods, as entered in the Custom-house books, *correspond with the representation made*, and that the goods *remain with their original marks unchanged;*‖ but, if, *on such examination*, the Intendant of Customs shall detect *any fraud on the revenue* in the case, then the goods shall be *subject to* confiscation *by the Chinese Government*.

Rule-Conditions.

The officer, deputed by the Intendant of Customs, shall ascertain by inspection that *the goods* are *the original goods imported*, and in the original package, and that *none have been withdrawn or exchanged*, . . . but, if *the goods* be found to be *other than the goods they are stated to be*, that *then they will be confiscated* [there and then], according to the Treaty.

(The offensive, arbitrary, and vexatious character of this Rule, objectionable in every sense, needs no further explanation).

Rule ii. proposes, in violation of Art. x. and xi. of the Tientsin Treaty, to do away with the merchants' right to carry on a direct trade, from Hongkong or abroad, with the ports of the Yang-tse river; and, at variance with Art. xlv, to restrict the re-exportation to foreign ports of foreign duty-paid imports from a second Chinese port, so far as Drawbacks are concerned, to a period of thirty months, to be reckoned from the time of the arrival of the goods at the first port.

Rule iii. is a tardy and unsatisfactory relaxation of a rule, hitherto enforced by the Foreign Customs-Authorities, and resting on no other foundation save their personal unacquaintance with the grammatical

---

that the period of one year for the granting of drawback on goods re-exported, was determined at the request of the mercantile body." Possibly, the Hon. Mr. Low misunderstood by "goods" (Chinese produce) "foreign goods."

‡ The American version renders: "the Superintendent of Customs,"—a term very usually employed, but which is apt to be confounded with "the Superintendent of Trade,"—a far higher charge.

‖ That is to say: the package of the goods remaining essentially intact.

usages of the English language.§ The Inspector-General now proposes to depart from the purely vexatious practice, unwarranted by any Treaty-provision, so far as to dispense with the signature of the dead.

Rule iv. contains a repetition of a portion of the objectionable paragraph of Rule i. respecting the conditions in violation of Art. XLV. of the Treaty of Tientsin, under which alone it is proposed that Drawback-Certificates shall be granted. The Rule, moreover, applies those conditions, without warranty, to Exemption-Certificates.

Passing on to a review of the proposed Rules touching "Transit-Passes": they are marked by the same contempt for Treaty engagements, intensified by duplicity, which we have found to characterise the preceding Rules relative to Drawbacks and Exemption-Certificates, and would appear to have been designed with the sole view of obstructing inland trade, and of curtailing the rights of the foreign merchant, to the utmost.

Rule i. demands, contrary to Treaty provisions, that all applications for Transit Passes shall be made by the original importer of the goods, and that the name of the person who is to carry them, must be given. *It tacitly assumes the applicant to be a foreigner.*

Rule ii., at variance with Rule i., admits applicants, not being the original importers; but, except when they are defunct, requires, without warranty, the signature of the latter. Compared with Rule i. and iv., it tacitly, like the preceding Rule, *assumes the applicant to be a foreigner.*

Rule iii. allows foreign goods to be conveyed for sale into the Interior, whether the trader, *conveying them*, be foreigner or native.

Rule iv., in flagrant violation of Treaty provisions, *firstly*, demands that all goods, intended for sale at a specified inland mart, shall be conveyed thither by a specified route; *secondly*, decrees that such goods, upon a departure from the proper route, shall be confiscated (there and then);¶ *thirdly*, decides that the Transit-Pass shall protect the goods from

§ The passage, from which the rule in question has been deduced, occurs at the commencement of ART. XLV of the Tientsin Treaty, and reads:—"British merchants, who may have imported merchandise into any of the open ports, and paid the duty thereon, if they desire to re-export the same, shall be entitled, &c." The Inspector-General has, strangely enough, taken the construction in a personal, instead of a generic sense, and has been followed in this ungrammatical and irrational view by the Chairman of the Committee of the Shanghai General Chamber of Commerce in his letter of March 12, 1872, to the Senior Consul, Mr. G. F. Seward.

¶ China is a country, containing, according to McCulloch and Dr Williams, an area of upwards of five million square miles, and its topography is not particularly familiar to

(illegal) taxation, in the shape of *li-kin*, between the port and the inland mart *in transitu* only; *fourthly*, orders the Transit-Pass, upon arrival, to be presented to the nearest authority, on pain of a fine to the amount of an additional half-Tariff duty; and *fifthly*, subjects the goods, on their sale to the native trader or retail-dealer, to the *Li-kin i.e.* a war-tax of undefined amount.

Rule v. leaves it to the native Intendant of Customs at Shanghai and the Inspector-General, Mr. Hart, to fix the number of days, within which foreign goods are to be conveyed to any given inland mart,—on what penalty, in case of default, the Ya-mên does not say;—and prescribes that, on the sale of such goods, the Transit-Pass shall be called in and cancelled.

Rule vi., abrogating the principal provision of Rule 7 of the Trade Rules incorporated with the Treaty of Tientsin, permits foreign goods to be sent for sale inland *uncertificated*, on the condition of their paying both Custom-House dues and *li-kin*.

These Rules simply propose to reduce existing Treaties with China, so far as their provisions bear on the inland trade in foreign goods, to a dead letter. They not only do *not* recognise the title of the native merchant to a Certificate, and maintain the untenable *in transitu* theory; but they attempt to legalise, moreover, *in addition* to the stipulated inland charges commutation-tax of half the Tariff import duty, the imposition upon foreign goods of those illegal and "over-burdensome" imposts, which, under the name of *li-kin*, the Chinese Government, in all cases in which, consequent on the Transit-Pass system, it fails to levy them *en route*, levy upon such goods on their passing into the hands of the native retail-dealer. For the foreign merchants to accede to these Rules concerning Transit Dues, framed by the Foreign Inspector-General, Mr. Hart, in concert with the Tau-tai of Shanghai, and by the Tsung-li Ya-mên proposed to the Representatives of Foreign Powers, would be to accede, on their part, to the ruin of Foreign Trade with the Interior of China, and deliberately to relinquish Treaty-rights, secured for them at the cost of two wars.

---

foreign merchants. Even the Inspector-General himself might be puzzled to decide upon the route, which it would be "proper" for him to take, or which he "ought to take" from Shanghai to Suchow,—a short distance of about 80 miles. Forsooth, if "propriety of route," 道理, were in this country made the standard for confiscating foreign goods sent for sale inland, as Rule IV proposes to make it, the chances are that not a yard of shirtings and not a catty of iron, despatched from a port, would ever reach its destination.

In the course of time a copy of the proposed Regulations would seem to have reached also the British Consulate. We have to infer this at least from the following letter, dated Shanghai, June 21st, 1872, which in reference to the subject was, after considerable delay, addressed to his Excellency Mr. Wade, by Mr. F. B. Johnson, as Chairman of the Committee of the Shanghai General Chamber of Commerce :—

SIR,—I have the honour to acknowledge the receipt, through Mr. Consul Alabaster, of a Draft of certain Rules proposed by the Chinese Government to govern and regulate the issue of Drawback Certificates and Transit Passes, and I am to convey to you the thanks of the Committee for the opportunity thus given to them of expressing the opinion of the Chamber upon this important document. The views of this Chamber with regard to the rules attaching to the issue of Drawbacks were expressed in my despatch to the address of the Senior Consul under date 12th March, and the Committee see no reason to change these. Practically, an extension to thirty months of the period during which foreign duty paid goods shall be entitled, on re-exportation to a foreign country, to a return of the Import duty, will satisfy the present requirements of trade, and therefore I have only to urge that as the Treaty prescribes no limitation by lapse of time of a right which it acknowledges, and which is universally recognized by civilized countries, the proposed rule should be accepted by the foreign ministers only on the understanding that the regulation in question shall be subject to relaxation, whenever the general course of trade shall call for it.

It is satisfactory to know that the claims of re-exporters who have been hitherto surcharged with duty contrary to Treaty stipulations will be examined and adjusted, but it is incumbent upon me to point out that the return of duty cannot with fairness be confined to those cases alone in which it is ascertained that drawbacks have been supplied for and refused. For, in consequence of the persistent determination of the Customs' Authorities not to grant the drawbacks in question during a period of nearly twelve years, it has latterly been considered useless to apply for them, and it will be obviously unjust if reparation be refused in any case in which it can be conclusively shown that the duty has been wrongfully detained. I reserve, for a separate communication at a future date, a consideration of the Rules applying to Drawbacks on duty-paid goods re-exported to Treaty Ports, as this subject has already been brought under discussion by my letter to the Senior Consul, dated the 12th March.*

With regard to the regulations for the issue of Transit Passes on foreign goods destined for the interior, I have to express the unqualified satisfaction felt by the Committee at the recognition now publicly made by the Chinese Government of the principle for which this Chamber has so long contended; viz., that the commutation of inland duties may be claimed on Imports of foreign origin without reference to ownership.

Rule 8 provides that traders, whether Chinese or Foreign, may convey goods inland under cover of a Transit Certificate, which will be issued on payment of the half duty, as provided by Treaty, and the recognition of this principle removes the main difficulty which has hitherto interfered with the successful working of the Transit system. I need hardly say that the Members of this Chamber are desirous to co-operate with the Native authorities in the adoption of all reasonable means to secure the revenue against fraud and smuggling.

Many of the Rules, however, which the Chinese Government have framed in order to subserve this purpose appear to the Committee to be not only unnecessary and vexatious, but calculated to defeat the object which Transit Certificates are taken out specially to promote. As long

* SIR,—The Secretary briefly acknowledged on the 27th ultimo your Letter of the 24th, and since then the Members of the Committee have considered the proposal of the Imperial Maritime Customs, with regard to Drawbacks on re-exported goods, which you have submitted to them for the consideration of the Chamber.

I have now the honour to state to you the unanimous opinion of the Committee, which is that as the terms of the British and German Treaties very clearly provide for the issue of Drawbacks of duty on re-exported goods, and as very great inconvenience and loss have been sustained by Importers in consequence of the refusal of the Customs to issue the necessary certificates after the lapse of twelve months from the date of importation, the fulfilment in their integrity of the Treaty stipulations should now be claimed.

The engagement appended to Mr. Hart's proposition for an extension of the time to two years, viz. that after that period each case shall be considered, "as it arises under a system which shall be just to the Merchant, and at the same time shall not interfere with the working of accounts" has not been overlooked, but the Committee conceive that this stipulation implies an inversion of the proper rule applicable to special cases, which may threaten an interference either with the safety of the Revenue or the working of the Customs' accounts.

It seems obvious that the burthen of proving the existence of an exceptional necessity to suspend privileges conferred by Treaty should be thrown upon the Customs, and inconsistent with justice that the Importer should in each application for Drawbacks, as proposed by Mr. Hart, be called upon to show that the exercise of his legal right will not be inconvenient to the arrangement of the Custom-house Accounts.

The Committee, moreover, are quite unable to understand why adequate protection to the Revenue, and a proper arrangement of accounts, should be dependent upon an arbitrary

as it was held that the right to commute inland taxation was a privilege to be enjoyed by foreigners alone, so long it might not be unnecessary to adopt rules in order to prevent a fraudulent ascription of foreign ownership by native traders; and the nature of the fraud to be guarded against may possibly have called for a practice of inquisitorial declarations which rendered the entire transit system one of very questionable advantage. But the privilege of commutation being now admitted to be one which may be claimed by natives and foreigners alike, the field for the commission of possible fraud is confined within very narrow boundaries, and the regulations may be simplified accordingly.

Before entering into a detailed examination of the Rules which the Yamên propose to adopt it will not be out of place to quote the article of the Treaty on which the transit system is based, and to state the opinion of the Chamber as to the rights which have been created by it.

The 28th Article of the Treaty of Tientsin provides that—

"It shall be at the option of any British subject desiring to convey imports from a port to an inland market to clear his goods of all transit duties by payment of a single charge. The amount of this charge shall be leviable on imports at the port at which they are landed: and on payment thereof, a Certificate shall be issued, which shall exempt the goods from all further inland charges whatsoever."

And the interpretation placed by Lord Elgin upon this provision is

---

limitation of the period during which Drawbacks can be freely claimed, and suggest that very simple regulations regarding the forms of application, and the conservancy of marks and numbers on the original packages will suffice to do all which Mr. Hart proposes to effect by an abrogation of Treaty rights.

With regard to the allegation of the Prince of Kung, that the existing arrangement was made by the authorities of this port, at the request of the Mercantile body, I observe that you consider the statement to be deprived of force by the fact that the arrangement was made prior to the ratification of the British and French Treaties of 1858. I append, however, copies of the correspondence which passed between this Chamber and H.B.M. Consul on the question in 1859, 1860, and you will not fail to perceive that the efforts of the Chamber were alone directed to procure an extension to "one year at least," of the period during which Drawbacks should be granted instead of the onerous limitation of it to three months, which was then imposed upon the Mercantile Community.

I further append a copy of a despatch from Lord Elgin, which shows that the clause in the English Treaty was framed to secure the recovery of the full amount of duties paid on Foreign Imports, and drawback *in any case*, when the goods are re-exported to a foreign country.

I trust that the Consular body will not only press the question to a speedy solution, but will also urge upon the Chinese Government the justice of returning the duties which they illegally detain. The whole amount of them forms no heavy claim upon the Revenue, but probably presses with considerable hardship upon individuals, and I need hardly add that the interests of the Chinese Government, and of foreign trade alike, demand that in an important centre of distribution such as the port of Shanghai, no vexatious hindrances should be imposed upon the ingress and egress of merchandize.

shown by his dispatch to the Foreign Office, dated Shanghai, November 8th, 1858. It writes—

"Henceforward, on payment of a sum in name of transit duty, which for simplicity's sake has been fixed at one half of the tariff rate of duty, goods, whether of export or import, will be free to pass between the port of shipment or entry to or from any part of China without further charge of toll octroi or tax of any description whatsoever."

And Rule 7 of the Rules and Regulations attached to the Treaty provides that—

"Merchandize shall be cleared of its transit dues under the following conditions. In the case of imports. Notice being given at the port of entry from which the imports are to be forwarded inland of the nature and quantity of the goods; the ship from which they have been landed; and the place inland to which they are bound, with all other necessary particulars, the collector of customs will on due inspection made, and on receipt of the transit duty due, issue a transit duty certificate. This must be produced at every barrier station and viséd. No further duty will be levied upon imports so certificated, no matter how distant the place of their destination."

The Committee do not disguise their conviction that it was as much the purpose of the treaty of Tientsin by this article to protect foreign imports from taxation throughout the country other than the customs duty to be levied on entry, and the half duty to be levied on transit, as it was one of the objects of the Commercial Treaty between Great Britain and France to limit the duty on French wines imported into Great Britain to a certain fixed sum per gallon. They therefore consider that on sufficient proof of foreign origin, and of the payment of Import and Transit duty being tendered, a simple stamp should be placed on the packages, in accordance with the general practice of the native excisemen, to denote that the commuted transit duty has been paid, and that the goods should then be freed from further impositions throughout the empire.

The terms of the Treaty are, however, unfortunately so loosely expressed as to admit of an interpretation, which, though opposed to the general bearing of the entire article, is claimed as justifying the Chinese in limiting the operation of the Transit Certificates to the protection of the goods from taxation *en route* to, and while they remain intact in, a place of destination to be named prior to their departure from the port of entry. In view of this ambiguity therefore the Committee, representing what they believe to be the sense of the foreign mercantile community on this question, and without abandoning the principle for which they have hitherto contended, are not unwilling to accept the instalment of reform offered by the Chinese, provided satisfactory guarantees shall be given that the system of commuted taxation, even in this limited degree, will be faithfully carried out by the Native Government—that is to say—provided the taxes for which commutation is made shall be guaranteed not to be subsequently levied in an indirect or a surreptitious form.

It is practically admitted by the Ya-mên, in the dispatch under consideration, that the only two conditions imposed by the Treaty upon the owners or carriers of goods transmitted to the interior under the protection of Transit Certificates are, that the goods themselves shall be of foreign origin, and shall be bound for a fixed destination, and it is therefore obvious that rules which are unnecessary to the fulfilment of these two conditions must be deemed superfluous and vexatious or be framed for ulterior purposes.

By this test I propose to consider the regulations suggested by the Ya-mên.

Rule 1.—Requires that the applications for Transit Passes must be made by the merchants who originally imported the goods. This requirement involves great waste of time and trouble; compliance with it may frequently be impossible, and it is wholly unnecessary for the purpose of identifying the goods. The Inspector-General has declared his readiness to recommend to the Yamên the abrogation of a similar condition in the case of applications for drawbacks on foreign imports, and the stipulation may be omitted from the regulations regarding Transit Passes without inconvenience. The Rule further requires a declaration as to the place to which the goods are to be carried and the name of the carrier. The first of these stipulations can only be defended on the ground of its necessity as a means of affording the Chinese Government a reasonable facility for protecting its revenue, but the second is quite unnecessary, and cannot be claimed in support of either of the conditions to which I have referred.

Rule 2.—The objections above named as to declarations from the original importer apply equally to the terms of this Rule.

Rule 3.—To this there is no objection to be made.

Rule 4.—Provides for the exhibition of the Transit Certificate at each barrier and duty station along the line of route, to be viséd and stamped, but it goes on to say that if the goods are not on the line where they ought to be, or prove to be other than the goods named in the Certificate, they shall be confiscated and the right of confiscation is claimed by virtue of Rule 7 attached to the tariff of the Treaty of Tientsin. The alleged offences which are to be subjected to so severe a penalty are essentially distinct in character, and must be considered separately. Should the goods covered by the Transit Pass prove to be of a description other than those which are entitled to the benefit of the transit system, that is to say to be of native origin, or if the quantity be found in excess of that named in the Certificate, or if fraud be attempted, or evasion of duty be in any way discovered, then confiscation might be a legitimate penalty. If, however, the discrepancy between the description of the packages in the Certificate, and the goods themselves be merely one of marks or numbers, be otherwise accidental, or involve no evasion of duty, in such cases the penalty of confiscation would be altogether an unjustifiable one, and the Committee suggest that a small fine be substituted for it.

As regards the proposed penalty of confiscation for deviation from line of route, I have to protest against it as being unreasonable and excessive, and not justified by Treaty, there being no fraud involved in such an irregularity. The certificate covers the goods, in the language of the Tariff Rules, "no matter how distant the place of their destination." If, as the Chinese claim, the destination must be fixed, and the goods be freed only along direct lines of route, then the only proper and a sufficient penalty for deviation will be the subjection of the goods to the ordinary levies at the various barriers, which are not cleared by the certificate, and through which they may pass. Let the case be supposed in which 10 bales of Cottons certificated for Soochow are found *en route* to Kashing. There would be and could be no fraud intended or practised by such a deviation. The goods would be simply in the position of being uncertificated, and would consequently be liable not to confiscation, but to the payment of the ordinary barrier dues.

In all cases moreover in which it can be shown that deviation has been occasioned by floods, obstructions of an extraordinary character, or other reasonable cause, the goods should be exempted from all penalty or extra charges whatever.

The second clause of Rule 4 provides that on the arrival of the goods at the place of destination the certificate shall be handed to the nearest authority, who will fix his seal to it and return it to the consignee as his protection against taxation on the goods so long as they remain unsold. If the certificate be not so presented an additional half tariff duty is to be levied as a fine. The Rule concludes with the strange announcement, that notwithstanding the commutation of the lekin duties, which has already been made, these duties will still be levied by the local government upon the buyer.

It appears scarcely possible that the Chinese Government gravely proposes to accept from the importer a commutation of specific duties, and afterwards to levy these duties upon the buyer of the goods; yet no other meaning can be attached to the last clause, while the unnecessary multiplication of Rules seems as if there were an intention to create offences, and goes far to excite a belief that the Yamên intends to raise from the natives, as soon as the goods shall have fairly passed out of foreign hands, the dues which have been professedly commuted. The intricate nature of the Rules gives rise in fact to a natural suspicion, more or less justified by the action of the authorities in more than one Province, that they have been framed in order that the goods may be carefully traced from the Port of entry to the place of destination, and be subjected through the medium of the ultimate recipient to the payment of all the barrier dues which are supposed to have been commuted.†

The Committee see no reason for the stipulation that the certificate shall be surrendered at the place of destination unless it be intended to indicate to the local authorities the name of the consignee of the goods for the purpose of subjecting him to special taxation. The certificate having been stamped at the various barriers will be virtually cancelled, and the provisions for the surrender of them contained in this Rule and in Rule 5 are therefore wholly unnecessary for the protection of the legitimate revenue.

Rule 6.—Appears to refer mainly to uncertificated goods, and in this respect the purpose of it does not seem very clear. The provision that in the event of irregularity appearing in the passes the goods they represent shall be detained at the barrier until communication be had with the Custom-House seems to be a reasonable one.

The Committee conceive that if the Chinese authorities intend to carry the transit system faithfully into effect, the Rules relating to it may be drawn up in a very simple form. The certificate to be issued in payment

† I have candidly to confess that, with the experience of many years of Chinese systematic obstructiveness and "over-burdening" illegal taxation before him, Mr. Johnson,—to judge from the above paragraph, in which the policy of the Tatar Government, whereof that long experience is but the faithful and practical exponent, still appears to him "scarcely possible," and has given rise, on his part, only to a "natural suspicion" as to its tendency,—seems to me to have been somewhat slow in opening his eyes to the stubborn evidence of facts and the actual state of things.

of the commuted duty should protect the parcel of goods it represents from the port of entry to any indicated place in the interior along a direct route, and at the place of destination so long as the parcel remains intact. Along any other route, when a reasonable cause of deviation cannot be shown, or at any other place than those named in the pass, and after distribution, the protection ceases, and the goods become liable to *ordinary*, but not special local taxation. The names of the owner, of the carrier, or of the recipient of the goods, should not be given. The certificates being *viséd*, and stamped at the various barriers, and thus rendered ineffective for use a second time, there is no valid reason to be given for requiring them to be surrendered.

It becomes my duty to urge your Excellency to withhold your assent to the proposed regulations unless the restrictions and penalties sought to be imposed by them be modified in respect to the various clauses to which I have taken exception, and unless satisfactory and explicit declarations be made by the Chinese Government, in order that no ground for dispute may exist hereafter as to the precise nature of the engagements which have been entered into.

The Transit system, even in its present partially regulated and ill-defined condition, is shown by recent Custom-House returns to be working in a progressive manner and with beneficial effect in those Provinces where it finds encouragement from enlightened native administrators. It is worthy of consideration therefore whether it be not better to allow the process already existing to gain gradual recognition throughout the Empire by the force of its inherent excellence, than in reality to run the risk of hindering its growth by the promulgation of regulations which in their proposed form I can only describe as crude, ill adapted to the requirements of the system, and vexatious to trade.

I observe that the regulations regarding Transit Passes on Exports have not yet been framed by the Yamên.‡ The Committee are aware that fraudulent irregularities are not uncommon in respect to applications for commutation certificates on native produce which is not a *bonâ fide* constituent of foreign trade, and they will readily support any reasonable rules which the Chinese Government may find it necessary to adopt for the protection of the national revenue. On the other hand, the illegal exactions of the Provincial Officers are not less notorious.

‡ The reader will remember that, at the date of Mr. Johnson's letter, even the amended Regulations (B) had not as yet been framed.

The Committee are of opinion that if the principle of commutation, as applied to inland dues, both on Imports and Exports, is to be settled on a durable and equitable basis, a comprehensive enquiry through the respective agencies of the Consular Authorities and the Customs' Officials, into the working of the present system of Transit Passes, and the practice of barrier taxation, should precede the adoption of any new code of regulations on the subject, and I am to bring this proposal to the attention of your Excellency.

The Committee earnestly desire that the Tsung-li Yamên may be led to see the advantages which will be reaped alike by the Chinese Government and people, and by foreign trade, from a scheme of equal and settled taxation. They believe that if, when the revision of the foreign Treaties shall again come under consideration, the Imperial Government would accept a first and final payment at the port of entry, which would free foreign merchandize from further taxation throughout the empire, an increased tariff would not be objected to by those interested in foreign trade. The plan of the recent abortive convention between Great Britain and China was unacceptable to the Chamber because commutation of transit duties was made compulsory without adequate guarantees, and its operation was incomplete. The plan which the Committee are prepared to propose, of an optional payment to be attested by a simple stamp or certificate which should be in force everywhere throughout the Empire, would in the opinion of the Chamber encourage trade, benefit the people, and largely augment the revenue of the country.

Leaving it to the reader to compare these comments of the Shanghai Chamber of Commerce upon the Regulations (A), here under discussion, with those Regulations themselves and my own analysis of the latter, which at the time was under the notice of the Chamber,—I desire to call his attention to what I cannot but consider the grave errors embodied in the Chamber's letter. To the most prominent of these errors, the writer himself assigns the most prominent place. Before even entering into an examination of the proposed Rules, he expresses "the unqualified satisfaction felt by the Committee (of the Chamber of Commerce) at the recognition now publicly made by the Chinese Government of the principle for which this Chamber has so long contended, viz., that the commutation of inland duties may be claimed on Imports of foreign origin without reference to ownership." He thereupon, without any grammatical or logical connection, begins a new paragraph, stating:—"Rule 3 provides that traders, whether Chinese or Foreign, may convey goods inland under cover of a Transit Certificate, which will be issued on payment of the half duty, as provided by Treaty, and the recognition of this principle removes the main difficulty which has hitherto interfered with the successful working of the Transit system. I need hardly say," he adds in a train of thought, which, notwithstanding the sequel, is not intelligible to me, "that the Members of this Chamber are desirous to co-operate with the Native authorities in the adoption of all reasonable means to secure the [Chinese] revenue against fraud and smuggling."

We are thus led to infer, that Mr. Johnson sees in the third of the proposed Rules the public recognition, on the part of the Chinese Government, of the long contended-for principle, to which he alludes, and the sole ground for the Committee's "unqualified satisfaction." I fear, however, that there exists no adequate reason for such a satisfaction, and that Mr. Johnson's construction of the Rule must rest on a misapprehension or some ground to me unknown and unintelligible. That Rule contains not even an expression, from which the principle under consideration could be rationally deduced. On the contrary. I have the original Chinese text before me, and the translation of this portion, as previously given, though it might have been worded more literally, is essentially correct. On referring to it, the reader will find that the only right it confers on the foreign and native trader in common, is the right to *convey*, in the capacity of *carriers*, foreign goods into the Interior; but the importer of such goods, the applicant for a duty-paid Certificate, and hence the owner of the goods, are tacitly supposed to be foreigners. And this is in accordance with the whole spirit of the Tsung-li Ya-mên's views and policy. Only in the case of foreign goods, destined for an inland market, having been imported from abroad by a Chinese merchant, —a case which was neither contemplated by the Ya-mên, nor had ever occurred,—a construction could, in my judgment, be placed upon the Rules proposed by the Ya-mên, which, though at variance with their spirit, might justify Mr. Johnson's interpretation of them. But in no other case.

The second error, prominent in Mr. Johnson's letter, is that, in the name of the Committee of the Shanghai Chamber of Commerce, he concedes,—contrary to the facts of the case, —that "the terms of the Treaty (of Tientsin) are unfortunately so loosely expressed as to admit of an interpretation, which, though opposed to the general bearing of the entire article, is claimed as justifying the Chinese in limiting the operation of the Transit Certificates to the protection of the goods from taxation *en route* to, and while they remain intact in, a place of destination to be named prior to their departure from the port of entry;" and that, "in view of this ambiguity," he expresses the not-unwillingness of the Chamber conditionally to waive, partially and temporarily at least, what I judge to be a clear and indubitable Treaty-right of the British and Foreign merchant. The question here at issue is not, whether a particular sentence of a particular Article of the Tientsin Treaty *can* be construed, but whether the Treaty of Tientsin can be *rationally and consistently* construed, in the sense forced upon it by the Tsung-li Ya-mên and the Inspector-General, Mr. Hart. I have proved, and shall further prove, to demonstration, that this is not the case, and that the Chinese Authorities themselves were from the first fully aware of the fact. Nay, when the very 28th Article of the Tientsin Treaty, quoted by Mr. Johnson, clearly provides that the agreed commutation-payment for all "transit"- (i. e. inland) duties "shall exempt *the goods* from all further inland charges whatsoever," there is virtually no room left for legitimate doubt; and I cannot but hold it to be a grave mistake, on the part of the mercantile community, more especially in the actual state of affairs, to yield so much as one single iota of the provisions of existing Treaties.

The third and by far most important error, however, committed by the Chamber, is embodied in the following passage:—"The Committee conceive that if the Chinese authorities intend to carry the transit system faithfully into effect, the Rules relating to it may be drawn up in a very simple form. The certificate to be issued in payment of the commuted duty should protect the parcel of goods it represents, from the port of entry to any indicated place in the interior along a direct route, and at the place of destination so long as the parcel remains intact. Along any other route, when a reasonable cause of deviation cannot be shown, or at any other place than those named in the pass, and after distribution, the protection ceases, and the goods become liable to *ordinary*, but not special local taxation." It can admit of no doubt, that a Rule, which binds the Foreign merchant, resident at one of the ports, to declare beforehand, or to declare at all, a specific place of destination for goods he intends to send to some inland market, interferes essentially with a free transit-system, and is positively opposed to the whole spirit and the main object of existing Treaties. The Chamber of Commerce, therefore, instead of submitting to a restriction of this nature, should have used its efforts to have it removed. But I wish to speak more especially of Mr. Johnson's fatal suggestion, that the protection of British duty-paid goods, sent for sale to an inland market, against the imposition of further duties, shall cease after their distribution at the place of destination; nay, that such goods shall then become liable to ordinary, but not special, local taxation.

Mr. Johnson, himself, falls here into that looseness and ambiguity of expression, which he deplores in the wording of the Treaty of Tientsin; and we are left to conjecture what he may understand by "local" taxation, and what by "ordinary," as distinguished from "special," local taxation. But it is certain that, as referred to any given locality, the Chinese Authorities now regard *le-kin* in the light of an item of "ordinary" local taxation; and hence, the real, practical purport of Mr. Johnson's suggestion appears to me to be this, that he would have the amount of illegal taxation, by which the Chinese Government is now over-burdening foreign trade in the Interior, paid, not by the Foreign or Chinese wholesale-, but by the Chinese retail-dealer. In other words, he would not only, like his Excellency Mr. Wade, maintain, but also legalize, the imposition of *le-kin* and other illegal taxes, and, abandoning the principle that the foreign goods, on which the inland commutation-tax has been paid, are thereby "exempted from all further inland charges *whatsoever*," only render it somewhat more troublesome for the Chinese Authorities to collect upon those goods illegal taxes which, heavy as they already are, would surely be increased in proportion to the increased trouble and expense involved in their collection. Mr. Johnson, whose theory is to all intents and purposes the *in-transitu* theory *pur et simple* of the British Minister, Mr. Wade, and the Inspector-General, Mr. Hart, had manifestly over-looked what should ever be borne in mind, viz.: that it is in truth a matter of indifference for the Foreign merchant to know how, and from what class of native traders or consumers, illegal taxes are levied upon his goods, the sale of which is thereby unlawfully restricted, if not altogether frustrated; but that the one thing, which really concerns him, is to see that such taxes *are not levied at all;* that they are exacted in no shape and from no one; and that his Goods, having once paid to the Chinese Government all taxes by Treaty payable upon them, shall thereafter be allowed to circulate freely, and without any further enhancement, by taxation, of their cost to the consumer, *throughout the Interior of China.*

There occur several passages of minor importance in the Chamber's letter, open to animadversion. Thus the indubitable Treaty-right of commuting inland charges by one single payment is represented as a *privilege;* the Chamber of Commerce is made to offer its assistance in the framing of *Rules* for the better protection of the Chinese Customs-revenue in reference to fraudulent export commutation-certificates, whereas no Rule can prevent the use of such certificates, their fraudulent character appearing only from the non-shipment to foreign ports of the produce to which they refer, and the remedy lying already in the hands of the Foreign Customs' Department, as will hereafter appear; and it is stated that "the plan of the recent abortive Convention between Great Britain and China was unacceptable to the Chamber because commutation of transit duties was made compulsory without adequate guarantees, and its operation was incomplete," whereas by Treaty the commutation in question was compulsory from the first, and constitutes one of the most important benefits conferred by the Treaty of Tientsin.

The severest comment, however, which that letter has manifestly provoked, are the modified Regulations (B), and the Regulations (C), by the Tsung-li Yamên submitted to the Foreign Representatives; and that such Regulations should have been mainly framed by a British subject, as "Inspector-General of Chinese Maritime Customs," is, considering their tendency and spirit so hostile to, and obstructive of, British legitimate trade with China, and so utterly regardless of existing Treaties, perhaps, not one of their least objectionable features. It is true, the indubitable Treaty-right of Chinamen to "apply for (lit. solicit) duty-certificates (usually styled *transit-passes*) *for the purpose of conveying* imports from foreign lands to the Interior of China," has at last been recognized in explicit terms; but this "privilege," which the sanguine and divinatory eye of the Chairman of the Shanghai General Chamber of Commerce had read, as we have seen, already in the text of the original Regulations (A), and hailed with so much unqualified satisfaction as "the recognition now publicly made by the Chinese Government of the *principle* for which the Chamber has so long contended, viz., that the commutation of inland duties may be claimed on Imports of foreign origin without reference to ownership:" what does it in reality amount to? Principles, more especially after having been for years contested, should be enounced in clear, precise, and unmistakeable language. The very contrary is here the case. That language, therefore, is not merely, it is of necessity also purposely, vague. By implication it might possibly be construed in Mr. Johnson's anticipated sense; according to grammar it admits of no such interpretation; in spirit it is diametrically opposed to it; *de facto* it is altogether silent as to "ownership," but speaks of "conveying," and only speaks of "conveying" foreign goods—(by historical implication foreign-owned foreign-goods)—inland, as the object, for which Chinamen also (in the quality of carriers, comp. also Regul. (A), Rule iii.) shall in future be permitted to apply for duty-certificates protecting such goods against illegal taxation *on the way to* their immediate destination, and no further.

Had it been the *bonâ fide* intention of the Tsung-li Ya-mên and the Inspector-General, Mr. Hart, who framed the Rules in question, to concede the principle, to which the Chamber justly attaches so much weight, and which would imply a desire on their part to facilitate instead of trammeling and obstructing Foreign trade with the Interior of China, we are justified in assuming that, for the sake of obtaining due credit for, and insuring to the Chinese Government the full benefit of, such an intention, they would have announced it in corresponding terms, and that the tenour of the Rules generally, proposed by them, would in some degree at least have been in harmony with it. Nor is it irrational to conclude that they would, moreover, have applied the same principle to the Regulations (C). The facts of the case are diametrically opposed to this legitimate reasoning, and lead to the almost unavoidable inference, that the authors of Rule i. § 1. of the Regulations (B), pouncing upon the fatal admission made to them on the part of the Chamber of Commerce; embodying, in language the most plain and concise, the principle of that admission in § 4 of the same Rule; relying on the facile belief and sanguine interpretation of the Chamber; and desirous to offer, in return for the substantial principle surrendered to them, the semblance at least of a similar principle—framed the paragraph in question accordingly.

The general tendency, and it must consequently be inferred, the contemplated aim, of the Regulations newly proposed, is not only the obstruction of the indirect, but also the final and total destruction of all direct, Chinese inland trade on the part of British and Foreign subjects at large. In other words: these Regulations, as framed by the Inspector-General, Mr. Hart, in communion with the native Intendant of Customs at Shanghai, and by the Tsung-li Yamên transmitted to the Representatives of Western Powers in Peking, follow out, to the full extent that in them lies, the policy of the Chinese Government to exclude all foreigners alike from the Interior of China; to confine all foreign intercourse to the Treaty-ports, and, so far as for the present may be found practicable, to the sea-borders; to obstruct foreign trade to the utmost; and, whilst thus obstructing, to the utmost to *tax* it, for the combined purpose of commercial restriction on the one hand, of military armament on the other, and with an ultimate view to the consummation of that fondly-cherished dream—the expulsion of the outer barbarian from "the bayonet-ploughed soil of Cathay." In order to conceal these aims and to give a certain colouring to the forcible measures designed for their attainment, the foreign merchant and, as in collusion with, and misguided by him the native merchant, are, in accordance with the Tsung-li Yamên's despatch of March 23, 1872, assumed to be intent only on defrauding the Chinese Customs, and to render it imperative, for the protection of the Imperial revenue, that such evil intent should be met by the infliction, regardless of existing Treaties, of disabilities (Regulations (B). Rule iv. § 2, § 3; Reg. (C). Rule iv. § 2.), heavy duties (Reg. (B). Rule i. § 3, § 5, Rule ii. § 1, § 2, Rule iii, § 3; Reg. (C). Rule ii. § 8), exorbitant fines (Reg. (C), Rule iii. § 1, § 2), and wholesale confiscation (Reg. (B), Rule ii. § 3, Rule iii. § 3, § 4, Rule iv. § 2; Reg. (C), Rule ii. § 5, § 7, § 8, Rule iii. § 3, Rule iv. § 3), on the principle: confiscation first; inquiry into the merits of the case afterwards (Reg. (B), Rule iii. § 4).

The extreme boldness—provoked, it would seem, by certain portions of the letter of June 21, 1872, addressed by the Shanghai General Chamber of Commerce to the Chief Superintendent of British Trade in China,—with which these iron Custom-house and Barrier fetters are proposed to be placed upon that trade by the Inspector-General and the Tsung-li Yamên, and which, if anything can, should open the eyes of the mercantile community and of Western Cabinets to the true commercial policy of the latter and the real tendency of the influence exercised in Peking by the former, render a detailed consideration of the Regulations in question, on my part, unnecessary. Some of the principal objections to the Regulations (B), moreover, have already been laid before the reader. They leave me only a few observations to add.

As to the proposed Regulations (C), relative to the purchase of Chinese produce in the Interior by foreign merchants and its conveyance, subject only to the half-duty stipulated by Treaty, to one of the open ports for shipment abroad, they render such a business-transaction practically impossible, and so reduce, in this respect, the provisions of existing Treaties absolutely to a dead letter.

No Chinese household includes foreigners. The meaning

of the 內人 of Rule i, § 2, therefore, *i.e.* persons of the foreign merchant's household, to whom and himself alone permission is granted to proceed inland for the purpose of buying produce of the soil, must be taken as restricted to foreign employés of his firm. But whether this be so or not: what foreign merchant, who, totally unacquainted with the exact geography and the productions of each single locality in the Interior of China, is on the one hand expected in his ignorance to state beforehand, not only the name of the very village or mart, at which, and no other, he intends and shall be allowed to purchase certain specified articles that may or may not be produced or offered for sale at that particular village or mart, but to declare also, as it were on oath, in what district the mart or village, in what prefecture the district, and in what province the prefecture, according to the 大淸一統志, is situated, while on the other hand he is threatened with civil disabilities, ruinous fines, and total confiscation of his property, if he fail in the observance of but one item of the Inspector-General's "directions," pass but one of the unrecognised Barriers on his road without displaying both his "tripartite" and his goods, and deviate on his return but one inch from the right way, —what foreign merchant, I ask, would under such conditions ever think of going himself, or sending any member of his household, whether foreigner or native, on such an errand? If the proposed Regulations (c). should be accepted, their framers will have succeeded not only in effectually securing to the Chinese Government the full and undisputed amount of illegal taxes, imposed by it on native produce destined for exportation abroad, to the local Authorities their share of local charges, and to the Customs' underlings a proportionate revenue in the shape of "squeezes;" but, what is of even greater moment, in *legalising* the aggregate of those imposts, which may to a certainty be expected to go on rapidly increasing; and in burdening with the yearly increasing sum total the British and foreign consumer.

One of the peculiar features of the Regulations (C), and the modified and improved Regulations (A) is, that they convert the foreign merchant, intending to purchase native produce or to dispose of foreign goods inland, to the use of a Chinese Customs' *employé* and check upon, respectively accuser against, himself (Regul. (B), Rule iv., § 1, § 3, § 4; Regulation (C), Rule iv., § 1, § 2, § 4, § 5); and he is expected to perform this somewhat novel duty, within stated limits of time, too, on pain of excommunication (Regul. (B), Rule iv., § 3; Regul. (C), Rule iv., § 2), and at the risk of causing his own property to be confiscated (Regul. (C), Rule iv., § 4). This is expecting not a little from traders, assumed to be intent only on defrauding the Chinese Customs; but the device, original, ingenuous, and inexpensive, reflects credit on the organizing and expectative faculties of the framers of the Regulations, and will no doubt be duly appreciated as well as faithfully followed out, in the event of those Regulations becoming law, by the body of British and foreign merchants.

In § 2 of Rule ii. of the Regulations (B), it is not positively stated that, as insisted on by the Inspector-General in his anonymous memorandum of November 1, 1871, the "*Agent*" as well as "Goods and Certificate must travel in company to secure exemption" from illegal taxation. This follows, however, from the words of the preceding § 1: "When they —persons conveying foreign goods inland—have taken out a certificate for a place previously designated, they must follow the direct road to it;"—whereupon we read § 2:—

"The duty-certificate and the goods conveyed under its protection must always travel and remain together," &c. It seems to me, therefore, plain that the Agent of the foreign merchant is, in § 2, tacitly assumed to accompany the goods, and that the omission can only serve, if it was not actually meant, to mislead.

A highly objectionable article is Rule ii. § 3, inasmuch as any foreign mark or writing on the packages of the foreign goods conveyed by Chinese merchants inland, might according to it, be construed into a sufficient ground or excuse for their confiscation; and such goods, whether the property of foreigners or Chinese, would at all times be at the mercy of the native Custom-house and Barrier officials. The looseness and vagueness of diction and the corresponding selection of Chinese characters in all cases, in which a latitudinarian sense is demanded by the Chinese trade and Custom-house policy, forms, throughout the Regulations, so striking a contrast with the concise and to-the-point language employed whenever Chinese interests require the latter, that it is in reason barely possible not to ascribe to this difference in style and expression a designed character.

I need do no more than call attention to §§ 4 & 5 of Rule i. Upon these two paragraphs hangs, as will be presently seen, a claim of indemnity for some £25,000,000, and more, which the British Government would be fully justified to enforce, in the event of a fresh war, against the Government of China; the Treaty-right of Western Powers to insist on the punishment of those Chinese officials, who, in violation of existing Treaty-engagements, have caused Foreign trade to be over-burdened with illegal taxes; the future prosperity and development of the entire foreign commerce with the Chinese people; and the maintenance or abandonment of the important principle involved in the question: Whether International Treaties, so long as they remain in force, have to be observed; or whether, on the part of both or either of the High Contracting Parties, they may be broken, at any time and in any manner, at their individual will and pleasure?

Touching Sir Rutherford Alcock's views in regard to this question, and on the ground of which he adopted, in May 1870, an opinion diametrically opposed to the opinion with more than usual warmth urged by him in July and November, 1868, and demanding consideration here, they are so intimately connected with the two antagonistic opinions themselves, that I am unable to separate the subject. It is not, I think, unfair to assume, considering the tenour of his own statements, that, in thus veering completely round, the late Representative of England at Peking has been to some extent influenced, on the one hand, by a petty spite against the merchants, who had caused his Revision Convention to fall to the ground, and who had thereby induced his shelvation, on the other hand, by a strong desire to ingratiate himself again with the Ministry of the day. Be this as it may, Sir Rutherford Alcock wrote, as we have already seen, as follows:—

In July 1868.

China, like most other countries, by entering into commercial Treaties with Foreign States, has, in consideration of a fixed payment of maritime and transit duties, *foregone all further right of taxation on whatever can be shown to constitute the foreign trade, import or export.*

In May 1870.

The merchants have persistently maintained an interpretation distinctly and authoritatively repudiated by the only competent authorities in such a matter—the two High Contracting Parties, the British and Chinese Governments. Neither the opinion of the Law

Otherwise, of what use could be the provisions of the Treaties so carefully fixing and limiting the Tariff rates, import, export, and transit? If the Territorial Government retained the right to surcharge these at pleasure, the whole trade could at any moment be stopped, or more gradually dwarfed and finally ruined by burdens it is unable to bear, or prohibitive duties. *The le-kin constitute a violation of Treaty rights*... On that one article, opium, *alone* the Chinese Government reserved its absolute right of (inland) taxation without limitation by Treaty... There is every desire on the British Minister's part to avoid...pressing for impracticable measures either beyond or within the limits of existing Treaties. But this one question of an assumed right of the Chinese Government to tax foreign trade *ad libitum* is one *of principle*, and of such vital moment to the interests of commerce, *that a British Minister can have no discretionary power in protesting against it as a violation of Treaty.*

In November 1868.

I still hope Your Imperial Highness (Prince Kung) and the Ministers of the Ya-mên, collectively, will see that the time has arrived for removing all just cause of complaint and placing the trading-relations of British subjects *in the Interior* on the footing of security and immu-

Officers of the Crown, as to the legal and proper interpretation of these Articles; nor the equally clear testimony of the late Sir F. Bruce and Mr. Wade, both engaged as the Secretaries of Lord Elgin in drawing up the several clauses of the Treaty, as to the true meaning and intent of those articles in his Lordship's conception, have availed to deter the merchants from reiterating *a fallacy*, and insisting upon an interpretation, which rests upon no better foundation than their own opinion against all evidence and authority.

But Treaties are not of private interpretation, according to the interest or *caprice of individuals trading under their stipulations.* What the Treaty of Tientsin does grant in this matter of transit both Governments are agreed, and their joint decision is without appeal. By that Treaty, the importer of foreign goods has the right to sell them at the port without liability, *while they remain his property*, to any other duty than the import duty, or to send them to any inland market which he may select, free from any other charge than the Customs dues on importation and the stipulated transit duty of 2½ per cent. But both at the port and at the internal market, *when once the goods have passed out of his hands, they are liable to bear whatever taxes*

nity from illegal taxation and obstruction, *without which the Treaty itself becomes a dead letter.* This day eight years ago Lord Elgin and the army that accompanied him, left the gates of Peking, *after having secured the ratification of the Treaty of Tientsin, and,* in negotiation with Your Imperial Highness a further Convention that, in the terms of your proclamation then issued, *'Hereafter the weapons of war may for ever be laid aside.'*

or duties the Chinese administration may see fit to levy on them (in common with similar goods of Chinese origin). This is the authoritative reading of the Articles in question, accepted by Her Majesty's Government...These are the conditions of Trade, as determined by the only authoritative reading of existing Treaties.

Whatever allowance we may be inclined to make for a diplomatist who, after having borne the greatness of England on his shoulders, had, after a long exposure to the debilitating effects of the climate of China, failed in the crowning effort of his public life, and returned home only to disappointment, neglect, and privacy: it is painful to see a man even in Sir Rutherford Alcock's present position, on grounds which are but too transparent, not only abandon without reason, but entirely ignore, a former view which he had deliberately formed, supported by valid, logical, and irrefutable arguments, and in the strongest conceivable language impressed, in the name of England, on (what he believed to be) the Government of China; nay, reduce that view, as adhered to by others, to a fallacy resting, against all evidence and authority, on the mere interested or capricious interpretation of "trading individuals." I doubt whether inconsistency, ill-judgment, and bad taste could be carried much further. There exists, to my knowledge, no authority whatever for attributing to Sir Frederick Bruce the opinion, imputed to him by his successor at Peking. The former Minister, certainly, never acted as Secretary to Lord Elgin's

Embassy. With the opinion of the Law Officers of the Crown "as to the legal and proper interpretation" of ART. xxviii. of the Treaty of Tientsin and RULE vii. of the Trade Rules, I have not the advantage of being acquainted; but, with every deference to their Lordships, I venture to think that no interpretation can be well considered, or rest on a sound basis, which is at variance with the clear testimony previously adduced by me.

The point which here concerns us is the strange and novel doctrine, advanced by Sir Rutherford Alcock, to the effect that "the two High Contracting Parties, the British and Chinese Governments, are the only competent authorities to agree and decide upon the meaning and purport of a Commercial Treaty, concluded through their Plenipotentiaries between the two nations, and that their joint decision is without appeal." Sir Rutherford would seem to have imbibed in "the Capital of the Son of Heaven" quite ultra-absolutistic ideas regarding the Powers that be. *Magna Charta*, Parliament, and the People of England, manifestly, had slipped from his memory. Imagine British merchants, who, on their faith in certain clearly expressed provisions of the international Treaty of Tientsin, have invested some ten million £ sterling worth of British property in Shanghai alone, to be told by Her Majesty's ex-Chief Superintendent of Trade in China, that, His Imperial Highness Commissioner-President Prince Kung, and Her Majesty's Secretary of State for Foreign Affairs the Earl of Granville, having agreed to reduce the said provisions to "a dead letter," there is "no appeal from their joint decision"! But, let the pleasantry pass.

Great Britain has thus far been content to allow her Representative in Peking to occupy the position of a most humble, yet unsuccessful petitioner for admittance to but the threshold of the Imperial Palace, for access to but the foot of the Dragon-throne of "the One Lord of the World." With the gates of the Emperor's Palace shut in his very face, almost ignored by the overweening Tatar Monarch, and unnoticed by his supercilious semi-barbarous Government, that Representative has been told by a *Deputy* :—You will for the present be *suffered* to stay in the Capital; but as to any business between your Outer Principality and the Government Universal, it can be transacted only with this temporary "Commission, Imperially appointed for the General Control of the Various Tributary States' Affairs," and a barbarian servant engaged for the purpose. Aye, and men having been found to accept, and feel proud of, such a position: Sir Rutherford Alcock set to revising the Treaty of Tientsin with the "barbarian servant" of a Commission appointed for the General Control of the Affairs of the British Dominions and other Dependencies of the Ta Ching Empire; and concluded the Supplementary Convention of Peking with the *Tsung-li Ya-mên*. With the Tsung-li Ya-mên also were the Treaties of Tientsin and other Treaties concluded. Is the Chinese Government, *i. e.* the Emperor of China, bound by those Treaties? Morally speaking: no doubt; legally speaking: hardly. There exists, according to Chinese notions, at any given period of time but one Ruler, Heaven's Representative on Earth, the reigning Sovereign, to whom the whole human race is subject, and whom we "outer barbarians" are wont to style "the Emperor of China." He is, so long as he occupies the throne, nameless. His reign alone is distinguished by a motto of good augury, or years' epithet, 年號, *niên 'hao*. That of the present reign is: 光緒; which may be rendered "Glory's Consummation," and is in the West generally mistaken for the Emperor's name. His historical or Temple-name, he will receive only after his death. Imperial Rescripts or Edicts, and similar State-papers, which are issued in the Emperor's name, neutrally, i. e. without the use of either the first or third personal pronoun,‖ have the concluding formula: 欽 此, "This from the Emperor," generally but erroneously rendered: "Respect this!" Even personal letters, in which the Emperor writes as 朕, "I, THE EMPEROR," which character no other Chinese is allowed to use on pain of death, bear no signature.

The validity and authenticity of all Chinese State documents is determined by the proper State seal being attached to them, in conclusion of the document and with the date, f. i. "Glory's Consummation, year the 10th, moon the 6th, day the 18th," written perpendicularly, downwards, through the midst of the seal. An international Treaty requires, on the part of China, the Great Imperial Seal, to render it valid and binding on the Emperor and his Government. To the Treaty of Tientsin and other Treaties this seal is not attached; but one of a very different character.

The inscription, in ancient writing, on the former seal, reads in modern Chinese characters and English:—

既 受 "The dominion of the World (I, THE EMPEROR, have)
壽 命 received from Heaven; The splendour of past ages
永 於 (of Dominion has) descended (on ME)." The seal,
昌 天 with a slightly varying inscription, was first intro-

‖ To give an illustration of this peculiar style, I will subjoin a literal translation of the Imperial Rescript, which ordered the appointment of the late Mr. Burlingame as (Chinese) State or Public Messenger (tantamount to "Queen's Messenger"):—

"It having been

Reverentially submitted by the Commission for the General Control of Individual (Tributary) States' affairs, that the Public Messenger P'u Ngan-chên (the Chinese transliteration of "Burlingame," usually named simply P'u) transacts business-matters in a conciliatory spirit, and is thoroughly conversant with the fundamental relations of the (Governing) Central (State) and the (Governed) Outer (States): it is hereby ordered, that

duced by the great founder of the Chin Dynasty, Shih 'Huang Ti. The one at present in use, is the third stone. The inscription on the second seal is in (Manchu and) Chinese: 皇帝之寶, which may be rendered: "The Emperor's gem." The character 寶, *páu*, "precious, resplendent," is an epithet, applied to the Imperial seal; as it is, *f. i.*, by one person to the family of another, of whom a Chinaman will speak as "Your *precious* family," or to the shop of another man, of which he will speak as "Your *resplendent* shop," in both cases using the same predicate 寶. The term for seal is *yin*, 印. The use of the latter seal has been assigned to the Tsung-li Ya-mên, in its intercourse with the Representatives of Outer (Tributary) States,—an act of great international impropriety.

Already on the signing of the Treaty of Tientsin, Mr. Wade, at that time Lord Elgin's Interpreter, had his misgivings on this subject, as will appear from the following documents:—

The Earl of Elgin to Lord J. Russell.

Peking, October 26, 1860.

My Lord,—I have the honour to inclose a translation of the Imperial Decree conferring full powers on Prince Kung, and of the certificate affixed to the ratified Treaty, and signed and sealed by him, declaring the apposition of the Emperor's Seal to the Treaty to be a full and valid act of Imperial ratification. Before consenting to be satisfied with the ratification in this form, I inquired what Baron Gros' views on the subject were, and I ascertained that he would be glad to have the certificate which I proposed to demand, but that he was quite willing to accept the Seal as a valid act of ratification, even without any such certificate.

(signed) Elgin and Kincardine.

---

he be appointed to proceed to the Individual (Tributary) States, bound by Treaty, in the capacity of an Official of rank, to manage such matters as have arisen, in reference to each Individual (Tributary) State, out of the (commercial) intercourse between the Central (State=China) and the Outer (barbarian States). The rest according to prevision. This from the Emperor. T'ung-chih, year 6, moon 10, day 26, ("Union and Order," November 21, 1867).

Decree produced by the Prince of Kung at the Court of the Board of Ceremonies before signing the Convention of the 24th October, 1860.

(Translation)

On the 7th day of the 8th moon of the 10th year of the reign of Hien-fung, (21st September, 1860) the Chief Secretariate had the honour to receive the following Imperial Decree :—

"We command Yih-su, Imperial Prince of Kung, to be Imperial Commissioner Plenipotentiary, with power to do whatever may be necessary to the exchanging of Treaties and the making of peace between the two nations. Respect this!"

NOTE.—The term "tsiuen-kiuen," translated "Plenipotentiary," is of foreign manufacture, and employed here, as on former occasions, out of deference to our prejudices. The plenipotentiary power, according to Chinese notions and usages, is really conferred by the words "pien-i-hing-sz,"—"to do the things which the occasion may demand as essential."—T. F. W.

Certificate appended to the Treaty of Tientsin by the Prince of Kung, October 24, 1860.

(Translation.)

The Prince of Kung, Commissioner and Plenipotentiary of his Majesty the Emperor of the Ta Tsing Dynasty, hereby executes a certificate :—

Be it known, that the impression of the 'Hwang Ti-chi P'au' (the fifth of the twenty-five seals of the Empire), which has been reverentially affixed to the foregoing Treaty, the same being the Treaty of Peace concluded at Tientsin in the year wu-wu (1858), is an attestation of the full assent of his Majesty the Emperor of China to, and his promise to abide by, all the Articles therein, and renders unnecessary any separate authorisation by the Imperial signature. This Certificate is accordingly appended to this Treaty, to serve as a record for evermore. Executed at Peking, on the 11th day, of the 9th moon, in the 10th year of the reign Hien-fung (20th October, 1860.)

How Prince Kung, the Mandarins, and the Tatar Court must have smiled, on this occasion, at the facile belief, and easily-led punctiliousness of "those outer barbarians!" How admirable the sarcasm, which lies in the analogy between the 皇帝之寶, and "the Emperor's full assent to, and promise to abide by, all the Articles of the Treaty of Tientsin!" Does not, moreover, the very Certificate state, that His Majesty is "the Emperor of the Ta Ching Empire," (by Mr. Wade erroneously rendered—a palpable absurdity—the Ta Ching "Dynasty"), *i. e.* of the entire habitable Earth? § And is "the Lord of the World"¶ bound by a promise, forced from him by some of his own rebellious subjects? Then, the laughable idea of Prince Kung, any more than a common coolie,* vouching for THE EMPEROR's assent; and the foreign-invented, senseless term "*tsiuen-kiuen*, translated *Plenipotentiary*," which reduces the whole certificate-affair to a mere farce.

But, even *assuming* the Decree, produced by Prince Kung, to have had the proper seal attached to it, Mr. Wade translates:—"WE (*i. e.* 朕, I, THE EMPEROR) command....Respect this!" The concluding formula itself, however,—correctly rendered: "This from the Emperor,"—proves that the supposed Edict was worded in the usual style, and that the true version would have been: "It is (hereby) ordered, that...." On account of the absent Imperial pronoun 朕, Mr. Wade cannot possibly have misapprehended the syntax; but, as he would seem to have done on another occasion,—with the view of making it appear that the present Inspector-General

§ To a large Atlas, *f. i.*, published in 1863 by Provincial Authority, and entitled: "Atlas of the Whole of the One Great Ching Empire," and also: "Atlas of the Whole Central and Outer Dominions of the (present) Exalted Dynasty," there is prefixed in the Introduction, a "General Map" of those Dominions in three divisions; the first comprehending "the Central State," *viz.*, China inclusive of a portion of Russia, of Corea, Japan, etc.; the two others comprehending both "the Central and the Outer States of the Ching Empire," *viz.*, *the two hemispheres of the Earth.*

¶ In his famous Edicts to the Eight Banner-Corps, the Emperor Shih Tsung Hsièn (Yung Chêng, 1723—1736) says:—朕身爲天下之主. "I, THE EMPEROR, individually, am the Lord of the World;" and by His Imperial Highness Prince Kung, in a recently printed volume of Essays, the same doctrine is, over and over again, impressed upon his readers in the very strongest language.

* In the same volume, just referred to, Prince Kung repeatedly adduces the old maxim: "The Emperor is the Emperor, and the subject subject," in other words: There are but the one Absolute Ruler of mankind, and,—reduced to the same level before him, all men, however high their rank relatively to each other—his slaves.

of Chinese Maritime Customs had been Imperially appointed, —he must be inferred to have introduced here the same Imperial WE, intentionally. Again, he explains "the words *pien-i-hing-sz* to signify:—"to do the things which the occasion may demand as essential," whilst he translates them: "with power to do whatever may be necessary to...." I am not in possession of the Chinese text of the Decree; but the reading can only be: 便宜行事, and Mr. Wade must have known, that its meaning is simply: "for the purpose of transacting business,"† although he appears not to have known, that, "according to Chinese notions and usages," Heaven's "plenipotentiary power," solely possessed by the Emperor, is never by him entrusted to a deputy for any purpose whatever. Lastly, Mr. Wade, though fully aware of the true nature of the difficulty, manifestly had allowed Lord Elgin to remain under the erroneous impression, that it was not the improper stamp attached to the Treaty for the Great Imperial Seal, but the absence of the Emperor's signature, which constituted that difficulty. The Emperor has no signature. Its place is taken by his seal.

According to the authoritative "Collective Code of the Ta Ching Dynasty,‡ the fifth of the twenty-five State seals,—the one assigned to the Tsung-li Ya-mên, is used 以肅法紀, "for awe-inspiring (documents), restraining (regulations), and yoke-imposing (bonds)." It is quite in harmony, therefore, with the title of the Tsung-li Ya-mên itself. It measures 4·8 Chinese inches square, and is exceptionally made of wood,—a particular kind of sandal-

† The sentence may, when the context justifies it, but not otherwise, be rendered: "with authority to transact business."

‡ 欽定大清會典, 16 vols. 8°, vol. i. ch. ii. fol. 6. I have only the first edition before me; the text in regard to our subject, however, has undergone no later alterations.

wood—; all the other seals, with the exception of the third, a small seal made of gold, being cut of precious stone, viz. jade, varying in color and quality.|| The first or great seal, made of white jade, and measuring 4·4 Chinese inches square, impressed in vermilion and used 以章皇序, "for statutes, etc., emanating from the Imperial Cabinet itself," as I understand the phrase. Its inscription, claiming the autocracy of the Earth for the Tatar Sovereign, is, no doubt, highly objectionable; the use, for which the *fifth* seal, which is impressed in black, is destined, renders its application to international treaties simply insulting. Altogether, nothing could be in a more unsatisfactory state than are, diplomatically, the treaty-relations of Western Powers with China,§ and, independently of other, as will be presently seen, even more fatal, objections, Sir Rutherford Alcock can but have advanced his theory, that "the two High Contracting Parties, the British and Chinese Governments, are the only competent authorities to agree and decide upon the interpretation to be placed on the various provisions of the Treaty of Tientsin," in perfect ignorance of the facts and bearings of the case.¶

A similar, and truly surprising degree of unacquaintance with the real merits of "the transit-system," upon which he advises the British Government, Mr. Wade exhibits in his often cited Memorandum,—a composition,

|| It cannot be the size of the fifth seal, which has determined the choice of its exceptional material, as the ninth, eleventh, and twenty-first seals are of the same size, while the twenty-second one, made of black jade, measures as much as 53 Chinese inches square.

§ Comp. my ssay. On the Universal Supremacy of the Emperors of China, as diplomatically enforced in their relations with Western Powers, and considered in its practical bearings and tendencies.—Shanghai, 1875, 8°.

¶ Sir Rutherford Alcock has shown, by some papers contributed to *Fraser's Magazine*, for March and April, 1871, that it is possible for a man of education to reside for years as British Minister in the Capital of China, and to take home from it, even relative to its Government, nothing but erroneous notions.

as he himself observes, "of immense length," but of neither breadth nor depth; in which the distinguished author inclines to all sides; affirms and negatives, emphasizes and "but" s, proposes and opposes, approves and disapproves, everything; extends his full hand, under the appearance of his little finger, to the Chinese official, and his little finger, under the appearance of his full hand, to the British merchant; would fain please God, and decidedly not displease the Devil. If Mr. Wade had been a Member of the Tsung-li Ya-mên, or been looking forward to the chances of another Burlingame Mission, he could hardly have argued more ingeniously than he does, in support of the continuance of a system of illegal inland taxation in China, which, so far as trade with the Interior is concerned, virtually reduces the Treaty of Tientsin to a dead letter. But his pro-Chinese bias and feelings, rising up to "mountains full two hundred *li* in height,"* are so well known as to require no further elucidation on my part.

To what extent, however, Mr. Wade was unfit, not only from his strong prejudices, but from defective information, to advise the British Board of Trade on the subject under consideration, will appear from the following statements, made by him, namely:—"A fair Tariff of import and export customs was (in virtue of the Treaty of Nanking) published in 1843, but the promised declaration by which the inland transit duty was to have been regulated never appeared." His Excellency, therefore, was manifestly ignorant of the official publication of the declaration in question, dated Hongkong June 26, 1843, as well as of the existence of the "Supplementary Treaty of Hooman-

* See Mr. Wade's *Tzŭ Erh Chi*, London, 1847, 4° p. 32; and Key, Exercise I, 13 p.p, 4-5. About three Chinese *li* are equal to an English mile.

Chai of October 8, 1843," and the Government Notification of February 20, 1844; although, strangely enough, he adds: "it was doubtless, of the rates to be charged at these—certain fixed points, or—barriers, a list of which is published in the Code of the Board of Revenue, that the declaration required by Sir Henry Pottinger, in 1842, was demanded."† There is nothing here but confusion. In the Treaty of Nanking of August 29, 1842, in which it is expressly stated that the amount to be levied as transit duties, "shall not exceed—per cent on the tariff value" of British imports, there is no allusion made to inland "Barriers," at which he rates of duties were then to have been payable according to measures of length, weight, and capacity. The Chinese tariff of inland taxes, at the period in question levied at the various inland Custom-houses—there existed then as yet no Barriers,—and published in the Code of the Board of Revenue,‡ was duly promulgated by the British Plenipotentiary.

Again, in reference to the optional clause in Art. xxviii. of the Treaty of Tientsin, Mr. Wade writes:—"This stipulation, like that in the Treaty of Nanking, had reference to the Barriers that had been sanctioned by the Board of Revenue." In the first place, this sentence includes a contradiction in terms, inasmuch as, at the conclusion of the Treaty of Nanking, no "Barriers" had been "invented," Mr. Wade apparently confounding them with the old Cus-

† The declaration or promulgation of the tariff of inland duties, of which Mr. Wade here speaks, can possibly refer only to Sir Henry Pottinger's "Declaration of June 26, 1843," which he has just asserted to have never appeared,—because in that document alone the tariff in question is alluded to. I find to my surprise also, that Mr. Wade, towards the conclusion of his memorandum, actually quotes the "Supplementary Treaty signed at Hoo Mun Chai, 1843." All I can say is, that his Excellency must, with that Treaty before him, be inferred to have read it very partially, and for a special purpose only.

‡ A translation of the Tariff is given also by the late Mr. Wingrove Cooke, in his correspondence from China in the years 1857-58, London 1859, 8° p.p. 191-5.

tom-houses.|| And, in the second place, the optional clause in ART. xxviii. of the Treaty of Tientsin had by no means reference to the Barriers only which, since the Treaty of Nanking, might, or might not, have been sanctioned by the Board of Revenue, but to the whole of the inland charges, including *le-kin*, which were being levied at the time, and were not to be increased thereafter. Had Mr. Wade read the Treaty-Article referred to with the least degree of attention, he would have avoided falling into an error, solely on the ground of *which* he was afterwards enabled to draw so fine a distinction between "transit"-taxes and *le-kin*, in favor of the legality of the latter impost.

"But it was found," Mr. Wade goes on to say, "that in the then conditions of the Interior and especially of the valley of the Great River, the required notification, if producible at all, could not be looked for without very considerable delay;" and that "*therefore*, by the 7th of the Rules appended to the Tariff, *the inland duty* on all imports and exports therein enumerated was limited to a sum equal to half the duty leviable upon them under Tariff, and that on duty-free goods, to a sum equal to 2½ per cent. upon value; exemption from any additional impost *in transitu* being secured by certificate." I hardly comprehend his Excellency. The notification in question might have been "produced" at any moment. Does Mr. Wade, then, mean to say, that a *fixed* inland commutation-tax was finally agreed upon, because the valley of the Yang-tze was at the time in the

|| The Tsung-li Ya-mên and the Superintendent of Trade for the Middle Ports, the late Tsêng Kuo Fan, do not participate in Mr. Wade's strange error. In the notification of the Governor-General of the Two Kiang, he states:—"I, Tsêng Kuo Fan....... in reference to a communication from the Tsung-li Ya-mêu, respecting the first article of the regulations, which were established in the 11th year of Hsien Fêng, and requiring that foreign merchandise, entering the Interior, shall pay *duty* at the *Custom-houses* 關 and *le-kin* at the Customs barriers 卡 &c."

possession of the Tai-pings? Legitimate trade in that quarter existed not: all intercourse with the rebels having been strictly forbidden. What advantage, therefore, could "a fixed tax" have presented to the Chinese Government over its accustomed "irregular and multiplied levies," in districts temporarily beyond the reach of its authority? Did Lord Elgin, perchance, conclude his Treaty with China solely with a view to her disturbed provinces? It would seem that Mr. Wade could have perused neither the Treaty itself with due attention, nor Lord Elgin's despatch to the Foreign Office, of November 8, 1858, at all. For ART. XXVIII. of the former, compared with RULE VII. of the appended Rules, distinctly says that one *fixed* inland duties commutation-tax it was adopted on account of "charges suddenly and arbitrarily imposed by the provincial authorities as transit duties upon produce on its way to the foreign market, and on imports on their way to the Interior, to the detriment of trade;" and the latter document as distinctly states, that it was in "the substitution of one fixed payment for the present irregular and multiplied levies, the remedy was to be sought against this grievance,"—a grievance, which had from all sides been pressed upon Lord Elgin by the mercantile bodies. Finally, Mr. Wade here admits, that the one fixed commutation tax was to absolutely commute "*the inland duty* on all imports and exports," and in the same breath maintains that the *certificate*, certifying the due payment of that inland duty, was *not* to exempt all imports and exports from "the inland duty," but from "any additional imposts *in transitu* only,"—a palpable contradiction in terms.

"I am not in a position," Mr. Wade remarks, "to state whether Sir Henry Pottinger supposed that the single payment, by which he stipulated that the Chinese merchant was to compound for his barrier dues, would exempt the goods he carried inland from all farther taxation. I suspect that he did; and the mercantile community, though, with reason, not sanguine that the promised scale of inland duties would ever be published at all, were, I think, under the same impression as to the sense of the Treaty stipulation." If his Excellency, when he wrote this, as Secretary of the British Legation in China on leave of absence in London, and with the very Archives of the Foreign Office at his disposal, was not in a position to ascertain the fact, which he "suspects": who could have been? His suspicion, however, is ill-founded. Sir Henry Pottinger, in his Declaration of June 26, 1843, did not compound the then leviable inland taxes—by Mr. Wade erroneously styled "*barrier* dues"—by one single fixed tax—but agreed that the British (the same as the Chinese) merchant should pay the whole of the actual inland taxes at that period levied upon native trade, to an extent *not exceeding the then rates*, such rates being upon a moderate scale. And how, with the said Declaration before it, could the mercantile community have participated in Mr. Wade's groundless impression? What *reason*, moreover, had merchants to apprehend that Sir Henry Pottinger would fail in causing the promised scale of inland duties—involuntarily Mr. Wade recurs again and again to the use of the true designation for taxes, to which he otherwise applies the misleading term of "barrier"- or "transit"-dues—to be published?

Mr. Wade further observes:—"Through the native trade, undoubtedly, the *le-kin* hits our own trade hard, and for more reasons than one we are justified in crying out; but again we must be careful to remember what the tax really is." Its nature appears to me to be singularly misunderstood.

"Since the last payment, "he writes," of our indemnity in 1865, only, has the Central Government caused two-fifths of the Customs receipts (the amount that the French and ourselves drew annually from 1860 to 1865) to be remitted to Peking. The remaining three-fifths are applied to the expenditure of the 'provinces.' So they were throughout the whole five years of indemnity payments; and except the Canton quota, which, up to a certain date, had always gone to the purse of the Imperial household, so, for the last fifteen years of trouble, have the whole of the maritime duties, collected on foreign trade, been applied."

"As I have before mentioned, the Central Government, it might be more proper, perhaps, here, to say the Court, now draws and applies nearly half the total of the Tariff duties. It has no other fund so large, and none so regularly paid. Be its alarm" (at the abolition of the import Tariff, proposed by his Excellency) "ever so great, the action taken by it will be slow. The Decree calling for the provincial return will be for a time disregarded, or at the best tardily obeyed."

"The "*squeezes" of the local authorities*, that is, *I presume*, the *le-kin* or war-tax, of the abuses connected with which I shall have enough to say, owe their existence and evil growth to the same demand for supplies, not to any action taken by or through the Customs Inspectorate. In some form or degree the impost is of far older birth than the Inspectorate, and must be at this moment *a chief resource of Government* in regions far beyond the influence of that Institution."

"The *le-kin* taxes are, and for years to come will be, indispensable to *the Chinese Government*...To find bread for its standing civil and military establishments, to say nothing of the large bodies of militia or volunteers, which are demanded of it to make head against the rebellion or brigandage incessantly troubling it in one quarter or another, *the State* has been driven to various abnormal ways of recruiting its means."

It is almost painful to follow Mr. Wade through the labyrinth of his illogic, inconsistency, self-contradiction, and verbose inaccuracy. After having incidentally stated that the *le-kin*, "though ostensibly a voluntary contribution, is in reality a tax of great elasticity upon all trade, and one which, in course of time, becomes as grievous in the arbitrariness of its imposition as the 'benevolence' of our Kings of old," his Excellency tells us, that it is only through the native trade it touches our own; asks us, in justification of the grievously-arbitrary impost, to carefully remember what the singularly misunderstood tax really is; thereupon presumes it to be the squeezes of local authorities; in the same breath positively affirms that it constitutes one of the chief fiscal resources of the Chinese Government, being the bread of the Chinese Army; and finally explains its true nature by warning the English Board of Trade, that it (the *le-kin*) is *no imposition of the Foreign Inspectorate-General*, but—considering that three-fifths of the Customs revenue, derived from British and foreign trade, have been regularly absorbed by the Provinces, whilst, during the period 1860 to 1865, the remaining two-fifths were appropriated by England and France for war expenses, and go now towards the support of the Peking Court,—simply a necessity, imposed upon the poor Chinese Government partly by Great Britain herself. Such,—however little of logic there may be in Mr. Wade's argument, if there be any at all,—appears to me to be the drift of his remarks; and this inference is confirmed by the whole tendency of his subsequent, less occult reasoning.

The statements here animadverted upon have, at all events, scarcely any foundation in truth. The *le-kin*, *chow-fang*, and similar imposts, are taxes, directly and in open violation of Treaty-engagements, levied upon British and foreign imports, and native exports destined for British and foreign ports. They are not the "squeezes" of local authorities, but illegal taxes imposed by the Chinese Government. And these taxes are not being levied to supply bread to the Chinese troops engaged in the suppression of rebellion and the restoration of order, but, partly for the obstruction of foreign inland trade, partly,—and for a number of years past, at least, this has been the case,—for the purpose of military armaments against Western Powers generally, and against England in particular,—a purpose, to which a large part of the three-fifths of the regular Customs revenue, alluded to by Mr. Wade, is equally applied in the Provinces. It is well for the Court of Peking, that Mr. Wade is so little acquainted with its resources; or else the Imperial Household must have had a hard time of it during the Franco-British-indemnity-paying period of 1860–1865. But what logical connection there exists between the Emperor's relief from penury in 1866, and his alarm at Mr. Wade's intended proposition to abolish the import Tariff in favor of a "*carte blanche* inland taxation," on the one hand, and His Majesty's *slow* action and "a Decree calling for the provincial return, which will for a time be disregarded or at the best tardily obeyed," on the other, is to me a mystery. Or had his Excellency here once more and suddenly been seized with the idea, that the *le-kin* taxes are nothing more nor less, than "the squeezes of local authorities"? Does he consider "the Court," *i. e.* the Emperor and his household, and "the Chinese Government," *i. e.* the Emperor and his State-Secretariate and Privy Council, to constitute in the divine-absolutistic Empire of the Ching, two distinct elements of power, independent of each other? And what relations existed there between Mr. Wade and the Foreign Inspectorate-General of Chinese Maritime Customs, that he should see occasion to disconnect from the *le-kin* "a department which, if not on other grounds as much above suspicion as his Excellency 'is happy to believe,' is entirely distinct from the receiving offices"? That there exists some connection between the levying of the *le-kin* taxes and Foreign

Custom-houses, "the foreign Commissioner of Customs at each port, being, it is true," as Mr. Wade himself remarks, "the subordinate of the Chinese Superintendent of Customs," I can positively affirm; to what an extent that connection goes,§ is a question I am not prepared to answer.

Mr. Wade states:—"By Article IX. of the Treaty of Tien-tsin, Lord Elgin obtained for the British merchant the right to travel with a pass-port, on business or for pleasure, to any part of the Empire. This gave him personal access to the markets whether as buyer or seller, and secured him, at all events, against false information....So far as Article IX. of the Treaty of Tientsin is concerned, it is my impression that the privilege it guarantees has been fairly enjoyed.... The personal access which it does authorise to whatever places the foreigner desires to visit, has been, with rare exceptions at all events, conceded him....At Shanghai, notwithstanding our power of visiting the producing districts, tea and silk are procurable on as good terms at the port as up the country, if not on better; but this because the native community have the wit to combine. The foreign community invariably compete. The combination of the tea-growers proves, I fancy, too much even for the native brokers." It is characteristic of the present Representative of England in China, that he represents the right of the British merchant

§ That the Foreign Commissioner of Customs at Shanghai, Mr. Dick, knows to a cash what is the exact annual product *f. i.* of the *chow-fang*, which he still calls the "Defence Tax" ("Suggestions for the Revision of the Chinese Customs Tariff and Trade Regulations," appended to the "Reports on Trade at the Treaty Ports in China" for the year 1869), Shanghai, 1870, 4°, p. 20, note), is, of course, no proof of such a connection. The office of the *chow-fang* being under the same roof with the Foreign Custom-house, the returns in question might easily be obtained. If we were to judge, however, from the confiscation-case of Messrs. Bower and Hambury, to which I shall have to revert in the sequel, foreign tide-waiters and tide-surveyors, being in the united service of the Foreign Maritime Customs and the Tau-tai, even act, occasionally at least, as *le-kin* officials; and the *le-kin* and "transit-" dues in that case appear to be inextricably mixed up together.

to travel, under a restrictive pass-port system, in the Interior, as a privilege, and the curtailment of his Treaty-right as a Chinnese concession. Not only were, up to within the lasts even or eight years, travellers' passports, with the terms "for purposes of trade" inserted in them, constantly refused or disregarded by the Provincial Authorities, but in certain provinces they were so by direct instructions from the Tsung-li Ya-mên. If, more recently, the "privilege" has been "fairly enjoyed," it is simply because foreign merchants have had to "concede" the point, and almost ceased to avail themselves of the privilege in question, for the reason indicated by Mr. Wade himself, namely, the chief staple articles of exportation from China, "tea and silk, being procurable on as good terms at the ports, as up the country, if not on better."

How is this fact to be explained? Manifestly, the foreign merchant finds it useless to incur,—pleasure in travelling, or travelling for pleasure, in China is out of the question—, the trouble, privation, and expense, of proceeding himself, or sending agents of his own, to the inland marts; useless, either because he finds it impossible to escape illegal taxation after all, or because the journey costs more than the amount which he is able to save in purchase-money and transit-charges, or because the native traders use bribery in order to evade a portion of those taxes; in short, because the desire of the Chinese to sell brings the produce to the British merchant's door at a cheaper rate than he could, by purchasing as a mere traveller, in the Interior, lay it down himself. Not so Mr. Wade. The present Chief Superintendent of British Trade in China contends that the foreign merchant can buy more advantageously at his own port than at the inland market, because there—"the native community have the wit to combine" against him *i.e.*, impliedly, against his dullness, manifested by "invariable competition." But there are two points, which reduce his Excellency's argument to its proper value. Of his extraordinary advocacy in favor of "combination," which is in principle identical with, and necessarily involves, monopoly, against "competition," the very soul of free trade—one of the principal conditions of England's commercial and industrial prosperity—, I will not even speak. The first of the points referred to, is that Mr. Wade overlooks how, in the same paragraph in which he lauds the Chinese wit of combination, he explains that:—"Article IX. of the Treaty of Tientsin does not accord us, nor, as I (Mr. Wade) have urged elsewhere, does any other Article accord, the right of residing otherwise than a tourist or mercantile traveller may reside, in any part of China, but the Consular ports." How, then, such being the case, can the British and foreign commercial tourist be rationally expected to, and how could be possibly, "combine," successfully combine, against the resident native tea-growers and silk-farmers? The preliminary and indispensable condition of such a combination, on the part of foreigners, is the right of residence in the Interior. They possess as yet no such right. Mr. Wade, personally, opposes it. Is it not amply sufficient that, in China, British merchants should be allowed "to visit any producing ground or import market they please; to contract, if it suit them, with the producer for exports, and to certificate them to the port of shipment; or to contract with the native dealer in imports, and to send their goods certificated from the port to his house?" Why, as his Excellency adds with paternal and quite touching solicitude, should they, moreover, "subject themselves to the *inconvenience* of that multiplication of establishments, which has already cost our China merchant so dear"? I am of opinion that, in regard to this matter, the individual merchant himself ought to be considered the only proper judge; but, at all events, let no sensible man talk of Foreigners combining, at an inland mart, against the native tea growers and silk farmers, so long as they continue deprived of the right of residence in the Interior.

The second point, to which I have alluded, lies in Mr. Wade's own remark, in "fancying, that the combination of (native) tea-growers proves too much even for (the combination of) the native brokers;" for surely, he would not have us understand that, in China, the native "wit" is peculiar to the tea-growing part of the population? Brokers, generally, have the reputation of not being wanting in that quality. But, if native brokers, inland, combine, or are made to combine, against native producers: is not this a case of "diamond cutting diamond," of "Greek meeting Greek," by which the British merchant may be fairly concluded to come out the chief gainer? For if, *at the port*, he do compete for the purchase of Chinese produce, the Chinese, eager to convert their accumulating stock into money, do combine in an equally fervent desire to dispose of it; and, were it not that the people of England, the United States, and other countries were so determined to drink new tea, and to wear fresh silks, at any price, it might be difficult to say on whose side the advantage would remain. As it is, there can be no doubt as to one thing, *viz.*, that the Chinese Government, in addition to the export and inland-duty on tea and silk fixed by Tariff, make the Western consumer of these commodities, in open violation of Treaty-provisions, pay about *twenty per cent ad valorem* over and above their fair market cost.

The view next expressed by Mr. Wade, and requiring notice, relates to the ownership of certificated British merchandise, intended for sale inland. "Article XXVIII. of the Treaty of Tientsin," he writes, "*promises* exemption from all charges *in transitu*.... ; provided always, as Sir Frederick Bruce read the Treaty, that such imports or produce, being *bonâ fide* British owned, were accompanied by a certificate....

"It is hard enough on the provincial Governments, that they must give up their tolls on goods that are foreign-owned, but it will be harder still if Chinese, armed with foreigners' certificates, are to carry Chinese-owned goods toll-free from one end of the Empire to the other...

It must be remembered that, with these local Governors (whose cupidity is not easily restrained) pleas for extraordinary expenditure abound,...and that for years they have been used to the appropriation, almost unquestioned, of the *le-kin* taxes,...so grievous to bear.

"I hold that the transit-duty, as defined by Treaty, once paid, the certificate thereon granted....will not exempt the goods, cleared under it, from the *le-kin* or from any other tax, once they have become Chinese property." Those poor provincial mandarins, whose cupidity even Mr. Wade is unable to restrain! Well may they congratulate themselves at possessing so warm and influential a friend in the present Chief Superintendent of British Trade in China. I fear, however, that his pro-Chinese enthusiasm carries him occasionally, as here, beyond the boundaries of prudence, if not of reason. When, in one page, he admits that "there has not been, to his knowledge, any instance but the one exposed at Ningpo, of such an abuse of the certificate," as I shall have to speak of in the sequel and is alluded to by Mr. Wade above, and in another page talks of the Chinese revenue, derived from the native inland taxation, being defrauded, throughout the Empire, by means of false certificates taken out by British and other foreign merchants, in order, it would seem, to create the greater sympathy, on the part of the British Government, for Chinese officials, who are systematically endeavouring to destroy the legitimate trade of England by illegal exactions, and whose rapacity he himself denounces: I am at a loss to account for so unaccountable a proceeding. On the other hand, his Excellency, missing no opportunity of gratifying "the Central Government" as well, greatly exaggerates the share of the *le-kin*, which "the Provincial Governments are allowed to appropriate," and forgets how he has just insisted, that "*le-kin* taxes are, and for years to come will be, indispensable to the Chinese (*i. e.* "the Central") Government....to find *bread* for its standing civil and military establishments." And the whole of Mr. Wade's preceding declamation is based on the *erroneous* view of his, that only British- and foreign-*owned* goods are entitled to a commutation of inland taxes and a corresponding certificate. He had read the provisions of the Treaty of Tientsin wrongly; and, if there was one man above all others in China, who ought to have read them aright, surely it was Mr. Wade. As to imports, even before he pressed his mistaken opinion, —so far as I know, never shared in, as he states, by Sir Frederick Bruce,—on the British Government, the very Tsung-li Ya-mên had formally proclaimed that opinion to be opposed to Treaty-stipulations; and in doing so, as the Inspector-General explains it, "merely honestly ordered subordinate offices to give full and proper effect to a previously existing right." Respecting exports, I have shown that the spirit of the Treaty of Tientsin, containing no condition of *ownership*, is equally plain; and it will, presently, be shown, that in practice it absolutely excludes the construction placed upon it by his Excellency.

"The immediate abolition of the *le-kin* contribution (the remedy urged by some of the physicians of this ailing Power)," Mr. Wade states, "is simply impracticable. I will state the ground of this conclusion. The provinces have revenues specially affected to their expenses, but the income with which the Empire assumes to support its establishments should, in normal times, amount to some 45,000,000 taels, say £15,000,000 sterling. It derives this from three sources, the land tax, the sundry taxes, and the Salt Gabelle. The Salt Gabelle, even in the most flourishing periods, appears always to have been in confusion; and in evil days, *such as those we live in*, it can even less be reckoned on: the collectors and monopolists" [the State is the only monopolist in salt] "make large fortunes, the smugglers also; the account with the State is always grievously in debt. But a large portion of the land-tax, which should yield nearly two-thirds of the

In the towns and cities, whether on the seaboard or inland, the ledger of the native dealer, merchant, broker, and tradesman alike, is subjected to an unsparing inquisition, and on all discoverable transactions the *le-kin* falls heavily and without relaxation.

total income of the State as above estimated, it must have been, for years past, impossible to collect at all, in any place where a population still existed to pay it; while, in many places, the country has been so thoroughly laid waste, that there is no longer a population to be taxed. The sundry taxes" [including foreign Maritime Customs], "of course, have fared no better. Of the provincial as distinguished from the Imperial revenues, we have no exact ac-

Although, thanks to the increase of trade since 1860,...the foreign customs have nearly doubled,... even now they amount to something less than 8,000,000 taels.

count. They are roundly put at some 6,000,000 £ sterling.... The foreign import and export duties (not the transit dues) are, perhaps, the only income on which, for some time past, the Central Government has been able to count with perfect certainty....It is this poverty of the exchequer, and this feebleness of the Government, which also explain, though they do not excuse, the disregard of the transit duty clause."

Mr. Wade's plea *ad misericordiam*, in favour of his *protégé* the *le-kin* tax, is made to rest, on the one hand, upon a great exaggeration of the temporary financial difficulties of China, and almost as great an exaggeration of the insignificance of her normal revenue ; on the other hand, upon his silence as to certain publicly-known or barely concealed purposes, to which a large portion of that revenue is applied. True, he remarks that " the most eager apologist of the Government will no more contend that the sources selected have been the best, than that the means drawn from these sources have been honestly or judiciously applied; very little indeed, considering the emergency, having been done to improve the effectiveness of the forces employed ostensibly to restore order in the provinces :" but he alludes with no syllable to, as though he were in utter ignorance of, the vast sums expended upon the arsenals at Tientsin, Shanghai, Nanking and Foochow, the purchase of gun-boats and foreign munitions of war *against Western Powers*, and the object of which, now patent to the world, was no longer a secret to the attentive observer, even at the time when Mr. Wade presented his memorandum to the British Government.

To judge from that memorandum, it might seem doubtful whether there did, or did not, then survive in China, out of a population estimated at 400 million people, as many tens of thousand tax-paying subjects of " the One Lord of the World," and whether the revenue of the Ching

Empire Universal had, or had not, dwindled down to the pittance, collected, "thanks to the Foreign Customs Inspectorate," from "the foreign import and export duties (not the transit dues)."

This is not the place to enter into a discussion regarding the normal amount of imposts, levied yearly in money and kind, by the Chinese Government; but, to put it down, as Mr. Wade does, at £6,000,000 for Provincial, and £15,000,000 for Imperial use, or £21,000,000 in all, betrays an apparent unacquaintance with the subject, which it is difficult to account for on his Excellency's part. Let it be remembered that the area of the Tatar Dominions, as estimated by McCulloch, exceeds 5,000,000 English square miles, and that, according to Dr. Williams, the area of the Eighteen Provinces, *i.e.* of China Proper, alone, cannot be much less than 2,000,000 square miles,—say 1200,000,000 English acres. If, then, we assume only one half of these lands to be under cultivation, the land-tax, which at the present time may be estimated at a mean rate of two shillings per acre, would yield a gross amount of £60,000,000; and this rough approximation agrees remarkably well with the statement of Dr. Medhurst, who, drawing his information from Chinese sources, valued the land-tax in money and grain, several years ago, at $198,984,032 Mexican, or about £45,000,000 sterling, *clear* revenue, of which *less* than £15,000,000 were transmitted to Peking. Sir George Staunton was informed that the entire income of the State amounted, at the time of his visit, to £66,000,000, being about three shillings and sixpence English, per head.

As regards the management of the Salt Gabelle, it is, no doubt, corrupt enough: but the revenue derived by the Government from this monopoly is, withal, not quite so poor as Mr. Wade represents, nor the administration so bad as the salt, which it supplies. Besides the support of a very large number of officials, employed in connection with the trade, it yields to the Chinese exchequer an annual income not much short of a couple of million pounds sterling. If it were productive of nothing but debts, would the "needy" Tatar Government be likely to cling to it with so much fondness and pertinacity as it does? On the large revenue, collected from *le-kin*, Mr. Wade observes a profound silence. Nor does he allude to the very handsome item which the Maritime Customs on commerce, carried on in *native*-built bottoms, contribute to the Treasury. It is quite instructive to see how hard his Excellency labours to make it appear as though the Foreign Inspector-General of Chinese Maritime Customs were the only financial pillar of "the Central Government, it might be more proper, perhaps, here, to say the Court."

The nominal expenditure of the Provinces is strictly regulated by the Board of Revenue; and so are the taxes to be levied. The corruption of the higher officials consists, with few exceptions, in this, that they "squeeze" *the revenue duly collected* and by Government or their superiors placed at their disposal for specified purposes, by not appropriating the whole of such sums to those purposes, or by applying them altogether for their own benefit; that of the inferior officials in this, that they "squeeze" *the tax-and-rate-payers* by levying unauthorised charges in addition to the prescribed taxes or rates. The latter are, *on paper*, never exceeded, and the Provincial appropriations most minutely accounted for. When Mr. Wade proposes that periodical "returns" of the *le-kin* taxes, collected in the various provinces, and of their application, should be made to "the Central Government," and communicated to the British Minister in Peking; when he imagines that thereby a check will be imposed on the Provincial Authorities; and when "his hope is, that the Central Government, once compelled to avow its cognizance of these burdens, will bestir itself to moderate the pressure which it now inclines to ignore, and this will be a first step towards the suppression of the war-tax, where there is no occasion for levying it:"—his Excellency shows but, that he is in perfect ignorance of the true state of the case. The returns in question most carefully prepared, are regularly sent up to Peking, and if the Board of Revenue were inclined to communicate them to Foreign Representatives, the latter need only apply for them. Mr. Wade is altogether under an erroneous impression, in stating to his Government that, "(wherever there is a centre of trade, trade becomes liable to taxation apparently without an appeal against the authority of the Provincial Government and without any other limit than the Provincial Government may see fit to prescribe; branch transit duty collectorates multiplying, and the tariff of each rising, of course, at the pleasure of the subordinate in charge." As I have already stated, imposition of taxes and their re-appropriation throughout the Empire is essentially regulated by the Board of Revenue. It is true that but a comparatively small proportion of the sum total, actually levied by the Government, is remitted to Peking for Imperial purposes: but this is simply a feature of the Chinese system of fiscal and financial administration, necessitated partly by the nature of the taxes, as paid in kind, partly by the vast extent of the Empire and its undeveloped means of communication. At the present time, the Imperial revenue, as distinguished from the revenue appropriated to Provincial wants, amounts, if I am well informed, to about £17,000,000; the Imperial expenditure to less than £15,000,000; and the accumulating annual surplus to something like £2,000,000 sterling.

I have already spoken of the second plea, advanced by Mr. Wade in support of the continuance, for at least years to come, of the *le-kin* tax,—the plea of "the weakness of the Central Government" of China. He states:—

The Central Government has not felt itself in a position to say to these (Provincial) Authorities:... You will not be allowed to resort to this measure or that...It is (this poverty of the exchequer, and) *this feebleness* of the Central Government, which also explain, though they do not excuse, the disregard of the transit duty clauses...Until the central power is better able than it believes itself to take the Provincial Governments in hand, we must not expect to see the amount of these (*le-kin*) taxes, now admittedly excessive, materially reduced.

The Central Government, though *not powerless, would* it but assert itself, has been scared by the bugbear of war expenditure from interference in provincial finance...I do not forget or unsay what I have earlier stated regarding the weakness and timidity of the Central Government; but I am not without hope that it may be *brought* to put forth *the power it certainly possesses*, in the manner I desire.

Considering, then, that Mr. Wade, though in contradiction with himself, here distinctly admits, that it is, not in the power but in the *will* to reduce or abrogate the *le-kin* taxes, that the Chinese Government is wanting, and that, in truth and reality, his Excellency quite agrees with me upon this point, I may leave it where it is. As to the alleged timidity of the Government to put forth its power, Mr. Wade, confounding the Chinese Government with Prince Kung, and investing him with the charge of a "Regency" which had no existence, remarks correctly, that this imagined

Regency, "except in the single act to which it owes its birth, has not been remarkable for vigour or boldness in the work of administration." The act alluded to is Prince Kung's *coup d'état* of 1861, by which he upset the Special Council of State, appointed by the late Emperor to assist his successor in the Government, and to some extent usurped that power himself. But his own turn came soon. In 1865, he was suddenly "removed from all his functions and no longer permitted to have a voice in public matters," ostensibly on account of his "having exhibited in the administration of affairs such favoritism and greediness for presents, such arrogance and grasping after power, that people are everywhere discussing his conduct," as we learn from the "Peking Gazette" for April 3, 1865. He was, however, soon restored to his title, and the presidency of "the Board for the General Control of Individual (Tributary) States' Affairs"—the Tsung-li Yamên,—and by Imperial Rescript of May 9, 1865, also to a place in the Privy Council and State Secretariate. In this Rescript it is said :—"At the audience held this day, Prince Kung, having been allowed to appear to return thanks for favours granted to him, prostrated himself to the ground, weeping bitterly, as if he had no way to conceal his mortification. We then personally admonished and warned him, and the Prince expressed himself to be deeply sensible of the grievous faults into which he had been led, and sincerely repentant and ashamed of his past conduct. It excited the utmost commiseration in Our heart." According to Mr. Wade, we should have to infer that it was "the Regency," *i.e.* Prince Kung himself, who thus reduced His Imperial Highness to the piteous state, into which he had fallen, and from which he has never again risen to his former position. Did "the Central Government" on that occasion evince any signs of timidity? Did it so, when, to say the least, it connived at the Plot of the Summer-Solstice of 1870, and took upon itself the responsibility of the Tientsin Massacre? Has it done so in firmly resisting European demands for further improvement and progress; in dictating the Tsung-li Yamên's "Missionary Despatch;" in setting international Treaties at defiance; and in openly preparing for war, offensive not defensive, against the West? Or, did Prince Kung, individually, betray any timidity in consigning the members of "the Regency," appointed by the late Emperor himself, and including two Princes of the blood Imperial,—his own—to the scaffold? Did he do so when, with a victorious British Army at the very gates of the Capital, he, in an official despatch, reproved the Representative of England, Lord Elgin, for using language unfit for *a subject* of "the One Autocrator of the World" to use? ¶ Overweening arrogance his Imperial Highness has shown but on too many occasions: timidity never; unless, perchance, on that memorable day when, soon after the Tientsin Massacre, Mr. Wade, then Her Britannic Majesty's Chargé d'Affaires, is reported, on the authority of Mr. Hart, to have "succeeded in frightening the Peking Government out of their wits."* It appears to me, that his Excellency would have rendered better service both to China and to England, had he succeeded in frightening the Tsung-li Ya-mên *into* its wits.

¶ The words of Prince Kung's despatch to Lord Elgin, dated the 27th September, 1860, are:—"The words in the despatch under acknowledgement regarding the attack on and destruction of the Capital, and the downfall of the Dynasty, are words which it is not fitting that *a subject* should use. Can it be right for the British Minister" [—I quote from Mr. Wade's translation, the original has undoubtedly "Messenger—"], "when declaring that he still entertains a desire for peace" [—*i. e.* peaceful submission—] "to employ them?"

* The Hongkong *Daily Press* as quoted in the *North-China Herald* for October 25, 1870.

Mr. Wade's third plea in favour of the *le-kin* tax is this:—"On the suggestions that it should be wholly, or even partially, suppressed, I shall offer but this additional remark, that, if we could drive the Chinese to admit that the present mode of levying the war tax is in breach of the Treaty, there is, in my belief, nothing to prevent them turning our flank by a change in its denomination. A house tax, shop tax, or corporation tax, would effect the same object, and press almost, if not quite, as grievously as the *le-kin* on our trade." Mr. Wade would seem to find some difficulty in dis-identifying himself from Chinese interests and tactics, and to entertain strange fiscal notions. Does his Excellency really fancy, that the burden of a tax lies in its denomination, and that there is no difference between a tax imposed upon Chinese houses, Chinese shops, or Chinese corporations, and a tax imposed upon British and Foreign manufacture? It seems hardly credible. Yet, when in another place he compares the *le-kin* with our income-tax at home, there can remain no doubt on the subject. Supposing, however, that the latter tax were levied under the name of "the national-wants-relieving tax:" would such a "change of denomination" afford any relief to the tax-payer? Or, suppose that, instead of an income-tax, a newly invented "war-tax" of from twenty to fifty per cent *ad valorem*, were, in violation of existing Treaty-stipulations, imposed on all French wines imported into England: would these two "modes" of raising *the same amount of revenue* to the English exchequer be identical in their "effects upon trade?" Would the English consumer of, and the English trader in, French wines think so? Would the French wine-grower and wine merchant be of the same opinion? Would the French Minister at the

Court of St. James' plead with his own Government in favour of the legality and the continuance of such a tax,—on the ground of old, poor, distracted Mother Britannia being hard up for funds, and that her home-made cider and holy water were, together with French wines, taxed at similar rates,—as we have seen the now British Minister in "the Capital of the Ching Empire Universal" plead to that end with his Government? And would the French Ministry have listened to fallacies so glaring and unprincipled, and said with the Gladstone administration :—Oh, its all right; and, were it not so, it would be manifestly both unjust and inexpedient to keep England to her Treaty-engagements, and interfere with her endeavours to destroy our trade, and simultaneously find therein the sinews for a new war with us?

Mr. Wade has not realised the fact, that the income-tax is, in principle at least, a *general* tax *i. e.* in its effects essentially a capitation-tax; that a house-tax is not necessarily so, but, as commonly understood, would fall on proprietors of houses only, as *a class* of the community; and that a shop- or corporation-tax would decidedly be a *class*-tax. Neither has he realised this second fact, that, the heavier the *general* Chinese taxation, the greater the chances for British and Foreign staple manufactures, on account of their comparative cheapness, to find a market in China. Suppose a Chinese family, resident at Sin-gan, the provincial capital of Shen-si, with a fixed income of Taels 1,000 or £300 sterling per annum, to expend for house-rent, say £40; taxes £20; indispensable articles for clothing (£60); other indispensables £150; luxuries and sundry expenses £30; suppose further a piece of English Grey Shirtings to cost at Sin-gan (inclusive of *le-kin*) eighteen shillings, a piece of home-made Shirtings of similar quality (on which no *le-kin* is paid) seventeen shillings, a piece of English woollen cloth (inclusive of *le-kin*) £9, and a piece of Russian cloth of similar quality £8. 10/–; † and lastly suppose, for the sake of simplicity of illustration, the wants of our Chinese family to necessitate the annual purchase of four pieces of cloth, and thirty pieces of cottons, the aggregate cost of which would, at the lowest market prices, just reach the sum of £60, allotted to the purpose. Why, is it not certain, that, under such circumstances, the cheaper home-made cottons and the Russian cloth will be bought, and that the English cloth and shirting will be excluded from the market by the *le-kin* tax? On the other hand, let us assume the *le-kin* tax to be removed from British manufactures in accordance with Treaty-stipulations, and, as Mr. Wade suggests, a corresponding additional tax to be imposed upon houses or in the general form of a capitation tax, whereby the house-rent of the Chinese family of our illustration will be raised from £40, say, to £52, or its quota of general contributions to the State from £20 to £32; whilst the price of English Grey Shirtings at Sin-gan will be reduced to about fourteen shillings a piece, and that of woollen cloth to about £7, not to speak of the probable increase in the cost of the home-made fabric, say only to seventeen shillings and six pence a piece. It is true, the Chinese consumer might still, retrenching his fund for luxuries and sundry expenses accordingly, choose to buy the *dearer* articles for clothing; but is there so much as the shadow of a probability that he will do so, and, with his house-rent or taxes increased by £12 annually, pay upwards of £60 for the very same Chinese- and Russian-manufactured goods, which, of British manufacture, he could purchase for

† Compare Art. iii. of the Russian Treaty of Peking, of November 14, 1860.

less than £50 ? ‡ Let the experiment only be made. Let Mr. Wade but persuade the Tsung-li Ya-mên of the truth of his fiscal theory, and induce "the Central Government" to "turn our flank," by relieving Foreign manufactures of *le-kin* and other illegal taxes, and imposing, in their stead, any Chinese house-, shop-, or corporation-taxes, it may think proper. I venture to anticipate that, so long as such manufactures are allowed, throughout China, to reach the hands of the native consumer, unenhanced in their fair market-price by other imposts than the stipulated import- and "transit"-duties, by Treaty payable to the Chinese Government: that both the native consumer and the foreign manufacturer will be equally grateful to his Excellency for his extraordinary wisdom and more extraordinary powers of persuasion.

Meantime, Mr. Wade's fancy, so fertile in resources and so inexhaustible in duplex views, proposes, on the one hand, facing Her Britannic Majesty's Board of Trade, "a strict enforcement of the transit-duty clauses of Article XXVIII. (of the Treaty of Tientsin) as it now stands,"—indeed, his Excellency would stand by *that Article* even "whether our transport of goods to or from the Treaty ports be placed under the foreign Inspectorate or no ;"—on the other hand, turning to the Chinese Provincial Governors, that, considering how little the Tariff protects our imports, it be abolished altogether, and "*carte blanche* in inland taxation be left to the Provinces,"—a measure which, he adds with a knowing glance towards his high mandarin friends, could

‡ The figures, here used for illustrative purposes, may appear to involve a considerable exaggeration ; but it must be remembered, that no direct trade has as yet been established with the capital of Shen-si, and that British manufactures, which may reach it through native channels, have to pay an accumulation of inland charges, probably far in excess of what I have assumed.

scarcely,—though he feels by no means sure it would not alarm the Central Government or rather the Court though the Tsung-li Yamên,—be *ill*-received by them. In other words, with the view of saving to British imports into China, on account of the bad faith of the Chinese Government, the stipulated Tariff-duty, the present Chief Superintendent of British Trade in China would see *that trade itself consigned to certain and speedy ruin* for the special advantage of the Provincial Governors. Suddenly facing round, therefore, to the British merchant, the "able," the "very able Minister" of Her Britannic Majesty's actual Government pours forth into his ear an abundance of *sympathy* with his "hard case." True, from a natural mandarin fellow-feeling, he looks upon the sale of official dignities in China, to which, —"the worst sign of the times,"—this dynasty, too, have recklessly recurred, as by far the most objectionable expedient for raising ill-applied funds, and "the other expedient"—I am quoting throughout Mr. Wade's own words almost literally,—extraordinary though it be, as of comparative little moment, nor so objectionable in its nature. Still, it is withal "over-burdensome in the degree, and vexatious in the method, of its employment," and what is so grievous to bear is this, that the war-tax never ceases; indeed, that, so far from abating, it seems always on the rise. Now, could there be a harder case than this? *Native* and foreigner are alike injured by the course pursued. Hence Mr. Wade's sympathy with the British merchant. He has not, however, as yet completed the circle. Turning, then, his countenance finally to "the Central Government" of China, whilst addressing his own, he observes:—"It may appear singular that, admitting as I do, the oppressiveness of the *le-kin* tax, the corruption and torpor which are responsible for its undue extension and ill-directed application, I should occupy myself at such length about the protection of revenue so collected and so applied. I have endeavoured to show that, however ill-gotten and ill-spent, these war-taxes are, and long will be, the main resource with which the Provincial Governments have to face, almost every one of them, an unusually heavy expenditure; and that, until the central power is better able than it believes itself, to take the Provincial Governments in hand, we must not expect to see the amount of these taxes, now admittedly excessive, materially reduced. *We must put up with them as an evil*, not incurable, but not soon or suddenly to be cured, and—turning towards Her Majesty's Government—"we must do our best to combat their influence upon our interests: first, by a strict exaction of our rights under the transit-duty clause, of which I would give up no part; and then"—resuming his previous position, and once more facing, with a significant smile, "the Central Power,"—"by certain supplementary concessions, which, *I think, the Chinese Government will not find it hard to yield.*"

There now remain for us, in this place, only the more important objections to consider, which have been urged against the unquestionable meaning of the so-called "transit-clauses" of the Treaty of Tientsin, as established by me in the previous section. The first point is, that the inland charges commutation-tax, stipulated by Art. xxviii. and Rule vii., is asserted to exempt from inland charges foreign merchandise from a port to a given mart, and native produce, destined for exportation abroad, from a mart to an open port, *in transitu* only. "The Certificate," the Inspector-General of Chinese Maritime Customs states, "is simply a

Transit certificate; it protects from *a Treaty port to a specified place*" (and *vice versâ*); "lapses on arrival at the place specified, and thereafter the goods, having once entered the stream of general Chinese trade, are liable to the incidence of local taxation."—"I hold," Mr. Wade writes, "that the transit duty, as defined by Treaty, once paid, the certificate, thereon granted, should clear the foreign payer's imports of transit dues to any inland market he may choose, or his exports purchased inland to any open port. But the certificate will not exempt the goods cleared under it from the *le-kin* or from any other tax, once they have become Chinese property." The British Board of Trade, also, submits, in very terse language, to the Foreign Office:—"My Lords (of the Committee of Privy Council for Trade) entertain no doubt that the view expressed in some of the Memorials, and even at one time by Sir R. Alcock himself, viz., that the payment of the transit dues ought to be held to exempt the goods, upon which it has been paid, from all subsequent internal taxation, and to insure the sale of the goods to their ultimate consumer with no enhancement of cost derived from taxation, save that represented by the import and transit duties, is a view which cannot be entertained by Her Majesty's Government. There is nothing in the terms of the treaty which appears to my Lords to justify such a sweeping demand, and in view of the internal taxation to which native goods are subject in China, it would be in their opinion both unjust and inexpedient to enforce such a demand, even if it were warranted by the terms of Treaty stipulations. All that Her Majesty's Government can claim in this respect, appears to my Lords to be, that in the Treaty ports, the importer shall have the right to sell his goods in the market, after payment of the Customs duties stipulated, and that he shall have the right to send goods to any internal market which he may select, free from any other charge than the Customs duty on importation, and the stipulated transit duty; but that both at the port, and at the internal market, when once the goods have passed out of his hands, they must take their chance in common with native goods, and bear whatever impositions the rapacity or necessities of Chinese administration may inflict."—What additional strength these views may, or may not, derive from the latest opinion of Sir Rutherford Alcock, I leave, after having expounded that opinion in a preceding page, for the reader to say.

Let us now, in the first place, consider what the views referred to, in practice, really imply, and, in order to bring the matter more closely home, assume that the commercial part of the Treaty of Tientsin has been negotiated between England and France, instead of between China and England. England has agreed to open the whole extent of the United Kingdom to French trade; allowing French merchants to import into certain sea-port towns French and other foreign merchandise on the payment, to the English Government, of certain fixed import-duties, and to have such goods conveyed, for sale, to any part of the Interior; also to export British produce and merchandise, bought inland, from the same sea-port towns, on the payment of certain fixed export-duties. And there being customarily levied in England upon inland trade, certain tolls and octrois, besides some newly imposed war- and other taxes, respecting the irregular and somewhat heavy rates of which there had arisen some difficulties previously, England has further agreed to commute the whole of these inland charges, in consideration of the payment, by France to the British Government, of a fixed tax in addition to both the stipulated import- and export-duties. Lastly, it has, on the part of the French plenipotentiary who framed the Treaty, been conceded in one of certain Rules of Trade subsequently appended to that Treaty, that the French merchant, desirous of sending foreign goods for sale or consumption inland, should specify the place or mart, to which he intended to have them conveyed; and that, after payment of the inland charges commutation-tax, a certificate, certifying this payment to have been duly made, and exempting the foreign goods "from all further inland charges whatsoever," shall be given by the proper English authorities, to accompany such goods in the form of a "transit-pass." And similarly so in regard to English produce or merchandise, to be conveyed from an inland mart to one of the Treaty ports for exportation abroad.

Assuming, I say, all these stipulations to have been solemnly agreed upon and embodied in an international Treaty,—and they are but a faithful transcript of the corresponding stipulations of the Treaty of Tientsin:—is there one member of the British Government, who could or would contest its obligations as regard the complete exemption of French imports, having duly paid the import-duties and commutation-tax, from all further inland taxation? Is there one English Customs official, who could or would misconstrue the sense and effect of a certificate, *in his own language designated as a receipt in full for all inland-taxes and imposts*, because, forsooth, the French, for want of a more convenient term, happened to style it a "transit"-certificate? And is there one rational Englishman, who could or would maintain that a pass, exempting *French merchandise* from all inland charges whatsoever, exempts them only "*in transitu*," say, from the London Custom-house to Cornhill E. C., or to

Regent street, or to Hampstead, or to Oxford, as the case may be, and that, once arrived at *the specified terminus* and passed out of French possession into *English hands*, it must take its chance in common with native goods, and bear whatever impositions the rapacity or the necessities of the English administration may, in the shape of inland "war"- and other taxes, inflict upon it? To make French *merchandise*, upon which the import duty and inland charges commutation-tax, stipulated by Treaty, had been duly paid, pay, *so long as that Treaty remains in force*, any tax whatever in addition to the Treaty-imposts, would not only constitute a flagrant breach of international faith: but involve, moreover, on the one hand, the truly pernicious doctrine, that such a breach of international faith is justifiable by any and every pretence of financial necessity, nay, by bare official rapacity; and, on the other hand, the more than absurd theory, that France, in concluding a commercial Treaty with England and agreeing to pay to the English Government certain duties and imposts upon her trade with the United Kingdom, had done so, not with a view to the sale of French merchandise, at a computable price promising to insure such a sale, to the British *consumer*, but with a view to the privilege of conveying it to an English *inland place*, to become the prey of English official and fiscal rapacity, or else to rot; not for the purpose of protecting from further imposts French *merchandise intended for sale to the English consumer*, but for the purpose of protecting from further imposts the *French possession* of such merchandise, *i. e.* to obstruct or rather *prevent* its sale to the British consumer, and to restrict its consumption to *French subjects resident in the Interior of the United Kingdom*. In short, if the doctrines and theories here under consideration were to prevail, international Treaties would become simply "a delusion and a snare"; and the sooner they be done away with altogether, the better.

But suppose the English Government, moreover, to be an overbearing, supercilious, and perfidious Government, hostile to France and bent on commercial isolation; suppose it to hold no direct intercourse with the French Ambassador in London, excluded from admittance to the Court of St. James, and to communicate with him only through a temporary "Commission for the General Control of the Affairs of France," which he imagines to be our "Foreign office;" suppose France to have concluded her commercial Treaty with this Commission, under the false impression of its identity with the British Government, and the Commission to have appended to the Treaty an improperseal, invalidating it as an international legal contract; and suppose the English Government, immediately after the signing of the Treaty, to have imposed upon trade *heavy additional inland charges* by raising the existing, and adding fresh, inland imposts under the designation of "war"- and other taxes, and relying on the unacquaintance of the French merchants with the English language and other circumstances, to have surreptitiously ordered these "overburdensome" taxes to be levied ostensibly upon inland trade in general, but virtually and more especially upon *French* inland trade, *with the twofold view of gradually ruining that trade, and meanwhile deriving from it the ways and means to arm, and defray the expenditure of an early-to-be-renewed war with France.* Lastly, suppose the community of French merchants in, and trading with England, to have called the attention of the French Government to this state of matters; suppose the French Government to have consulted its Representative in London, and the first Secretary of the Embassy,—famed for his English scholarship, his intimate acquaintance with the members of the English "Commission for the General Control of the Affairs of France," and his knowledge of England generally,—happening at the time to be on leave of absence in Paris; suppose the French Secretary to have submitted to his Government views analogous to those which were by Mr. Wade submitted to the British Government upon an analogous question; suppose him, on the strength of those views, to have been appointed to the post of French Ambassador in London; suppose the French Government to have, through the Foreign Office, told the community of French merchants in, and trading with, England,—who, *on their faith in the Treaty concluded between England and France*, have invested millions of money in French Wines which, *solely owing to the heavy and illegal inland taxes, levied upon them by the English Government in violation of Treaty-stipulations*, they cannot sell in England except at a loss, and millions of money in British coal and iron which, for the same reason, they cannot dispose of in France save at a ruinous price,—that "the French Government entertains no doubt that the view expressed by the merchants and at one time by the former Ambassador of France in London himself, viz., that the payment of the inland charges commutation-tax ought to be held to exempt the goods, upon which it has been paid, from all further inland taxation, is a view which cannot be entertained by the French Government, there being nothing in the terms of the Treaty, which appears to the Government of France to justify *such a sweeping demand*, and that *all* the French Government can claim from the Government of England is, that the English administration continue to inflict on French inland trade whatever impositions its rapacity or its necessities may judge *à propos* ;" and suppose the former Ambassador of France in London, distinguished for his versatility and duplicity of view, to have decided that " the High Contracting Parties, the British and French Governments, are the only competent authorities to agree upon the meaning and purport of a Treaty, and that their joint decision is without appeal."

Supposing, again, all this, I ask: What an opinion would all honorable Englishmen have to form of the assumed action of the British Government? What a view would all fair and rationally-thinking Englishmen have to take of the supposed conduct of the French Government, and its supposed former and actual Representatives in London? And must not the members of the English Government, such as I have assumed to be its character, needs be concluded to have chuckled to their heart's content over the credulity, blindness, and infatuation of the supposed French Ministry and its Representatives? Now, this is precisely what the members of the Chinese Government and the Tsung-li Ya-mên *are* doing: in secret they chuckle over the credulity, blindness, and infatuation of the British Board of Trade and the distinguished sinologue in whom it places so unbounded a political reliance; they marvel at, and deride, the inconsistency of Sir Rutherford Alcock; they rejoice equally in their own superiority and cunning, and the spoil, which they and their provincial fellow-mandarins are accumulating from the inland trade of the British and foreign merchant; and whilst they thus triumph, in secret for the present, they grudge not to devote a large portion of their plunder to the support of the Government for the purpose of warlike preparations, and look forward, with impatience, to the time when, having cleared the polluted, "bayonet-ploughed soil of Cathay" from the hated presence of "the outer barbarian," they may triumph in the full light of day.

Speaking with the utmost deference of the Lords of the Committee of Her Britannic Majesty's Privy Council for Trade, I cannot help thinking that their Lordships, instead of investigating the question under consideration for themsemselves and using their own judgment, have allowed themselves to be led, without due consideration, to adopt the peculiar, ill-matured, and strongly biassed views of Mr. Wade, "with whom, in accordance with Lord Clarendon's suggestion, they conferred on this subject." Indeed, the opinions expressed by them are but a literal re-echo of the opinions of the present British Representative at Peking and Chief Superintendent of British Trade in China. And if I be not mistaken in this, the "*in transitu*"-interpretation, forced upon ART. xxviii. of the Treaty of Tientsin and RULE vii. of the appended Trade Rules, is in reality the exclusive interpretation of Mr. Wade and the Foreign Inspector-General of Chinese Maritime Customs, Mr. Hart. His Excellency, it is true, contends that Lord Elgin himself placed the same construction upon the Tientsin Treaty; but such a statement is hardly reconcileable with Lord Elgin's own clear words :—

Mr. Wade, in his Memorandum to H. M. Government of Dec. 1868.	*Lord Elgin in his despatch to the Foreign Office of Nov. 8, 1858.*
"Lord Elgin, *I am certain*, did not look for more than the protection, *in transitu*, of certificated goods... Lord Elgin did hope that imports so certificated, might not only be carried by *travellers (!)* from one centre of traffic to another, but dis-	"Henceforward, on payment of a sum in *name* of transit-duty,... *goods*, whether of export or import, will be free to pass between the port of shipment or entry *to or from any part of China*, without farther charge of toll, octroi, *or tax of any descrip-*

posed of in parcels along the line" — [this would have been in diametrical opposition to the provisions of Rule vii.] —"an order of proceeding not impossible in quieter times; but I remember his Lordship expressly stating, that he did not see his way to the further protection of imports against taxation once they had passed into the hands of a Chinese purchaser. They must then, said he, take their chance."

Mr. Wade, at a Meeting in Shanghai on Nov. 16, 1869.

"Mr. Wade rose and said, that he *could* not be mistaken as to Lord Elgin's intention, which was to avoid taking under British jurisdiction, or interfering with, Chinese subjects or Chinese property."||

tion whatsoever. I confess that I consider this a *most important* point gained in the future interest of foreign trade with China...I have always thought that the remedy (against the grievance pressed upon me by mercantile bodies or individuals since I came to China), was to be sought in *the substitution* of one fixed payment for the present *irregular and multiplied levies;*...(although) it was obviously difficult to devise a scheme for *the commutation* of transit [*i. e.* inland] duties which without creating great financial disturbance, *should prove an effectual protection to the importing and exporting merchants.*"

On comparing these passages, it appears to me manifest, that Mr. Wade's memory as to Lord Elgin's *intentions* must be at fault, and that his reminiscences and impressions, after a lapse of ten years and more, cannot be placed in the balance against his Lordship's clear, positive, and contemporaneous *written testimony.* The British Plenipotentiary's conviction was, that he had protected, and effectually protected British and foreign *merchandise,* intended for sale or consumption in China, and Chinese *merchandise* intended for exportation abroad by British (and foreign) subjects, in consideration of the payment of fixed and specified duties, from all further charge of "toll, octroi, or tax of any description whatsoever." An imbecile alone can be supposed to have meant such an effectual protection to constitute and afford no protection at all; *i. e.* to protect simply "*in transitu* from

|| The *North-China Herald* for Nov. 8, 1871.

a Treaty-port to a specified inland place," (and *vice versâ*), in order that the goods, once conveyed into the Interior, might the more certainly become a prey to Chinese rapacity. Lord Elgin was inferior to few men in power of intellect, perspicuity, and practical common-sense. He may have had his *misgivings* as to the action of the cunning and deceitful Chinese Government; but that he *meant* to, and by Treaty *did*, "insure the sale of British and foreign goods to their ultimate consumer in China, with no enhancement of cost derived from direct taxation, save that represented by the import-duties and inland charges commutation-tax," is a fact, which admits not even of the shadow of a doubt.

The best additional comment, perhaps, I can offer on Mr. Wade's differing view, are his own words. "The foreigner," he states in his frequently cited Memorandum, "pays on his imports about 5 per cent. in the shape of Tariff duties, not for the mere privilege of housing them on his premises, but, as it was believed, to enable him to sell them free of farther charges on all ground between his port and the inland Custom-houses nearest the port; and for passing them inland of these barriers he should pay 2½ per cent. upon value in addition to the Tariff duty. Yet he finds at Amoy, for example, that charges of one kind or another range from 5 to 90 per cent. upon value, and his imports are consequently unsaleable. If the Tariff protects imports so little, why not abolish the import Tariff?"

There remains, thus, as the only authority for, and apparently the first originator of, our "*in transitu*" construction, the Foreign Inspector-General of Chinese Maritime Customs, Mr. Hart. Unfortunately, however, for him and his followers, their interpretation, though still upheld by Mr. Hart in his anonymous memorandum of November 1, 1871, had long previously been disavowed by his own immediate native superiors. For, I have already shown that, in October 1862, the Tsung-li Ya-mên, as well as the then Governor-General of 'Hu-kuang, Kuan-Wên, and again, in November 1868, Tsêng Kuo-Fan, in his capacity of Superintendent of Trade, freely admitted that, by the Treaty of Tientsin, the war-taxes (*le-kin*, *chow-fang*, etc.),—the only taxes upon foreign inland trade levied by the Chinese Government and complained of by the British and Foreign merchant,—are, and were meant to be, included in the inland charges commutation-tax or the so-called "transit"-dues, agreed upon and fixed by Art. xxviii. of the Treaty and Rule vii. of the appended Trade Rules, and that consequently, those "war"- and all other inland taxes, in so far as in the aggregate they exceed the said commutation-tax, have been, and are being, levied upon foreign inland trade in China, *illegally and in violation of Treaty-stipulations.* To leave, however, no manner of doubt on this point, I will quote from Tsêng Kuo-Fan's despatch of Nov. 5, 1868, the following passages:—

"Thus it is evident that foreign goods entering the Interior, whether in the hands of Chinese or foreign merchants, when accompanied by a certificate that the half-duty has been paid, then no further tax or *le-kin* shall be levied on them. If it be argued that, were Chinese merchants, having purchased foreign merchandise accompanied by a certificate that the half duty has been paid, not to pay the *le-kin* also, they would defraud the revenue:—this (latter tax) is a regulation of the *le-kin* barriers; but is by no means a Treaty stipulation....It is imperative to act in accordance with Treaty-stipulations, and on no account must the *le-kin* be made to violate existing Treaties, and provoke constant disputes with the Consuls. To this end I have written to the Customs, (instructing them) to act accordingly."§ This passage alone, it appears to me, should have sufficed to settle, as it does settle, the entire question.

The second point, however, to which I have alluded, consists in the argument, that the Chinese Government possess *the legal right* to impose upon foreign merchandise, the moment it has become Chinese property, whatever imposts it may judge fit; and that the English Government is not entitled to interfere in the internal administration of the Chinese Empire. Now, I as loyally accept the latter, as I emphatically reject the former, proposition. There absolutely exists no connection between the two. Mr. Wade and others, in muddling them up together and impressing the British Board of Trade with their own confused ideas, have created a difficulty of a purely imaginary character. Sir Frederick Bruce would seem to have given the occasion for the misconception. In speaking of "RULE 7, which was substituted for Art. XXVIII. of the Treaty of Tientsin," he remarks in a despatch, dated December 2, 1862, to the Foreign Office:—"I conceive that most embarrassing questions will be avoided by adhering strictly

§ The corresponding original text reads:—

是洋貨入內地無論華商洋商但執有半稅單均不得再征厘稅若謂華商販運洋貨執有半稅單若不交厘卽屬影射偷漏 此係厘卡章程並非條約所載…須按約辦理斷不可因厘背約徒啟領事爭論等因札關移行遵辦.—I may just remark, that the translator of the despatch, as printed in "the *North-China Herald*" for August 18, 1871, has altogether mistaken the sense of one of the paragraphs, and rendered it unintelligible. What he translates: "with reference to foreign merchants, purchasing foreign goods for an interior market, the gist of it consists in two points," should read: "as to foreign merchants, who enter the Interior to sell, themselves, foreign merchandise, and [for the supposed purpose of evading *all* "transit" duties] lay stress on there being two alternatives, it is thus:"—"if the foreign merchant should prefer not to pay the half-duty at the sea-port, then he must pay it as well as the *le-(kin)* tax at the inland barriers; if he be unwilling to pay the charges inland, then he must pay the half-duty in advance. Herein he has his choice."

to it. The object of the Rule was to substitute one unvarying charge for the arbitrary exactions of provincial authorities, where Her Majesty's subjects bought or sold goods in the interior. *But it was not intended to interfere between the Chinese Government and its own subjects.*" Again, in a later despatch of April 30, 1863, he observes in reference to the publication of a certain letter :—"It has done good by clearing up the misapprehension that prevailed as to the real position of foreigners at the Chinese ports open to trade, and as evidence that Her Majesty's Government will not agree to any system, which does not respect the *territorial* rights of the Chinese Government, and its exclusive *jurisdiction over its own subjects.* This exclusive jurisdiction of China over Chinese, and of each foreign nation over its subjects, is the foundation on which the international relations of China with the outer world is based." Sir Frederick Bruce's view, however, is explained by his despatch to Mr. Medhurst, H.M.'s Consul at Shanghai, of November 5, 1862, which I have had previously occasion to transcribe, and from which it will be seen, that the essential condition of the decision, then given by the British Representative in Peking, was, that the taxes, which in his opinion the Tau-tai, as an official of the Chinese Government, was entitled to levy on Chinese subjects even "within the limits of the so-called British Concession," be "taxes imposed on *persons* resident in the Concession, and paid by those living in the (Chinese) city and suburb." Now, this is the point which has escaped the attention of Sir Rutherford Alcock, Mr. Wade, and others, who refer to the opinion of Sir Frederick Bruce in support of their own untenable views. There is just the same difference between the right of the Chinese Government to tax the persons of Chinese subjects, to tax whom it possesses, or assumes to possess the limitless right, and its right to tax *British Merchandise* imported into China for sale or consumption under Treaty-stipulations, and to tax which beyond fixed limit it has by international Treaties, recognised to be as binding as the Laws of the Empire themselves, positively waived the right,—as there is between a Chinaman and a bale of English shirting ; and to protect the latter from unlawful spoliation by the Chinese Government and its officials, is no more to interfere between the Chinese Government and the former, his property, and his duties as a subject, than to lawfully defend one's own is to commit a crime. Yet, Mr. Wade, in his Memorandum of December 1868, states in regard to *le-kin* :— "this impost, although in its excessive degree objectionable, is not in is nature more open to objection than our own income-tax, nor, indeed, than any extraordinary tax, by which a State short of money may recruit its finances... The merchants conceive that transit dues and *le-kin* are identical... I have laboured at great length to show, that the *le-kin* and the transit dues are, so far as we are concerned, imposts of a totally different character ; that we may fight any augmentation of the latter by Treaty, but that the Treaty will not help us against the *le-kin*." And at the Meeting in Shanghai, on November 16, 1869, *en route* from England to Peking as Chargé d'Affaires, he is reported to have said :—" Lord Elgin's intention was to avoid taking under British jurisdiction, or interfering with, Chinese subjects or Chinese property. This is the keynote to the whole question. There was at the time a political objection to unnecessary interference, and although the fears that then existed may be shown to be groundless, it is by no means certain that the British Government are even now prepared to accept a concession that may leave them, if it is to be effective, no alternative but to force the local authorities to forego the taxation of their own subjects. Whilst the imports continue British property, the aggrieved have a *locus standi* with the British Consul and the British Minister, but when the goods pass into Chinese hands, we must trust in great measure to the strictness, with which the Peking Government hold in check the taxing propensities of their subordinates."

On analysing these passages, we find: *1*,—that his Excellency appears unable to, and does not, distinguish between a *capitation*-tax, lawfully levied by the British Government upon *British subjects*, and a tax upon *foreign goods*, unlawfully levied,—supposedly here by the British Government also,—in violation of the Treaty-rights of the foreign Power, by whose subjects those goods had been, under the guarantee of international Treaty-stipulations, imported into England; *2*,—that his Excellency, by implication, advances and maintains the doctrine, that financial difficulties at any time justify and warrant a State to violate, and repudiate, in any manner it may think proper, the international obligations which, by solemn Treaty, it has engaged to observe and keep towards other States; *3*,—that his Excellency holds the British merchant to be so dull and inconsistent, as to cry against "*Illegal* Exactions in the Interior" and "Local Taxes *in excess of* Tariff Duties,"¶ on the ground of their identity with the *legal* "transit-dues," as commuted by

¶ The very contrary, I need hardly say, is the case. See *f.i.* the Shanghai, Hongkong, and other "Memorials, addressed to H.E. the British Minister at Peking, on the approaching Revision of the Treaty of Tientsin, and Sir Rutherford Alcock's Reply," Shanghai, 1868, 8°.

Treaty;* *4*,—that his Excellency is seemingly unable to, and does not, see that, in arguing the "totally different character" of the *le-kin* imposts from the unquestionably *legal* character of the "transit"- or inland charges commutation-tax, he argues the *illegal* character of the former; *5*,—that his Excellency, from a manifest confusion of his own ideas, conceives that, when a fixed inland tax upon merchandise is doubled and trebled by further inland taxes, *differently denominated*, upon the same merchandise, this constitutes *no augmentation of the said inland tax*,—by Treaty, moreover, stipulated and fixed to include all inland taxes whatsoever; *6*,—that his Excellency is of opinion, that an international Treaty is of no use or avail against infractions and violations of the provisions of such a Treaty; *7*,—that his Excellency,—if his words have been correctly reported†—looks upon the due fulfilment of Treaty-stipulations on the part of the Chinese Government, and its desisting from the illegal taxation of British merchandise, as *a concession* made or offered by the Chinese to the British Government, and which Her Britannic Majesty's present Advisers may by no means be prepared to accept; *8*,—that his Excellency appears to entertain so exalted an opinion of "the local (Chinese) authorities"—the Provincial Governors, I presume,—as to look upon the Emperor's subjects as their own; and *9*,—that his Excellency is unaware of the fact, that the increased rates of *le-kin* and other unlawful taxes upon British and foreign merchandise were imposed, immediately after

* Mr. Wade, elsewhere, too, sneers at "those, who should know their own business," viz., the body of foreign merchants in China; and assumes an air of superiority in knowledge over them, to which his Memorandum presents so striking and remarkable a contrast.

† They are quoted by me on the authority of Mr. J. Barr Robertson,—who was present at the meeting in question,—from his letter to "*The North China Herald*," dated November 6, 1871, and published in No. 236 of that journal.

the ratification of the Tientsin Treaty, not by "the subordinates of the Peking Government," but by the Chinese Government itself.

Mr. Wade's "Key-note to the whole question" clearly emits a false and very discordant sound. The question is simply one of *mutual Treaty obligations, binding the two Governments of England and China.* Both Governments should solely keep these obligations in view; observe and respect them; and cause them to be observed and respected by their subjects, mutually. In a general sense no other duties devolve on either Government from existing Treaty-obligations. That the English Government has no more the right to "take under British jurisdiction, or interfere with Chinese subjects or Chinese property" *in China*, than the Chinese Government has the right to "take under Chinese jurisdiction, or interfere with, British subjects or British property" *in England*, is no Article of Treaty-agreement, but a maxim of International Law. *In England*, Chinese subjects and Chinese property are as much under British jurisdiction, as are British property and British subjects themselves. And properly so: because English Law and Justice protect both equally. *In China*, British subjects and British property have, by Treaty, been withdrawn from Chinese jurisdiction. And properly so: because the Chinese Government is a semi-barbarous Government, and Chinese Law and Justice afford neither protection to foreign property, nor security to the foreigner's life. Is there any one personally acquainted with the condition of China and her most recent history, who will contest the absolute necessity continuing to exist for this state of "exterritoriality," as it is usually designated? That very necessity, universally recognised, imposes on the English Government even a more rigid observance of its special duties, involved in the Treaty of Tientsin, than might otherwise be the case. Hence, certainly, on the one hand it should not only carefully abstain, itself, from any interference, practically, between the Chinese Government and its subjects, their duties, and their property, but should interdict also the maudlin bias of its pro-Chinese functionaries from indulging in such an interference in theory,—assuming the form of Memoranda and Despatches of "immense length," and tending to blind the British Government as to the true state of matters, to mislead public opinion, and to throw confusion and perplexity into a subject of itself perfectly simple and clear. But, on the other hand, too, the British Government should, so long as the Treaty of Tientsin remains in force, firmly and consistently uphold its provisions,‡ see them upheld, and, in accordance with them, insure effective protection to British subjects and *their* property, invested in China, it cannot be too often repeated, on the faith of those provisions, from the lawless rapacity of the Chinese Government and of Chinese officials. A clearer, and under existing circumstances more imperative, duty no Government could have to perform; and in performing it by insisting upon the due observance, by the Chinese Government, of Treaty-obligations solemnly entered into, and, to use the words

‡ Lord Clarendon, the British Secretary of State for Foreign affairs, in his despatch of December 28, 1868 to the late Mr. Burlingame, as "envoy of Chinese empire," while assuring him of "the friendly feelings entertained towards the Government of Peking by the British Government," insists :—"But Her Majesty's Government, I said, expects from China faithful observance of the stipulations of existing treaties;" and in the Queen's speech from the throne, on the prorogation of Parliament on August 7, 1874, Her Britannic Majesty states :—"My relations with all foreign Powers continue to be friendly, and the influence of those cordial relations will be employed, as heretofore, in maintaining the obligations imposed by Treaties."

Upon the Government of China, the influence of friendly feeling and "cordial relations," an already too long experience has shown to produce only the opposite results expected from them; and it is to be hoped, therefore, that the present British Administration may be disposed to reconsider, without much farther delay, a policy that has tended towards

of Mr. Wade, its "holding in check the taxing propensities of its subordinates," the English Government would no more interfere between the Chinese Government and its subjects, than, by doing so, it would exceed its public duty to itself and the community of British merchants in, and trading with, China *on their faith in existing Treaties.*

Mr. Wade, however, still contends that the course just indicated, "if it is to be effective, might leave Her Majesty's Government no alternative but to force the Chinese local authorities to forego the taxation of their own subjects;" in other words, to *interfere*, if necessary by force of arms, between "the Central Government" and its subjects, the Provincial Governors. And this leads me to a consideration of the third and last point, to which I have previously alluded, namely, the question of *expediency.* "It would be in the opinion of my Lords," the Secretary of the British Board of Trade writes to the Foreign Office, "both unjust and *inexpedient* to enforce such a demand" (the abrogation of the *le-kin* impost on British merchandise, upon which the stipulated commutation-tax has been paid), "even if it were warranted by the terms of Treaty stipulations." Mr. Wade's argument hardly calls for any farther notice. A bale of English shirting, as I have once before had occasion to observe, is not a "Chinese subject." With Chinese subjects and their taxation or that of their property by the Chinese Government, Her Britannic Majesty's Government has no concern whatever. It is nei-

the ruin of British trade with China, and has brought England to the verge of another war with the Government of Peking,—a war, which, should it unhappily become inevitable, will involve, on the part of England, the greater sacrifices in human life and treasure, the longer it is delayed. In my humble opinion, it may yet be averted by a policy of firmness, decision, and *action.* A most important and effective measure in this sense, would undoubtedly prove the annexation of Burmah to the Indian Empire of Great Britain

ther one of the Chinese Government Boards, nor in charge of the Chinese Police Administration. Its sole concern is with the Imperial Government of China, the provisions of existing Treaties between the two countries, and their due fulfilment, here in regard to *British merchandise, over-taxed in violation of those Treaty-provisions.* This, and this alone, is the question. It requires no key-note. That the Chinese Government possesses, if it had but the *will* to exert, the power to "check the taxing propensities of its subordinates," Mr. Wade, as we have previously seen, himself admits. Nor will "the Central Government, of course, avow," he tells us, "that feebleness," to which his Excellency, one of the most eminent of the "foreign physicians of this ailing Power," is determined "*nolens volens*" to reduce its strength. And in the Minute of a Meeting of the Mixed Commission on the Revision of the Treaty of Tientsin, on June 5, 1868, we read:—"On the first point, the abolition of all taxes upon foreign export and import trade within thirty *li* of the Custom-house, the Chinese Commissioners refused to supplement the system of transit-passes already in force, *declaring that nothing better could be invented.* It was replied that the scheme had in effect seemed well adapted, but had fallen through by the unwillingness of the local Mandarins to understand and carry it out, and they were asked *whether they were prepared to force their officials to do so.* They answered: *Yes;* the passes had failed by the fault of the merchants, and the separation of the goods from the passes; but they were prepared to have issued and published an Imperial Proclamation, setting forth proper penalties for any infraction of the existing Treaty Rules for the taxation of goods forming part of foreign trade. They were asked, whether this had not already been done? and said: No.|| It is, therefore, simply a fact, that the levying in China of inland duties upon British and Foreign Merchandise—whether such merchandise be in the hands of British and Foreign or Chinese subjects,—in excess of the inland charges commutation-tax, is a positive violation of the Treaty of Tientsin, and by the Tsung-li Ya-mên and high Chinese Officials *acknowledged to be so*; that such illegal duties, to an "over-burdensome" extent, are levied upon British and Foreign merchandise, having paid the stipulated inland commutation-tax, systematically, and by order of the Chinese Government; and that the Chinese Government, (supported by Her Britannic Majesty's present representative in Peking, and Chief Superintendent of British Trade in China), persist in continuing to levy them, not because it wants the power, but because it wants the *will*, to fulfil its Treaty-obligations.

After Sir Rutherford Alcock had *à priori* insured the failure of the Revision of the Treaty of Tientsin, by entrusting the preliminary negociations on the part of England solely to the incompetency of Mr. Hugh Fraser, Second Secretary of Legation, and allowing, on the part of China, the Foreign Inspector-General of Chinese Maritime Customs, Mr. Hart, to sit on the Committee together with five experienced native Officials, and that failure, to all intents and purposes, had once become a *fait accompli*: it was, possibly, a matter of sound expediency for the Lords of the Committee of Her Britannic Majesty's Privy Council for Trade, "under existing circumstances to recommend for the consideration of

|| The sequel reads:—"They (the Chinese Commissioners) were then told, that it had been the duty of the Chinese Government to publish such obligations effectively, and that the *proposed* Proclamation, if effective now, would have been equally so *then*." It was Mr. Hugh Fraser, Secretary of Legation and only English member of the Revision-Committee, who spoke thus, and wrote as he had spoken.

Her Majesty's Government, to endeavour to arrive at an understanding with the Government of China, by which the formal revision of the Treaty might be deferred until the majority of the Emperor, which Sir R. Alcock stated would take place in 1872 or 1873." § But, that their Lordships, although under the influence of Mr. Wade's representations and strongly-pronounced pro-Chinese bias, yet manifestly *doubtful* as to the true position of the "transit-question," should have unconditionally submitted to the British Government in reference to the demand of British merchants for relief from illegal taxation in China, that "it would be in their opinion both unjust and inexpedient to enforce such a demand, even if it *were* warranted by the terms of Treaty-stipulations," appears to me almost in the light of an infatuation. I will say nothing of the utter inexpediency, in Western relations with such a Government as the Chinese,¶ to recede a single step from a position once deliberately taken up, or to waive a single point of rights once legally acquired by Treaty; nor of the striking fact that, whilst full of solici-

§ It is characteristic of Sir Rutherford Alcock and the manner in which British Diplomacy is being conducted in China, that an English Minister, who had for years resided in Peking, should have been as vaguely informed, as was the general foreign public, of the important date of the epoch of the late Emperor's majority,—a date and an event to which "one third of the human race" looked forward with anxious expectation, and upon which, for England, might have turned the question of continued peace, or a new war, with a great and distant Empire.

¶ Even Mr. Hart, in his "Note on Chinese Matters" states :—"However advanced the Chinese may be in civilization, it is not to be forgotten that their civilization is not a Christian civilization; they are Asiatics, too, and there is a pride of race about them that leads them to tread upon the neck that bends, rather than to lift the head that touches the dust, when its owner is an alien.

"It is the keen-sighted policy that will not permit shuffling—the just policy that will not claim what it has not a right to—the firm policy that will not retract from a demand once made—and the personal policy which bases its just requirements on its own, and does not argue for their satisfaction from the point of view of Chinese interests, that will be most likely to command success; any winking at obligations neglected—any claiming of what cannot fairly be laid claim to—any retreating from a position taken up—and any advocacy of measures as favoring Chinese rather than foreign interests, only tend to cause misunderstanding, breed wrangling, invite insult, arouse suspicion, and evoke an unexpressed, but action-inspiring scorn."

tude for justice to the Chinese, the idea of justice to the British merchant would seem not to have occurred to their Lordships' mind. But had their Lordships, indeed, "carefully considered" the true import and wider significance of their words? They could only mean this: that Her Britannic Majesty's Government should be prepared to inform the country, that the national policy in China, pursued by Lord Palmerston,—a policy which extended the commerce, the industry, the prosperity, and the power of England, and caused the British name to be respected from one extremity of the Ta Ching Empire to the other,—was a *false* policy, which the Rt. Hon. W. E. Gladstone considered it "expedient" to reverse; and that the two Chinese wars, undertaken by England with the view of breaking through that system of isolation by which, in opposition to the wishes of the Chinese people, its overweening and semi-barbarous Tatar Government was, and to this day is, striving to exclude "one third of the human race" from intercourse with the rest of God's world, and of effectually opening up the vast Empire of the Manchu usurper to the legitimate commerce of the West, were *unjust* wars, in which English blood and treasure have been expended to an unholy end, and which Her Britannic Majesty's late Administration felt it to be their Christian duty to expiate by again resigning the commercial Treaty-rights, secured by those wars, into the hands of the "Imperially appointed Commission for the General Control of Individual (Tributary) States' Affairs," through which "the One Autocrator of the World" condescends to communicate with "His Loyal Eng Principality,"* and by surrendering

* Thus, as has been already observed, England was designated in the body of the Letter of Credence, presented from "the Great Exalted Monarch and Highpriest of the Great Ching Empire of the World" to "the Great Lady" (the Queen of Great Britain and

British and foreign trade with the Interior of China to "whatever impositions the rapacity or necessities of Chinese administration may inflict upon it." Were Her Britannic Majesty's late Advisers, in accordance with the opinion expressed by the Lords of the Committee of Privy Council for Trade, to avow less than what I have just stated, they would but disavow the true import and bearing of their China policy of "Justice and Expediency." Can their Lordships be doubtful as to the view, which Parliament and the People of England,—for, despite of Sir Rutherford Alcock's latest theory, there exist as yet such Powers,—will take of that policy? †

Ireland) "of the Great Eng State" (England as one of the "Ten-thousand" Tributary States of the Ching Empire Universal).

† This was written before the fall of the Gladstone Ministry and the accession of the conservative party to power.

VI.

PRACTICAL WORKING OF THE TRANSIT-SYSTEM.

Alleged abuse of Treaty-provisions on the part of Foreign merchants—Sale of Transit-certificates, in 1866, at Ningpo—The Commissioner of Customs' unfair statement of the case—The Foreign Custom-house responsible for the practice of Discrepancies in the open infringement of Customs' rules—Customs' Revenue—Fines and Confiscations—The Chinese Customs, Mr. Wade, and the British Merchant—Tendency of British Representatives in Peking to favor the Chinese—History of a confiscation-case—How the British Merchant in China is protected by the British Minister—Disadvantages, under which foreign merchants are placed touching the payment of *le-kin*—The Tsung-li Ya-mên's "own Hart"—First-fruits of Mr. Hart's appointment—The Ya-mên proposes new regulations respecting trade on the river Yang-tze, the Transit-System, and the Coast-Trade—Sir Frederick Bruce's Notification of his "Revised Provisional Regulations for British Trade on the Yangtze River," and "Regulations (sanctioned by Mr. Bruce) regarding Transit-Dues, Exemption Certificates, and Coast Trade Duties"—Promulgation of corresponding documents by the Tsung-li Ya-mên—Sir Frederick Bruce represented as in the Service of China—The Ya-mên's proposed "Five Regulations respecting War-Taxes payable at inland stations, Coast-Trade Duties, and Exemption Certificates" apparently withheld from the knowledge of the British Government—Essential discrepancies between the English text of Sir Frederick Bruce's "Regulations regarding Transit-Dues," etc., and Mr. Wade's Chinese version, as officially published by the Tsung-li Ya-mên—The latter grants to China the unrestricted imposition of *le-kin*—Both the English text and the Chinese version violate Treaty-provisions and mislead the mercantile community—Imperative necessity for an explanation on Mr. Wade's part—"T'u's five Rules"—Attempt, made by the Native Intendant, and Foreign Commissioner, of Customs at Shanghai, to place the Transit-System on a new basis—Tsêng Kuo-Fan's despatch of Nov. 5, 1868, to the Shanghai Customs Authorities—Responsibilities incurred by the Inspector-General and the Shanghai Commissioner of Customs—"A new and valuable Chinese Concession"—The Transit-dues question, and the local Press.

The next element of the subject under discussion, which now remains for me to consider, is the practical manner, in which the provisions of the Treaty of Tientsin relative to British and Foreign trade with the Interior of China have been carried out, both on the one side and the other. The Tsung-li Ya-mên's earlier despatches abound in complaints or rather recriminations as to infringements or abuses of Treaty-provisions on the merchants' part. Those complaints have now, so far as my knowledge goes, altogether ceased.‡ But Mr. Wade, on imaginary grounds, continues to look with a kind of shudder at the "unclean hands" of his countrymen, *possibly* intent on defrauding, at some future time, the Ta Ching revenue by false certificates, throughout the Empire; and, these alarming anticipations of his morbid philosinensic fancy having communicated themselves to the British Board of Trade, their Lordships state in all seriousness:—"It has also to be remembered, that the imperfect execution of the Treaty of Tientsin in this particular (the imposition of *le-kin*) is due not alone to the weakness or inaction of the Chinese Government, but also to the fraudulent evasion by British merchants of the obligations and conditions which it imposed. My Lords refer to the sale of transit certifi-

‡ An exceptional charge, however, has recently again been preferred by the Acting Commissioner of Customs at Chinkiang, Mr. G. Detring, whose ultra zeal I have had occasion to notice elsewhere. Attempting to be sarcastic, if not witty, he writes in the "Customs Gazette" for October—December, 1871, p. 45, as follows:—"The Transit Pass Trade, or rather the trade under Transit Pass, has flourished more than ever. During the year 17,750 Passes were issued (against 10,059 in 1870) for the conveyance of foreign produce to the interior, and 880 Passes for the conveyance of native produce to this port. It will be remarked that hardly one third of the produce thus brought to Chinkiang under Transit Pass appears in the Export Tables. It being mostly intended for local consumption, the produce is bought, owned and sold by natives, *to whom foreigners continue selling outward Passes to the detriment of the inland Revenue.* There is, however, no case on record, where the validity of these outward Passes has been contested." The articles, to which Mr. Detring refers, are Raw Cotton, Dates, Dried Lily Flowers, Melon Seeds, Oil, and Animal Tallow. As to Raw Cotton, the arrivals from the Interior under Transit-Passes amounted, according to his own returns, to Piculs 1,601; the shipments to Piculs 3,483. Of dried Lily flowers, it is true the exports are put down at only Piculs 3,010, while the arrivals under Certificate were Piculs 8,217; but there is no evidence to show, that a large quantity was not, *in native Junks*, shipped to Shanghai, whence, during

cates to the Chinese, by which malpractice the difficulties in the way of a just administration were greatly increased. A stricter execution of the stipulation on the English side should be, if possible, enforced, as well as on the part of China."

Let us examine the sole foundation, upon which this broad charge of "fraudulent evasion" of Treaty-obligations on the part of "British merchants" is avowedly made to rest. It consists in certain paragraphs touching Cotton in the Report on the Trade at Ningpo for the year 1866, addressed by Mr. Jas. K. Leonard, the then Commissioner of Customs at that port, to the Inspector-General.|| I will, italicising the more notable passages, quote those paragraphs at length :—

The Cotton crop has been a large one, but the quantity is not so good as last year. Prices, which have ruled high throughout the season so far, are maintained by the growers being, after last year's profitable business, so independent as to feel no necessity of forcing sales. The large exportation of this article is in Native craft Coastwise, Chinchew and Wanchew being both large consumers. A considerable quantity has gone to Hankow to replace what has been destroyed there by the

---

the last quarter of 1871 alone, Piculs 5,164 were exported to Foreign Countries. The same remark applies to Oil, and may also apply to the remaining articles. The "Returns" are so unsystematic and imperfect, as to defy control. Mr. Detring has failed to explain why it is that the validity of these, as he alleges, fraudulent outward passes is never contested by the Chinese authorities; namely, because, in the shape of a Produce-tax or the like, the latter had already at the inland mart, and *beforehand*, taxed the produce to an extent *much exceeding the rate they were lawfully entitled to levy upon it*, and probably little if at all below the amount of charges, to which the goods as Chinese property would have been subject. The Chinese trader, even without any other pecuniary advantage, prefers to avail himself of transit-passes, on account of the "squeezes" and the trouble they save him. Moreover, Mr. Detring overlooks, *firstly*, that the Foreign Customs is but a *branch* of the Chinese Customs-Service; and *secondly*, that for any open infringement of Treaty-regulations relative to the Transit-System on the part of Foreign merchants, *the Foreign Commissioner of Customs is, and is alone, responsible.* In accusing the Foreign merchant of selling fraudulent Transit-Passes to the detriment of the Chinese Revenue, *freely and without impunity*: Mr. Detring accuses *himself* of passively conniving at the alleged fraud.

|| Reports on Trade at the Ports in China open by Treaty to Foreign Trade, for the year 1866. Published by order of the Inspector-General of Customs. Shanghai: Printed at the Imperial Maritime Customs' Press, 1867, 1°.—p.p. 18-19.

floods, and a short crop in Japan has afforded another new outlet. In ordinary times Foreign traffic is principally confined to supplying the Cotton market in Hongkong.

EXPORT OF COTTON.

	1861.	1862.	1863.	1864.	1865.	1866.
Peculs	5,849	19,648	125,155	103,201	33,568	33,727

It is in connection with this staple more especially, that *the utter futility of the Transit Pass system becomes apparent.* The export of Cotton from this port by Foreign merchants is *trifling in the extreme;* yet, notwithstanding, almost the entire produce of this article comes down from the Interior *declared Foreign property.* The *sale* of Transit Passes is assuming almost sufficient importance *to be a business of itself;* merchants obtain them for thousands of bales *per month*, and at the rate of 5 cents a bale they are eagerly sought for by Native merchants, who thus are enabled to evade payment of many local imposts, to which as Chinese subjects they are *lawfully* liable. This *misinterpretation of the Treaty* might be met by placing the Native on the same footing as the Foreigner so far as regards Inland Dues, and till some such measure is adopted there is little chance of alteration; but how difficult it is to introduce reforms of that nature requires no comment.

The following table illustrative of the above remarks, shows the amount of "declared Foreign owned" Cotton passed from the interior, as compared with the quantity shipped by each Foreign merchant:—

	Bales	*Bales*	*Bales*	*Bales*	*Bales*	*Bales*	*Bales*	*Bales*	*Bales*	TOTAL.
September	2,885	1,640	4,965	1,470	215	380	270	25	...	11.850
October	3,388	3,374	7,238	2,680	405	1,555	1,565	1,350	...	21.555
November	4,670	1,410	3,775	280	255	2,420	1,110	1,820	685	16,325
December	5,085	1,765	4,395	955	635	1,920	735	1,570	415	17,505
Bales...	16,028	8,189	20,378	5.385	1,510	6.275	3,680	4.765	1.130	67.335
	Peculs	*Peculs*	*Peculs*	*Peculs*	*Peculs*	*Peculs*	*Peculs*	*Peculs*	*Peculs*	
At 120 catties per bale equal to ...	19,233	9,826	24,447	6,462	1,812	7,530	4,416	5,718	1,356	
Ship'd from N'po during 4 months	6,169	2,147	604	404	...	656	4,415	...	139 §	

Logic is manifestly not Mr. Leonard's *forte.* Since, however, his exposure of the fraudulent abuse, connected

§ Mr. Leonard adds :—"The importation of Opium has reached peculs 4,189, being fully peculs 1,000 over that of last year. Of this quantity only about 2,550 peculs have paid War Tax, showing clearly that the system of evasion, which it was endeavoured to suppress last year, still obtains.

with the certificated importation of Cotton into Ningpo, would seem to have remedied a "misinterpretation of the Treaty," which produced symptoms so alarming in high places, I have no desire to be severe upon that gentleman; yet, inasmuch as His Excellency Mr. Wade maintains that there exists no connection whatever between the Foreign Customs Inspectorate and *le-kin*, we may well be permitted to ask what business, in that case, had the Foreign Commissioner of Customs at Ningpo, in a public official report on the Foreign trade at that port, to meddle with the Chinese "War Tax"? But, turn we to the particulars of the case. In the first place, Mr. Leonard does not put that case honestly. He selects for illustration those very four months of the year, during which the far greater part of the annual cotton imports arrive from the Interior and accumulate at the port, and foreign shipments keep no proportionate pace with the arrivals. In fairness, his Table should have extended over a whole year at least. In

"The continuance of the exaction of this tax, *so long after the necessity for its imposition has ceased to exist*"—this was written in 1866—"excites no little discontent among Native dealers, and inclines them *naturally* to seek the aid of Foreigners in evading payment. This is to be regretted, as these persons run constant risk of collision with the authorities, which might at any time give rise to *grave complications with the Foreign Consuls*. The abuse, therefore, is *suffered* to exist unchecked, the *Tax Officers being unable* to devise or carry out any plan for its suppression."

Did Mr. Leonard, really, means to say, that foreign Opium-smugglers, brought before their Consuls, would or might have been granted official Consular protection from the consequences of assumed guilt, and that it was only from a fear that such a protection was almost certain to be extended to the guilty, that the Chinese Intendant of Customs, with the knowledge of his immediate subordinate the Foreign Commissioner of Customs, at Ningpo, suffered the Imperial revenue to be defrauded? I am unable to put any other construction upon his statement; and since the Inspector-General ordered it to be printed, he, of course, must have approved of it. Taken at the Shanghai rates of *le-kin* and *chow-fang*, the assumed fraud here in question,—a somewhat more profitable "business" than the sale of Cotton-certificates at 5 cents a bale, and which has yet escaped the sensitive apprehensiveness of His Excellency Mr. Wade and the British Board of Trade,—would have amounted to upwards of £35,000 sterling. For Chinese Custom-house Officials to have "suffered" such a sum to escape, unharmed, to the pockets of "barbarian" smugglers, from a fear of "grave complications with the Foreign Consuls":—why, Mr. Leonard must have meant his remarks for sarcasm; and, no doubt, the Inspector-General ordered them to be printed in a similar satirical mood.

the second place, he exaggerates flagrantly and in two opposite directions. In comparison with the total imports of Cotton into Ningpo, in 1866, which may be estimated at about 150,000 bales, he designates the aggregate of foreign exports, exceeding 40,000 bales, as a proportion "trifling in the extreme." Even during the four months, to which he specially refers, we find the proportion to be as Piculs 14,534 to Piculs 80,740. The difference between these two quantities, equal to about 80,000 bales, represents the aggregate of Transit-Passes, the sale of which, at 5 cents a bale, producing a sum total of $4,000 or less than £900 *for division among nine foreign merchants*, Mr. Leonard pronounces to be of "almost sufficient importance to be a business of itself." A small enough business it must have been, at all events, to that highly dishonest merchant, "illustrative of the Commissioner's remarks," who, according to the computation of the latter, exported to foreign parts just one bale less than he certificated to have imported, and thereby made an illegal income of 5 cents American, or 2½d. English money, being at the rate of seven pence half-penny *per annum*, at the best. Again, Mr. Leonard concludes "the utter futility of the Transit Pass system," not from the overburdensome taxation resorted to by the Chinese Government, and the discontent of the native traders who "naturally" seek to evade an imposition "for which the necessity has long ceased to exist" or from other causes to which I shall presently refer; but from the fact that certain foreign merchants at Ningpo, "misinterpreting the Treaty," allowed themselves to be induced by those native traders to assist them in defrauding the Chinese Government of taxes, to which they, as Chinese subjects, were lawfully liable."

Apart, however, from Mr. Leonard's exaggeration, illogic, and bias, there are one or two features, peculiar to this case, which demand notice. That British merchants should have offered for sale to native traders, as the report of the Ningpo Commissioner of Customs implies, fraudulent certificates at 5 cents per bale of Cotton, is simply a libel on the name *of a British merchant.* Nor will I ask, how,—having regard to the Inspector-General's view, that "the Foreigner, who has purchased Chinese produce in the Interior, need not accompany his goods, being at liberty to employ any agents for their conveyance; but that Agent, Goods, and Certificate must travel in company, to secure exemption" from *li-kin* and other inland dues,—it became possible for any English mercantile firm at Ningpo, simply by the loan of its name, to assist native merchants in passing their Cotton as "Foreign-owned property" from the inland mart to the port of shipment. I need only recall here to the reader's memory the clause, relative to Exports, of RULE VII. of the Trade Rules appended to the Treaty of Tientsin. It reads thus:—"Produce purchased by a British subject in the Interior will be inspected, and taken account of, at the first barrier it passes on its way to the port of shipment. A memorandum, showing the amount of the produce, and the port at which it is to be shipped, will be deposited there by the person in charge of the produce; he will then receive a certificate, which must be exhibited and *visé* at every barrier, on his way to the port of shipment. *On the arrival of the produce at the barrier nearest the port, and the transit dues due thereon being paid, it will be passed. On exportation the produce will pay the tariff duty.* Any attempt to pass goods inwards or outwards, otherwise than in compliance with the rule here laid down, *will render them liable to confiscation.*" Assuming, then, that English firms in Ningpo had furnished Chinese traders with letters, falsely representing them to be their Agents, authorized to purchase and convey for them to the port of Ningpo Cotton intended for exportation to foreign parts, and that the goods had arrived under certificate, duly *viséd* at every barrier passed, at the last barrier on its way to Ningpo: it is clear that by RULE VII. of the Trade Rules, notice had thereupon to be given to the Foreign Commissioner of Customs at Ningpo; and that the Cotton could not be "passed" until the "transit-duty," leviable upon it by Treaty, viz. one half the Tariff export duty of Tls. 0.3.5.0 being Tls. 0.1.7.5 per picul, had been paid to the Foreign Customs by the importing English firm, in accordance with the distinct provisions of the Rule referred to.

Now, there are two questions which here present themselves. The first is: Was the commutation-tax of Tls. 0.1.7.5 per picul, upon "the amount of 'declared Foreign-owned' Cotton, passed from the Interior" in 1866, paid to the Foreign Customs? Mr. Leonard's elaborate statement for the months of September, October, November and December, and the fact that the quantities therein named did "pass," leave us no room for doubt on the subject. Supposing the entire quantity of Cotton, thus imported into Ningpo during the year 1866, to have amounted to only 100,000 piculs: the transit-duty thereon would have been Tls. 17,500 or £5,250. But, on turning to page 138 of the Inspector-General's "Report on Trade" for 1866, which is occupied by a Table of "Duties collected at the Ports open to Foreign Flags in 1866 and 1865," there is no corresponding entry. We find the "Import" and "Export" Duties, the "Tonnage Dues," and the "Coast Trade

Duty" returned for each Port, and after the sums total have been given to a cash, we read :—

	1866.	1865.
Haikwan Tls.	8,658,381.8.3.3.—	8,208,582.5.4.2.
Add Transit Dues, at Shanghai	21,966.0.0.3.—	82,966.7.5.5.
Do. Do. Foochow	4,911.1.1.0.—	4,167.5.3.9.
Do. Do. Chinkiang	370.8.5.6.—	558.5.4.2.
Total Tls.	8,685,629.8.0.2.—	8,297,275.3.7.8.

Of the Tls. 17,500.0.0.0 or more, which must have been levied as Transit Dues on Cotton at Ningpo, there is no trace to be found in the Reports; and what does not diminish our perplexity, is that, whilst in a Table at page 126 the Ningpo Exports of Cotton are stated, within a picul, in accordance with Mr. Leonard's Table, to have been "Peculs 33,726," they are, at page 131, in a "Summary of the Principal Articles of Export, exported at all the Treaty Ports, in 1866," returned to the limited extent of "Peculs 1,039." Altogether the logic and arithmetic of the official "Returns of Trade," published by order of the Inspector-General, are of the most unreliable kind.¶

To revert, however, to our immediate subject. The officially published statement of duties collected by the Foreign Customs in 1866,—I wish to confine myself here to the case under discussion—does not include the amount of transit dues, amounting to upwards of £5,000 sterling, payable on Cotton by the Commissioner of Customs at Ningpo officially stated to have been imported into that port from the Interior as "declared Foreign-owned" property. It cannot be argued, that the dues in question, being dues upon native merchandise, which had been con-

¶ See: "The Returns of Trade at the Treaty-ports in China, as published by order of the Inspector-General of Customs, critically examined. Shanghai, 1875, 8°., p. 81.

veyed to Ningpo from inland marts, was not payable to the *Foreign* Custom-house, because it *is* so payable by Treaty-stipulation; the same as similar inland-charges-commutation-dues upon foreign merchandise, conveyed from a port to an inland mart, are so payable. Moreover, I find *f.i.* in the final "General Table" of the Returns for 1870, geographically arranged "Statistics of the Transit Trade as carried on under Treaty," of which the sums total, which alone it will suffice to adduce, are as follows:—"INWARDS: Passes 24,124 (including 17,796 "British"); value of Trade Tls. 6,370,004; Transit Dues Tls. 121,107.9.4.4; OUTWARDS: Passes 306 (including 99 "British"; value of Trade Tls. 1,097,175; Transit Dues Tls. 37,522.9.8.2. This alone would settle the point just raised. Are we, then, to conclude that the commutation-tax of upwards of Tls. 17,000 under discussion was *not* paid to the Foreign Customs, *i.e.* that "the sale of Transit passes by British merchants at Ningpo, in 1866, for thousands of bales of Cotton per month at the rate of 5 cents a bale," was virtually nothing but a hollow outcry? Or, are we to conclude, that those duties were paid to the Foreign Customs, and ask: What, then, became of the money? *

The second question, which suggests itself in connection with Mr. Leonard's strictures is: Not only suspecting, but, to give full credence to his own words, knowing what he did, viz., that Cotton was imported into Ningpo in large quantities under fraudulent certificates, and that, instead of being intended for exportation, and exported, abroad by British merchants, it was exported, in native craft by native traders to Chinchew, and other Chinese

* It will have been observed, that the Inspector-General returns of Transit-Dues, in 1866, include even the small sum of Tls. 370—little more than a hundred pounds—for Chinkiang.

marts,—was it not the duty of the Foreign Commissioner of Customs, and did he not possess the required authority and means, at once to check malpractices of the kind, and to put a stop to an unlawful evasion of the payment of Foreign export duties, leviable upon goods expressly imported, under certificate, for exportation by Foreign merchants to foreign parts, by the consfiscation of such goods, on their being attempted to be shipped in contravention of Rule vii. of the Trade Rules appended to the Treaty of Tientsin? As indubitably the Commissioner of Customs possessed the authority and the means to that end, as it was his duty, to employ them; and one single seizure would have remedied the evil complained of. Perhaps, a mere warning might have effected the purpose.

Under any circumstances, I am justified in affirming,—and I do so without fear of contradiction,—that a state of matters at Ningpo such as Mr. Leonard describes, in 1866, touching the sale of Transit-Passes, could have arisen and endured only *with the indirect concurrence, or by the direct sufferance of the Foreign Customs Authorities.* If we are to believe the Report of the Ningpo Commissioner, it amounted to nothing less than a system, or rather a "business" of *fraud and smuggling*, carried on by British merchants, in broad day-light, under a "misinterpretation" of Treaty-provisions, which the Inspectorate General not only took no means to rectify, but, in connection with which it failed either to collect, or to account for, Transit-dues to the extent of £5,000 sterling or thereabout, which were, in 1866 alone, unquestionably payable to the Foreign Customs by the conductors of that "business," according to Mr. Leonard's statement. Whatever amount of blame, then, there really may have been incurred, the larger share fell, obviously, upon the Customs Authorities, who so grossly neglected their duty, rather than upon the merchants, who only "misinterpreted the Treaty." The case, like any ordinary case of smuggling, was one of Customs administration, discipline, and responsibility. And what renders these apparent defalcations of the Revenue to the extent of something like £5,000, at one of the minor ports and in one single year, the more remarkable, is the extreme vigilance and strictness, manifested by the "Seizing Officers" of the Inspectorate-General as to trifles, at all the ports. If the natives be but half as alive and pouncing in this respect, as are the foreign *employés:* one would conclude, from a glance at Part III. of the "Customs Gazette,"† headed: "Precis of Fines and Confiscations," that not so much as the value of a pin's head could, without their good-will or consent, escape "Imperial" or any other "lawful" taxation in China.

Thus, we find, in looking over the lists for the three first quarters of 1871, that at Ningpo, "a Passenger" by the good "vessel *Ta-Lee,*" carrying some "Cuttle Fish Bones," these "Goods" were "sentenced" to be "confiscated" by the "Seizing Officer A. Sharpe," for the "Offense" of "False declaration of weight to Ship;" and that the "Sum realised" amounted to H. Tls. 0. 1*m.* 7*c.* 0*c.* being in English money about one shilling two pence farthing. This was a case of labour of pure love or duty; for the "Sum paid to Seizing Officer"—being 10 per cent on "Sum realised,"—is here left a blank. The same officer, however, on the same ground, having obtained a "sentence" of "Fined 10 times Duty" upon some "Joss

† Customs Gazette. Published (quarterly) by order of the Inspector-General of Customs, Shanghai, printed at the Customs Press, 4°.

Stick Powder," received his due share of the fine, amounting to H. Tls. 0.4.2.0, or about half-a-crown. But, with all their severity upon "Bamboo shoots," the Ningpo Tax Officers appear to be as "unable to devise or carry out any plan for the *suppression*" of attempts at modifiedly smuggling this very obnoxious article, as they are in regard to Opium; for, Bamboo shoots are repeatedly sentenced to be "confiscated,"—for "False declaration of weight to Ship,"—whether of the value of H. Tls. 0.3.4.0 or H. Tls. 0.6.8.0, unless they are, exceptionally, let off with a "Fine of treble Duty" to the extent of H. Tls. 0.4.1.0. On a "Passenger," however, happening to "Present false application," they are again, without mercy, and though but H. Tls. 0.5.1.0 in amount, doomed to confiscation. Fish Nets, Bird's Nests, Leather Boots, Silk Shoes, Fungus, Umbrellas, Hams, Cakes, Medicines—nothing has a chance of escaping the due payment of imposts at Ningpo. On the slightest "breach of regulations," every trifle is seized and sold, or fined "double," "treble," "5 times," "10 times Duty," as the case may be, for the benefit of the Chinese Maritime Customs, its seizing Officers, and mercantile morality.

Nor is all this laudable zeal confined to the open port of Ningpo and Tax Officers, whether foreign or native. At Chinkiang, the master of the "*Lor. Annie*" is mulcted in a fine of H. Tls. 10.0.0.0 or £3. for "shipping without special permission," by way of Goods, "Two old guns"; and the "Seizing Officer" in this case is the "Office," which generously presents its share of the fine inflicted, to the "needy" Imperial Revenue. The same exemplary "Office"—under the Inspection of Acting Commissioner of Customs, Mr. G. Detring—manifests, free of percentage, its unselfish dutifulness by a fine of H. Tls. 10.0.0.0 on some "Bamboo shoots" for "false valuation," and another fine of H. Tls. 30.0.0.0 on a parcel of "Mushrooms," the "Offence" being "Goods in excess of Cargo Certificate." For "Landing without Permit," the Assistant in Charge at Takow (Formosa) confiscates a lot of "Old Hemp Bags." Examiner Brackenridge at Tientsin effects the seizure, for the offense of "Goods in excess of Import application," of "Dye, 35 cups," which realize H. Tls. 2.0.0.0; whilst a nameless "Customs Watcher" confiscates Rice to the value of H. Tls. 3.0.0.0. At Hankow, "Linguist Got" makes an extra H. Tl. 1.0.0.0 by discovering a "False Declaration of Value" of Medicine, for which a fine of H. Tls. 10.0.0.0 is imposed; and "Customs native night watchmen" realise H. Tls. 0.5.0.0 out of a fine of H. Tls. 5.0.0.0 on Sundries, including "1 doz. Nail Brushes, 6 doz. Spoons, 10 prs. Spectacles, 8 tassels for do.," for the offense of "landing without permission"; whilst "Customs Boatmen" make H. Tls. 1.0.0.0, H. Tls. 1.8.0.0, and H. Tls. 2.0.0.0, at different times by "Sentences" on the same ground. At Fuchow, a "Customs Spy" obtains a sentence of confiscation for some Preserved Ginger, by which he realises a percentage of H. Tls. 0.6.5.0; and at Shanghai, "Ah-yew, Chinese detective" is so lucky as to add to his income Haikuan Tls. 2.4.5.0 through an "Offender unkown" for "Importing a contraband article," viz., "6 bags Salpetre," which are, of course, "sentenced" to confiscation, and disposed of at H. Tls. 24.5.0.0. Of the seizures effected by Tide-Waiters and Tax Officers I need say nothing,‡ but will only transcribe, in ad-

‡ Their strictness appears sometimes to border on injustice. I will only take Swatow,—where M. A. Huber, formerly Interpreter at the French Legation in Peking, was Acting Commissioner of Customs,—during the last quarter, for which I happen to have the "Precis of Fines and Confiscations" before me, by way of illustration. The Table reads as follow:—

PRECIS of FINES & CONFISCATIONS at the Port of *Swatow*, for the Qr. ending Sept. 30, 1871.

DATE.	OFFENDER.	VESSEL.	OFFENCE.	SEIZING OFFICER	GOODS.	SENTENCE.	SUM REALIZED.	SUM PAID TO SEIZING OFFICER.
1871.							*H. Tls.*	*H. Tls.*
July 4	Ho-E-Loong	*Yesso*	False declaration of value	S. Herton	1 pkg. Medicine, declared as Tls. 23.6, proved to be Tls. 37	Fined ...	15.0.0.0	1.5.0.0
,, 5	Sampan Man	,,	Breach of Regulations	,,	Not bringing Passenger's luggage to examination shed	,, ...	5.0.0.0	0.5.0.0
,, 5	,,	,,	,, ,,	,,	,, ,, ,,	,, ...	2.5.0.0	0.2.5.0
,, 5	Chinese Passenger	*Yearering Bell*	Attempt to smuggle	,,	33 pces. *T*-Cloths, 18 pces. Dyed Shirtings	Confiscated ...	64.9.5.0	5.9.7.4
,, 14	E-kee	*Derwent*	False declaration of quality	,,	Shark' Fins, pls. 8.64 declared as Black, proved to be { White 4.32 Black 4.32	Fined 3 times the difference in duty.........	12.9.6.0	1.2.9.6
,, 18	Ye-wah	,,	Breach of Regulations	,,	Carrying Sticks not brought to examination shed	Fined ...	20.0.0.0	2.0.0.0
,, 26	Sing-chang	*Douglus*	False declaration of value	,,	Medicine, pls. 1.50 declared as Tls. 42, proved to be Tls. 52.3.6.3	,, ...	6.4.3.6	6.4.3.0
Aug. 5	Yung-hip-wo	*Sophia*	False declaration of weight	J. Keymeulen	Shark' Fins White declared as pls. 3.39, proved to be peculs 4.29	Fined 3 times the difference in duty.........	4.0.5.0	4.0.5.0
,, 9	Supercargo	*Ping On*	Breach of Regulations	G. Bond	Discharging Rice on Sunday	Fined ...	25.0.0.0	2.5.0.0
,, 9	Sugar Boat	*Rebecca*	Breach of Harbour Regulations	J.S. Halsey	Fastenened by a long line astern, and refusing to move when ordered	,, ...	10.0.0.0	1.0.0.0
,, 9	Cargo Boat	*Star of the North*	,, ,,	,,	,, ,, ,,	,, ...	10.0.0.0	1.0.0.0
,, 10	,,	,,	,, ,,	,,	,, ,, ,,	,, ...	10.0.0.0	1.0.0.0
,, 10	,,	,,	,, ,,	,,	,, ,, ,,	,, ...	10.0.0.0	1.0.0.0
,, 14	Sampan	,,	,, ,,	,,	,, ,, ,,	,, ...	5.0.0.0	0.5.0.0
,, 18	Sugar Boat	*Catherine*	,, ,,	,,	,, ,, ,,	,, ...	5.0.0.0	0.5.0.0
,, 28	Lorcha	,,	,, ,,	,,	Moor'd in a wrong position, and refusing to move when ordered	,, ...	10.0.0.0	1.0.0.0
Sept. 1	Cargo Boat	,,	,, ,,	,,	Fastened by a long line astern, and refusing to move when ordered	,, ...	5.0.0.0	0.5.0.0
,, 1	,,	,,	,, ,,	,,	,, ,, ,,	,, ...	5.0.0.0	0.5.0.0
,, 1	,,	,,	,, ,,	,,	,, ,, ,,	,, ...	5.0.0.0	0.5.0.0
,, 1	,,	,,	,, ,,	,,	,, ,, ,,	,, ...	5.0.0.0	0.5.0.0
Aug. 6	Sampan	*Ping On*	Loading on Sunday	G. Bond	16 packages Rice sweepings landed without permit	Confiscated ...	13.2.3.0	1.3.2.3
					Total.........	*H. Tls.*...	249.1.2.6	24.3.9.1

dition, two foot-notes of the Commissioner of Customs at Hankow. They read thus:—"An exceptionally heavy fine|| (H. Tls. 30.0.0.0) was inflicted in this case (a native, "landing without permission), as the fraudulent intention was manifest, the articles (Silk piece goods) being found concealed on the offender's person." And: "It must be distinctly understood that the foreign merchants, whose names are mentioned in the table for the September Quarter, were completely innocent of any fraudulent intentions. In such cases they are misled, and not unfrequently defrauded by their native constituents."

This, certainly, sounds re-assuring. The chief feature, however, to which I have desired to call here attention, is the extraordinary variety of talent, zeal, and vigilance, employed by the Foreign Inspectorate-General for the protection of the foreign branch of the Chinese Customs Revenue, and the effective preservation of the duty-paying morality of British and other foreign merchants. We find there are Customs Boatmen, Customs Night Watchmen, Customs Watchers, Customs Spies, and Customs Detectives, besides Tide-waiters, Tax Officers, Examiners, Linguists, Assistants in Charge, nay the "Offices," *i.e.* the Commissioners of Customs themselves,—all equally intent upon the accomplishment of that praiseworthy object. Is it, then, reasonable to assume, that a thousand eyes, to whose quick glance, in 1871, neither nail-brush nor fungus, an old hemp bag no more than an old gun, escaped, should, in 1866,

I should remark that Passengers' Luggage is by Treaty exempt from duty. It reads amusingly, when, under the heading of "Goods," there are enumerated:—"Fastened by long line astern;" or: "Moored in a wrong position, and refusing to move when ordered;" and "Discharging rice on Sunday";—the latter in contradistinction to "*Loading* (rice-sweepings) on Sunday," which, in M. Huber's sight and judgment, is an offence, whilst "*Discharging* rice on a Sunday" constitutes a package of merchandise.

|| It is greatly exceeded in severity by the first line in the preceding table.

have been shut to a quantity of one hundred and twenty thousand bales, or thereabout, of "declared Foreign-owned" Cotton, and a commutation-tax of some £5,000 sterling, leviable upon it? If not, we have once more to ask: Why, then, is the money not included in the Inspector-General's published account of "Duties Collected" in that year? And what has become of it? §

Mr. Wade, as has been seen, submits to the British Government, that he is happy in believing the Foreign Inspectorate-General of Chinese Maritime Customs to be above suspicion; and it would grieve me indeed, to see his Excellency shaken in a belief, which contributes to his happiness: but is the honorable and long-sustained reputation of the *British merchant* a matter of less moment to Her Britannic Majesty's Chief Superintendent of British Trade in China, than is the fair repute of *a foreign Branch*

§ I have confined myself in the text to the one item of approximately £5,000, although but a small fraction of the discrepancies, which appear in the published revenue-accounts of the Foreign Inspectorate-General. The reader, who takes an interest in these matters, is referred to the writer's critical review of the "Returns of Trade," already quoted (page 232, note). It is there shown, amidst a mass of contradiction, error, and confusion, systematic and otherwise, probably without a parallel in the history of official statistics, that *f. i.* the returns of revenue from *Transit-dues*, *Import-duties*, and *Tonnage-dues*, according to the "Abstract of Trade and Customs Revenue Statistics" for 1871, compared with the "Abstract" for 1868, exhibit discrepancies discovered to the amount of Tls. 317,636 for the two years 1864 and 1865 alone, and that of this total only Tls. 21,898 appear, in the latter year, to have been placed to the credit of the public revenue, leaving a remainder of Tls. 295,738, or nearly £100,000 unaccounted for; while, seemingly in order to simply balance the accounts, we find the revenue, returned in the Abstract for 1868, as having been actually collected from *Coast-trade-duties* in the years 1864 and 1865, in the Abstract for 1871, *silently* reduced for those two years from Tls. 1,192,864 to Tls. 897,126, *i. e.* by exactly the discrepancy of Tls. 295,738, referred to above,—a falling off in the revenue from Coast-trade duties, within two years, of more than 40 cent., while the foreign trade generally, within the same period, had increased by 16 per cent.

Again, as regard the Transit-dues collected in the three succeding years 1866–1868, there appear fresh discrepancies to the aggregate amount of Tls. 245,253, or upwards of £70,000, returned short in the Abstracts up to the year 1870. In the Abstract for 1871, under an altered form which does not facilitate comparison, they have, within small the sum of Tls. 1,511, been added to the revenue, it is true; but once more so without one word of explanation; and whether in this case with real benefit to the Chinese Exchequer or also but nominally, it is hard to say.

The most serious discrepancies in the revenue accounts, however, appear on a comparison of Part II. of the "Returns of Trade" or the Returns proper, containing the "Statistics of

of the Chinese Customs service?¶ Could he, in the particular case under consideration, and with the Customs Reports before him, reasonably suspect the one, without suspecting the other? No doubt, there exist commercial firms in China, as there do elsewhere, which possess no title to a name, respected for honor and integrity throughout the world; no doubt, in China as in England, attempts are made, and will continue to be made, at smuggling and a partial evasion of the payment of national imposts; but there is, certainly, no greater tendency in this direction observeable among the Foreign mercantile community in China, where a provokingly heavy burden of *illegal* taxation is by the Chinese Government laid upon foreign trade with the Interior, than there is among the mercantile communities at home, where inland trade is free, and the imposts are sanctioned by the Representatives of the people. Almost from the very commencement, the British and Foreign merchant in China, favourable to the Institution of the Foreign Customs Service, has given to it his loyal and steady support, without which, indeed, it could not

---

the Trade at each Port," and extending to several hundred pages, with Part I., or the Abstract, occupying twenty pages only. The latter, in fact, is a methodical summary of the former, and, so far as I know, alone translated into Chinese for the information of the native Authorities in Peking. On calculating the amount of duties payable to the Chinese Government from the quantities of merchandise imported and exported, etc., as returned in Part II., at the fixed tariff-rates, and comparing the totals, thus found, with the totals, returned in Part I.: there results an apparent *annual* deficit in the latter returns of considerably more than Tls. 1,000,000 (about £350,000 *per annum* in the mean) for the Inspector-General to explain.

I may just add, that *f. i.* in the year 1871, the real value of the "Home," *i. e.* the Coasting-Trade of China, carrried on in foreign-built vessels, instead of Tls. 229,818,037, as returned by Mr. Hart, was Tls. 20,885,489; and the value of the whole trade,—import-, export-, and "home"-trade,—Tls. 178,561,584, instead of Tls. 394,131,056, as returned; the latter value being exaggerated by the Inspector-General to the extent of upwards of Tls. 200,000,000, *annually*.

¶ In a measure, perhaps, this bias is explained by the fact that, like the Inspector-General, Mr. Hart, and a large proportion of his "Foreign In-door Staff." Mr. Wade is Irish. In the official list of that staff, made up and printed, at the suggestion of "the Chinese Secretary," by order of the Inspector-General's Circular No. 20 of 1873, the Irish element disappears under the loyal denomination; "British."

have prospered; and, under trying circumstances, his conduct in regard to its Administration has been even ultra-exemplary and over-considerate. Resignedly and without murmuring he has put up with great hardship, and greater injustice. He has submitted to the Coast-Trade duties; and has not rebelled against the *chow-fang* and "ever-increasing" *le-kin*. He has paid his Tonnage-Dues regularly; and patiently seen the larger portion of its revenue squandered,—worse than squandered,—upon the Burlingame Mission and other similar and dissimilar anti-foreign inventions. Trustingly he has accepted the Inspector-General's repeated promises of amendment in the application of those Dues; and vainly, to this day, he applies, again and again, for a safer and more certain access to the very port of Shanghai for his richly-laden argosies.* Nay, at the same time that he exercises so much consideration and forbearance towards the Foreign Administration of the Customs in all these and many other matters, to which I need not allude, and, in claiming for his native constituents the right of sending foreign merchandise into the Interior under a "transit"-certificate, enforces but a clear Treaty-right, arbitrarily withheld from the Chinese by their Foreign Customs Authorities: the latter assail, or until very recently have assailed, the character of the British and Foreign merchant by accusing him, in thus acting, of illegal proceedings and fraudulent abuse of Treaties; whilst all along, they must have known those

* Compare: The Tonnage-Dues Fund, the Harbour of Shanghai, and the Wusung Bar. Shanghai, 1872, 4°.—Recently Prince Kung has officially declared the Bar of the Wusung river to be, in a military sense, a protection to China, instituted by Heaven; whilst the Inspector-General, Mr. Hart, in his pseudo-prophetic memorandum of March 5, 1874, foretells the approaching downfall of Shanghai as a place of *foreign* commerce, and throws out some dark and mysterious hints about "no one being able to say, *how* soon commerce may cease to ask for access to Shanghai."

rights to have been acknowledged by the Chinese Government itself, and instructions to act in accordance with them from the native Superintendent of Trade, their superior, to slumber, unheeded, in "the archives of each Custom-house."

Taking, then, into account the various facts and circumstances, to which I have referred, the reader will, no doubt, consider it with me simply prepostorous that, on the sole ground of Mr. Leonard's Report in 1866, Mr. Wade should have made the gong of alarm—lest the whole Chinese Revenue be defrauded by British merchants, and the bankrupt Government of the Ta Ching Empire be disabled from prosecuting its warlike preparations, may be for further massacre and the expulsion of us "outer barbarians" from the "bayonet-ploughed soil of Cathay,—to resound through the sensitive minds of the Lords of the British Privy Council for Trade. But that Her Britannic Majesty's Board, too readily listening to, and crediting, the tale of those deceptive sounds, should, without examination and in language, the confusion of which is but the reflection of confused ideas touching the subject, have connected certain malpractices of certain Ningpo traders for a while apparently suffered to prosper by the Foreign Customs Authorities, with "greatly increased difficulties in the way of a just administration," —of the Customs, or else of what?—and, in an official document submitted to the consideration of the British Government, have ascribed the illegal imposition of the *le-kin* and other war-taxes upon Foreign merchandise, and the imperfect execution of the Treaty of Tientsin "in this particular," not only to "the weakness or inaction," instead of the perfidy and rapacity, "of the

Chinese Government, *but also to the fraudulent evasion by British merchants of the obligations and conditions which that Treaty imposes:* this has appeared to my judgment a matter so grave and, in its more or less probable consequences, fraught with so much danger, not only to the British and Foreign commerce with China, but to the best interests of China herself, as to deserve a full exposure,—even in reference to "the sale of transit certificates to the Chinese,"—of the utterly frail or wholly baseless grounds, on which the views, adopted by Her Britannic Majesty's Board of Trade, actually rest.

They may possibly, however, have received additional strength from a despatch of Sir Rutherford Alcock to Consul Medhurst of June 17, 1869, copies of which were communicated to the Chamber of Commerce of Shanghai and the late Lord Clarendon, then English Secretary of State for Foreign Affairs. In this despatch Sir Rutherford Alcock, in reference to the minutes of proceedings at a Meeting of the Chamber, held on May 7, 1869, and the terms of a resolution passed, and conveyed for the information of the British Minister to Mr. Medhurst, expresses himself thus:—

The Defence of Traffic in Transit Certificates.—I confess the arguments employed are to my apprehension only tenable in a total oblivion or disregard of the Treaty stipulations. By treaty, a right was given to foreigners to commute all Transit Dues by a fixed payment of 2½ per cent. for any merchandise constituting their foreign trade, whether import or export. But to make any produce an element or a part of foreign trade, a foreign merchant must own it or at least have a *bonâ fide* property interest in it either as an import or export. No right was given to a native to share in this, which was a treaty privilege exclusively granted to foreigners, no right, in a word, was given to a native dealer to withdraw native produce in transit for native consumption, from the powers of taxation exercised over all Chinese subjects and trade, by the Emperor in his own territories. No foreigner could transfer his privilege to a native and so enable him to defraud the native collector (!), evade his own revenue laws, and, under a false pretext, that the merchandise was foreign property, pay less than he otherwise would. And this under the clauses of a Treaty exclusively applicable to foreigners and foreign trade.

To call such a collusion as this between foreign and native honest trade, or anything but a fraud, and a breach of Treaty, can only be considered a perversion of terms.

The result of such a practice being resorted to by certain foreigners is bad enough, since it renders any system of transit certificates impracticable; but to me it seems even worse, that by any sophistry it should be possible for a respectable body like the Chamber of Commerce at Shanghai to defend it.

If the Chinese had any right, as one of the speakers assumed, to take out exemption certificates, that is transit-passes, to commute the inland dues in like manner as foreigners had by Treaty, why should they have *bought* them of the foreigner? The fact of a traffic existing through and by the foreigner alone is a sufficient answer to any such plea.

If they had the perfect right to take them out, as the Chairman inferred, of which I do not think he was a very competent judge as between Chinese subjects and their rulers, why did they not exercise this right, I repeat, instead of seeking the foreign dealers? Between those, who "could not see the injustice done to the Chinese Revenue" by the sale of transit passes to the Chinese, or any fraud on the revenue, and the seller of such ware, I fear little distinction will be made. It will be thought in England that there must be something peculiarly blinding in the air of Shanghai on commercial questions.

All I can say is, that to sell a privilege, granted to foreigners only by Treaty, to natives under false pretences and declarations, and in order that he may pass native produce through the inland customs at a cheaper rate than he would be otherwise entitled to do, if this be not fraudulent *ab initio*, and a designed fraud on the Chinese Revenue, words have no recognised meaning, and if the Chinese adopt a similar view of Treaty rights, and what is fraudulent or honest, there is not much to be hoped I fear from any further revision of Treaties, for these instruments are only valuable in so far as they are interpreted in good faith, and acted upon with honesty of purpose."

Sir Rutherford Alcock having remarked :—"The Chamber will, I trust, for its own sake see fit to repudiate (the views imputed to the Chamber by the then Representative of England) as in any sense giving the deliberate opinion of the largest and most important mercantile community in China :" a reply on the part of the Chamber was thus rendered necessary. In it, the Chamber says :—

No little surprise has been felt by the members of the Committee at the extraordinary interpretation placed upon the words of the speakers at the meeting of May 7th, by his Excellency. They deplore, what they cannot but feel, its misrepresentation of their expressed sentiments, and take the strongest exception to the conclusions at which his Excellency arrives, as being founded, partly on this misconception and partly on an exaggerated statement of their arguments...

The use of Transit Passes by Chinese.—It is to be regretted that Sir Rutherford should have gone out of his way, as it seems to the Committee, to put into the mouths of the speakers at the General Meeting of May 7th, sentiments which they did not utter, and then to express the hope that the Chamber would disown or detract them, in terms which cannot be acceptable to any respectable body of merchants. For the intimation is most distinct, that dishonesty is openly declared as a principle, and that unless the Chamber accepts his reproof and listens to his admonition, its character is lost. The truth is, and the statement can be immediately verified by reference to the debate,... As therefore the Chamber has never expressed or adopted the views, ascribed to it by Sir Rutherford Alcock, it has nothing to repudiate, and can safely leave its reputation in the hands of any fair reader of its debates."

The despatch of Sir Rutherford Alcock is characteristic of the former British Minister,—Rhodes-colossus-like, hollow but "bestriding the narrow world." He could hardly, in a fewer words, have given a greater proof of superficiality and onesidedness, of presumption, unfairness, and incapacity. He had failed to seize the true and final determination of the transit duties question by Treaty, and its importance to Trade. He was labouring under the delusion, that international Treaties of Commerce are concluded for the personal benefit of merchants. He was unable to distinguish between the transit-clauses relative to native produce intended for exportation to foreign parts, and those relative to foreign manufactures destined for native consumption in the Interior of China. He was blind to the difference between a bale of English Shirtings protected from illegal taxation by Treaty-rights secured by two wars, and an unprotected Chinaman subject to the despotic powers of taxation of "the One Lord of the World." He contended that the Chinese were not possessed of a "privilege," which the Chinese authorities themselves had long since admitted them to possess. He could not realize, that an international Treaty might confer rights on the native as well as on the foreign merchant, nor perceive, why the native merchant, being deprived of the exercise of his rights by an unscrupulous and despotic Government, should desire to avail himself of his "privilege," notwithstanding. He was incapable of seeing, that, *abuses* of the "Transit-System" having been provided against by Treaty, it rested simply with the Foreign and Native Customs Authorities to deal with, and prevent, them. And on the ground of all this misapprehension and incompetence, associated with less pardonable elements, Sir Rutherford Alcock hesitated not, to accuse the British Merchant in China of designed fraud on the Chinese Revenue; to contrast his non-appreciation of the solemn nature of Treaty-stipulations and of "what is fraudulent or honest," with the implied honesty of purpose and good faith of *the Chinese Government;* and to call upon the Chamber of Commerce of Shanghai to repudiate views and doctrines, which his "extraordinary interpretation" alone had ascribed to it. Possibly, Sir Rutherford Alcock had read the discussion of the Chamber by the light of his own grammar, syntax, and logic. This would go far towards explaining that interpretation.

The Representatives of England in Peking have ever been but too willing to favor the Chinese Government, when in conflict with, or at the expense of, the British merchant. A remarkable and characteristic illustration of this tendency offers a case of confiscation of sixty-three (out of sixty-four) bales of silk, worth upwards of £5,000, the property of the wealthy and highly respected firm of Messrs. Bower & Hanbury of Shanghai, which occurred in 1862. They were seized by James Kennard, "*tide-waiter in the Imperial Maritime Customs*," and—an ominous name—Moses Jagger, "*tide-surveyor to the Imperial Maritime Customs*," on the ground that the European, in charge of the Silk, had attempted to evade the payment upon it of, what we shall find to have been, *the le-kin tax*, and under circumstances, which will be best gathered from the following "Declaration of Thomas Hanbury," Esq.:—

I, Thomas Hanbury, English merchant, of Shanghae, in the Empire of China, do solemnly and sincerely declare as follows:—

That I have been resident in Shanghae for a period of nine years; that during that time I have carried on business as partner in two mercantile firms. That during those nine years no case of attempted smuggling was ever charged against myself, or the firm in which I was a partner. That my present and former firm has always paid duties regularly and punctually, according to the established tariff rates.

That as regards the seizure of sixty-four bales of silk on the eighteenth of January last as they were being conveyed from the interior to Shanghae, I declare that no instructions were given by myself or any one in my office to attempt the evasion of duty, or to run past the barrier; further, I declare that those accompanying the silk, and in the employ of my firm, would not have been benefited by the evasion of transit duty. Also, that the position of the barrier had been recently changed, and a junk anchored in the stream employed, instead of a station on shore, and that those in the boats coming from the interior were not aware of this fact. Forty-two bales of silk coming from another district were lying at the barrier at the time the sixty-four bales were seized, thus proving what was the custom of my firm in regard to stopping at the barrier.

At the same time I was of the opinion that the levying of transit dues from British merchants at said barrier, on produce brought down by them without certificate, was illegal, and totally at variance with the notification of Her Majesty's Minister Plenipotentiary, published for general guidance by Her Majesty's Consul on the 23rd September, 1861, and which reads as follows:—

"1st. That the British merchant has nothing to do with the payment of transit duties, unless the goods are carried into the country, or brought down from the place of production under certificate as British property. It is optional to the British merchant to take out the certificate or not as he pleases, but if he does not, and he buys or sells at the port of shipment, he has nothing to do with the payment of any duty but the one specified in the Tariff on imports and exports."

And I make this solemn declaration conscientiously believing the same to be true.

(Signed) THOMAS HANBURY.

To enable us to judge of the further merits of the case, we have the views of Sir Frederick Bruce, the then British Minister in Peking, as stated in despatches, from which I quote what is necessary for the purpose, together with a letter addressed by Messrs. Bower & Hanbury to Consul Medhurst:—

Mr. Bruce to Earl Russell.

Peking, December 2, 1862.

MY LORD,—I think it advisable to inform your Lordship of the course I have pursued in cases of seizure and confiscation of goods for evasion of duties by the Chinese Custom-house. I therefore inclose the particulars of a case in which sixty-three bales of silk belonging to Messrs. Hanbury & Co., for which no transit-duty certificate had been taken out, were seized by the Chinese and confiscated for having attempted to evade the Customs barrier near Shanghae, established for the collection of inland duties.

The principle I have laid down is, that in such cases the Chinese authorities are bound to prove that the breach of regulation which exposes the goods to confiscation has been committed, and that if the fact is denied on affidavit they must furnish equally satisfactory evidence on their side in support of their charge. If not, I consider that restitution may be demanded or compensation required.

I do not find that there is any disposition on the part of the Chinese authorities to throw difficulties in the way of a full investigation, and as in such cases it is not difficult to ascertain whether the offence has been committed or not, I do not apprehend that the foreign merchant is likely to suffer injustice.

I may observe that a case arising out of a charge of evading inland duties is not likely to recur; for I have stated as the rule to be observed in future, that if a British subject purchases produce on his own account in the interior, and intends to have his property recognized and protected as British property on its way to the port of shipment, he is bound to cover it by taking out a transit-duty certificate. If, on the other hand he thinks it more for his interest to buy produce and bring it down uncertificated, it will not be entitled to any special protection as British property, but will be subject to such charges and regulations as the Chinese authorities may choose to impose.

I conceive this to be the meaning of Rule No. 7, which was substituted for Art. XXVIII. of the Treaty of Tientsin, and that most embarrassing questions will be avoided by adhering strictly to it. The object of the Rule was to substitute one unvarying charge for the arbitrary exactions of provincial authorities, where Her Majesty's subjects bought or sold goods in the interior. But it was not intended to interfere between the Chinese Government and its own subjects.

I may also remark, that if the Chinese are satisfied with this interpretation of the Rule, they waive, in some degree, the right they might claim on a strict interpretation of its terms; for it is expressly agreed that permission to export produce which cannot be proved to have paid the transit dues may be refused until payment is made of the amount, whereas, hitherto, the Chinese Government has not insisted on proof of such payment in the case of produce which is bought by the exporter at the port of shipment....

(Signed) FREDERICK W. A. BRUCE.

Mr. Bruce to Consul Medhurst.

Peking, May 2, 1862.

Sir,—With reference to the sixty-three bales of silk belonging to Messrs. Bower, Hanbury & Co., reported to you to be confiscated, I have to observe that the account of the transaction given in the Taoutae's letter differs entirely from that given by the Chinese boatmen.

The depositions of Mr. Hanbury and Mr. Leech, as they were not in the boats at the time, have no bearing on the question at issue, which is simply, Did the boats attempt to pass the barrier without reporting, or not?

The Taoutae asserts that the boats containing the sixty-three bales forced their way by the barrier; that they were pursued for a *le*, and taken; and that there was a foreigner on board, who declared there were no goods, and that they were discovered on examination.

The Taoutae is bound to support these statements by the evidence of the persons who made the seizure.

If he does not, I must assume that the statements of Messrs. Bower & Hanbury's boatmen are correct. You cannot insist on hearing the case in a Consular Court, but you are entitled to have the evidence on which the Taoutae proceeds communicated to you.

The Chinese authorities are entitled to levy the half transit-duty on silk brought down uncertificated; and you will warn Her Majesty's subjects that non-compliance with the system laid down in the Tariff-rules for their protection exposes them to increased risk and detention.

I am bound to state that the disappearance of Leech from the boats, taken in connection with the pretension that the half-duty was not legally leviable on uncertificated produce, is a suspicious feature in the case.

(Signed) Frederick W. A. Bruce.

Messrs. Hanbury & Co. to Consul Medhurst.

Shanghai, July 12, 1862.

Sir,—We beg permission to offer a few remarks after a perusal of the affidavits on the strength of which his Excellency the Taoutae has thought fit to confiscate and sell off sixty-four bales of silk belonging to ourselves, without any trial or hearing of our defence.

Inclosed is declaration of our Mr. Hanbury, showing that for a period of nine years' trading at this port, this is the first accusation of an attempt to evade duty that has been brought against him. It is, therefore, a peculiarly hard case that 5,000*l.* worth of property should be summarily confiscated by virtue of the statement of two tide-waiters in the employ of the Taoutae, who, as they receive a share of the spoil, are interested in the confiscation, but whose evidence is totally at variance with the four affidavits handed you some time since; viz:—

Two from boatmen in our employ who were on the boats at the time of seizure;

Charles Brooks, Englishman, in our employ, present at the seizure;

De Wit C. Deming, American, not in our employ, but present at the time of seizure.

We feel sure Her Majesty's Minister Plenipotentiary will not permit this gross violation of all rules of English law and equity, and will not allow us to suffer so severely because the Taoutae chooses to ignore the evidence we produce to rebut the charge of his two interested employés, and to judge the matter by Chinese law, not even allowing us, the defendants, a hearing.

We particularly call attention to the fact that the tide-waiter James Kennard, who boarded the boats, in his declarations fails to state how far the boats were from the Custom-house junk, called the barrier, when they were seized, and that Moses Jagger, the other tide-waiter, only speaks from hearsay on this point; while, on the other hand, all our witnesses are most explicit in declaring that the boats, when seized, were close to the barrier, "within hail," "within stone's throw," &c. The case turns on this point altogether, in our opinion, and the balance of the evidence in regard to it we submit is largely in our favour.

We further beg distinctly to state that there is no barrier at the place where the boats were seized, but a junk anchored in the river, and the existence of which was unknown to our employés when coming down the river, the Custom-house business formerly being done entirely on shore.

(Signed) BOWER & HANBURY.

Mr. Bruce to Consul Medhurst.

Peking, November 5, 1862.

SIR,—I have gone carefully through the papers bearing on the claim of Messrs. Hanbury & Son for restitution of sixty-three bales of silk confiscated by the Taoutae of Shanghae for attempted evasion of the inland dues.

I regret to say that a perusal of the evidence forwarded in your despatch of the 12th of July last leaves no doubt in my mind that the boats formed part of a number that attempted to pass the Custom-house barrier without reporting, and that they were overtaken and seized in the act.

The evidence of Brooks and Deming is untrustworthy. According to their account they were neither pursued, boarded, nor searched. It is evident that they felt the attempt to evade payment of the duties would be established were it admitted that they had past the barrier to such a distance as rendered it necessary to send a boat after them, and had denied the existence of the silk on board; and they have consequently suppressed the facts in their affidavits, although they have not positively denied them.

There is nothing to shake the testimony of Kennard and Jagger, and the facts deposed to by them establish a clear case of attempted evasion of duties, subjecting the articles to confiscation.

You will therefore inform Messrs. Hanbury that I cannot bring forward their claim for restitution.

(Signed) Frederick W. A. Bruce.

The "Declaration of James Kennard" states :—"That on or about the 18th day of January last I was on duty on board the Custom-house junk stationed at the south barrier, when, between the hours of 5 and 6 P.M., I observed *several* boats passing down the Pootung side of the river. All the boats which pass down the river are bound to pull up at my station, *in order to pay the transit Dues ;* and if they refuse to stop, one of my duties is to follow them up. That accordingly I started with two Chinaman from the said junk, and overtook three of the said boats, and immediately boarded them and inquired if they had any silk on board, to which they [the boats ?] replied in the negative. That I searched the whole of the three boats, and on board two of them I discovered a large quantity of silk, amounting on the whole to sixty-three bales . . . That a few days afterwards I received orders from Mr. Jagger to take both the said boats *up to the Custom-house at Shanghai*, which I accordingly did." The similar "Declaration of Moses Jagger" has it:—"That on or about the 18th day of January last I was at my station at the south barrier, in the performance of my duty, which is to inspect all boats passing down the south barrier on their stopping to pay the transit dues. That between the hours of 5 and 6 P.M. on that day I observed *a large convoy* of boats passing on the Pootung side of the river, instead of pulling up at my station as they were bound to do. That *some of the men* in my employ on board the Custom-house junk accordingly followed up the said boats and searched them, to ascertain if there was any silk concealed on board any of them. That when the said boats had gone about three-quarters of a mile past the station three of them were, as I am informed and verily believe, overtaken by the men in the Custom-house junk who had pursued them, and were boarded, and the *men* in charge were asked if *they* had any silk on board,—to which they replied in the negative. That James Kennard, *one of the men* who had pursued the said boats, *then* searched them; and lifting up the hatchways discovered sixty-three bales of silk in two of the boats, but none in the other... And I further solemnly and sincerely declare that I reported the same to *the official mandarin who acts with me at the said station*; and he, as I am informed and verily believe, thereupon wrote to *the Taoutae* of Shanghai, who instructed me to have the said boats brought up to Shanghai and *delivered over to the Imperial Maritime Customs*, which was accordingly done."

On the other hand, the "Declaration of Charles Brooks," the European in charge of the three Boats in question, states:—"On the 19th day of January last, I arrived from the Interior with a quantity of silk, about sixty-four bales in all, I believe ... In coming down the river, usually I have been *in the habit* of stopping at the Customs-house, near the Tong-ka-doo French Cathedral, and *the boats were proceeding there on this occasion*, and they were hailed by the Custom-house junk anchored in the stream; *this junk was newly placed there*, and until hailed I was not aware it belonged to the Custom-house. We stopped at once, and our boats with the silk in came alongside the Custom-house junk. I never received any instructions to attempt the evasion of any duty, and I had no intention of doing so on this occasion; when the boats were seized, they were *between the Custom-house junk and the Custom-house*, within stone's throw of both. When the boats were seized the Custom-house officer did not accuse us of attempting to evade any duty; he said other boats had lately passed without paying duty, and probably the Taoutae would seize our boats in consequence." The position of the boats, when being hailed, assigned to them by Mr. Brooks, and their going alongside the junk, *the distance being no more than thirty yards*, is confirmed also, as well as that the day was the 19th of January, by the Declaration of a Mr. De Wit C. Deming, an American, who happened to be in the boat with Mr. Brooks at the time of the occurrence.

Now, Mr. Hanbury's testimony, to the effect that his Agent had neither instructions to evade, nor any interest in evading, the payment of duty on the Silk in question, must be implicitly accepted. There, consequently, existed no adequate motive for smuggling on the Agent's part. Whether it was his *intention* to proceed, as usual, to a native Custom-house higher up the river, and he was really not aware of the character and position of the junk, from which pursuit was made, is a question which it might have been more difficult to answer in the affirmative, had the Agent's statement that the junk had been newly placed in the river, been denied by the "seizing officers." The latter, on the contrary, had a great and very tempting interest in causing so valuable a cargo to be confiscated. Their Declarations contain flagrant contradictions, more especially that of Moses Jagger; whilst to the Tautai there appears to have been given a version of the affair entirely differing from the depositions. The distance of "pursuit,"—an essential point—which the Declaration of Jagger extends to three quarters of a mile, was even in the mandarin's report reduced to a *li* or one third of a mile: the European witnesses denying the *pursuit* altogether, and estimating their distance from the junk, on being boarded, at only thirty yards or a stone's throw. Indeed, this is fully confirmed by the Declaration of Kennard himself, as well as by the corresponding part of that of his immediate superior. Both these accounts agree in stating that, *immediately* on the barges being perceived on the Pootung side of the river, Kennard, with two Chinamen, started (in a light boat) to *board* them. But, during the hours of 5 and 6 in the evening about the middle of January, at Shanghai, it is either pretty dark, and in that case the barges could not have been seen at any distance; or else the moon shone, and in this event, Moses Jagger, being "at his station and in the performance of his duty," can hardly have failed to espy the boats even before passing the newly placed floating "barrier." He would seem, moreover, to have been on the look-out for them, unless he and his subordinate knew by instinct that they were laden with Silk,—Kennard's first question on boarding and before he had proceeded to a search, being: had they any *silk* on board? He himself says nothing of a chase; and there can be no rational doubt, but that the additional "pursuit for three-quarters of a mile"—a distance which of itself would suffice to discredit the statement,—spoken of in Moses Jagger's Declaration and forming a very awkward and ill-fitting episode in his narrative, was simply the offspring of his own "verily believing" imagination. There are Moses Jaggers of far higher position and renown than Kennard's superior; and know we not that, in certain quarters, "Lying" is regarded as a mere "social necessity," in fact as "an accomplishment?"

In all human probability, the truth here lies between the two depositions of Charles Brooks and Moses Jagger, but greatly towards the side of the former; and the fact was, that the silk-boats did pass the junk-barrier without reporting, but were immediately, thereupon, boarded and seized by Kennard. In Sir Frederick Bruce's judgment, the whole issue of the question depended on the former fact. The view is an obviously erroneous one; and the British Minister altogether treats the case with a degree of levity, carelessness, and partiality, which appear to me to assume a character of culpability. He himself observes "that the account of the transaction, given in the Taoutae's letter, differs entirely from that given by the Chinese boatmen;" yet allows the discrepancy to go for nothing. He pronounces "the evidence of Brooks and Deming to be untrustworthy," because they *truly*, and in accordance with Kennard's Declaration, state that they were not pursued, and *omit* stating that they were boarded and searched; and decides, that "there is nothing to shake the testimony of Kennard and Jagger," although the latter contradicts himself, and *falsely* asserts that the silk-boats were pursued for three quarters of a mile, and the former *omits* to say, that—

which it would be unreasonable to question,—he hailed the boats, which consequently must have been within hailing distance, immediately before he, (after starting overtook and) boarded them. "The depositions," Sir Frederick Bruce declares, "of Mr. Hanbury and Mr. Leech, [should be Mr. Leeds] as they were not in the boats at the time, have no bearing on the question at issue"; and he fails to notice that Mr. Leeds made no deposition at all, and Moses Jagger, whose testimony he accepts *in toto*, was no more in the boats at the time, than were Mr. Hanbury and Mr. Leeds. He feels "bound to state that the disappearance of Leech [should be: Leeds] from the boats is a suspicious feature in the case;" and does not perceive, that "the suspicious feature in the case" has, like the person or name of Leech, no other foundation save his inattentive reading, Mr. Leeds not having "disappeared from the silk-boats" and the charge of Mr. Brooks, but *preceded* him in other boats under his own charge.

The more important elements of the case, however, are these. In the first place it is explicitly declared by Mr. Brooks, that the Custom-house junk, anchored in the stream, *had been newly placed there*, and that he was not aware of its character,—the novel character of *a floating* barrier for levying *inland* tolls or taxes; and the *fact*, started by him, has never been denied by the "seizing officers;" whilst Mr. Hanbury declared that there had been no intention to evade, and that his agent had had no interest in evading, the payment of the customary impost on entering Shanghai. Indeed, as the silk came under no certificate, it has necessarily to be assumed that all other inland taxes upon it between the place of purchase and the port had been discharged; and it has, therefore, to be judged highly improbable, that the property should have been risked by any attempt to evade the last fraction of the imposts leviable. On the other hand, Mr. Kennard as explicitly declares, that his duty was to follow up boats, passing down the river and "bound to pull up at his (newly established floating) station in order to pay *the transit dues,*" only *on their refusing to stop.* But, no proof that they were called upon, and refused, to stop, has been so much as tendered by Kennard, who, on the contrary, admits that he immediately boarded and seized; whilst the depositions of Mr. Brooks and Mr. Deming, supported by the testimony of the seizing officer himself, prove that they allowed themselves to be taken alongside the Customs' junk without any resistance whatever. What value we have to attach to Moses Jagger's "pursuit to about three quarters of a mile" has already been seen. Under the peculiar circumstances of the case, therefore, and keeping in view the admitted fact that the anomalous floating "barrier" presented quite a new phenomenon in the stream, and exhibited no sign to warn the hurried traveller of that phenomenon being the station of "a tide-surveyor to the Imperial Maritime Customs in the performance of his duty:" it appears to me unquestionable, that the latter had no right whatsoever to *seize* the boats, or the produce conveyed in them, but was only and simply justified in *constraining the boats to go alongside "the barrier nearest the port, and, notice having been given to the Customs at the port, to pay the transit dues due on the produce;"* provided always, that such transit dues *were* payable on the produce in question.

But, in the second place, there were in this case no "transit-dues," *i.e.* no inland charges commutation tax, to which the "seizing officers" ostensibly refer, and for the attempted evasion of which the goods were seized, if not confiscated, leviable at all; simply because, contrary to RULE VII. of the Trade Rules, but in accordance with the optional clause of ART. XXVIII. of the Treaty of Tientsin (superseded by the Rule), the practice favored by the Tsung-li Ya-mên, and the public notification of the British Minister and his despatch to Earl Russell of December 2, 1862, Messrs. Bower & Hanbury, instead of bringing down their goods under a certificate, had preferred to bring them down uncertificated, not, as Sir Frederick Bruce states, "subject to such charges and regulations, as the Chinese authorities *might choose to impose*," but subject to such customary inland charges as were lawfully payable upon silk between the place of purchase and the port. The whole of these inland dues must be supposed to have been levied upon the goods under Mr. Brooks' charge up to "the south barrier"; because those goods, being uncertificated, had actually come thus far. What, then, were the further dues, demandable upon them, at the "south barrier"? *The le-kin or war-tax.* No other tax is levied at "barriers," 卡. It is a striking circumstance, and one not unattended with a painful impression, that Sir Frederick Bruce speaks of this tax, instead of designating it by its proper name, as "the *half transit*-duty," and that he looks upon Mr. Hanbury's "pretention that the *half-duty* was not legally leviable on uncertificated produce, as a suspicious feature in the case." That he did not confound it with commutation-tax or half Tariff export-duty, is but too plain from his own words. Why, then, disguise the *le-kin* under the name of "the half *transit*-duty," which existed not, and "the half (export) duty," which it was *in amount* only? Let us conclude that the British Representative in Peking was, at the time, somewhat bewildered as to the true merits and bearings of the case under consideration. We have already seen that the Chief Superintendent of British Trade in China continued, for four years after the conclusion of the Supplementary Treaty of Shanghai, which did away with the optional clause of Art. xxviii. of the Treaty of Tientsin, in ignorance of the true import of the stipulation finally agreed upon, *and came to read it aright only in 1863.*

Three questions, then, arise here, namely:—Were the silk-boats really bound to pull up at "the south-barrier," *i.e.* the floating *le-kin* barrier, newly placed in the stream, "in order to pay the transit-dues," as asserted in the Declarations of James Kennard and Moses Jagger? Had these tide-waiters in the Foreign Chinese Maritime Customs Service the legal right to board and seize the property of British subjects, for an alleged attempt to evade the payment of *le-kin* at a newly launched "barrier?" And was the Tau-tai of Shang-'hai lawfully authorised to confiscate the property of British subjects for such an alleged attempt, "without," as the Messrs. Bower and Hanbury forcibly urge, "any trial or hearing of their defence," and "in gross violation of all rules of English law and equity"? We have to answer all these questions in the negative. Mr. Hanbury, in corroboration of the deposition of his agent, "distinctly states that there was no barrier where the boats were seized, but a junk anchored in the river, and *the existence of which was unknown to Mr. Brooks when coming down the river*, the Custom-house business formerly being done entirely on shore." The boats, Mr. Brooks declares, *were on their way to the old Chinese Custom-house*, (where the final inland imposts used to be levied and paid). *There were no "transit-dues," i.e.* no commutation tax, *payable* upon British property, which was being conveyed without a certificate, *either at "the south" or any other "barrier."* No British-owned property, though uncertificated, was *legally subject to the payment of le-kin*, most certainly not, as I have previously shown (pages 56-58) at barriers erected since the ratification of the Treaty of Tien-tsin in October, 1860; and "the south-barrier" had been created and set afloat long afterwards,—for the *illegal* purpose, moreover, of levying, contrary to Treaty, upon British-owned (and other) native produce (and British and other foreign goods) a heavy war-tax. Hence, the boats under the charge of Mr. Brooks were *not* bound to pull up at the south barrier in order to pay the transit-dues. As to the second point: No tide-waiter or tide-surveyor in the *Foreign* Chinese Maritime Customs Service had any business whatever with the collection of Chinese *inland* imposts, *solely and alone excepting the commutation-tax*, fixed by Treaty, upon *certificated* foreign merchandise or foreign-owned or to-be-owned, native produce; much less had they any business with the collection of *le-kin*,—a tax *unlawfully* and in open violation of Treaty-provisions imposed upon Foreign and Foreign-owned property. Hence, Moses Jagger and James Kennard, so far from having a legal right to board the boats and seize the cargo, overstepped, in so doing, and exceeded their duty in every sense; and, instead of being allowed to share in the spoil, should have been prosecuted and punished for their unlawful proceedings.

Regarding the third point: Art. xvi of the Treaty of Tien-tsin contains these words: "British subjects, who may commit" (or be accused of having committed) "any crime in China, shall be tried and punished by the Consul, or other public functionary authorised thereto, according to the laws of Great Britain;" and it was in direct violation of this Treaty-provision, that the British Minister in Peking directed Consul Medhurst:—"You cannot insist on hearing the case in a Consular Court, but you are" (i.e. are only) "entitled to have the evidence, on which the Taoutae proceeds, communicated to you." A more ill-considered and culpable abandonment of a most important principle, established by Treaty and dictated by necessity—a necessity involved in the semi-barbarous condition of China and the moral and legal depravity of her Officials,—could hardly have been made to rest on more untenable grounds, namely: that the Chinese Authorities were, despite of Treaty stipulations, entitled to levy the illegal *le-kin* tax on silk brought down uncertificated, but in accordance with the British Minister's own Notification and the Tsung-li Ya-mên's own interpretation of the Treaty; and that the disappearance of Leech (Mr. Leeds, who never disappeared) from the boats, taken in connection with the pretension that "the half duty," i.e. the *le-kin*, was not legally leviable on uncertificated produce, formed a suspicious feature in the case. Nor is this all. The silk of the Messrs. Bower and Hanbury was not lawfully liable to pay *le-kin* at the newly invented floating-barrier; or, for argument's sake assuming that it was, there existed neither ground nor excuse whatsoever for seizing, much less for confiscating, the property; but simply occasion for its detention until the payment of *le-kin*, if legally due on it, should be effected. The Taoutai of Shanghai, therefore, possessed no lawful authority to confiscate British property under any circumstances; and in the particular case under consideration, not only in violation of international Treaty-stipulations, but also in utter disregard of Chinese law and universal principles of justice. And in this course of arbitrary illegality and defiance of Treaty-obligations, adopted against one of the most wealthy, respected, and honorable British merchants of Shang-'hai, the corrupt and unscrupulous Chinese Official, whose rapacity was as well known as the integrity of Messrs. Bower and Hanbury, was supported by the Chief Superintendent of British trade in China, and Her Majesty's Representative in Pe-king.

There is only one of the extraordinary, feeble, and ill-considered reasons finally assigned by Sir Frederick Bruce in explanation of his decision, to which I have still to refer. It is, that "a perusal of the evidence had left no doubt in his mind, that the boats formed part of a number that attempted to pass the Custom-house barrier without reporting." Waiving our right to expect logic and lucidity of expression from a British Minister in Pe-king: what he, I presume, meant to imply or to say was, that the boats, under the charge of Mr. Leeds, which had *preceded* those under the charge of Mr. Brooks, and did pass "the south-barrier" without reporting, actually *had defrauded the Chinese revenue*; and that, consequently, the latter, in attempting the same thing, must have had the same object in view, or, belonging to the same convoy, were equally guilty. There would have been at least *some* degree of apparent force in such an argument, had it been proved, 1stly that Mr. Leeds, on that occasion, *had* defrauded the Imperial revenue, and 2ndly, that Mr. Brooks stood, and acted, under his orders. But no such proof had been given in evidence; and the merits of the case had to be judged, not from *impressions* which might be created *in Sir Frederick Bruce's mind*, but from *facts*, which should been substantiated *in the Consular Court*. The only foundation for these impressions rested on the Declarations of Moses Jagger and James Kennard, the "seizing officers." The former states that, on or about the 18th of January, 1862, "he observed *a large convoy of boats* passing on the Pootung side of the river, instead of pulling up at his station, as they were" (not) "bound to do;" the former, that "*he observed several* boats passing down the Pootung side of the river; overtook three of the said boats, and immediately boarded them;"....that "the boats so searched by him, *formed part of a large convoy* consisting altogether of twelve boats or thereabouts, all sailing under the English Union jack, and in charge of two Europeans;" and that he was unable to state whether the remainder had any silk"—his whole mind appears to be absorbed in *silk*,—"on board or not." Now, it is manifest from Mr. Kennard's own words, that he, as well as his superior, stated partially as a matter of personal observation what they could have subsequently learned only from hear-say; but even *they* imply in no manner or way, that, from what they had been able to ascertain,—and nothing was easier for them to ascertain than every particular respecting the "large convoy of boats" they had seen pass, and their cargo,—that any attempt at evading the imposts legally payable at the Chinese Custom-house, had been made *by Mr. Leeds*. We are, consequently, fully justified in inferring that no such attempt was made; and a circumstance, which at a first cursory glance, *seems* to militate, however slightly, against my former reasoning, lends in reality but additional strength to it.

That, notwithstanding all these striking and prominent features of the case, Earl Russell, then Secretary of State for Foreign Affairs, should have "entirely concurred" in

Sir Frederick Bruce's views and "approved of" his action, needed hardly be said. I will subjoin his official despatch to this effect:—

Earl Russell to Sir F. Bruce.

Foreign Office, April 8, 1863.

SIR,—I have to state to you that Her Majesty's Government entirely concur in your views and approve the instructions which you have addressed to Her Majesty's Consul at Shanghae, as reported in your despatch of the 5th November last, with regard to the proposals made by the Taoutae for taxing *Chinese subjects* who reside within the limits of the so-called British Concessions.

The lands situated within the limits of the British Settlement are without doubt Chinese territory, and it cannot reasonably be held that the mere fact of a residence within those limits exempts Chinese subjects from fulfilling their natural obligations.

(Signed) RUSSELL.

It may possibly be thought that I have devoted too much space to an incident almost "dead and forgotten;" but I have done so for various cogent reasons, *viz.*: in vindicating one of the most respected firms of Shanghai from the charge of smuggling or a wilful evasion of the payment of imposts legally and legitimately due to the Chinese Government,—a charge which I conscientiously believe, and from the published evidence before me have *proved*, to be devoid of all foundation,—preferred against it by the Chinese Intendant of Trade and supported by the British Minister in Peking, to vindicate the character of *the British merchant in China* from such an accusation; to show, how inextricably, under certain circumstances, the Foreign Customs Service appears to be mixed up with the

† As a special instance I may here allude to the well-known Sung-Yang claims of Messrs. Jardine, Matheson & Co., for which Sir Rutherford Alcock has failed to obtain compensation, whilst the similar claims of Russian merchants were successfully enforced by the Russian Minister, General Vlangaly. The case has been fully reported by me elsewhere, and forms one of the most striking instances of the repudiating force of the Chinese Government, and the absence of every sense of honor and justice on its part, on record.

levying of illegal inland taxes, which over-burden British trade with the Interior and render the Treaty of Tientsin in this respect "a dead letter;" to furnish from the period of office of Sir Frederick Bruce, as I have done, here and elsewhere, from that of his successors Sir Rutherford Alcock† and Mr. Wade, an illustration of the kind of protection and countenance, which British merchants in China have thus far enjoyed at the hands of Her Britannic Majesty's Representatives and Chief Superintendents of Trade in Peking; to indicate both the necessity and the expediency of the separation of the two charges, and the appointment to Shanghai of a Consul-General for China, entrusted with extensive powers, and in all matters and decisions touching Commerce and Trade independent of the British Minister; and, lastly, to contrast with the action of the Representatives of England and the British Government, relative to the obligations imposed by the Treaty of Tientsin, the action of the Chinese Government and the Tsung-li Ya-mên.

I have already had occasion to remark, that the *le-kin*, after its first introduction about the year 1843, at the rate of $\frac{1}{10}$ per cent., was soon and steadily raised, until, 1856, it reached "per station" 2½ per cent. *ad valorem*. An official tariff of *le-kin* payable at each "barrier" upon "foreign goods," 洋貨, with the taxes calculated on this scale, or rather, inclusive of a small "squeeze," at "Tls. 2.5.5.0 for every Tls. 100 upon the value of all such merchandise," and dated "the —th day of the 6th month of the 8th year of S'ien Fêng (1858), is now before me. Subsequently to the ratification of the Treaty of Tientsin, the rate was made equal to that of the commutation-tax then agreed upon, *i. e.* to half the Tariff import- and export-duties, except on "duty-free" or such goods as are not mentioned in the Tariff, and on which about 3 per cent. "per station," or half that rate, *i.e.* about 1½ per cent. at certain intermediate stations or "half-barriers," are now levied. These rates it had apparently been judged expedient at the time not to exceed; and the method adopted for a further augmentation of the tax, has been to multiply the barriers, or to double the tax at the same barrier, by giving to the additional "half duty" a different name, such as *chow-fang* at Shanghai and other ports. The highest rates prevail in those provinces, in those districts, and along those lines of communication, where the largest amount of foreign trade, *i.e.* trade in foreign goods and native goods foreign-owned or intended for exportation to foreign parts, is carried on, or where it is intended to impede or stop such a commerce altogether. Along lines commanding a trade only or chiefly in merchandise of the country, the tax is even nominally much lighter, and for the same line of road *within the same province* restricted to nominally 10 or 12, hence in reality to 5 or 6 per cent. as a *maximum*. For, in practice, native goods enjoy a still greater advantage, as compared with foreign goods, and native goods destined for foreign parts: inasmuch as there prevails a custom, on the part of the Tax-officials, to allow, in consideration of the payment of a very moderate "squeeze" or bribe, the native merchant to declare, for articles of home-trade, a fictitious value, which, as a rule, may be taken to reduce the tax to one half its nominal amount;‡ whereas, not only

‡ Mr. Edward B. Drew, Commissioner of Customs at Kiukiang, in a Memorandum on *le-kin*, of which I shall presently have occasion to speak, states:—"The practice is to declare about 80 per cent. of the whole quantity if the cargo be a small one, and some 60 per cent. if it is large." But, not only does he adduce a case, which had come under his personal observation, and in which only 50 per cent. of the value of a cargo of charcoal were declared; but his Tables, embodying the results of his own calculations, show that, for twenty-six articles of foreign cotton and woollen manufactures, and three kinds of foreign

is no such reduction allowed for foreign goods and native produce intended for exportation to foreign parts or foreign consumption in China, but official "squeezes" are levied upon them to the utmost extent to which it is found practicable. They vary from 5 per cent. to 30 per cent. or more, and may, in the mean, be estimated at about 20 per cent. upon the nominal *duty*. Thus, suppose a given quantity of Chinese manufactures, N, and a similar quantity of foreign manufactures, F, each of the taxation-value of £100, to be sent from a port A to an inland mart B, and the nominal or Tariff amount of *le-kin*, payable upon it, to be 20 per cent.; or let a given quantity of native produce, say tea, intended for native consumption, N, and a similar quantity, destined for foreign consumption, F, each of the taxation-value of £100, be supposed to be sent from an inland mart D to a port C, and the *le-kin* payable upon it to be 20 per cent. also. In either case, the value of the goods N would be allowed, on the part of the Chinese Tax-officers, to be declared at one half or £50, and the *le-kin*, actually levied upon them, would be besides "squeezes," say 10s., £10. 10s.; whereas the value of the goods F would have to be declared in full at £100, and the *le-kin*, levied upon them, would be £20, besides 20 per cent. "squeezes" = £4; making in all £24: *so that foreign inland trade in China, touching le-kin, is under a disadvantage of at least from 13 to 14 per cent. on each line of road, where such trade is carried on, within each Province, as compared with native inland trade.*

---

metals, the declared value, in the mean, deduced from the number of articles and the duties computed by Mr. Drew, is only 46 per cent. He also seems not to be aware of the difference *in practice* made by the Chinese Tax-officers between foreign goods and native produce destined for foreign consumption, and native goods intended for native consumption. Nor is it easy to obtain correct information upon points like these. It, certainly, is not obtainable from Chinese *officials*.

But this is not the principal point. China differs somewhat from Western countries. We have seen that the Tsung-li Ya-mên allows to a foreign merchant, who intends purchasing native produce at some stated mart in one of the provinces, separated by a second province from the one in which his sea port residence is situated, just 400 days, *i. e.* one year and thirty-five days, to go, transact his business, and return. Locomotion is not carried to a high rate of speed in the Celestial lands. The enterprising merchant may travel from one end of the empire to the other, safe from any danger of a steam-boiler exploding or the engine running off the rail. China has no Manchester or Sheffield distributing its manufactures all over the country. Almost every city is, in a manufacturing sense, isolated, and supplies its own wants alone. Few fabrics and articles such as silk, raw-cotton, grass-cloth, samshu, tobacco, opium, etc., have any large sale beyond local consumption. Even the book trade is to a great extent carried on locally in local editions. As regards the great staple-articles which England sends out to China, Cotton- and Woollen-Goods, they have mainly to compete with home-made stuffs only. The Chinese inter-provincial trade in these manufactures is altogether insignificant. Hence, since no native Cotton- and Woollen-manufactures pass the Custom-houses and Barriers, neither *le-kin*, tolls, nor any other duties levied at those establishments, fall upon them; and hence again, the inland imposts just alluded to burden in reality, so far as British and foreign imports into China are concerned, *almost exclusively the British and foreign trade.*

This shows the fallacy *per se* of Mr. Wade's argument,—adopted also by the British Board of Trade, and resting on the assumption that the *le-kin* tax weighs equally upon native and foreign inland traffic. Above all, however, the facts, here adduced, on the one hand prove to evidence, that the tax in question was, as Mr. Tsai has it, "invented" by the Chinese Government for the special purpose of obstructing *foreign* inland trade, whilst simultaneously deriving the largest possible amount of revenue from it; and on the other hand, in combination with the fact that *le-kin* is included, and was by the Chinese Government distinctly understood to be included, in the inland charges commutation-tax finally agreed upon by RULE vii. of the Supplementary Treaty of Shanghai, they fully explain the anxious efforts of the Tsung-li Ya-mên and the high Provincial Authorities to uphold, despite of that Rule, the optional clause of ART. XXVIII. of the Treaty of Tientsin,—palming their obstructive disingenuousness upon the facile belief of Sir Frederick Bruce, Sir Rutherford Alcock, and Mr. Wade, and through them upon the English Government and the public, for generosity;—to discourage the "transit system" under certificate in every possible way; and to withhold from the Chinese themselves their right, as clear as that of foreigners, to take out certificates both for foreign merchandise intended for sale inland and native produce destined for foreign consumption,—a disingenuousness and Treaty-misconstruing efforts, in which they were, and to this day, as we have seen, continue to be, zealously supported by the foreign Inspector-General, Mr. Hart, and his subordinates.

In 1861, Mr. Horatio N. Lay, who then held the position just referred to, had to go home on sick-leave. He appointed as his representative an English gentleman, the late Mr. FitzRoy, at the time Commissioner of Customs at Shanghai, and, conjointly with him, Mr. Hart, on account of Mr. FitzRoy's unacquaintance with the Chinese language. Mr.

Hart, in this capacity, went on a short visit up to Peking, where he arrived on the 5th June, 1861; had, on the 15th, a first interview with Prince Kung; and before the end of the month had became the Tsung-li Ya-mên's "own Hart."‖ His supposed influence or subservience in this capacity made itself soon felt, as will be seen from the subjoined Custom-house Notice of July 22, 1861, followed by the Correspondence and Consular Notification, to which it led:—

NOTICE.

RULES REGARDING THE IMPORTATION AND EXPORTATION OF CHINESE PRODUCE.

1. Foreign Merchants in exporting Chinese produce from Shanghae pay, as it is provided in the Treaty, the inland or half-duty, and the export tariff duty.

2. Foreign Merchants in bringing merchandise from the Yang-tse River have only to pay the inland or half-duty at the time of importation, but if such goods should be exported the export duty will be levied.

3. Foreign Merchants in conveying Chinese produce from Shanghae into the Yang-tse River have to pay the inland or half duty.

4. When Foreign Merchants bring Chinese goods from the Yang-tse River to Shanghae, if such goods should not be landed but transhipped for exportation, both the inland or half-duty and the export tariff duty will be levied.

5. When Foreign goods arrive at Shanghae, if such goods be not landed but transhipped for the Yang-tse River, the import tariff duty and the inland or half duty will be levied on them.

6. Goods imported to Shanghae by Foreign Merchants from Ningpo, Foochow, Canton, Tientsin, and any of the Treaty ports, should pay the import tariff duty; but if such goods should be reshipped for exportation the export tariff duty will not for the present be enforced.

Office of Maritime Customs,

Shanghae, 22nd July, 1861.

‖ See Note ‖ to page 68, above. Sir Frederick Bruce's version, in an official despatch, as quoted by Mr. Wilson (History of the "Tai-ping Rebellion," London, 1868, 8°, p. 260) is:—"By his tact, good sense, and modesty, he (Mr. Hart) *obtained access* to the Prince of Kung, and *turned to useful account* the favorable impression he made upon His Royal Highness and his advisers." Let it be remembered, that it is the patron of Mr. Hart, who writes thus; and the diplomatist's language appears plain enough. In 1863, Mr. Lay's dismissal was obtained by the late Mr. Burlingame under circumstances which I shall relate in another place.

BRITISH CHAMBER OF COMMERCE,

SHANGHAI, 25th July, 1861.

SIR,—Enclosed I have the honour of handing to you a copy of certain new Regulations, bearing date the 22nd July, which have been posted up in the Custom-house, and in accordance with which that Office now claims that all the duties in question should be paid.

It is not the intention of the Chamber on the present occasion to enter at length upon the subject of these Regulations, but it loses no time in addressing you to protest: *Firstly*—Against the act of the Custom-house in framing and attempting to put into force new Regulations without the consent previously obtained of the British Authorities, to whose subjects, trading under Treaty protection, such new Rules must apply; and, *secondly*—Against the manner in which, under the Regulations alluded to, the Custom-house Authorities interpret the Treaty-clause respecting Transit-duties, which, in the opinion of the Chamber, are very clearly defined by Treaty as only leviable upon the transit of either imports or exports the property of Foreigners, and in those cases in which they exercise their option of commuting the transit-duties for one-half of the Tariff-duties, *between the Treaty ports and the interior of the country*, and certainly *not between* one *Treaty port and another.*

Further, the Chamber considers that the system of granting exemption certificates on the re-export of goods, whether Foreign or Native, has become by long usage the established custom of this port, many operations being entered into with this knowledge and in reliance upon this fact, which must be seriously interfered with by any sudden alteration; that on these grounds alone, without alluding to the right to claim such exemption certificate under the Treaty which the Chamber considers to exist, it is not competent for the Chinese Authorities to alter such established usage without due notice to the Mercantile Community, and certainly not without previously consulting at least the local British Authority, if not Her Majesty's Minister at Pekin.

Moreover, in the opinion of the Chamber, Clause 6 of the Regulations enclosed contains an implication that the Custom-house has a right to impose a duty (which for the present it intends not to enforce), which appears to be quite at variance with Clause 15 of the Treaty of Tientsin.

For these reasons the Chamber does hereby protest against such new and unauthorised regulations and alterations; it requests your immediate attention to the matter, and begs that this its protest may be brought without delay before the notice of Her Majesty's Minister and Chief Superintendent of Trade at Pekin.

I have the honour to be, &c.,

(signed) R. C. Antrobus,
Chairman.

To W. H. Medhurst, Esquire,
Her Majesty's Consul,
Shanghai.

British Consulate,
Shanghai, July 27th, 1861.

Sir,—I have had the honour to receive your letter dated the 25th instant, calling my attention to a Code of Regulations under date the 22nd July lately posted up in the Custom-house, and requesting me, on behalf of the Chamber, to convey to H.M.'s Minister at Peking their formal protest against the irregular manner in which the said Regulations have been promulgated, and the construction which they place on Treaty stipulations.

The Superintendent of Customs addressed me a letter on the 20th instant, announcing his receipt of instructions from Prince Kung to stop the issue of exemption certificates on China produce carried from one port to another from the 17th instant, and he followed up his notice by a second letter on the 22nd instant, enclosing a copy of the Regulations you allude to, which he declared were necessary as a temporary measure, until Prince Kung could decide how to treat Chinese produce brought into port after having been before imported elsewhere.

As I looked upon the issue of Exemption Certificates on Chinese produce as a long-established usage of the port, whether permissible under the 45th Article of the Treaty or not, and therefore not revocable without the assent of H.M.'s Minister and due notice to all persons concerned, and as I considered the Regulations in themselves objectionable on many grounds, I informed the Superintendent of Customs, in a reply dated the 23rd instant, that I could recognize neither innovation, but that I was prepared, if any alteration were desired, to take it into consideration, and refer it for Mr. Bruce's opinion by the next northward mail.

The Superintendent declined my offer, and persisted in maintaining the correctness of his proceedings, allowing the Regulations meanwhile to be posted at the Custom-house in the English language, and to be put in force in several instances on goods landed and shipped by British subjects.

Under these circumstances I had no alternative than to issue the Notification of the 25th instant, which you have doubtless seen, and to lodge a formal protest stated the 26th instant, against the Superintendent's acts, in which I remonstrated not only against the abrupt and discourteous manner in which the innovation had been made, but pointed out the objectionable character of the Regulations themselves.

That protest, together will all correspondence connected with it, will be transmitted to H.M.'s Minister by the next northward mail, and I shall take the same opportunity of conveying a copy of your letter under acknowledgment, for the information of the Honourable Mr. Bruce.

I have the honour to be, etc.,

(Signed) W. H. Medhurst,
H. M. Consul.

To R. C. Antrobus, Esq.,
Chairman of the British Chamber of Commerce.

Notification.

British Consulate, Shanghae,
23rd September, 1861.

H. M.'s Minister Plenipotentiary, &c., &c., at Peking, has pronounced an opinion on the question at issue between the Chinese Superintendent of Customs of this Port, and the Undersigned, relative to the indiscriminate levy of transit-duties on all Chinese Produce, whether brought down from the interior or purchased at a sea-port, and the abolition of Exemption Certificates.

With respect to the six Rules issued by the Custom-house, on the 22nd July, 1861, H. M.'s Minister decides:—

1st, That the British Merchant has nothing to do with the payment of transit-duties, unless the goods are carried into the country, or brought down from the place of production, under Certificate as British property. It is optional to the British Merchant to take out the Certificate or not as he pleases; but if he does not, and he buys or sells at the port of shipment, he has nothing to do with the payment of any duty, but the one specified in the Tariff on Imports and Exports.

2nd, When Chinese Produce is procured at one port, and carried thence to be shipped at another port for the Foreign market, such produce is only liable to the Export duty at the first port of shipment, where all duties in the nature of transit duties due by the British Merchant ought also to be levied.

H. M.'s MINISTER thinks the above is the fair construction of the Treaty.

As regards the exaction of transit-dues at Shanghai on goods despatched up or brought down the Yang-tse River, H. M.'s MINISTER does not admit the principle on which it is founded, as he considers the arrangement adopted for payment of tariff-duties at Shanghae as one eminently favorable to the Chinese Government, and the payment of Transit-dues by the Foreign Merchant is dependent, as has been stated, on his taking out a certificate at the port of shipment, which is in this case either Hankow or Kinkiang.

As to Exemption Certificates on produce carried coast-wise from one Chinese port for consumption in another, H. M.'s MINISTER is ready to agree that tariff-duty be paid at the port of shipment, which shall be brought to account for indemnity, and half-duty at the port of discharge, which being in the nature of a transit-duty, shall not be subject to deduction for indemnity. This rule will apply to cargo of the above denomination carried up or down the River Yang-tse.

Imports and Exports in the Coast Trade being liable, under the understanding now declared, to pay a half tariff duty more than Imports and Exports in the Trade between China and Foreign Countries, H. M.'s MINISTER thinks that the Custom-house will be entitled to make such arrangements as shall prevent the loss to the Revenue that would be occasioned, were goods, nominally imported for re-shipment outwards, detained and consumed within the Port.

Pulse and Beancake are declared by H. M.'s MINISTER to be separately provided for by the 5th Article of the Tariff Rules.

The Superintendent of Customs has received instructions from Peking corresponding to the opinion above detailed, and the Undersigned is now in consultation with him regarding a few Rules which he proposes to issue in pursuance thereof, as also in respect to arrangements for the refund of all duties which have of late been levied in contravention of the principles now laid down by H. M.'s MINISTER.

(Signed) W. H. MEDHURST, *Consul.*

The entire incident here related, would seem to have lapsed from the Inspector-General's memory, when he wrote his "communicated article on the Transit-System for the *North-China Herald.*" It is from the above Notification, that Mr. Hanbury in his deposition quoted the first paragraph regarding the optional clause of ART. XXVIII. of the Treaty of Tientsin. The first paragraph of the final "Regulations, sanctioned by Sir Frederick Bruce, regarding Transit Dues etc.," and promulgated at Shanghai by Mr. Markham, H.M.'s Vice Consul in charge, on October 30, 1861, would have been even more to the purpose, but appears to have escaped his attention. I have to speak of those Regulations now.

By ART. X. of the Treaty of Tientsin it was conceded that, on account of the Upper and Lower Valley of the river being then "disturbed by out-laws,—the *Tai-pings* were not acknowledged as "belligerents,"—the only port to be opened to trade, within a year's time, was Chin-kiang. In the early part of 1861, however, "Provisional Regulations for Foreign Trade on the Yang-tsze-kiang" were issued by Sir James Hope and Mr., now Sir Harry, Parkes; Sir Frederick Bruce having, in November, 1860, proposed to the Tsung-li Ya-mên the opening of Kiukiang and Hankow as well. On the 21st September, 1861, the Tsung-li Ya-mên, having now the benefit of Mr. Hart's advice, counter-proposed to the British Minister "certain necessary *alterations* in the Regulations provisionally agreed to," trusting "that his Excellency would call on Merchants trading on the Great River, to abide by them (the proposed alterations)."

At the same time, the Tsung-li Ya-mên further proposed certain Regulations affecting the "Transit-System" and the Coast-Trade. Sir Frederick Bruce, having revised the former and formulated the latter, communicated his "Revised Provisional Regulations for British Trade in the Yangtze River," and "Regulations (sanctioned by Mr. Bruce) regarding Transit Dues, Exemption Certificates, and Coast Trade Duties" to the Tsung-li Ya-mên, the Home Government, and, by Notification published at Shanghai in October 30, 1861, to the British community in China. In his despatch of October 26, 1861, to Earl Russell, he gave "a short statement of the considerations which had induced him to issue these Notifications."

On the part of the Tsung-li Ya-mên, too, the Chinese versions of these documents were communicated to the native Superintendents of Trade and, it is to be presumed, to the Foreign Inspectorate-General. The Superintendent of Trade for the Southern Ports imparted them to the Intendants of Customs and others for their guidance, in a Notification dated "S'ien Fêng, the 11th year, the 9th month, the 30th day" (Oct. 4, 1861). In the former Notification England is simply styled 英國 "the Eng or rather *Ying*) State" and, at the first occurrence of the term, placed contemptuously at the foot of the Tsung-li Ya-mên, which, of course, is duly raised two lines; whilst in other places, the same as the name of the British Minister 卜大臣, "the Honourable Pu" (Sir Frederick Bruce), itis, also in disregard of every Chinese rule of propriety and respect, written on the common level of the lines, or embodied in the running text. Then follow the "Twelve Temporary Regulations for Trade on the Great River," as understood, and originally proposed, *by the Tsung-li Ya-mên*, succeeded by the "Eng State's Notification," 英國告示, (Sir Frederick Bruce's emendations), wherein England appears, from being again placed on the common level of the lines, in the position of a subordinate Tributary State, to whose "Notifications" the Chinese Officials are, in view of the Ya-mên's Regulations, expected to pay what heed they may judge proper. Next come, similarly arranged, the Tsung-li Ya-mên's "Five General Regulations regarding Trade" touching 納稅, "the payment of duties," as understood by the Ya-mên; and finally the "Eng State's Notification" regarding them, in which 大英欽差大臣卜, "the Great Eng (lish) (Chinese-) Imperially appointed Commissioner, the Hon. Pu" (raised two lines), says so and so. Sir Frederick Bruce's name is here raised, because he is designated, not as the Envoy of "the Great Eng State," 大英國 [欽差], but as 欽差, a (Chinese) "Imperially appointed Commissioner,"—so the term is usually translated when applied to an Envoy or Authorised Agent of the Emperor of China,—being 大英 [國人] a native of the Great (Tributary) State Eng. The character 欽 "Imperial" is exclusively used in relation to the Emperor of China, and never applied to, or in connection with, any other Prince. Our phrase, therefore, describes Sir Frederick Bruce as being in the special service of "the one Lord of the World." So greatly the Tsung-li Ya-mên must have been pleased with his "Regulations regarding Transit Dues, etc.," or with their Chinese version as composed or sanctioned by the then Interpreter of the British Legation in Peking, Mr. Wade; or with both, and other matters connected with the subject.

Now, it is distinctly stated in the Tsung-li Ya-mên's despatch to the British Minister of September 31, (also printed in the Blue Book, but which should be Sept. 21), 1871, that the proposed Regulations as regards 納稅, "the payment of duties," also, shall be forwarded, together with the proposed Temporary Regulations for Trade on the Great River, in a separate despatch. The translation of this despatch, of the same date, appears in the printed Official Correspondence, and has the following concluding paragraph:—"A necessary communication, to which are appended the Regulations of Trade on the Great River, addressed to the Hon. Mr. Bruce, *etc.*" Even without the preceding notice, I could have safely affirmed, that the "*etc.*" of the translation will not be found in the original; but, instead of it, and preceding the words "addressed to the Hon. Mr. Bruce," the "Five General Regulations for Trade," 通商各口通共章程五款, touching 納稅, "the payment of duties." But no translation of these proposed Regulations is printed in the official correspondence, presented to the House of Commons; and to all appearance their contents have been actually withheld from the knowledge of the British Government. The proposed "Provisional Regulations for Foreign Trade on the Yang-tsze-kiang" alone are appended to the English version of the Tsung-li Ya-mên's despatch.

The omission and the apparent corresponding mutilation, of the concluding sentence of the Tsung-li Ya-mên's despatch referred to, may not unreasonably be accounted for by the fact, that the Ya-mên's proposed Regulations state distinctly and repeatedly, that "the foreign as well as the Chinese merchant shall equally, on coming to any Custom-house pay duty, *and on passing any barrier pay le-kin,*" 洋商華商均逢關納稅過卡抽釐, both upon foreign goods intended for inland consumption, and upon native produce destined for exportation to foreign ports. This is sufficiently startling. But what is still more so is the Chinese version of the "Regulations sanctioned by Mr. Bruce regarding Transit Dues, Exemption Certificates, and Coast Trade Duties," communicated, in the original text, by the British Minister to his Government, and by public Notification,—at Shanghai on October 30, 1861,—to the English mercantile community in China. I will subjoin this text, so far as it relates to "Transit-Dues," and side by side with it a faithful translation of the corresponding Chinese version, rendered as literally as possible:—

Regulations sanctioned by Mr. Bruce regarding Transit Dues, Exemption Certificates, and Coast Trade Duties.	*The Great-English (Chinese-) Imperially-appointed Commissioner the Honourable Pu, hereby gives*
NOTICE is hereby given, that the following are the arrangements sanctioned by Her Britannic Majesty's Envoy Extraordinary, Chief Superintendent of Trade, &c., &c., regarding Transit-Dues, Exemption Certificates, and Coast-Trade Duties:—	PUBLIC NOTICE respecting *War-Taxes payable at Inland Stations,* Coast-Trade (literally: Second-Port Entrance) Duties, and Exemption Certificates, as now clearly fixed by his Excellency under Three Heads of Regulations for the due observance of all English merchants.
1. *Transit Dues.*	1. *War-Taxes payable at Inland Stations.*
1. It is at the option of the British merchant to clear foreign imports to an inland market, or native produce to a port of shipment, either by payment of the different	1. English merchants desiring to send foreign goods into the Interior for trade and barter, or to convey native produce to a seaport for shipment,§ shall be allow-

§ This, and a similar, passage in the next paragraph of the Chinese version, show, as previously intimated, that the Tsung-li Ya-mên looked upon native produce being simply and *bonâ fide* intended for shipment at a sea-port, as the one essential condition, which entitled and entitles it to a Certificate. Indeed, when the Ya-mên, in § 4, incidentally only, supposes the produce to have been *purchased* at the inland mart: we find, that it takes the very same view of the whole subject, which has been vindicated by me as the true one, from the English texts of the Treaties themselves.

charges demanded at the inland Custom-house, or by one payment of a half-Tariff duty as provided in Tariff Rule 7.

ed to do so, on either conforming with inland law and paying (by way of tribute) duties at each Custom-house they meet, and *le-kin at each Barrier they pass;* or else, according to the provisions of Rule vii. of the Supplementary Treaty (literally: Bond),—which states that, on application (more literally: on supplication), foreign goods shall be granted a Duties (-paid) Certificate, and native goods a Conveyance-Pass (undertaking) that Duties shall be paid according to Treaty,—by the single payment of one half of the Tariff (literally: normal) Duties. With these two alternatives (or essentials) all are bound to comply.

2. In the case of native produce the memorandum to be presented at the first inland barrier may be there deposited by the merchant himself or his agent, native or foreign; but whereas it is alleged, that both native and foreign transit-dues have been totally evaded by the sale of produce *in transitu* after entry at a barrier as for shipment at a Treaty port, the memorandum tendered must be in the form of a Declaration, signed by the firm or merchant interested, and to the effect that the produce therein specified and entered on —— date, at —— barrier, for shipment at —— port, is the property of the Undersigned firm or mer-

2. English merchants, conveying native produce to a port, shall, on arriving at the first station, enter a special declaration, clearly stating particulars. Either the merchant himself, being present and proceeding (to the port), or the agent whom he may employ, whether a native of his own State or a native of the Central State (literally: of the Interior) may make this statement. There are cases, in which goods have arrived at a station and, having been falsely declared to be on their way to a seaport, have been allowed to pass, whereas afterwards they have been clandestinely sold *in transitu* without paying any Government-duties

chant, and that the said firm or merchant engages to pay the half-Tariff transit dues thereon.

This form will be provided gratis by the Maritime Customs at every Treaty port, and issued on the Consul's application by the Superintendent of Customs.

whatever.¶ Considering these constant and unlawful evasions, it is now stipulated that the goods shall be clearly specified in the Declaration, as also the day of their arrival at such and such a station, the port to which the merchandise is really to be conveyed, and where the merchant, who owns the native produce, engages to pay (by way of tribute) the half duty thereon. All of which having been clearly stated in the Declaration, there is then at the foot of the document to be affixed the merchant's name and surname, or else the letter of authority from the mercantile firm concerned, by way of proof.*

This form of declaration will be provided to any merchant by the Custom-house at each port, and issued at the Consul's request in writing,—free, moreover, of expense.

3. Native produce carried inwards from a port cannot be cleared by a transit-duty certificate, whether in charge of native or foreigner; it is liable to all charges imposed on goods *in transitu* by the Provincial Governments through whose jurisdiction it passes.

3. Native produce conveyed into the Interior, cannot be franchised by the (tribute-) payment of the half duty. It shall pay, in accordance with the inland law of each Province (tribute-) duty at each Custom-house it meets, *and le-kin at each Barrier it passes.*

¶ The blame of these evasions, in the English text only *alleged*, and by the Tsung-li Ya-mên stated to Sir Frederick Bruce to have been effected by *Chinese* (see page 91, above) are laid to the charge of the foreign merchant and his agents.

* Here we have another positive proof, on the part of the Tsung-li Ya-mên, against the assertion of the Inspector-General that "Agent, Goods, and Certificate must travel in company, to secure exemption" (see page 88, above).

4. Foreign imports not protected by transit-duty certificates, are liable to the same charges.	4. [In the Chinese version omitted].
5. No transit duty is leviable on foreign imports or native produce carried up or down the Yang-tze-kiang between Shanghai and the ports on that river now open under provisional rules; but foreign imports, carried inland from either of these ports, pay foreign or native transit dues, according as they are certificated or uncertificated.	5. If, under the temporarily granted Regulations for the Great River, merchant-vessels, proceeding from Shanghai to Hankow or Kiukiang for trade and barter and carrying produce down, or foreign goods up, the river, buy or sell whilst just touching at the port, they shall in neither case have to pay (by way of tribute) Government-duties. But foreign goods, which arrive in Hankow or Kiukiang, and are stored and subsequently conveyed into the Interior, or native produce purchased in the Interior, shall, when accompanied by a Certificate *en règle*, pay the half duty; or else, when holding no Certificate, they shall pay (tribute-) duty at each Custom-house they meet, *and le-kin at each Barrier they pass*—in accordance with (Chinese) principles of administration.

It would be difficult to assign any reason for this Notice in so far as it relates to the "Transit-System," considering that the latter had been distinctly regulated by ART. XXVIII. of the Treaty of Tientsin and RULE VII. of the Supplementary Treaty of Shanghai; but what renders the Notice still more unintelligible is, that it violates those Treaties in material points, and in a sense altogether favourable to the Chinese and detrimental to the interests of British and Foreign Trade. For, in the first place, it upholds the optional clause of Art. xxviii. against the final stipulation of Rule vii. I have already shown, that this was an object stealthily but persistently sought to be accomplished by the Tsung-li Ya-mên and the Provincial Authorities, burning for the *le-kin* and the "squeezes" bound up in it, and as yet without a machinery to secure at the inland mart, to which foreign goods might be sent under Certificate, the booty which would thus escape them *in transitu*,—a point to which I shall revert in the sequel. In the second place, the Notice admits upon uncertificated goods the payment of all "the different charges demanded at the Inland Custom-house," than which a more latitudinarian, unstatesmanlike, and irrational concession of the kind could hardly be imagined. True, only the inland Custom-house (關, to be distinguished from 卡, a Barrier) is spoken of; but in the following paragraph "barriers" are mentioned, and here to insist, therefore, on the distinction alluded to, would be a mere quibble. What the Notice really grants are *all* charges, of whatever kind, "which the rapacity or the necessities of Chinese officials may impose upon foreign trade," and *demand*, at the various inland stations, barriers as well as Custom-houses. And hence, it sanctions, *by implication*, as in the Chinese version of the Notification it does in direct terms, the payment of *le-kin* upon all uncertificated merchandise, whether foreign goods intended for sale in the Interior, or native produce destined for exportation to foreign ports.

In a former section of this essay, I have produced to evidence:—1, That the Treaty of Tientsin, taken, as it should be (Art. i. and liv.), in connection with the Treaty of Nanking, renders the levying of *le-kin* altogether, and that of other inland charges, in the aggregate exceeding the stipulated Treaty-rate upon foreign inland trade, (whether carried on under Certificate or not,) illegal.—2, That the Treaty of Tientsin, even when read by itself, renders the levying of *le-kin*, at other stations, and at higher rates, than those established or in legal use *at the time*, and the levying of any inland charges whatsoever, in the aggregate exceeding the stipulated commutation-tax upon foreign inland trade, (whether carried on under Certificate or not,) equally illegal. —3, That the Tsung-li Ya-mên and the Chinese Provincial Authorities themselves distinctly understand the *le-kin* and other "war-taxes" to be included in the stipulated inland charges commutation-tax.—4, That, by the payment of this commutation-tax, *the goods*, upon which it had been, or had to be, paid, whether foreign manufactures or native produce, and whether in the possession, or the property, of British *or Chinese* subjects, were to be exempted from all *further* inland imposts *whatsoever*. And—5, that the whole of the foreign inland trade was to be carried on under Certificate; in other words, that, independently of the stipulated import- and export-duties, the Chinese Government *should* be free to levy upon that trade one-half of such duties, respectively, in addition, and in the shape of inland taxes, but that it should *not* be free to levy upon it one single cash in excess of this additional half-duty.

Under these circumstances, two not unimportant questions arise, namely: Are arrangements, come to between the Tsung-li Ya-mên and a Representative of England at Peking and approved of, whether silently or otherwise, by Her Britannic Majesty's Secretary of State for Foreign Affairs, *at variance with Treaty-stipulations*, lawful and binding? And: Who, in the present case, is responsible for the arrangements of this nature, more especially for the levying of *le-kin* and other illegal imposts upon British inland trade in China, conceded, in violation of the clear Treaty-rights of the Merchant, to the Chinese Government? The former question may be positively answered in the negative. No international Treaty, once concluded, can, so long as it continues in force, be essentially modified in its provisions by the mere action of a British Envoy abroad, though afterwards concurred in or sanctioned by the Foreign Office at home.

As to the second question, we have to assume, on the one hand, that the Chinese version of Sir Frederick Bruce's Notification regarding Transit-Dues, etc., communicated in English to the British Government in his despatch to Earl Russell of October 12, 1861, is the correct and genuine text, as translated, or approved of, by the Chinese Secretary and Interpreter of the British Legation in Peking, at that time Mr. Wade; and, on the other hand, that the papers relative to this matter, presented to the House of Commons by order of Her Majesty, are full, correct, and genuine transcripts of Sir Frederick Bruce's correspondence. Both suppositions may, I think, be here unhesitatingly adopted.

Proceeding, then, to argue on the basis of these suppositions: it is clear from the published official correspondence, that a translation of the important draft of Regulations respecting War-Taxes payable at Inland Stations, etc., submitted by the Tsung-li Ya-mên on September 21, 1861, to the British Minister, has been designedly withheld from the knowledge of the British Government; and that the same is the case as regards the positive right, conceded to the Tsung-li Ya-mên, to levy *ad libitum*, and in violation of existing Treaties, *le-kin* and other war-taxes upon British inland trade —in opposition to Rule vii. of the Supplementary Treaty of Shanghai distinctly allowed, and thus encouraged to be—

carried on without Certificate: a right, *conceded in an unfaithful Chinese version* of a Notification, officially promulgated in English for the guidance of the British mercantile community in China.

It may possible be urged, that the terms of the original Notification: "by payment of the different charges demanded at the Inland Custom-house," include *le-kin* and taxes of any kind whatsoever; and, consequently, that neither the British Government nor the British mercantile community have been deceived by the special terms, employed in the Chinese version. But such an argument will not hold good. The British Government, no more than the Merchants, can be expected to be acquainted with the working of the fiscal system of the Chinese. It has to trust, in this as in numerous other respects, to its Representative and the Members of the Legation. But in reading Sir Frederick Bruce's Notification, the natural impression, produced on the European mind by the sentence referred to, is that it speaks of the ordinary road-charges,....tolls, octrois, etc.,—ordinarily levied on inland traffic, and as the English Minister's explanatory despatch to the Foreign Office contains not a syllable to the contrary, not a word indicative of the true nature and amount of the "different charges demanded": that impression has to be taken as the actual meaning, which Sir Frederick Bruce *intended* to convey both to his own Government and the mercantile community in China. Both, therefore, in presence of the Chinese version determining the real construction placed by the Tsung-li Ya-mên upon the words of the original Notice, were deceived; and there is here not mere neglect, somewhere, on the part of the British Legation,—there is culpability. How little the Merchants had understood the clause under consideration, is best proved by the incessant and unanimous complaints which the imposition of the *le-kin* and other "illegal" imposts have subsequently elicited from them as a body.

Sir Frederick Bruce possessed, personally, no knowledge of the Chinese language. Hence, he could not possibly have carried out the apparent deception, commented on, without the participation of his Chinese Secretary and Interpreter, then, Mr. Wade. What presents itself to us as the only subject for inquiry, is: Whether Sir Frederick Bruce was at all aware of the real state of the case? whether the translation of the Tsung-li Ya-mên's proposed Regulations regarding War-Taxes payable at the Inland Stations, was by him withheld from the knowledge of the British Government, and the apparent substitution of "etc." for the title of that document in the translation of the Ya-mên's despatch of September 21, 1861, effected by his order or at his instance? and whether, having been duly made acquainted with the true sense and purport of the official version into Chinese of the Regulations regarding Transit Dues, Exemption Certificates, and Coast Trade Duties, sanctioned and publicly notified by him, the British Minister at Peking kept Her Majesty's Seeretary of State for Foreign Affairs and the British merchants in ignorance of that sense and purport? Or: Whether Sir Frederick Bruce himself was left in ignorance touching the points in question, end the entire responsibility of the matter falls, and falls solely, upon his Chinese Secretary and Interpreter? I am not in a position to solve the problem. Nor have I the desire to do so. There occur expressions in Sir Frederick Bruce's official correspondence, more especially in connection with the confiscation-case of Messrs. Bower and Hanbury, which *seem* to betray his consciousness of the *le-kin* tax as an impost upon British goods, which the Chinese Government was entitled to levy, and an example of great want of national scrupulosity on his part I have had occasion to adduce elsewhere: still, the expressions alluded to are, after all, quite reconcileable with the hypothesis of his having acted, in the Transit-Dues affair, although with extreme laxity and partiality, yet with perfect sincerity and good faith. On the other hand, the Interpreter's participation in the assumed deception appears hardly deniable; and what gives a worse colouring to the actual extent of his responsibility, is the extraordinary and, it appears to me, irrational warmth with which, in his Memorandum on the Revision of the Treaty of Tientsin, by Mr. Wade submitted to his Government in December, 1868, he, in disapproving of, defends, and, in condemning, advocates and upholds the *le-kin* tax. In simple fairness towards Mr. Wade, however, I have once more to call the reader's attention to the *premisses*, on which the whole of this argument is made to rest. It would pain me for one moment to doubt his Excellency's ability to offer a perfectly satisfactory explanation of the points at issue. All I have wished here to insist on, is *the imperative necessity for such an explanation on his part.*

Meantime, it will add not a little to Mr. Wade's difficulties in this respect ‡ that, whilst he lays all the blame, connected with the *le-kin* tax, on the Provincial Authorities, the Chinese version of Sir Frederick Bruce's Regulations, which, until evidence shall have been offered to the contrary, must be regarded as Mr. Wade's own composition, transfers that blame almost entirely to the Tsung-li Ya-mên

‡ These difficulties are far from being restricted to the point here mooted. I abstain, however, from further alluding to them, as they are inseparably connected with matters foreign to the subject of the present treatise.

and the British Legation. Indeed, it turns the tables completely upon himself. With the instructions of the Ya-mên and Superintendents of Trade before them: what choice had the native Customs' Officials but to obey? True, in Chinese fashion, they have made and make the most of the opportunity; but the responsibility rests with the higher Authorities just named, and through the Ya-mên with the Chinese Government. The action of the latter, so far from finding an excuse in the complaisance of the British Minister and/or his Chinese Secretary and Interpreter, is but aggravated thereby, inasmuch as it *knew* that the points conceded involved a positive violation of the international Treaty, solemnly concluded with Great Britain; that they could not hold good in law; and that, on the day of reckoning, the Government might, and it is to be hoped will, have to refund the large sums, unlawfully levied upon British and Foreign trade.

And had not also the Inspector-General, Mr. Hart, cognizance of the real state of matters? He was acquainted not only with the Treaties and both the Chinese and English texts of Sir Frederick Bruce's Regulations, but also with the fact that the Tsung-li Ya-mên and one of his immediate superiors, the then Superintendent of Trade for the Southern Ports, Tsêng Kuo-fan, fully admitted the illegality of the *le-kin* tax on foreign trade, nay, as will be presently seen, that the latter warned, or rather instructed his subordinates to avoid every collision with foreign Consuls, on account of that tax being contrary to treaty-stipulations. In his very memorandum, in which he so strongly defends the "in transitu" theory, i.e. the tax in question, he refers to the collection of Ying, in which Tsêng's despatch is printed.‖

‖ See the part, entitled: 長江各口通商暫訂章程, fol. 16-17*a*.—Comp. p. 17, above.

Reserving the determination of the actual amount of the illegal exactions here under consideration for the next section, I have, in this place, to speak of only two more attempts, made by the Customs to modify the practical working of the Trade Rules, attached to the Treaty of Tientsin, in a spirit diametrically opposed to the stipulations of that Treaty, and regarding which the Inspector-General in his Memorandum on the "Transit-System" observes silence. The first of these attempts dates from the month of May, 1870, and originated in an application to the Tau-tai of Shanghai, (in his capacity of Intendant of Customs) from —if I am well informed—the American Consul-General, Mr. Seward, for permission to one of his nationals to send some coals, in a lorcha owned by the latter, to the island of Tsung-ming, opposite Wu-sung. The application was promptly and peremptorily refused, on the ground of a document, on that occasion framed by the Tau-t'ai T'u for general guidance in future, and which is now known as "T'u's Five Rules for the prevention of Smuggling." The following translation of the Chinese text was published, at the time, in the *Shanghai Evening Courier* :—

1.—Whenever a foreign merchant desires to send foreign goods into the interior of China, he must make a written application through the Commissioner of Customs, stating distinctly what kind of goods he wishes to send; the quantity, the name of the vessel by which such goods were imported, the name of the place to which they are destined, the route by which the goods are to travel, and a description of the boat by which they are to be sent. The Customs will then send a person to examine the boat; and after his report, a permit may be issued for these goods specified to proceed on their route; said permit is to state the name of the boat-captain; and if in passing the barriers, there be found no discrepancy between the goods and the permit, said boat may be allowed to proceed; but if any discrepancy be found between the cargo and the permit, the goods and boat shall be detained, and sent to their place of departure for adjudication.

2.—Foreign goods proceeding into the interior will not be allowed to proceed by any other than the interior routes; nor be allowed on any other than boats used for inland travel; no sea-going boats can receive such permission to convey goods; nor can the goods proceed by the sea-coast—so as to allow of smuggling; and any deviation from this rule will render the boat and goods liable to seizure and confiscation,—and the master of the boat liable to punishment by the Chinese authorities, so soon as any attempt is made to pass the barrier at the sea-coast.

3.—Whenever any person wishes to obtain a pass for goods proceeding into the interior, application must be made by the person or hong immediately concerned, and no person or hong may apply for a permit for any other person or hong; and if any foreigner disposes of his pass to a Chinese, the goods covered by their pass shall all be confiscated; and the foreigner so disposing of his permit shall be sent to the Consul of the nation of which he belongs, for fine and punishment, and the Chinaman who purchases such permit shall be punished by the Chinese authorities.

4.—Whenever a boat having foreign goods arrives at a barrier, the permit must be handed to the officer in charge of the barrier for verification; and if satisfactory, the seal of the barrier shall be affixed, and the goods allowed to proceed. But if any person fail to hand in his pass, or refuse to allow such verification, or carry any goods not enumerated on the permit, the person in charge of the barrier may detain the person, and confiscate the goods, and send the master of the boat to the nearest Chinese magistrate for punishment, and send a report of the case to the officer granting the permit.

5.—When the foreigner has received a pass for goods to go into the interior, the pass shall state distinctly the name of the place to which the goods are to be sent, and when the goods have arrived at their destination, the permit must be handed either to the officer in charge of the barrier there, or to the local Magistrate; who shall cut off a corner of said permit, and send it to the place whence it issued. And if any person should conceal his permit and attempt to use it a second time, he will render himself liable to fine and punishment.

These Rules have since, in his correspondence with the Consuls, been frequently referred to by the Chinese Intendant of Customs as authoritative; have given some trouble; and are still, if I am not mistaken, under the consideration of the Peking Authorities, foreign and native, respectively. In a place, where Memoranda of the Tsung-li Ya-mên are liable to turn into "etc.," Copies of the Treaty of Nanking cannot be found on the one hand, and proposed Solutions of the Missionary Question are misplaced on the other, "T'u's Five Rules" stand a fair chance of going altogether astray.

A second and more ambitious attempt of Chinese encroachment upon the Treaty of Tientsin, to which allusion has already been made in an earlier portion of this treatise, was undertaken in the summer of 1871, by the native Intendant T'u, and the Foreign Commissioner, of Customs at Shanghai, Mr. Dick, combinedly. The latter Official namely, under instructions from the former, desired to enforce a new form of "Transit Pass to Interior," of which I subjoin a literal copy :—

TRANSIT PASS TO INTERIOR.

Shanghai,........................187 .

Customs No.......

Commissioner of Customs,

Applicants....................................

Please apply to the Superintendent of Customs for a Transit Pass to enable the undermentioned merchandise to be sent to ....*

[Table setting forth No. of packages and description of goods.]

......hereby declare that the above mentioned merchandise is wholly...... own property, that ...... have purchased it from ...., and that, ... intend sending it to.............................., * for the purpose of being sold by ...., * solely on ...... own account.

(Signature of applicants.)

* Name of place and of agent to be given in Chinese.

The following correspondence relative to this innovating form of declaration, as published in the *North-China*

Herald for July 21, and July 28, 1871, will fully explain its tendency and bearing, whilst carrying down its history to the action taken in regard to it by the Tsung-li Ya-mên, previously referred to in connection with Mr. Hart's anonymous Memorandum on "the Transit-System":—

TAOUTAI TO CONSULS.

Shanghai, June 20, 1871.

H. E. Too, Tautai of Shaughai, makes the following communication to the several Consuls of Treaty Powers:—

In regard to Customs passes for transporting foreign merchandise into the interior; if the merchandise is the *bonâ fide* property of a foreign merchant, purchased for the purpose of sending it to an interior market, a Customs pass can be granted.

At present there are at Shanghai a lot of foreign merchants of small capital, who not unfrequently pass goods at the Customs for Chinese, and apply for a Customs pass, in their own name, to transport the said goods into the interior, whereas the said goods are not their own property, and they are simply acting for the Chinese owner; for which service they receive a certain consideration. Thus, the Chinese, by borrowing the name of others, defraud the Gavernment out of the taxes that would otherwise be collected, by the way, [*in transitu*], on the said goods: therefore it is necessary that some regulations should be established by which a stop may be put to this fraud.

In future, a foreign merchant applying for a Customs pass, if the merchandise is not his *bonâ fide* property, two things must be expressed in the Customs pass. 1st, From what hong the goods were purchased. 2nd, The name of the place and the name of the hong or the person to whom the said goods are consigned for sale, These two regulations cannot in any way be annoying to the foreign merchants, while it will enable the Customs to arrive at the true state of things. There is no difficulty in stating, in the Customs pass, the hongs from which the goods were purchased, while the Customs having this information can be easily satisfied by inquiries at the hong. Thus, when the goods are transported to the interior, to a certain place, and consigned to a certain hong or person for sale, it will be easy for the Customs at such place to inquire of such hong or person, and verify the truth or falsity of the statements made.

In addition to forwarding by the Superintendent of Customs a blank form of application for Customs passes, and instructing him to act according to the above regulations, I have the honour to enclose the said form of application for your Excellency's inspection, and have to request that you will act accordingly.

CHAMBER OF COMMERCE TO CONSULS.

Shanghai, June 24, 1871.

SIR,—I have the honor to solicit the attention of the Consular Body to the accompanying form of application recently adopted by the Customs at this port, in cases where merchants desire to procure Transit Passes for foreign goods to the interior of the country, and I beg reference especially to the declaration required, to the effect that the goods are the property of the person making the application, and to the additional information demanded as to their purchase, the agents' name to whom they are consigned, and the person on whose account they are to be disposed of.

The Chamber has already so fully expressed the views and the wants of its members with reference to the general question of Transit-dues, that I will not ask your Committee to peruse a reiteration of them; but as the action of the Customs appears distinctly to point to their insistence upon the practice of withholding Transit passes for foreign Imports in the hands of Chinese, I have to request that you will kindly bring the matter to the notice of the Foreign Ministers at Peking, in order that a clear declaration of the intentions of the Chinese Government may be elicited; and should the Government purpose to apply the articles of the Treaties in a manner to exclude foreign Imports in any case from the privileges accorded by the 10th Article of the Nanking Treaty and the 28th of that of Tientsin, the Chamber trusts that their Excellencies will take steps to enforce the right of traders under the clauses named.

Sir Rutherford Alcock has left us no doubt as to the interpretation he attached to the British Treaty in this respect, which by the most favoured nation clause in other Treaties applies equally to Foreigners of other nationalities; for in his despatch dated "On the Yang-tsze November 24th 1869" addressed to Her Britannic Majesty's Consul, his Excellency, contrasting foreign imports with native produce writes: "It is otherwise with Foreign Imports. These are entitled to the protection of Transit passes, whether in Chinese or foreign hands."

This point the Chamber has always maintained; and an attempt to limit the privilege to goods still in the possession of Foreigners it is constrained to view as an infraction of the Treaty stipulations.

It cannot be urged by the Chinese Government that Art. 28 of the British Treaty of Tientsin overruled the 10th clause of the Nanking Treaty, for it is expressly stated in Art. I. that: "The Treaty of Peace and Amity between the two nations, signed at Nanking on the 29th day of August, 1842, is hereby renewed and confirmed." And Art. 54 reads: "The British Government and its subjects are hereby confirmed in all privileges, immunities and advantages conferred on them by previous Treaties."

This being the case, reference is made to the plain language of the Nanking Treaty, wherein it is stipulated that: "When British merchandise shall have once paid" [etc., see above p. 73]; and this renders it difficult to conceive what plea can be used to authorize the withdrawal of the privilege thus explicitly granted in 1842 and confirmed in 1858–60.

A minor objection to the declaration demanded from applicants for Transit-passes is its inquisitorial character, for unnecessary inquiries into the details of the business of merchants are regarded as obstacles to trading; but the main point on which the consideration and action of the Foreign Diplomatic Representatives is asked, is the important question above brought forward, of the limitation of Treaty rights concerning foreign Imports.

I have the honor, etc.,

(Signed) F. Porter, *Chairman.*

To the Chairman of the Committee of Consuls, etc.

Consuls to Taoutai.

Shanghai, July 13, 1871.

Sir,—The undersigned have received your letter of the 20th June, in which you propose certain changes in the transit passes system.

The undersigned believe that one set of rules for the issue of transit passes should be observed at all the ports. They believe also that the changes proposed by you are essential innovations, likely to be very detrimental to trade. For both reasons they believe that the subject should be considered at Peking between the Ministers and the Imperial Government, in order that a perfect and indisputable understanding may be arrived at.

The undersigned therefore invite your Excellency to take the instructions of the Government in the matter. They will, on their part, bring the subject before their respective superiors.

The undersigned insist that until instructions shall be received, there ought to be no variation from the system which has been hitherto observed at this port, and they respectfully request you to advise the Commissioner of Customs accordingly.

The undersigned have the honor to be, etc.

TAOUTAI TO CONSULS.

His Excellency Too, Shanghai Taoutai, to the several Consuls of Treaty Powers.

I received on the 30th of the 5th moon the reply of the twelve Consuls, and understand it.

My propositions in regard to Transit passes are not innovations, and in no way at variance with the Treaty, and could in no way be detrimental to the interests of Foreign merchants.

Now, since the various Consuls are not satisfied, let the custom, which has hitherto been observed, stand in force,

In addition to informing the Superintendent of Trade and requesting Tsêng-kwo-fan to communicate the matter to the Tsung-li Ya-mên and await an answer, I have the honor to make this reply.

That the Tsung-li Ya-mên must have virtually decided against the innovation, proposed by the Taoutai T'u and Mr. Dick, who would hardly have acted in such a matter without instructions from the Inspector-General, appears from the fact that, practically, Chinamen have since been permitted, the same as Foreigners, to convey, under Certificate, foreign goods to stated marts in the Interior, from Shanghai and one or two other ports. But no public Notification, recognizing, on the part of the Chinese Government, the Treaty-right and the principle involved, has appeared; and that the Tsung-li Ya-mên "issued (to the effect in question) its instructions in 1868, and repeated them to the Shanghai Customs in 1871," is an assertion which rests solely on the anonymous authority of the Inspector-General, who, when "communicating" this information to a local newspaper, cannot but have known, that the Tsung-li Ya-mên does *not* correspond with, and does *not* issue instructions to, "the Shanghai Customs." The Ya-mên corresponded *on equal terms* with Tsêng Kwo-fan; who, as Superintendent of Trade for the Southern Ports (east of Canton), issued instructions to his subordinates the (native) Intendants of Customs; who, in their turn, issued instructions to *their* subordinates the Foreign Commissioners of Customs, in this case by the Foreign Inspector-General somewhat vaguely designated as "the Shanghai Customs." He must also have known that Tsêng Kwo-fan's despatch of November 5, 1868, does not state, that, in issuing his instructions to the Shanghai Intendant of Customs, he had been "instructed" to do so, much less that he had been instructed by *the Tsung-li Ya-mên*, from which he received, and would have accepted, no instructions. Lastly, the Inspector-General knew that, at the period in question (June, 1871), the important instructions of the Superintendent of Trade for the Southern Ports, so essentially affecting the practical working of the Treaty of Tientsin, and a *copy* of which was, no doubt, in the archives of the Inspector-General, as well as of "every Custom-house," had *for nearly three years past* been allowed, a dead letter, to lie in those archives ignored and unheeded.

Nor is this all. With positive instructions to act in accordance with Treaty stipulations, insuring to the Chinese merchant the right to take out "Transit"-Certificates, and, consequently, to the foreign agent to do so on the former's behalf, in his possession, Tan-t'ai T'u, in an official despatch to the Body of Foreign Consuls, had the assurance to accuse such agents—"a lot of foreign merchants of small capital" as he styles them,—in using their admitted Treaty-rights, of *defrauding* the Chinese Government of taxes, fraudulently levied by its own officials upon Foreign Trade; and he was permitted to do so without even a retractation of, and an apology for, his false charge being demanded of him. Nay, with the same instructions "in the archives of the Shanghai Custom-house," the Foreign Commissioner, in concert with the native Intendant, of Customs at Shanghai, and in order that "a stop might be put to the" (falsely alleged) "fraud," lends his aid to his native superior, and proposes a new form of declaration, by which the British and Foreign merchant is expected to sign away recognized Treaty-rights, which both the native and the foreign official had, so long as three years previously, been instructed by the Superintendent of Trade for the Southern Ports and Governor-General of the Two Kiang to respect and to act up to, but had ignored and disregarded. The translation of Tsêng Kwo-fan's despatch, as published in the *North-China Herald*, says:—"To this end I have written to the Customs and to the Intendant of Trade to act accordingly." But, there exists no Intendant *of Trade;* and the text says only, that Tsêng wrote to "the Customs," 關, *i.e.* to the native Intendants of Customs,—with whom alone, on Customs-matters, the Superintendent of Trade corresponds,—*implicitly* with instructions to direct the Foreign Commissioner of Customs accordingly. And that this must have been done, appears from the statement of the Inspector-General, who, possessing no knowledge of what the archives of the native Intendancies, but only what those of the

Foreign Commissioners, of Customs contain, could otherwise not have been aware of the fact alleged by him.

Were it not for Mr. Hart's positive statement, I should have been inclined to look upon Tsêng Kwo-fan's "instructions" as a mere empty *form,* and to exonerate the Shanghai Commissioner from responsibility, in this case, at least so far as the assumption of those instructions having never been communicated to the Foreign branch of the Customs could have done so. Not the least important question now is: whether the Commissioner of Customs acted in so grave a matter without the knowledge, or with the sanction, of the Inspector-General; and it appears to me, that both these officials owe it to themselves as well as to the mercantile community, to give a clear explanation of the facts of the case. It can hardly be a matter of indifference to the British Government, whether British subjects in foreign employ do or do not, over-stepping the proper limits of their spheres of official duty, neglect or observe their natural duties of loyalty to, and act or do not act against, the positive interests of, their own country. In various and sometimes startling forms, this problem has recently forced itself upon public notice; and it appears desirable that, in England too, it should at an early date receive that attention on the part of the Legislature, which has been given to it, long since, in the Law-Codes of other countries.

One more remarkable feature in connection with this subject, I cannot altogether pass over in silence. The practical carrying into effect of the inland-charges-commutation-clause of the Supplementary Treaty of Shanghai, which, so far as foreign goods are concerned, has demonstrated, by the rapidly progressive development of inland trade attending even its slowly extended application, the wisdom of its provision, it was, on this very account, as I have previously shown, the object of the clear-seeing Chinese Authorities to obstruct, if they could not put it down, from the first. Hence, the Tsung-li Ya-mên insisted on every fitting occasion, that it remained perfectly *optional* for the Foreign merchant to commute inland charges (inclusive of *le-kin*) or not, as he might judge proper; hence, Sir Frederick Bruce was persuaded to take for a while at least, the same view; hence, every means was resorted to, in order to surround the "Transit"-Certificates with vexatious obstacles and difficulties, or to render them of none effect; and hence, and thus, *for the space of more than ten years*, the native Authorities succeeded in virtually depriving the Foreign merchant, together with the native trader, of the exercise of one of the most important of their undisputed Treaty-rights, and in subjecting Foreign inland trade to what they knew to be *illegal* exactions. In none of the documents already adduced by me, is this so clearly expressed as in the instructions of Tsêng Kwo-fan, when he states:—"It is imperative that the Treaty stipulations be observed, and under no circumstances should the *le-kin* be made to violate existing engagements, thus provoking constant disputes with the Consuls." It is true, that the Chinese Government provided against any "loss" of Revenue from the commutation principle, by having recourse to complementary "Stationary" taxes, "Grower's" taxes, and similar imposts. In the case of foreign manufactures, however, much additional expense, squeezing, delay and uncertainty of income attended the latter process; and it was considered more convenient to keep "stopping the fraudulent practices of the outer barbarian."

Yet, in the face of all these facts, there are not only individual merchants in Shanghai, who look upon the informal and merely temperary *desistance* of the Customs-officials at this and, may-be, one or two other ports, from opposing and acting in defiance of recognized Treaty-rights, for a space of ten years unlawfully withheld from the mercantile community, as "a valuable concession" on the part of "the Chinese Government"; the local Press, moreover, usually supposed to express, and to have an interest in expressing, on matters of public importance the sentiments of the local public, unites in congratulating itself on, and spreading abroad the singular and almost ludicrous idea of, "the Transit Dues Question having been fairly settled." Thus, Mr. J. Barr Robertson writes on November 6, 1871, to the *North-China Herald*:—"Of course, the Chinese Government have the most complete liberty to grant what they please so long as it is in the right direction, but by all means let us call things by their right names, and therefore this *extension of the Transit Pass system*, long and loudly demanded, *a new and valuable concession*." And the Editor of the *North-China Herald*, in almost literally reproducing on February 1, 1871, a "Retrospect of the year 1870, published by Messrs. Da Costa & Co. on January 31, 1872, in *its* "Retrospect for 1871," purporting to emanate from the Editor's own pen, observes :—

"If there is any subject for congratulation, it is, that the Transit Dues question has been fairly settled, thanks to the exertions of an active Consul. Too much importance can hardly be attached to this fact, nor to the benefit which will, through it, accrue to the importers of foreign manufactures. It may take time to get the machinery into working order, but once this is done, the benefit to foreign trade will be distinctly visible. The very fact of Chinese being able to send foreign goods into the interior under a pass issued by their own government (corrupt as it is known to be) is a subject for congratulation, and a step in the right direction.

Had England a right-minded Minister at Peking,—(the *North-China Herald* pluralises and modifies: "Had we more vigorous Ministers at Peking,")—the wedge might be still further inserted, and permission obtained for small draft but roomy steamers to convey European goods up the creeks, to such trade centres as Soochow, Hoo-chow and Hangchow, but this, we fear, is only a dream of the future—(according to the *North-China Herald's* no-dreamy-fears-indulging version: "to the trade centres of new districts.")"

The "fair settlement of the Transit Dues Question," to which in the opinion of the Editor of the *North-China Herald*, supported by that of the *Evening Courier*, § too much importance can hardly be attached, amounted just to this, that, previously to the latter part of 1871, applications for Certificates, *i.e.* for "Receipts for inland taxes duly paid" upon foreign goods about to be conveyed to an inland mart, had to be, and were, signed by the foreign merchant, whether for himself or on behalf of his native constituent; and that now—pending further decisions, and, at any rate, at Shanghai—the native merchant is graciously permitted by the Chinese Superintendent of Trade for the Southern Ports to sign such applications personally, and, after having duly and in advance paid to his Government the full amount of inland charges by Treaty leviable upon foreign goods, to accept a Receipt for the same. This Receipt, however, or "Pass," issued accordingly, is not issued by the Chinese Government "corrupt as it is known to be"—the logic

§ The Editor of the *Shanghai Evening Courier* appears to have partly relied on an error in the version of Tsêng Kwo-fan's despatch of Nov. 5, 1868. as copied from the *Shanghai News-Letter* in the *North-China Herald*. The translator, probably overlooking that the despatch is printed as registered by the Tau-tai Ying, has erroneously connected the date of the despatch, T'ung Chih, 7th year, 9th month, 21st day (Nov. 5, 1868) with certain "Regulations" of the Tsung-li Ya-mên, issued S'ien Fêng 11th year (1861), referred to immediately afterwards, and which, omitting the latter date and applying to them the former, he renders "a communnication." The fact that the despatch was received in Shanghai on T'ung Chih, 7th year, 9th month, 26th day, (Nov. 10, 1868), as he himself translates, should have called his attention to the mistake into which he falls, since no despatch from Peking could possibly have reached Shanghai, *via* Nanking, in five days.

of the *North-China Herald* is occasionally unintelligible—but, which is a very different thing, by an Intendant or Intendants of Customs, acting under instructions only from a local Superintendent of Trade; and how far this may, or may not, be "a subject for congratulation, and a step in the right direction" I will leave for the reader to say. Statements such as those here referred to, playing as they do into the hands of the Chinese Government, can only tend to mislead public opinion both in China and at home. The best comment upon them are the new Transit-Regulations, framed by the Inspector-General, and proposed by the Tsung-li Ya-mên.

VII.

ILLEGAL TAXATION.

Tabular view of the amount of illegal taxation and total amount of imposts, levied, within the importing Province, on Foreign Trade, during the year 1870, by the Chinese Government—Complementary "Stationary"-trade taxes—Produce tax—A "strike" of Chinese merchants—Comparison of the Table with the similar Table, published in 1869, by the Shanghai Commissioner of Customs, Mr. Dick—Taxes on Opium and Cotton Goods—Principle of Chinese illegal taxation—Taxes on Woollen Goods, Metals and sundry articles of importation—Taxes on Silk, Tea, and sundry articles of exportation—General Remarks—The Commissioner of Customs at Kiukiang on *le-kin*—Unreliability of his special data—Examination of details, on which Mr. Dick's Table is based—His Table officially admitted to be restricted to inland charges, collected at, or near, the ports—Its arithmetical errors and incongruities—Object of its publication—Alleged "loss to Chinese Revenue by Hongkong being a free port"—Mr. Dick's "Hongkong Claims"—Smuggling in Opium—Corruption of Chinese officials—India *versus* China—The British Possession of Victoria a thorn in Mr. Dick's side—His "Hongkong Claims" examined—The Chinese Customs-tariff compared with the tariffs of some other countries—Opium not taxed more heavily in China, than are imports generally—Defence of the Opium trade—Deceptive character of the Tsung-li Ya-mên's Opium Memorial—The Memorial essentially the composition of a foreigner—Its leading motive—The growth of the poppy in India a legitimate branch of agricultural industry—Annual amount of illegal taxation to which Foreign Trade is subject in China—The Tonnage Dues—Systematic fabrication of Chinese public accounts—Differential Coast-trade duties—Mr. Dick's threatened "Withdrawal of the Department from its connection with the Home trade"—Amount of imposts, by the Chinese Government annually levied on Foreign Trade in open and systematic violation of Treaty-stipulations—Estimate of the accumulated debt, thus surreptitiously contracted by China towards England since the Treaty of Nanking.

THE by far most important item, connected with the practical working of the Treaty of Tientsin, is the actual amount of illegal taxation to which Foreign Trade is at present subject in China, and to which, to a greater or less extent, it has been subject ever since the conclusion of the Treaty of Nanking. Its determination is, as to details, attended with unusual difficulties. I have spared, however, no trouble in endeavouring to obtain official and other trustworthy information from every source, both native and foreign, accessible to me; and from the concurrence of many elements and tests, independently collected and applied, I venture to affirm with a degree of confidence amounting to certainty, that the *general* results at which I have arrived may be accepted as perfectly reliable. They are, for the year 1870, contained in the succeeding annexed table, in which, for the sake of avoiding exaggeration, the 'Hai-kuan' tael has been converted into English money at the rate of only 6/– a tael.

Among the documents which I have been able to procure, and which have been used by me, I may mention an official list of all the taxes levied within the Foreign Settlements, by the Taou-t'ai, as Intendant of Customs at Shanghai,—洋涇浜各局收捐章程冊; an authentic list, obtained from the Chow-fang Office.

The table, it will be noticed, contains only the taxes collected on Imports within the importing province, and on Exports for the producing province. If the merchandize pass through other provinces, it becomes liable to a double and treble amount of such charges. That is to say, if *f. i.* uncertificated foreign goods, after having paid, within the importing province, besides the import-duty and treaty commutation- or "transit"-tax, 10 per cent. or more *ad valorem* for *le-kin* and other illegal taxes, they are, on entering a second province, liable to additional illegal imposts of 10 per cent. or more *ad valorem;* and, having thus paid upwards of fully 20 per cent., over and above treaty-rates, on entering a third province, they become liable to further illegal taxes of 10 per cent. or more *ad valorem*, exclusive of about 20 per cent. in each case, upon the illegal amount of *imposts levied*, for "squeezes." Similarly so in regard to Chinese produce, destined for exportation to foreign countries.

The local consumption at the ports is, comparatively speaking, so small that the whole of the imports, the same as the exports, may be considered for our purpose as subject to inland taxation. The additional imposts levied, both in amount and name, differ at the different ports to a greater or less extent; and so do the inland charges on uncertificated imports and intended exports in each province. But, so far as I have been able to ascertain, the aggregate of the dues illegally imposed on foreign goods at Shanghai, being the chief centre of foreign trade in China, *represent a fair mean;* and it is on this account that the fiscal documents of which I have been able to avail myself possess, as to details, a greater and more general value than would otherwise be the case. They may to some extent be considered as normal. The wharfage-dues at the port in question are nominally only 1 per mille. Actually, however, they are levied at the approximate rate of 1 per cent. *ad valorem;* and as a similar tax, though differing in name, is imposed, I learn, at all the other open ports, its excess has been carried uniformly through the table.

When the goods are accompanied by a "transit"-certificate, they pay ostensibly, and should pay only about 2½ per cent., in accordance with Treaty-provisions. In reality they pay 12½ per cent. *ad valorem* and upwards, just as though they had been uncertificated. The difference is made up, in the case of native produce intended for exportation abroad, chiefly by the "grower's tax," 落地捐 or 落地税, besides Licenses, etc.; in case of foreign imports by the "Stationary trade tax," 坐賈, the former in the producing districts altogether, the latter, in various forms, mostly levied inland. It is with this view and for this purpose, that the merchant has to state, at the port, particulars of goods to be sent into the interior, as well as the place of their destination, in order that a copy of such particulars may be at once forwarded by the Intendant of Customs to the officials of that place, and thus "the goods" may, to use the words of the Inspector-general, Mr. Hart, "after having once entered the stream of general Chinese trade, *become liable to the incidence of local taxation.*" That is to say, in violation of the clearest Treaty-rights of the Foreign Merchant, the Chinese Government having, through the certificate, been prevented from levying *in transitu* its illegal imposts in full, does so the moment the goods have arrived at their destination, by submitting them, in addition to the half-duty paid, to a complementary duty, to which the general name of "Stationary trade taxes" is given.* Hence, in some shape or another, the whole of the illegal charges, with which the Chinese Government is "overburdening" foreign trade, are finally levied upon it despite of Treaties and "Transit-Certificates." The total value of British trade with China, in 1870, amounted, according to the In-

* Mr. Drew, in speaking of this "Stationary Trade Tax," remarks:—"It was established at Kiukiang a few months after the recapture of the city in 1858, simultaneously with the other form of *le-kin*... The tax consisted of the levy upon every shop of a certain fixed number of cash per diem, greater or less for each according to the supposed amount of its daily business. In theory this levy was 2 per cent. of that business. To show what it was practically, it may be mentioned that a certain small grocery, whose receipts were from 15,000 to 20,000 cash, was assessed 66 cash, afterwards 35 cash a day; and that one of the largest piece good hongs paid 600 cash a day; the smallest shops paid only 8 or 10 cash. Payments were made once every five days. The principal abuses said to have been connected with it were those which, at the inception of the plan, attended the fixing of the sum each shop should pay. Then and later, partiality was shown by the deputy in the sum assessed—in consideration of value received. This branch of the *le-kin* continued in operation (at Kiukiang) until the summer of 1868, when it was abolished as no longer necessary (at Kiukiang)." My own information is at variance with the latter statement.

spector-General's Returns, to H. Taels 185,417,000; the trade, carried on under Certificate, reaching H. Taels 4,804,000, or less than $2\frac{2}{3}$ per cent. on imports, and only H. Taels 341,000 or between $\frac{1}{5}$ and $\frac{1}{6}$ per cent. on exports. For the reasons stated, the certificated inland trade, generally, does not affect the amount of illegal taxation, unless it be, perchance, in the case of Russia, the "Total Value" of whose trade, "coast-wise, inwards, and outwards," according to the Statistics published by order of the Inspector-General, and to the unreliability of which I have already had more than once occasion to refer, amounted, in 1870, to H. Taels 194,544, whilst her "Transit-Trade inwards" was of the value of H. Taels 16,530, "outwards" of the value of H. Taels 621,088, together H. Taels 637,618, or more than three times the value of her total trade.

At an early period of this year (1875) a regular strike on the part of the native merchants at Tientsin and, almost immediately afterwards, at Shanghai, was provoked by an attempted change in the present system of levying the so-called transit-duties. The merchants shut their offices for several days, refusing either to ship or to take delivery of foreign goods, and their guilds declared point-blank to the Intendants of Customs, that they would rather relinquish business than yield. Differences between Chinese guilds and Chinese authorities are not laid bare to the "outer barbarian;" and by the foreign public the real merits of the case were, as usually, altogether misapprehended. If I am correctly informed, the question was, and is, a grave one, although for the present settled by the obnoxious measure being withdrawn by the Intendants of Customs both at Shanghai and Tientsin.

For some time past the *le-kin* tax is understood to have

been again the subject of repeated conversations between the foreign Ministers at Peking and the Tsung-li Ya-mên, and, as the time for the revision of the German Treaty is approaching, the Chinese Government would seem to have bethought itself of the best manner in which not only to keep up the *tax*, but to save also the heavy expense of its present method of collection, by "sacrificing" the inland *barriers* to the urgent demands of Western diplomacy and the Treaty-*rights* of Foreign trade, against a fair *compensation* in the shape of an increased rate of import-duty on opium, or the like. With this end in view, the Intendants of Customs at Tientsin and Shanghai appear to have received orders from the Tsung-li Ya-mên—it may not unreasonably be supposed with the cognizance of the Foreign Inspector-General,—to levy the *whole* of the charges, now levied on foreign Trade at the ports and inland, *at the ports*. The idea was a brilliant one. No doubt the Chinese Government calculated, on the part of the foreign merchants, either upon their indifference, having for years past allowed a variety of heavy illegal taxes to be imposed on their trade in the very Foreign Settlements, or upon their ignorance of what is going on, in the way of taxing foreign goods, at their own ports; on the part of Western Powers and their Representatives, upon the theory of the British Board of Trade, supported by the British Minister in Peking and the Foreign Inspector-General of Chinese Maritime Customs, that, in a fiscal sense at least, a bale of shirtings or a chest of tea and a Chinaman being identical things, Western Governments have no right to interfere, in the matter of taxing, between the Emperor of China and "his subjects." Unfortunately for the success of the measure, it placed the whole burden of the taxes in question on the shoulders of *the native merchants at the ports;* and the native merchants at the ports being less philosophical and logical than the Lords of Her Britannic Majesty's Privy Council for Trade, and less loyal to "the Son of Heaven" than the Representative of England and the Tsung-li Ya-mên's foreign confidential adviser, they rebelled against that measure† and thus, *for the time being*, it fell to the ground.

Annexed is the Table referred to:—

† At Shanghai the "Grower's tax" had been levied for some time past, and so far as this particular impost is concerned, it was at the port in question rather against the conti- [illegible] of the merchants was directed.

Denomination of Goods.	Quantity.		Value in £ Sterling.	Tariff Import and Export Duties levied at Port.		Additional Imposts Levied. At Port. Wharfage in Excess.	Le-kin.	Chau-fung.	Le-kin, &c. At Stations between Port and central Centre of Trade.	At Stations beyond.		In all.	Amount levied within the Importing Province on Imports; on Exports in each Province through which they pass.	Amount of Illegal Taxation.		Total Amount of Imposts, levied on Foreign Trade, within the Importing Province on Imports; on Exports in each Province through which they pass.	
				Amount.	%	Per-centage on Value.								%	Amount.	%	Amount.
Imports.			£	£									£				£
Opium,—Malwa	Piculs	84,690	5,292,230	312,910	6·0	0·0	10·0	8·0	..	..	..	18·0	733,150	..	..	19·0	1,056,930
Patna	,,	18,240	1,611,740	119,180	7·4	0·9	10·0	3·7	..	..	..	14·6	283,390	..	..	21·0	364,480
Benares	,,	6,130	747,31[illegible]	58,770	7·7	0·9	10·0	3·9	..	..	..	14·6	113,58[illegible]	..	..	21·5	17[illegible]
Other kinds	,,	1,220	161,990	10,850	7·1	0·0	10·0	3·6	..	..	..	14·8	24,040	..	..	21·6	33,480
			7,783,360	600,950	6·18							14·16	1,004,020			20·68	1,604,970
Cottons,—Grey Shirtings	Pieces	4,435,190	2,594,140	105,210	4·0	0·9	..	2·8	9·6	9·6	4·0	12·5	330,150	10·2	277,040	19·3	436,250
White ,,	,,	790,470	435,470	17,540	8·6	0·9	..	2·0	2·0	2·0	4·0	13·6	58,390	9·7	49,210	15·0	74,500
T-Cloths	,,	8,016,230	1,376,420	54,370	3·9	0·9	..	2·2	2·6	2·5	4·0	13·1	185,500	10·1	139,190	16·9	[illegible]
Drills	,,	626,440	815,350	31,800	3·4	0·9	..	1·0	2·2	2·2	4·0	11·6	70,070	9·6	60,170	16·7	91,970
			5,181,820	199,020	3·84							12·05	631,550	10·15	524,640	15·99	[illegible]3,370
Woollens,—Camlets	Pieces	84,990	616,290	19,920	6·5	0·9	..	8·6	8·8	8·7	4·0	15·9	40,910	12·7	30,900	22·3	69,8[illegible]
Cloth *	,,	46,920	411,390	8,900	2·2	0·9	..	1·4	1·6	1·6	4·0	9·5	39,010	8·3	34,120	12·0	[illegible]
Spanish Stripes	,,	71,840	235,600	13,[illegible]	5·7	0·9	..	3·1	3·4	3·4	4·0	14·8	34,370	11·0	25,920	20·5	[illegible]
Lastings	,,	59,440	159,020	5,900	5·7	0·9	..	2·0	2·2	2·2	4·0	11·4	18,2[illegible]	9·5	15,250	15·3	24,1[illegible]
Long Ells	,,	302,500	300,150	16,[illegible]	5·8	0·9	..	3·0	3·5	3·5	4·0	14·5	44,790	11·8	30,130	19·8	50,730
Lustres, &c.	,,	240,770	250,220	14,810	5·7	0·9	..	3·1	3·4	3·4	4·0	14·3	35,300	12·0	30,060	20·5	50,170
			1,874,040	79,780	4·76							13·35	223,200	8·69	1[illegible]3,310	16·99	302,9[illegible]
Metals,—Copper	Piculs	30,140	98,650	9,180	9·3	0·9	..	4·0	6·0	6·0	4·0	19·4	19,240	11·9	14,710	28·7	28,[illegible]
Iron	,,	322,150	304,0[illegible]	19,340	6·1	0·9	..	8·0	3·5	3·8	4·0	14·6	30,5[illegible]	11·5	33,420	20·5	41,930
Steel	,,	20,340	10,950	1,350	7·6	0·9	..	3·8	1·3	1·3	4·0	11·1	6,400	13·8	3,640	31·7	4,9[illegible]
Lead	,,	166,[illegible]	365,430	19,390	5·8	0·9	..	2·6	2·3	2·3	4·0	15·5	61,0[illegible]	10·7	41,100	19·6	70,990
Tin	,,	60,700	365,360	18,050	5·4	0·9	..	2·0	2·9	2·8	4·0	13·3	48,900	10·7	39,120	18·6	67,300
			1,071,430	61,870	5·77							14·15	151,930	11·28	130,[illegible]30	19·06	218,700
Sundries	....	......	5,196,120	229,210	4·17	0·9	..	2·6	2·5	2·5	4·0	13·26	625,890	9·06	510,760	16·67	654,600
		Total....	20,707,230	1,070,780	5·15							15·06	2,718,790	10·26	1,530,850	16·[illegible]	3,709,570
		Opium deducted	7,783,361	600,950									1,094,030				
			13,058,060	569,830									1,624,710				
Exports.																	
Silk,—Raw	Piculs	45,920	6,389,740	187,460	2·1	0·9	..	..	..	..	10·0	10·9	695,800	9·8	626,770	13·1	833,270
Piece Goods	,,	3,790	60[illegible]	15,040	2·4	0·9	..	..	..	..	10·0	10·9	62,010	9·7	55,190	15·5	75,450
			6,949,630	151,100	2·17							10·90	757,810	9·6	681,960	13·47	908,510
Tea,—Black	Piculs	1,076,180	6,510,070	905,830	13·4	0·9	..	6·2	..	..	10·0	17·1	1,114,760	10·9	711,360	29·8	1,921,180
Green	,,	227,690	2,306,150	170,610	7·1	0·9	..	5·0	..	..	10·0	14·5	348,890	11·0	263,590	21·6	510,540
Brick	,,	52,000	161,150	11,330	7·0	0·9	..	3·5	..	..	10·0	14·5	21,920	10·8	16,[illegible]60	21·8	33,280
Dust	,,	5,500	8,800	2,080	31·3	..	..	..	..	..	..	..	..	..	..	31·8	2,680
			9,084,700	990,850	10·91							16·35	1,485,570	10·24	931,430	27·26	2,476,320
Sundries	....	......	2,470,220	185,790	6·33	0·9	..	2·6	..	..	10·0	13·70	338,420	10·90	270,060	19·26	475,190
		Total....	18,504,545	1,279,750	6·91							15·35	2,581,600	10·50	1,943,450	20·86	3,860,250
Imports and Exports		......Grand Total....	39,291,860	2,349,530	5·98							15·45	5,300,390	10·40	3,383,280	19·47	7,649,920
Probable Approximate Amount of Duties levied on Foreign Commerce in toto....................													(6,177,000)	16[illegible]	5,207,[illegible] (exclusive of duties on opium)	25 [illegible]	9,835,000

* No particulars being given in the Customs' Returns of the various kinds of Cloth imported, the corresponding amount of Import-duty has been calculated at the lowest rates. The "Quantities" and "Values (in £ sterling)" are taken from the Customs' Returns. From the former and the Tariff rates of duty, the "Amount of Tariff-Duty,"—from the latter and the Amount of Duty, the corresponding Per-centage—is computed; whilst from the "Total per-centage of additional imposts levied," the corresponding "Amount" has been deduced. By deducting from this Amount half the Amount of the corresponding Tariff-Duty, the "Amount of Illegal Taxation,"—and by adding to the same amount the corresponding of Tariff-Duty, the "Total Amount of Revenue"—has been obtained; whilst in both cases the corresponding Per-centage is computed from each Amount and the corresponding Value in £ sterling.

It will be interesting as well as instructive to compare the preceding table with a similar, though more general and less complete one, given by Mr. Dick, Commissioner of Customs at Shanghai, in his "Suggestions for the Revision of the Chinese Customs Tariff and Trade Regulations," appended to the "Reports on Trade at the Treaty Ports in China for the year 1869, published by order of the Inspector-General of Customs," and to which special attention was invited, at the time, by the latter. "It will be seen," Mr. Hart in his short Introduction, dated July 21, 1870, remarks, "that Mr. Dick has worked up his subject with much thoroughness, and that the form in which he presents it is not less calculated to awaken interest, than is the matter, thus brought together, to be of public utility. I desire to take advantage of this opportunity to thank Mr. Dick for the work done by him in this connection." Hence, Mr. Dick's Table may be safely inferred to represent no overdrawn picture of Chinese surcharges. Indeed, the chief results arrived at by both of us differ widely; but, then, this difference will be fully explained by me, and, as I have already had occasion to point out, neither the Inspector-General nor the Commissioner of Customs at Shanghai, any more than the Commissioner at Kiukiang, Mr. Drew,—whose "Memorandum on the Le-kin Taxing System of the Province of Kiangsi," previously quoted, I shall have further to refer to,—are over-strong in arithmetic and arithmetical logic.

The arrangement of the two Tables is not altogether the same. Whilst, in the first place, my own professes to give the mean imposts levied on imports at a port and in the province in which the port is situated, (taking for a main basis the imposts levied on foreign goods at Shanghai, on the way to Su-chow, and at and beyond Su-chow, the nearest inland centre of commerce or principal mart in the Province of Kiangsu, in which Shanghai is situated, and the whole of the imposts levied on exports,—the table of Mr. Dick professes to give the mean amount of imposts levied on imports and exports both at the ports and *throughout the Interior*. But it really gives the mean imposts, except on Metals, chiefly as levied at the ports alone. His Table is headed thus:—"Estimated Chinese Revenue from foreign trade, in the shape of import- and export-duties, collected by the Foreign Customs, and native charges collected by native offices, on merchandise passing through the Treaty Ports; excess of the total thus collected over the total due if the Treaty commutation of inland charges were carried into effect; and estimate of the loss caused to the Chinese revenue by Hongkong being a free port." This language is unmistakeable; and, as though it were to remove every doubt on the subject, Mr. Dick observes:—"The information about inland charges is unavoidably very imperfect, but it is the result of a set of Returns obtained from all the Treaty Ports last year, and is the nearest approximation to facts that it is possible to make at present. Against the excess over Treaty rates we have on the other side of the account the heavy loss caused to the Chinese revenue by Hongkong being a free port....On the inland and other native charges generally, the expense and waste of collection must be excessive, as the principal feature of the system is that several officers are kept to do piecemeal what could be done by one, as is exemplified on a small scale by the opium charges levied at Foochow and Shanghai." Finally, in a Table of "Comparison of Tariffs," Mr. Dick states the "Duties (Tariff and Native charges) in China, 1868, on

ESTIMATED CHINESE REVENUE FROM FOREIGN TRADE, IN THE SHAPE OF IMPORT AND EXPORT DUTIES, COLLECTED BY THE FOREIGN CUSTOMS, AND NATIVE CHARGES COLLECTED BY NATIVE OFFICES, ON MERCHANDISE PASSING THROUGH THE *TREATY PORTS*;
EXCESS OF THE TOTAL THUS COLLECTED OVER THE TOTAL DUE IF THE TREATY COMMUTATION OF INLAND CHARGES WERE CARRIED INTO EFFECT, AND ESTIMATE OF THE LOSS CAUSED TO THE CHINESE REVENUE BY HONGKONG BEING A FREE PORT.

1868.	*Tariff Duty.*		*Native Charges, together with commuted Transit Dues on such goods as paid the latter.*		*Total of Tariff and Native Charges.*			*Amount leviable if Native charges were commuted at Treaty rate of half Tariff Duty.*		*Excess at present collected.*	*Total Quantities Imported or Exported of some of the articles.*	*Quantities sent into or brought from the Interior under Transit Passes.*
IMPORTS. (*Value in Haikwan Taels, like the Duties.*)	Per-Centage.	Total.	Per-Centage.	Total.	*Percentage without allowing for goods paying commuted Transit Dues.*	*Percentage after allowing for goods that paid commuted Transit Dues.*	Total.	Per-Centage.	Total.			
		Tls.		Tls.			Tls		Tls.			
OPIUM: average value Tls. 411 per picul; Tariff Duty Tls. 30 per picul	7.69	3,017,611	11.20	2,461,615	..	18.50	4,099,426	..	4,099,426	(*Not entitled at present to commutation.*)	Pcls. 53,915	
COTTON GOODS: taking Grey Shirtings as an example; average value Tls. 2 1 0.0, Tariff Duty 8 cand. per piece	3.81	703,180	4.65	613,365	6.50	7.96	1,376,505	5.71	1,146,769	481,796	Grey Shirtings, Pcs. 4,765,131	Pcs. 533,159
WOOLLEN GOODS: taking Camlets as an example; average value Tls. 12 per piece; Tariff Duty, 0.3.5.	6.04	349,919	4.41	254,930	10.96	10.45	603,849	9.06	523,429	80,420	Camlets, Pcs. 104,696	" 8,139
METALS: taking Nail Rod Iron as an example; value Tls. 2.1.0.0 per picul; Tariff Duty, 0.1.2.5.	5.63	160,541	11.72	404,715	21.46	22.00	565,256	8.43	210,913	354,474	Nail Rod & Bar, Pcls. 233,130	Pcls. 30,636
SUNDRIES, ...	3.50	604,841	1.50	313,867	..	5.00	924,218	5.25	606,613	317,807	..	
(*Import Duties actually collected by Foreign Customs, Taels 3,257,679 A.*)	..	A. 5,296,094	..	4,474,649	..		7,771,254	..	6,616,947	1,154,307	..	..
EXPORTS.												
TEA: average value Tls. 22 per picul: Tariff Duty Tls. 2.5.0.0.	10.87	5,817,350	8.85	2,778,787	19.82	19.23	8,396,087	16.30	8,424,061	971,720	Pcls. 1,461,825	Pcls. 97,869
SILK: average value Tls. 418 per picul; Tariff Duty Tls. 10, ..	2.80	401,540	4.20	1,051,503	..	6.65	1,646,048	5.59	890,161	756,281	..	..
SUNDRIES, ...	4.00	156,787	4.60	176,820	..	8.60	333,066	6.00	235,106	97,960	..	..
(*Export Duties actually collected by Foreign Customs, Taels 4,202,397 B.*)	..	B. 4,360,837	..	4,009,468			5,575,265	..	5,540,884	1,038,348	..	..
GRAND TOTAL, ...Tls	..	C. 7,664,931	..	8,484,128			D. 10,146,629	..	13,156,806	2,380,251	..	..
(*Total I. and E. Duties collected by Foreign Customs,* Tls. 7,470,076 (C.)) Transit Dues do. " 116,008	..	..						..	..			..

Total collected by Foreign Customs, Tls. 7,797,384
Out of a total revenue as estimated at D. of " 10,146,029

The loss to the Chinese Revenue by Hongkong being a free Port is estimated at upwards of Tls. 1,000,000.

The Revenue collected at nine Chinese stations round Hongkong and Macao last Chinese year, from February 11th, 1869, to January 30th, 1870, amounted to Tls. 221,669, being on 19,513 chests Opium.

whole commerce," to have amounted to 12 per cent. As Mr. Dick cannot possibly have been unacquainted with the fact that inland imposts are levied both upon Exports, and upon Cottons, Woollens, etc., as well as upon Metals, not at the ports alone but throughout the Interior, there exists no alternative for us but to conclude, that the Shanghai Commissioner of Customs has knowingly excluded the far greater proportion of the latter taxes,—a very important item,—from his Estimate of Chinese Revenue derived from Foreign Trade, and "Excess at present collected." Indeed the truth of this conclusion will be proved, in the sequel, out of his own mouth.

In the second place, Mr. Dick's Table gives that "Excess" over the "Amount leviable if Native charges were commuted at Treaty rate of half Tariff duty," *i.e.* over the total of imposts legally leviable in China upon foreign Trade,—import- or export-duties and the inland charges commutation-tax. In other words, it gives directly the amount of illegal taxation to which Foreign Trade is subject; whilst my Table gives the imposts levied in addition to the Tariff import- and export-duties, and finally, by deduction of the half-duty, reduces the total to the standard in question. The other features, in which the two Tables either differ or agree, speak for themselves, and require no observation. For the sake of comparison, I subjoin Mr. Dick's Table *in extenso* :—

I will now go over the two tables *seriatim*, after observing that Mr. Dick's results are of themselves less exact, because they are based on "average values," and Grey Shirtings, "taken as an example" for Cottons, Camlets taken in the same sense for Woollens, and Nail Rod Iron for Metals. As regards OPIUM, which does not affect the "Amount of Illegal Taxation," Mr. Dick makes the Native charges 11·20 per cent., whilst I make them 14·15 per cent., or 2·95 per cent. more ‡ than he does. The difference arises from this, that Mr. Dick calculates the *chow-fang*, which he still terms "a Defence tax," at Taels 5.5.0.0. and the Wharfage dues at Tl. 0.4.4.0. per chest, *i.e.* the former impost at about one fifth, instead of Tls. 15 per picul or one half, the import duty, the latter at its *nominal* rate of 1 per mille. But it is a well-known fact that the Tau-t'ai of Shanghai, as Intendant of Customs, actually levies just ten times that rate, or 1 per cent. At Foochow this charge appears to be collected upon Opium under the name of "Kuan-hang" at the *nominal* rate of Tls. 1.4.4.0. per picul, or about $\frac{3}{10}$ per cent., as mentioned by Mr. Dick himself. It would be, indeed, strange if some such impost of questionable accountability were not resorted to by a Chinese official in the position of an Intendant of Customs. As to the amount of *chow-fang*, it certainly figures in an official list, furnished by the Tau-t'ai of Shanghai, and of which I have a copy before me, not at Tls. 5.5.0.0., but plainly at Tls. 5.0.0.0. per chest. In a list, however, indirectly obtained from "the Defence Tax Office" itself, the *chow-fang* levied on Opium is returned at Tls. 15.0.0.0. per picul, and, as though for the purpose of

‡ At variance herewith, the difference between Mr. Dick's percentage of Total Revenue of 18.50 per cent., and mine of 20.63 per cent., is only 2.13 instead of 2.95 per cent: difference 0.82 per cent. This arises from the corresponding difference in the percentage of import duty, in Mr. Dick's table = 7.50, in mine = 6.48 per cent. in the mean.

preventing any mistake about it, the chief figure is written in full, viz.: 拾五兩, "ten and five taels" per picul. As this charge is in accordance with the established rule, by which *chow-fang* is levied at the rate of one half the import- or export-duty, respectively, and moreover brings the total percentage of the "Transit-," as distinguished from the "Stationary"-imposts, up to the normal rate of 20 per cent., I have unhesitatingly adopted it. As to the amount of *le-kin* Mr. Dick very closely agrees with me. The whole difference between us here, amounts to 2·13 per cent., for 1870 = about £165,000, by which he estimates the (tabular) Revenue || from Opium short of the truth.

The mean rate of import duties on COTTON, as given by Mr. Dick = 3·85 per cent., and myself = 3·84 per cent., is virtually identical. But, whilst I make the additional charges = 12·05, the total revenue = 15·89, and the amount of illegal taxation (within the importing province) = 10·13 per cent, he makes the same items = 4·05 for native i.e. additional charges, = 7·86 for the total revenue, and = 2·15 for illegal taxation (throughout China), or 8 per cent in each case less. He omits to state of what elements his 4·05 per cent native charges consist. I make the Port taxes only 3·1 per cent; but it is quite possible that *they* alone, inclusive of the native Custom-house charges, which I have not taken into consideration, may amount to about 1 per cent additional. More probably the difference rests on some error of his own.§ It is simply a fact, however, and one which cannot possibly have been unknown to the Commis-

|| It should be borne in mind that my Table gives only the Total Revenue which is derived from Foreign Imports *within the importing Province*, and, more especially as regards Opium, independently of all "Stationary Taxes."

§ This, as the sequel will show, is positively so; information, subsequently obtained, furnishing the proof. I leave the whole of my argument as it originally stood, since it will not lose in force by independent confirmation.

sioner of Customs, that between Shanghai and Su-chow, the nearest centre of trade in the Interior, the amount of *le-kin* actually levied upon Shirtings and other Foreign Cottons, is about 6 per cent. According to the established rule of levying *le-kin*, the same as *chow-fang*, at fractions of the Tariff import- or export-duties, adding 10 or 20 per cent., respectively, for collecting and other "squeezes," I have put it down at 5·2 per cent only.

The native consumption of foreign goods at the ports and the nearest centres of trade themselves is comparatively trifling: it mainly takes place beyond the latter places, from which the goods are further dispersed. But, if I am well informed,—and I have every reason to believe that I am,—the Board of Revenue at Peking have adopted the principle of levying within the importing province, upon Foreign Trade, a *clear* 10 per cent. in addition to *chow-fang* and the import- or export-duties stipulated by Treaty, in the shape of *le-kin*; of having this tax, together with the *chow-fang* tax, collected upon opium exclusively at the ports, because, so far as Opium is concerned, there is no legal objection to it; upon other Imports, exclusive of *chow-fang*, which appears to be not an Imperial but a Provincial tax, solely in the Interior,—namely, three-fifths of the full amount before and at the nearest centre of trade, and two-fifths at inland stations beyond,—because the impost is an illegal one; and upon Exports, for the same reason,—the *chow-fang* tax excepted,—exclusively at the place of produce and inland stations. Finally, I learn, that the Board of Revenue have laid down the rule that the total amount of taxes levied upon Foreign Trade, whether Imports or Exports, shall, exclusive of tariff import- and export-duty, for the present at least, *not exceed* twenty per cent. *ad valorem*. And all this is so completely in accordance with the character of Chinese administration, the policy of the present Government, and facts actually known, as to exclude every reasonable doubt as to the literal truth of the system here delineated. What tends further to complete the proof is this, that Mr. Dick himself admits the total charges upon Metals, within the importing province, to be 20·00 per cent.; whilst, computing them on the basis of Tariff and other official lists of duties levied at Shanghai, and positive rates of taxes imposed at Su-chow and intermediate stations, complemented by the charge of two-fifths of 10 per cent. = 4 per cent., raised, according to the system indicated, at stations further inland, I find those total imposts to amount to 19·15 per cent. But a general principle of transaction, which holds good of Metals (and opium besides): what reason is there to assume that it should not hold good of all other articles of commerce as well? It will be seen that such is, indeed, the case.

To revert now to the special article of *Cotton goods.* The first 8 per cent. additional imposts, levied upon them at the port and inland up to the nearest centre of trade, are a positively ascertained fact. So is the existence of *le-kin* Barriers beyond the nearest centre of trade, both in the importing, and other, provinces. That further war-taxes, therefore, are paid within the importing province, is certain. But the particular amount of 4 per cent., which I have adopted for the complement of these charges, is fully warranted,—and that in the sense of a *minimum*, by the information obtained, and the fact of an analogous tax being admittedly levied upon Metals,—a class of goods far less objectionable to the Chinese Government than are cotton manufactures. Mr. Dick, consequently, estimates the amount of Chinese (tabular) Revenue from Cottons as applied to 1870, by 8·03 per cent., or about £446,000 short of the truth.

For WOOLLENS Mr. Dick takes Camlets as an example, and the import-duty, which I make for Camlets 6·3 per cent., in near accordance with me, at 6·04 per cent. The mean duty amounts to only 4·76 per cent.; but, as Mr. Dick deducts the duty and half duty, according to his own standard, from the total revenue, the difference does not materially affect the result. The native or additional charges, however, which I find to amount to 13·33 per cent., he makes, again without stating of what elements they are composed, 4·41 per cent. only. My charges "at Port" reach 3·5 per cent. The difference, as before, is hardly 1 per cent., and it would appear that Mr. Dick's "native charges" either include Custom-house dues, which I have neglected, or that the difference in question is connected with the difference between his "allowing" and "not allowing" for goods "paying" or "that paid commuted Transit-Dues." There is confusion here in Mr. Dick's ideas; for, it is plain that his "native charges" represent a definite amount of taxes actually levied, whether in part at 4·4, in part at 3·0, per cent., or at any other rate of per-centage, upon goods of a given value; that, consequently, the sum of the imposts levied bears but one absolute proportion to the value given; and that there is no room for either "allowing" or "disallowing;" while I have previously shown that the commutation-tax does not affect the amount of illegal taxation, and, hence, that the *value* of goods sent under transit-passes should not be deducted from the respective total values. His differences, therefore, between 8.50 and 7·86 = 0·64 per cent. on Cottons, between 10·98 and 10·45

= 0·53 per cent. on Woollens, etc., rest on an erroneous principle of calculation; and to all appearance he has computed a percentage for native imposts by those differences, respectively, short of what he should have done, so that the charges in question represent, for Cottons and Woollens, very nearly the imposts levied at the port alone. The next additional 6 per cent. of my Table are taxes positively known to be levied on the latter class of goods; while the same remarks, which have been offered on the analogous tax on Cottons, apply to the complementary 4·0 per cent. for *le-kin*, levied at Barriers beyond the centre of trade nearest to the port, in the importing province. Mr. Dick's estimate of the amount of Chinese (tabular) Revenue from Woollens, applied to 1870, falls by 7·64 per cent. or about £128,000 short of the truth.

In connection with the article of METALS, an entirely new feature in Mr. Dick's Table forces itself upon our attention. He makes the import-duty 5.68, whilst I make it 5.77, per cent. He makes the native or additional charges 14.32, whilst I make them 14.18, per cent. He makes the total of Tariff and native charges 20.00, whils I make them 19.95 per cent. There is here, essentially, *a complete accord between us*. But while Mr. Dick as usual does not state of what elements his 14.32 per cent. of native charges are made up, my corresponding percentage of 14.18 per cent. is made up of the same elements, and computed on the same principles, which constitute the basis of the Chinese system of taxing Foreign Trade. *In this particular instance, therefore, Mr. Dick fully and literally confirms that system, as applied by me*; and at the same time, more especially when considering that he makes his "Total of Tariff and Native Charges, without allowing for goods paying commuted

Transit-Dues," 21·45 per cent., testifies to my having kept *within* the limits of actual taxation, as it has been throughout my plan and purpose to do. Exaggeration in a case like the present could only tend to cast suspicion upon the result arrived at, and the cause advocated. Besides which, I am not given to exaggerate in any shape or form. Neither have I the remotest personal interest in the whole question at issue. My "additional imposts known to be levied at the port" amount to 3.85 per cent.; those known to be levied at, and between the port and the nearest centre of trade, 6·33 per cent., together 10·18 per cent.; whilst the complementary imposts which I am informed are levied beyond the nearest centre of trade, within the limits of the importing province, are taken, as before, at 4·00 per cent. *Mr. Dick, therefore, must, so far as metals are concerned, have had a knowledge, in accordance with my own information, of the whole of these charges.* Why, then, he should have ignored, and excluded from his table, with the exception of the Port charges, the further analogous imposts upon Cottons, Woollens, and other articles of commerce, I am not in a position to explain. In regard to Metals, he estimates the Chinese (tabular) Revenue, as collected in the importing Province, at fully its true amount.

The import-duties on Sundries I find to be 4·47 per cent., whilst Mr. Dick erroneously adopts only 3·50 per cent. for this item. The reason is chiefly that he has taken the duty upon Opium for 1868 too high, namely, 7·50, whereas I make it from actual returns for 1870 only 6·48 per cent. Hence, as we both compute the percentage of duty for Sundries from the remainders of the given Value of Imports and Amount of Duties actually levied by the Foreign Customs, he necessarily finds this percentage too low by a corresponding fraction. I make the additional imposts, with the exception of the complementary 4·00 per cent. which have now been fully established, actually known to be levied, 12.20 per cent.; Mr. Dick, without furnishing any details, makes them only 3·50 per cent., being, within 0·20, the amount of charges = 3·30 per cent., levied at the ports alone. The total charges, therefore, which he takes at 8·00 per cent., amounting in reality to 16·67 per cent., he estimates the Chinese (tabular) Revenue, as applied to 1870, from Sundry Imports by 8·67 per cent. or about £444,000 short of the truth.

While from actual returns I find the export-duty on SILKS, for 1870, to be 2·17, Mr. Dick makes it, for 1868, = 2.39 per cent. The additional charges, according to him, amount to 4·26 per cent. As he does not state what items they consist of, it is possible that they include charges levied at the ports only. In none of the official lists which have become known to me, is the amount of *chow-fang* on this article given; nor have I succeeded in collecting any positive information on the subject, and, therefore, omitted from my Table the charge altogether. Instead of Mr. Dick's percentage, just alluded to, I make the *le-kin*, inclusive of produce-tax, trade-licences, etc., levied in the producing locality and at inland stations = 10 per cent., partly on the ground of information obtained, partly on that of positive facts. The former is supported by the circumstance, that the *le-kin* of 10 per cent. levied upon Silks *inland*, because illegally levied, is but the counterpart of the *le-kin* of 10 per cent. levied upon Opium *at the ports*, and corresponds to the mean amount of *le-kin*, *known* to be levied,—for the reason just stated, inland—upon all other articles of importation. As to the positive facts alluded to, Mr. Dick assures us, it is true, that the charges as given by him are the nearest approximations which it is possible to make at present: but we have seen, that this statement is not consistent with the proofs adduced by me; nor can Mr. Dick have remembered, that already his predecessor, the late Mr. FitzRoy, in his official report, dated March 15th, 1867, stated that Silk, coming from the Interior to Shanghai, was even at that time paying *upwards* of Tls. 30 per bale, or Tls. 37·5 per picul, by way of transit-dues. Now, taking the import-duty with Mr. Dick at 2·4 per cent., being Tls. 10 per picul, the rate of Tls. 37·5 itself would make $3\frac{3}{4} \times 2\frac{2}{5} = 9$ per cent. *ad valorem*, *known* to have been levied inland upon Silk, in 1866 and at the commencement of 1867, in the shape of *le-kin*; and if we add to it but Tls. 5 per picul for either the margin left by Mr. FitzRoy or for subsequent increase of taxation, we obtain the full impost of 10 per cent., in perfect accordance with the system which has been found to obtain in all preceding cases. It will be recollected also, from the confiscation-case of the Messrs. Bower and Hanbury, that the Barriers levying the *le-kin* tax upon Silk extended (from the Interior) to the immediate vicinity of Shanghai, and, it may hence be safely inferred, to that of every other silk-exporting port. It is, therefore, certain that the total percentage of charges upon Silks, amounting to 13·07°/o, adopted in my table, is *below* the rate actually levied; and that Mr. Dick's estimate of the Chinese (tabular) Revenue from this staple article of produce, applied to 1870, falls by at least 6·42 per cent. or about £446,000 short of the truth.

In regard to Tea, Mr. Dick makes the export-duty 10.87, while I make it 10.91, per cent., the accord being as good as perfect. The *chow-fang* in my Table is taken from official lists, and the charges levied at the port of 5·45 per cent. are, therefore, proven. Mr. Dick states the whole of the native or additional charges to amount to 8·35 per cent., without, as usual, saying of what elements they consist. They leave only 2·90 per cent. for inland charges proper, which I make 10·94 per cent., and hence Mr. Dick's total imposts reach only 19·22, whilst mine amount to 27·26 per cent.: the difference being,—as they are approximately throughout save in the case of Metals (and opium),—8·04 per cent. The principal item of the inland charges is the Produce or "Grower's Tax." From the information I have collected, it amounts on Tea in the mean to about 6 per cent. Adding to this and the charges levied at the Port only 5 per cent. for trade-licences and *le-kin*, we obtain a total of 16·45 per cent., which coincides as nearly as possible with the mean total of my table. And this, from all I can learn, is *below* the truth. Thus, I find it stated in the "Annual Review of the Shanghai Tea Market for the year 1870," issued by the Messrs. Little & Co. who have taken special trouble in inquiring into the amount of native charges actually levied upon Tea in the Interior, that, calculated for the pound, they may be estimated at 3½ cents; or more correctly at $3.5 per picul, being as nearly as possible 20 per cent. *ad valorem.* The total amount of taxation of 27·3 per cent., to which, according to my Table, Tea is subject in China, may at first sight appear excessive; but it must be remembered that it represents, for the year 1870, a value of £2,476,520 sterling on Piculs 1,369,060, being in round numbers equal to 182,541,000 lbs., that is to say, a value of three pence farthing per lb., and no more. Yet, though out of this tax, the proportion of Illegal Taxation amount actually to a penny farthing per pound only;

it is just so much which the consumer pays above what he ought to pay, and in the aggregate comes to nearly one million pounds sterling, year after year taken by China out of England's pocket.

As regards *le-kin* payable upon Tea, Mr. Drew, it is true, incidentally remarks, in speaking of "the Hohow Tea paying 1·40 taels Lo-te-shwuy"—Grower's Tax—"besides the usual Ta-ku-t'ang duty," on the character or amount, of which he is silent:—"Tea, unlike other articles, does not [*sic*] appear to elude native revenue officers. It is well-known, too, that it does not pay Likin." But Mr. Drew's knowledge, like his logic, I fear, is of a somewhat unreliable nature; and, certainly, does not extend to his colleagues and the Inspector-general. On mere names or designations, moreover, little importance can be attached in the history of Chinese taxation of Foreign Trade. The *chow-fang*, at most of the ports, vanishes to the Western eye, because it is levied by *the Le-kin Office*; and the *le-kin* occasionally disappears in certain localities and in connection with certain articles of commerce, because it is collected either *at the Port or at the mart of production*: but the impost itself remains; and this is, after all, the principal point which concerns us. Mr. Dick estimates the Chinese (tabular) Revenue, as applied to 1870, from Tea, by 8·04 per cent., or about £730,000, short of truth.

The Export-duty on Sundries Mr. Dick takes at 4·00 per cent., while from a careful calculation based on the actual Returns of the Custom-house, I make it for 1870 = 5·53 per cent.; and whilst he adopts, without any reason, for the native charges on Sundry Exports, the same low percentage which he had adopted for "Sundry Imports," namely, 4·50 per cent., I find it to be 13·70 per cent., calculating on the basis of known facts or established principles. The Chinese (tabular) Revenue, as applied to 1870, derived from Sundry Exports, Mr. Dick estimates by 19·23 – 8·50 = 10·73 per cent., or about £265,000, short of the truth.

These remarks leave me only some few observations of a more general character to add. It may possibly be argued that the details of my "additional" taxation are, so far at least as Imports are concerned, chiefly derived from the system practised at Shanghai and between Shanghai and Su-chow; and that they do not apply generally. But I am able to return a most satisfactory answer to such an objection. For, in the first place, my information as to details is by no means restricted to Shanghai; the system of taxation, though to some extent its practical application be left optional with the Governors of each province, emanates from the Board of Revenue in Peking, and is essentially a uniform one; and the details, collected, are in perfect accordance with that system, as it has been delineated to me by a reliable informant, and professedly from the most authentic source. In the second place, the port of Shanghai, from its greater importance, may not unreasonably be concluded to represent the *normal* port for Chinese taxation. And this is fully borne out, in the case of Opium, by a list of "Total charges," furnished by Mr. Dick himself, and which I will here transcribe :—

CHARGES LEVIED AT THE DIFFERENT TREATY PORTS ON OPIUM,

(After Payment of the Treaty Import Duty of Tls. 30 per Pecul.)

PORTS.	AMOUNT OF NATIVE CHARGES PER PECUL.			QUANTITY Imported in 1868.
	At the Port.	On the way to the Principal Market in the Interior.	Total.	
Newchwang	Tls. 18.6.0.0	Tls. 10.1.9.7	Tls. 28.7.9.7	Pcls. 2,685.41
Tientsin	" 17.0.0.0	" 36.0.0.0 to Peking " 17.0.0.0 to Shansi	" 53.0.0.0 to Peking " 34.0.0.0 to Shansi	" 7,421.86¼
Chefoo	" 18.6.0.0	....	" 18.6.0.0	" 3,370.85
Hankow	" 13.9.2.0	" 16.5.6.4	" 30.4.8.4	" 2,915.00
Kiukiang	" 34.0.0.0	" 16.9.6.0	" 50.9.6.0	" 1,925.00
Chinkiang	" 38.4.0.0	" 24.0.0.0	" 62.4.0.0	" 4,877.99
Shanghai	" 37.2.8.7	....	" 37.2.8.7	" 10,779.00
Ningpo...........	" 34.0.0.0	....	" 34.0.0.0	" 4,505.23
Foochow	" 84.6.4.0	" 20.8.6.0	" 105.5.0.0	" 4,968.52
Tamsui	" 32.1.3.6	....	" 32.1.3.6	" 931.41
Takow	" 45.3.4.0	....	" 45.3.4.0	" 1,020.01
Amoy	" 90.2.9.0	....	" 90.2.9.0	" 3,316.40
Swatow..........	" 11.0.5.0	" 3.7.1.0	" 14.7.6.0	" 4,272.00
Canton	" 23.0.0.0	" 25.3.4.0	" 48.3.4.0	" 807.00

Imperfect, and, as has been seen, in its details unreliable as this table is, it yet furnishes a fair proof, that the charges at Shanghai upon Opium,—and hence we are justified in inferring, generally,—are, if anything, below, certainly not above, the mean of the charges levied at the different open ports. For, on adding the principal columns of Mr. Dick's Table, we find by a general process :—

Amount of Native Charges per picul.

	At the Port.	Total.
14 Ports.........................	(Tls. 497. 6. 6. 3.)	Tls. 685. 8. 9. 4.
Mean, for each Port......	(Tls. 35. 5. 4. 7.)	Tls. 48. 9. 9. 2.
Shanghai	(" 37. 2. 8. 7.)	" 37. 2. 8. 7.

Or, adopting a more correct method, apportioning, of the quantity imported into Tientsin, 6,000 piculs to Peking, and neglecting fractions of taels and piculs below 0.5 while taking them at and above 0.5 for units, we find :—

Tls. 29	× Piculs	2,685	=	Tls.	77,865
53	,,	6,000	=	,,	318,000
34	,,	1,422	=	,,	48,348
19	,,	3,371	=	,,	64,049
30	,,	2,915	=	,,	87,450
51	,,	1,925	=	,,	98,175
62	,,	4,878	=	,,	302,436
37	,,	10,779	=	,,	398,723
34	,,	4,505	=	,,	153,170
106	,,	4,964	=	,,	526,170
32	,,	931	=	,,	29,792
45	,,	1,102	=	,,	49,590
90	,,	3,316	=	,,	298,440
15	,,	4,272	=	,,	64,080
48	,,	807	=	,,	38,736
for 14 Ports	......Piculs	53,872	=	Tls.	2,555,038

Mean for each Port... per picul Tls. 47
Shanghai .... ,, ,, ,, 37

The charge at Shanghai, as above, is thus shown to be below the general mean; which more than confirms the correctness of my assumption, and the utmost probability, not to say the certainty, that the results exhibited in my Table do *not exceed* the truth.

Mr. Drew, however, states the full inland charges for the province of Kiang-si to be *nominally* only 10 per cent. *ad valorem* (with 2 per cent. additional on certain routes), and *exclusive* of the charges at the port of Kiukiang; but he generalises somewhat too readily on unreliable data, and is himself, apparently, as unreliable in his statements as he is in his arithmetic. This, in one page he writes:—"In no case that I can learn have the representations of merchants been brought to bear to effect a reduction of the li-kin tariff since it was made, excepting in the instance of grass-cloth, where their arguments were successful, the high rate on sandalwood, pepper, etc., appearing to be tolerated without murmuring, probably because false declaration of quantity makes it possible to avoid the *entire* payment due" (!); and in the next-following page:—"It has already been mentioned that the tso-koo was abolished (at Kiukiang) two years ago; the same is true of a tax on the owners of houses, know as "fang-li," the same "li" as in li-kin; further, at the close of 1868 the maximum leviable as li-kin, which had formerly been 13 fên,—equal to so many per cent. *ad valorem* —"for Kiang-si was reduced to 10 fên." Nay, in the very page in which he advances his former opinion, we read:— "In regard to foreign goods it has not been difficult to ascertain the way in which the now prevailing li-kin tariff came to be as it is.¶ At the opening of this port in 1861 special exertions were put forth by the wealthy native dealers in foreign textile fabrics who came here"—before the opening of the port,—"in order to get as low a tariff on them as possible, and the influence and various modes of effecting the purpose brought to bear obtained in behalf of these goods a remarkably low valuation, and by consequence a tariff" [—to native merchants—] "far lower actually than the 10 per cent which it nominally is. A similar course was hardly less successful in regard to metals and sugars. But sandalwood, pepper, cuttlefish, and seaweed had no weighty intercessors to speak for them, and a *valor* was allowed to be fixed at the discretion of the wei-yuen without external influence. . . The le-kin rates thus esta-

¶ There is nothing more difficult in China than to obtain *correct* information respecting any point of Chinese fiscal administration; and to obtain such information relative to foreign trade is more difficult than anything else. Chinese officials, as a rule, take a delight in imposing whatever stories may best suit their momentary purposes on European credulity, and chuckle over their success. Mr. Kopsch also, the Commissioner of Customs at Chinkiang, decides *ex cathedrâ*:—"Transit Dues are *not remitted* to Peking, as is generally supposed, but are retained by the Provincial Treasurer."

blished at Kin-kiang have, as would naturally be expected in regard to foreign goods (!), come to prevail generally throughout Kiang-si." Again Mr. Drew affirms:—"No li-kin tariff has ever been published,* but the equivalent of a fixed tariff has gradually grown up in respect of all the important commodities in the shape of *a settled custom* (!) of paying so-and-so much per package, per pecul, or per piece, according to the article, at the 3 fên barriers, and the amount to be paid at the 2 fên places is calculated from the 3 fên certificate." I judge it unnecessary to offer any remark on statements which speak for, and are best left to confute, themselves. When Mr. Drew qualifies the Chinese Atlas,—executed in the most miserable style imaginable,—to which I have alluded in a preceding note, as "the excellent Chinese *map of the world*—the 大清中外一統輿圖—published at Wu-ch'ang by Kwan Wên in 1863, while Governor-General of Hu-kwang, and *based on Jesuit surveys*," he betrays thereby that, occasionally, he not only judges of things which he cannot reasonably be supposed to have seen himself, but indulges in observations which indicate a more than ordinary degree of thoughtlessness, and are hardly consistent with the stand-point of a social philosopher, a fiscal scientist, an economist, and a moralist, he unitedly claims to occupy. Still, Mr. Drew's paper contains, withal, much interesting information: and what it undoubtedly proves is that, in the province of Kiang-si also, the principle of levying, independently of *chow-fang*

* Every *le-kin* Office and Barrier is in possession of a copy or copies of the official *le-kin* Tariff, printed on paper of Imperial yellow; although the officials may not choose to produce it or even to own the fact. Mr. Drew writes, without a word of explanation, 牙釐 instead of 釐; and styles "Li-kin General Bureau 牙釐總局 instead of 釐捐總局. Can the former be the popular designation, as the Head-Office of the *Grinding* Cash-(Contribution)"? I find it so named also in the "Returns of Native charges" for Ningpo.

and other purely provincial or local charges, a clear 10 per cent upon foreign trade, is in force; although of its application the writer has, manifestly, been led to form an altogether erroneous opinion.

Mr. Drew does not mention *chow-fang* as levied at Kiukiang, and Mr. Dick states:—"The Defence-Tax, levied only on goods landed and shipped by Chinese, is *a local one*, imposed by the authorities here with the concurrence of Foreign Powers in 1862, for the purpose of raising funds for the defence of the place against the rebels"; whilst in my table it is applied—except upon Silk—to all the ports. On reference to the history of the origin of the "Defence-Tax," which I have given above from official documents, the reader will perceive that Mr. Dick has somewhat misapprehended the facts of the case, and that the "concurrence of Foreign Powers," of which he speaks, really consisted in nothing but the qualified concurrence of Sir Frederick Bruce in a temporary capitation-tax to be imposed on Chinese subjects resident in the Foreign Settlement. The Commissioner of Customs sees fit to ignore that the excuse for such a tax has long since ceased to exist; that when its name was changed from *'Húi-fang* to *Chow-fang*, its character was changed also; and though, at Shanghai, it continues to be professedly levied only on goods landed and shipped by Chinese subjects, in our sense of the term, that, according to the views of Celestial Officials, that term includes the "barbarian" subjects of the One Autocrator of the Earth as well. It is true, from the inquiries I have made, that at the various ports it assumes various names, and that, being collected by the *Le-kin* Offices, it is frequently known by no distinguishing name at all, but included in the general designation of *le-kin*. That, however, as a tax distinct from the *le-kin* tax properly so called, it is in some shape or other levied at all the ports—which is the main point here,—I feel warranted in affirming positively, on the ground of reliable information collected, and confirmed, by independent testimony. Thus, Mr. Dick gives a list of the imposts levied on Opium at Fuchow, including "The Le-kin proper, collected by the Le-kin Office Tls. 16, *Military tax*, ("fang-chow"), collected by the same office, Tls. 9, per pecul." In an official publication of the Customs, to which I shall presently refer, the "*chow-fang*" or Defence Tax (ostensibly Tls. 5 per pecul on Opium) is specially named as being levied at Chingkiang; although the head of the leading mercantile firm at that port, having vainly endeavoured to ascertain the fact, denied it to me. At Ningpo, his native compradore—a Ningpo man—stated from personal knowledge, that it was levied,—in confirmation of what, unknown to him, I had affirmed; notwithstanding which the Foreign Inspector-General of Customs has naturally remained in ignorance of the fact. His subordinate, the Commissioner at Kiukiang, also, so late as in 1869, returned *le-kin* as the *only* tax levied at that port; yet, in a foot-"Note," he remarks :—"The collector of the Le-kin tax on Opium is the same one, who collects *the other war taxes.*" And in the case of Metals, in which, as we have seen, Mr. Dick makes the mean total of charges, levied at all the ports, amount to 20 per cent. *ad valorem*, these 20 per cent *include chow-fang*, computed at the rate of half the import-duty, and, therefore, include it as *a tax actually levied, at the mean rate named, at all the ports.* But what is true of Metals may here be reasonably concluded to be equally true of every other article of commerce.

In his Memorandum on the Transit Dues, Mr. Johnson

speaks of an "arrangement between the Shanghai Opium Guild and the native authorities, whereby Opium, which has paid the *le-kin* and other taxes at Shanghai, may pass absolutely free from further impost through all the barriers in the province of Keangsoo, *Nganwhy, and Kiangsi;*" and Mr. Dick quotes the passage with *tacit* approval. Mr. Johnson, indeed, is so high an authority on the subject under consideration, and so well informed upon all matters relative to it, that it is not without hesitation I question the correctness of his information on this particular point, though it differs from my own. I am supported, however, by Mr. Dick, who writes in 1869:—"Opium having paid the Taxes at the Opium Office called 洋藥稅捐總局 Yang-yo-shui-chuen-tsung-chü in Yang-hong-kai, outside the little East Gate of Shanghai, is furnished with a Transit Pass 分運單 Fen Yuen Tan, exempting it from further charges *within the jurisdiction of the said Office, i.e.* all parts of the Kiangsu province South of the Yangtsze." I state this, lest any doubt should arise as to the fact that the scale of imposts, on which my table is based, is *restricted to the importing province*, and that, on entering a second province, additional duties have to be paid. Mr. Drew also observes, in reference to what he terms this system of *crescit eundo* taxation, that *f.i.*, "the officials of Kiangsi will not recognize passes issued in Hankow, and *vice versâ* the Hupeh authorities dishonor the passes of Kiukiang." This is the general rule throughout China, although occasional exceptions to it may occur.

Having thus, I venture to think, firmly established the basis on which my table is made to rest, and met the objections to which it appeared liable, I may in conclusion proceed to notice an official publication, only just come into my possession, and directly bearing on our subject. It is entitled: "Returns of the Native Charges, as far as they can be ascertained, levied on the principal Imports and Exports, at and near the different Treaty Ports in China; and of the quantities of goods on which such charges are levied, as compared with the quantities paying the transit-dues specified by Treaty. Published by order of the Inspector-General of Customs. Shanghai, printed at the Customs' Press, December, 1869," pp. 63 and iv., in 4to. The Table of "Charges levied on the Principal Imports (after payment of Import Duty)—Opium," which occupies page i, is identical with Mr. Dick's Table of "Charges levied at the different Treaty Ports on Opium," transcribed above. In fact, the main body of the "Tables of Treaty and Extra-Treaty Charges levied at each Port" appear to contain simply *the details, from, and on the ground of, which Mr. Dick had, a few months previously, constructed his own Table*, also published in 1869, by order of, and, as has been seen, specially recommended to public notice by, the Inspector-General, Mr. Hart. But, while the latter professed to give the aggregate native charges levied upon Foreign Trade *throughout China*, the former tables profess to give the native charges only, according to the general title-page levied "*at and near the ports*," according to the special title-page of the tabular details "*at each port*,"—in perfect accordance with the independent conclusion,† drawn by me from Mr. Dick's Table itself. Both the Inspector-General and the Commissioner of Customs at Shanghai, therefore, appear to me to have laid

† When analysing Mr. Dick's Table, I was still unacquainted with the existence of the subsequent publication, containing the details, which have obviously served as a foundation for the former. Having in vain applied to the courtesy of the Commissioner of Customs for such information on the subject, as had been *published* by order of the Inspector-General: I am indebted to one of the leading mercantile firms of Shanghai for the communication of the printed "Returns" in question.

themselves open, by the publication of the earlier table, to the suspicion, not to say the charge, of having *wilfully desired to mislead their readers as to the actual extent of illegal taxation, to which Foreign Trade is subject in China;* and this would seem the more to call for an explanation on their part, as I have reason to believe that copies of separate impressions of Mr. Dick's "Suggestions," including his Table, have been communicated to Her Majesty's Board of Trade and distributed in other influential quarters, whilst the details of the "Returns" have been kept back and become very little known.

It would be a work of supererogation, certainly so far as imports are concerned, to enter into a critical examination of the whole of these fragmentary and more or less unreliable details, since, in a general sense, they have been already reduced to their proper value, and are now *acknowledged to be restricted to imposts levied at, or at and near, the ports.* One or two of the additional general tables alone, occupying page ii. to iv., deserve notice, to indicate and illustrate the manner in which the details in question have been "made up." For this purpose, I will literally transcribe the first portion of Table ii., "Charges levied on the Provincial Imports, after payment of Import Duty," relative to Cotton Goods :—

AMOUNT OF NATIVE CHARGES AT AND ON THE WAY FROM EACH PORT, AND COMPARISON OF QUANTITIES PAYING TREATY TRANSIT DUES WITH QUANTITIES PAYING NATIVE CHARGES.

Ports.	Amount of Native Charges per Piece.			Total Quantity Imported in 1868.	Portion Paying Treaty Transit Dues.	Portion presumably paying Native Charges.
	At the Port.	On the way to the Principal Market in the Interior.	Total.			
	Tl.m.c.c.	Tl.m.c.c.	Tl.m.c.c.	Pieces.	Pieces.	Pieces.
Newchwang..	..	0.0.0.9.6	0.0.0.9.6	121,395	..	121,395
Tientsin	0.0.4.0	{ 0.0.1.5 to Shansi 0.2.0.0 to Peking	0.0.5.5 to Shansi 0.2.4.0 to Peking }	1,393,377	..	1,393,377
Chefoo	..	..	*None*	536,618	..	536,613
Hankow	0.0.2.3.2	0.0.6.9.6	0.0.9.2.8	1,050,720	303,582	720,138
Kiukiang	0.0.3.7.1	0.0.8.6.5	0.1.2.8.6	220,104	2,000	218,104
Chinkiang ..	..	0.3.5.4.5	0.3.5.4.5	174,780	68,340	106,410
Shanghai	0.0.4.2.1	0.1.2.0.6	0.1.6.2.7	563,177	..	563,177
Ningpo	0.0.5.9.9	0.1.3.6.5	0.1.9.6.4	205,236	156,596	138,640
Foochow	0.0.5.2.7	0.1.1.3	0.1.6.5.7	65,147	650	64,497
Tamsui......	..	..	*None*	24,065	..	24,065
Takow	..	..	"	13,900	..	13,900
Amoy *	0.1.6.0	..	0.1.6.0	32,840	..	32,840
Swatow	..	0.0.3.1	0.0.3.1	85,169	..	85,169
Canton	*not stated*	*not stated*	..	111,358	..	114,358
			(0.0.4.0 being the Treaty rate).	4,090,890	558,168	4,132,722

COTTON GOODS.—*Grey Shirtings.*—Treaty Import Duty 8 candareens per piece.
Treaty Transit Dues 4 " "
Per piece not exceeding 40 yards by 31 inches.

* In addition to this amount is paid the Ta Hang Tax, Five per cent. *ad valorem*.

In the first place it will be observed, that the expressions "on the way from each Port" and "on the way to the principal market in the interior," are somewhat equivocal, if not deceptive; for, were it not for the explanation on the title-page that they are to signify: "*near* the port," they, certainly, would be misunderstood to include all inland charges, or all inland charges up to the principal market in the Interior, respectively. In the second place, it appears unintelligible why, in the case of Amoy, a tax which exceeds by one per cent. the import-duty should have been omitted from the "Total Amount of Native Charges," and consigned to neglect in a foot-note. And lastly, it seems equally strange, that for Canton, where the native charges upon Cotton goods are known to be multifarious and very high, we find them "not stated." That at Niu-chuang, Tam-sui, Ta-kow, and even at Swatow foreign Cotton manufactures should be subject to no imposts at the ports, is not less remarkable; but that at Chi-fu, one of the principal importing ports, they escape, both at the port and on the way to the principal market in the Interior, all taxation whatever, is quite surprising. What is only more so, is that, under the circumstances, instead of nearly a million and a half of pieces, a single bale of Grey Shirtings should be sent up to Tientsin, and pay "Tls. 0.0.5.5 per piece to Shan-si or Tls. 0.2.0.0 per piece to Peking," without the Inspectorate-General being apparently able to ascertain which. Yet, whether, out of the 1,393,377 pieces of Grey Shirtings in 1868 imported into Tientsin, a million pieces went to Peking and the remainder to Shansi or *vice versâ*, would involve a difference in the "Amount of Native Charges" of nearly £40,000 sterling, and allow a corresponding latitude to the Commissioner of Customs in the Returns, and the result deduced from them.

Although it is, of course, unknown to me what process has actually been adopted by Mr. Dick: yet, with the preceding table before us, it is not difficult to trace. Supposing him to have taken of the 1,393,377 pieces of Shirtings alluded to, four-fifths to have gone to Shan-si, *i.e.* to have paid the trifling imposts of Tls. 0.0.5.5, and one-fifth only to have gone, not to "Peking" as stated by Mr. Dick, but to Chih-li and the North of China beyond Peking, *i.e.* to have paid the (nearly five times higher) charge of Tls. 0.2.4.0—which I presume to be about the reverse of the truth—we then, treating fractions of a cash, or the ten-thousandth part of a tael, as before, arrive at the following result:—

"Portion presumably paying native charges."	Total charges. Per piece.	Product.
Pieces 121,395	Tl. 0.0.1.0	Tls. 1,214
{ 278,675	,, 0.2.4.0	,, 66,882
{ 1,114,702	,, 0.0.5.5	,, 61,309
536,613	,, 0.0.0.0	,, ...
720,138	,, 0.0.9.3	,, 66,973
218,104	,, 0.1.2.4	,, 27,045
106,440	,, 0.3.5.5	,, 37,786
563,177	,, 0.1.6.3	,, 91,798
138,640	,, 0.1.9.6	,, 27,173
64,497	,, 0.1.6.6	,, 10,707
24,065	,, 0.0.0.0	,, ...
13,900	,, 0.0.0.0	,, ...
32,849	,, 0.1.6.0	,, 5,256
85,169	,, 0.0.3.1	,, 2,640
114,358	,, 0.0.0.0	,, ...
Pieces 4,132,722	Mean per piece Tl. 0.0.9.7	Tls. 398,783
Total quantity imported (Pieces 4,690,890	,, ,, 0.0.8.5)	

Now, it is plain that, in order to obtain the correct mean amount of charges per piece—such a mean as is derived from such elements—the product of Tls. 398,783 should be divided by the proper multiplicand, *viz.* Pieces 4,132,722, showing the charges in question to be Tls. 0.9.9.7 per piece. But Mr.Dick has manifestly taken the improper divisor of Pieces 4,690,890, being the total quantity imported,—upon 558,168 Pieces of which the charges, amounting to Tls. 88,054, have been excluded from the Product,—and thus obtained the lesser mean rate of Tls. 0.0.8.5 per piece; because, since he makes Tls. 0.0.8.0 per piece = 3.81 per cent. *ad valorem*, if we reduce the mean of Tls. 0.0.8.5 in this proportion, we find exactly the percentage of 4.05, at which the total charges are calculated by him in his table; whilst, "without allowing for goods paying commuted Transit Dues," he makes the mean rate = 8.50 – 7.86 = 0.64 + 4.05 = 4.69 per cent., showing that, in this instance, he has used the proper divisor. For, on reducing the mean rate of Tls. 0.0.9.7 per piece in the proportion of Tls. 0.0.8.0 to 3.81 per cent., we find its equivalent to be 4.62 per cent. which nearly enough coincides with Mr. Dick's rate to further prove what his process has been. The difference of 0.64 per cent. is thus seen to rest on his part, as I suspected, upon an error in computation, which any tyro in arithmetic should have avoid. Had Mr. Dick calculated correctly, he would have arrived, *from his own figures,* at the following results :—

Allowing for goods paying Commuted Transit-Dues—

Pieces 4,132,722—Tls. 398,783—Per pce. Tl. 0.0.9.7 = 4·62 instead of 4·05 °/o

Not allowing for goods paying Commuted Transit-Dues—

Pieces 4,690,890—Tls. 481,837—Per pce. Tl. 0,1.0.3 = 4·90 instead of 4·69 °/o

the equivalent of a difference of 0.57 per cent. on Cotton goods, for 1870, being upwards of £29,500.

But, also the elements used by Mr. Dick are, independently of their deficiency, incorrect. I am not speaking of the circumstance that, *f. i.* in regard to Shanghai, the Commissioner of Customs keeps lingering, "on the way to the principal market in the interior," so close to the gates of the city, as to find it "impossible" even to reach the second barrier up the Su-chow Creek, much less the principal market itself, thus escaping, for the greater economy of his table, the heavy rates of *le-kin* which he knew to be levied at each ; nor of the Ta Hang Tax at Amoy, so easily disposed of in a foot-note. I am speaking of the facts, that Shan-si takes nothing like four-fifths of the imports of Cotton goods from Tientsin; that Mr. Dick includes in his divisor 121,395 pieces of Shirtings for Niu-chuang with a mere nominal equivalent in the product, and 536,613 pieces for Chi-fu, 24,065 pieces for Tam-sui, 13,900 pieces for Takow, and 114,358 pieces for Canton, together 688,936 pieces without any equivalent at all, thereby vitiating his result to a corresponding extent; and that, not satisfied with all this, he *still* further reduces his "True Amount of Native Charges" on Cottons by using a wrong divisor in determining their final proportion, and confounding the effects of "allowing," and "not allowing, for goods paying commuted Transit-Dues." In a similar manner Woollens and other imports are treated.

The taxes which burden the two staple articles of Export, Tea and Silk, are a matter of too great importance not to claim our special attention.

The Tables vi. of "Charges levied on the Principal Export-Duty," read literally as subjoined :—

AMOUNT OF NATIVE CHARGES AT AND ON THE WAY TO EACH PORT, AND COMPARISON OF QUANTITIES PAYING TREATY TRANSIT DUES WITH QUANTITIES PAYING NATIVE CHARGES.

Ports.	Amount of Native Charges per Pecul.			Total Quantity Exported in 1868.	Portion Paying Treaty Transit Dues.	Portion presumably Paying Native Charges, and not Paying Ty. T'sit Dues.
	En route from the place of production	At the Port.	Total.			
TEA.	Tls.m.c.c.	Tls.m.c.c.	Tls.m.c.c.	Peculs.	Peculs.	Peculs.
Hankow	1.2.5.0	0.3.5.0	1.6.0.0	403,901	97,862	306,039
Kiukiang { Black Ningchow & Wuning	1 6.2.1	..	1.6.2.1 *	192,477	..	192,477
Kiukiang { " Hohow	1.4.7.1	..	1.4 7.1		..	
Kiukiang { Green "	2.7.0.1	..	2.7 0.1		..	
Ningpo	2.0.6.7	..	2.0.6.7	125,493	..	125,493
Foochow	0.1.9.2	2.2.0.0	2.3.9.2	603,771	..	603,771
Tamsui	..	0.0.2.0.6	0.0.2.0.6	3,962	..	3,962
Amoy	0.2.8.0	1.3.6.0	1.6.4.0	35,721	..	35,721
Canton	0.4.0.0	0.2.4.0	0.6.4.0	96,497	..	96,497
				1,461,823	97,863	1,363,960
SILK.						
Chefoo	..	..	..	295.57	..	295.57
Hankow	12.4.0.0	1.6.0.0	14.0.0.0	1,907	..	1,907
Shanghai	21.2.3.7	..	21.2.3.7	42,146	1,914.22	40,231.78
Ningpo	22.0.6.4	..	22.0.6.4	1,531.40	..	1,531.40
Canton	..	5.6.2.0	5.6.2.0	11,683	..	11,683
				57,562.97	1,914.22	55,648.75

TEA.—Export Duty Tls. 2.5.0.0 per pecul.
Treaty Transit Dues Tls. 1.2.5.0 per pecul.

SILK.—Export Duty Tls. 10.0.0 0 per pecul.
Treaty Transit Dues Tls 5.0.0.0 per pecul.

* According to the special Table for Kiukiang, all those rates are expressed in Ku-ping taels, and should have been reduced to Hai-kwan taels at the rate of 101·88 : 100.

We have here again to notice the equivocal and misleading character of the expression "at and *on* the way to" each Port, more particularly in combination with the heading: "Amount of Native Charges, en route from the place of production," and the respective headings of the special Tables: "Taxes levied en route from the principal place of production to the Port," and: name and locality of *each* Barrier where a Tax is collected, name of each Tax, and date of its imposition." When compared with the general title of the special Tables, as "of Treaty and extra-Treaty charges levied *at each Port*," and the title-page of the publication itself, stating that the Returns refer to native charges "so far as they can be ascertained" and are "levied *at and near* the different Treaty Ports": there is an amount of slipperiness, confusion, and contradiction in these various indices, which, with all the want of system, method, and lucidity distinguishing Mr. Hart's administration and statistics, it is difficult to conceive might not have been avoided. On turning to the special tables, we find them to present some curious features.

Chi-foo appears to be the paradise of freedom from taxation. With the exception of opium, on which the inland charges have been reduced from Tls. 30 to Tls. 18.6 per picul,—including a "Commission paid by (Chinese) guild *to (foreign) importers, for reporting* opium imported and sold by them" of Tls. 1.6.0.0,—with the view, the Commissioner of Customs informs us, of increasing the revenue (by means of an enlarged importation): there is no such thing as an impost or a "squeeze" known in that happy region. Taxes payable at the Port: "None." Though inland Barriers, it is true, exist in sundry localities: "No taxes are levied en route to any of these places"; "No taxes levied on transit into the interior"; "No taxes levied en route from place of production." It must have been a matter of regret to Mr. Dick's Table to find itself unable to increase its divisor by even the unit of a picul of Tea, and no more than Piculs $6\frac{32}{100}$ of Wild Raw, and Piculs $280\frac{25}{100}$ of Yellow, together $295\frac{57}{100}$ Piculs of Silk.

HANKOW, on the contrary, exports chiefly Tea. At the Port, the only tax returned is one of Tls. 0.3.5.0 per picul on Leaf, and Tls. 0.0.6.0. per picul on Tea Dust, which latter, in 1868 levied on 11,349 Piculs, is *omitted* from the general Table. So is the heavier *le-kin* tax of Tls. 0.3.0.0 per picul, levied en route; whilst for Leaf it is returned at Tls, 1.2.5.0, the Transit Treaty-rate, only. This would, according to Mr. Dick's Table, be equal to 5·44 per cent., or, as it is stated to be levied at three Barriers to 1·81 per cent., no doubt more correctly 2 per cent., the *lowest* of the usual full Barrier rates, for each Barrier. But that *le-kin* should be levied at only three Barriers on produce, conveyed for exportation abroad, from two provinces into a third one, is more than improbable; and we may safely double and treble the number. The "Amount derived from that known as 'the Grower's Tax' on Tea," is returned as "Uncertain," and *excluded*, on 294,877 Piculs, from the General Table. Taking it as given for Kiukiang, in the mean at only Tls. 1.2.5.0 per picul, or 5·44 per cent, it would, together with the other charges referred to, bring the total of inland imposts on Tea, shipped at Hankow, up to *at least* 17 per cent,,—in very near accordance with my table, which makes the mean = 16·35 per cent. *ad valorem.*

As to Silk, the only tax levied at the Port is stated to be *le-kin* at the rate of Tl. 1.6.0.0 per picul, or, according to Mr. Dick's table, 0·38 per cent. The rate needs no comment. *Le-kin*, except on Opium, is not levied at a Port. The tax meant, is probably the *nominal* rate of *Chow-fang*, levied by the *Le-kin* Office. The *le-kin* proper is said to be levied at four barriers, at the rates of Tls. 7.0.0.0 per picul, or 1·47 per cent.; Tls. 1.6.0.0, or 0·38 per cent., respectively, making in all Tls. 12.4.0.0 per picul, or 2·96 per cent. *ad valorem.* Barriers could barely support themselves on a tax of little more than one-half per cent. upon inland traffic. At the *lowest* full rate known to be levied at them, the *le-kin* tax at four barriers would amount to 8 per cent. The "Grower's Tax," as in the case of Tea, being returned "Uncertain," is *omitted* from the General Table. Taking it at 5 per cent., the inland charges on Silk come to about 13 per cent.; which is probably near the truth. Omitting the *chow-fang* tax, for which I have no positive data in the case of Silk, I make the total 10·90 per cent.

Kiukiang exports tea alone. The taxes levied at the port are stated to be "Nil"; although upon imports there is the "le-kin" tax,—no doubt *chow-fang*, levied by the *Le-kin* Office. An unnamed charge is returned for two barriers at Tls. 0.2.2.1, or more correctly H. Tls. 0.2.1.9 per picul = 0·88 per cent. *in all.* It seems to include "an extra payment made to the Customs' officials at Ta-ku-t'ang of one or two candareens per pecul"; unless this extra payment be identical with "a tax collected at Ta-koo-t'ang, at a branch office of the Kiukiang Native Custom House, being a *shuy* and dating from early in the reigning dynasty," mentioned in the special Table, but for which *no amount* is returned. On the other hand, the "Amount derived from that known as 'the Grower's Tax' on Tea" is made up of the following items:—two charges "imposed with the name of "Local Tax" by proclamation of Tsêng Kwo-fan in July, 1863, the Viceroy plainly asserting that it is distinct from the Transit Dues, and it would be levied, were passes taken out, in addition to the half Tariff Duty," *viz.*, of Kuping Tls. 1.4.0.0 per picul = 6·1 per cent. on Black Ningchow and Wuning, and of Kuping Tls. 1.2.5.0 (which Mr. Drew elsewhere stated to be Tls. 1.4.0.0 also) per picul = 5·4 per cent. on Black Hohow. Besides which there is "the Grower's Tax" of Kuping Tls. 2.4.8.0 per picul = 10·8 per cent. on Green Hohow,—the per-centage being here taken in the mean proportion of Tls. 2.5.0.0 per picul = 10·87 per cent. The total product of this tax upon 192,477.29 piculs is returned at H. Tls. 334,649.1.5; which gives a mean of Tls. 1.7.9.1 per picul, or 7·79 per cent. *ad valorem.* If to this we add *le-kin*, etc., at the lowest full barrier rate of 2 per cent., for Ening, Wuning, Takut'ang, and the Kiukiang Native Custom-house, 8 per cent., we obtain a probable total of 15·79 per cent. for inland charges upon Tea, shipped at Kiukiang, which includes no *chow-fang*, and yet leaves only 0·56 per cent to bring it up to the 16·35 per cent. of my table.

Shanghai exports both Tea and Silk. In the special Table we find the "Taxes levied at the Port" to amount to "...." on Tea, and to "Nil" on Silk, although independently of the notorious Wharfage Dues, levied in excess on both, the official lists certify that *chow-fang* is paid on Tea at the rate of Tls. 1.2.5.0 per picul, or 5·46 per cent. *ad valorem*, "within the (Foreign) Settlement of Yang-king-pang." In the shape of "Taxes levied in the Interior" are given, as "imposed in 1865," on Fychow Teas, coming by way of Hangchow: Produce Tax, per picul Kuping Tls. 2.4.8.0 (= 10·8 per cent.), Local Tax Tls. 0.1.0.0 (= 0·4 per cent.), Hangchow Sea Wall Tax Tls. 1.2.0.0

(= 5·2 per cent.), together Kuping Tls. 3.7.8.0 per picul = 16·3 % mean per-centage. To lessen the effects of this heavy Tax, it is observed by the Commissioners of Customs, Mr. Dick, that "Very little Fychow Tea comes to Shanghai, as by going to Ningpo it avoids some of the charges here enumerated." Instead of supplying, however, the necessary data, he not only keeps his information back, but, on turning to the special Table for Ningpo, we find no taxes upon Tea corresponding to those enumerated in the table for Shanghai, much less taxes "imposed in 1865." Moreover, Mr. Drew in his Report for 1869, published in the same volume, which contains Mr. Dick's "Suggestions," states :—"The Fychow district sent of Green Tea from the country in 1868 : *viâ* Ningpo to Shanghai Peculs 74,271.78; *direct to Shanghai* Peculs 12,783.0.0 ; and *viâ* Kiukiang to Shanghai Peculs 68,191:04." According to this statement, *the whole quantity* of Tea, viz., Peculs 12,783, which Mr. Dick, in the special table, returns as having been exported from Shanghai in 1868, were Green *Fychow* Teas, subject to the higher Grower's Tax of 16·3 per cent. To settle this striking discrepancy between the Commissioners of Customs at Kiukiang and Shanghai, I must leave to themselves. The inland taxes, also said to be "imposed in 1865," which Mr. Dick states to be levied on "Huchow and Hangchow Teas" are more moderate, viz., "Produce Tax, per pecul Kuping Tls. 0.3.3.6, Li (-kin) Tax, Tls. 0.5.0.4, Measure Tax Tls. 0.1.6.0, and Hangchow Sea Wall Tax Tls. 1.2.0.0, together Kuping Tls. 2.2.0.0 per picul = 9·5 per cent. *ad valorem*. Mr. Dick remarks :—"On Huchow and Hangchow Teas the charges are levied, and Passes issued at those places ; the Passes enabling the Teas to come to Shanghai without further charge." What the

Commissioner of Customs, then, means to say is, that on Fychow Teas coming to Shanghai no *le-kin* is levied at all; on Huchow and Hangchow Teas only 2·2 per cent. *en route;* that there are no charges on Tea payable at the Port; and that, previously to the year 1865, Teas coming to Shanghai, for shipment abroad, were subject to no taxation whatsoever, that is to say "so far as can be ascertained." And such a statement is officially "published by order of the Inspector-General of Customs"! If we take the mean of the charges on Fychow and other Teas, however, or if we take the former Teas in quantity only in the proportion of one-fifth, and the latter in that of four-fifths, and add the charges actually levied at the port, we find the probable total of inland taxation on Teas, shipped at Shanghai, to be 17·3 per cent., which is still somewhat above the mean rate of my table. It will have struck the reader that, although for Tamsui the small quantity of Peculs 3,962, taxed Tls. 0.0.2.0.6 per picul, is duly incorporated in the General Table, the quantity of Peculs 12,783, exported in 1868 from Shanghai and taxed at least Tls. 2.5.0.0 per picul, has been *omitted* from it; the tendency of which, I need not say, is to reduce the "Excess of charges at present collected" of Mr. Dick's Table accordingly.

As regards Silk, the by far larger proportion of which is exported from this port, the article, like Tea, is returned as free from taxation of any kind, anterior to the year 1865. Nor do the charges, imposed at this recent period, include the obnoxious and much-complained-of *le-kin* tax. How, under the circumstances, it *f. i.* happened that, in 1862, the 63 bales of Silk, belonging to Messrs. Bower & Hanbury and of which I have previously spoken, were confiscated for an alleged attempt to avoid the payment of *le-kin* at "the South

Barrier" contiguous to Shanghai, I must leave to the Commissioner of Customs to explain. He also is, under the Inspector-General, responsible for the statement, that *no le-kin* is leviable and levied upon Silk, or, indeed, ever has been leviable and levied upon this staple article of Chinese export,—of course, "so far as can be ascertained." The only "Taxes levied (since 1865) in the Interior," he states, are the following:—"Produce Tax, per Bale of 80 cts. $16, Sea Embankment Tax $4, Hangchow Public Works or Reparation Tax $2, Shanghai Tax $4—equal to Kuping Tls. 22.1.5.0 per picul;" and remarks:—"These taxes are collected of the vendors at the inland markets, who get a Pass exempting the Silk from further exactions *en route* to the port." Whether the silk-producing districts supplying the Shanghai market have become American dependencies or simply adopted the American standard of currency, I know not; but the taxes in question, taking Mr. Dick's mean import per-centage of 2·39 for a basis, correspond to 3·23, 0·81, 0·40, and 0·81 (together 5·25) per cent., respectively, and the whole system of Chinese taxation indicates a discrepancy in the former charge. It *might* be 3 per cent; but, comparing the similar tax levied upon Tea, is more likely to be considerably higher. Of trading-licenses we discover here no trace. Still, the united testimony of the Inspector-General and Commissioner of Customs at Shanghai upon a point like the above, would be entitled to consideration, had we not found it to be in other respects and in most instances of doubtful reliability, and tending to improperly reduce the illegal charges, levied by the Chinese Government upon foreign trade, to a minimum; did not the information furnished point to an indirect source, and ignore the Imperial *le-kin* tax, which no local Authority can abrogate; and were it not at positive variance with the data obtained and officially published by the late Mr. FitzRoy,‡ Mr. Dick's predecessor, which, instead of a total of 5·25, gives, at the commencement of 1867, moreover, a total of *upwards of* 9 per cent., as the amount of taxes on Silk levied in the Interior,—in perfect accordance with the information I have, myself, collected from various sources, both native and foreign. It appears to me, therefore, that the details furnished by the special Table under review are in no sense of a nature to cast a doubt upon the corresponding percentage of 10·90 of my own table, mainly dependent on the inland charges, levied on Silk exported from Shanghai.

NINGPO exports Tea and Silk, the latter produce in but a small quantity. For Tea, "Taxes levied *at* the Port" are returned:—"Nil"; "Amount derived from the Tax known as 'the Grower's Tax' on Tea":—"None." The only "Taxes levied *en route*" are stated to be the following:— "On Kiangnan Teas: Yin-fei Tls. 0.3.0.0, Li-chao Tls. 0.7.6.6, Chüan-chao Tls. 1.0.0.0, together Tls. 2.0.6.7 per picul = 9·0 per cent.; with the remark: "First levied in 1856. The Chüan-chao was increased 4 mace (Tls. 0.4.0.0) in 1863, ..." : but *without* the increase of rate, = 1·7 per cent. being taken into account. "On Chê-kiang Teas: Nei-ti-cha-chüan" (inland tea-tax) Tls. 1.4.0.0, Chih-tsao (for the purveyor of Clothing to the Court) Tls. 0.1.3.4," together Tls. 1.5.3.4 per picul, = 6·7 per cent. "On Tea Leaf: Nei-ti-cha-chüan Tls. 0.7.0.0, Chi-tsao Tls. 0.1.3.4," together Tls. 0.8.3.4 per picul = 3·6 per cent., with the remark: "First levied in 1859." The whole amount of such

‡ The late Mr. FitzRoy, being an English gentleman, bred and born, was incapable of an untruth or a wilful misrepresentation. A faithful servant of the Chinese Government as Commissioner of Customs at Shanghai, and, for a time, as the then Inspector-General Mr. Lay's chief representative, he, at the same time, never forgot that he was a British subject, and owed allegiance to his country and his Queen.

taxes, collected in 1858, is "estimated" at Tls. 152,466.7.6.7, Tls. 15,340, and Tls. 34,783, together Tls. 202,609.7.6.7, on Piculs 125,493.14; being, in the mean, Tls. 1.6.1.5 per picul = 7·0 per cent. *ad valorem.* The *le-kin* tax is ignored. Its probable amount would make up the per-centage of my table.

Silk at Ningpo presents the curious phenomenon, that the "Taxes levied (upon it) *at* the Port," consist in "Ssü-ch'a-chüan, (a Silken Tea tax), 絲茶捐, 1861," producing, on "Peculs 1,531.40, at the rate of Haikwan Tls. 22.0.6.4 per picul," the diminutive sum of Tls. 1,579.0.0.0. The inland imposts are *identical with those on Silk shipped from Shanghai,* even as regards the "Shanghai Tax," and their being rated in American currency per 80 catties; only that "the Produce Tax," is here termed "the Silk Tax," that, while there "imposed in 1865," they were here "first levied in 1859," and that, while in Ningpo a "Pass exempting the Silk from further exactions *en route* to the Port," known at Shanghai, is unknown: the existence of *Le-kin* Offices in the cities of Huchow and Shao-hsing-fu, by which the charges in question are collected, unknown at Shanghai, is known at Ningpo. True, these offices would, in that particular part of China, seem to attend—"so far as can be ascertained"—to any save their own business: yet, if we assume them to collect, after all,—though, may-be, on the sly,—their proper share of inland taxes, say only 5 per cent., and add the latter to the admitted charges of 5·25 and (apparently) 0·24 per cent.: we shall already obtain a total of inland taxes on Silk, shipped from Ningpo, within 0·41 per cent. of that of my table.

Fu-chow, of all the Treaty-Ports, exports the largest quantity of Tea. But this is by no means the only thing, for which the place is remarkable. It is at least equally so for the circumstance that, in the special table, the sphere of action of its *Le-kin* Office is extended to exports, and that the "Taxes levied *at* the Port," for the first time in this instance traced back to about the real date of their introduction, consist of: "*Le-kin*" (either *chow-fang*, levied by the *Le-kin* Office, or *le-kin* proper, levied in the close vicinity of the Port) per picul Tls. 0.9.0.0 = 5·9 per cent., "Kwang-hseang Le-kin" (1854) Tls. 0.3.0.0, "Hwa-chĕng-shuey" (1855) Tls. 0.6.7.2, and "Ka-kwan-hseang" (1858) Tls. 0.3.2.8, together Tls. 2.2.0.0 per picul, or 9·6 per cent. *ad valorem.* Of inland barriers only two, at Yen-ping-fu and Chu-ki-wan, are named, and stated to levy "*le-kin,*" designated "a *local* tax" (1854), at Tls. 0.0.2.8 and Tls .0.0.1.4, respectively, together Tls. 0.0.4.2 per picul = 0·18 per cent., —manifestly some small local charge, or more probably a "squeeze," levied *besides* the *le-kin*, not returned. The "Amount derived from the Tax known as 'the Grower's Tax' on Tea" is stated to be "not procurable," with the remark "Rate Tls. 0.1.5.0 (Tls. 1.5.0.0?) per picul." Taxation on Foreign Trade at Fu-chow is high in general. If we take the Grower's tax at the Kiukiang mean of 7·8 per cent., we obtain, even without taking the probable amount of *le-kin*, collected in the Interior, into consideration, for the total of inland charges on Tea, shipped at Fu-chow, 17·4 per cent.; being 1 per cent. above the mean rate of my table.

AMOY exports only Tea, and also pays "taxes levied *at* the Port," viz., Tls. 0.1.6.0 "by the Hackwan (Custom-house), and Tls. 1.2.0.0 "by the War tax 釐金 authorities," together Tls. 1.3.6.0 per picul = 5·9 per cent. The column "Name and locality of each Barrier where a tax is collected (inland), name of each tax, and date of its imposition" furnishes the following information: "At the Poo-nan barrier, Ning Yang and Loong Yen teas are charged per picul Tls. 0.1.5.0 (=0·7 per cent.). At the Pai-ton barrier, An-c'heih Teas are examined, but no tax is charged." In certain parts of China, the foreign Commissioners of Customs would seem to look upon the 卡, or barriers, as simply intended for either ornamental purposes, or finger-posts, or what-nots. And under the heading of "Amount derived from the tax known as 'the Grower's tax on Tea,' we read: —"*A* 'Grower's tax' of Tls. 0.1.3.0 per picul is levied at Ning Yang and Loong Yen. Teas from An-c'heih pay no Grower's tax. Amount derived not ascertainable."

CANTON exports both Tea and Silk. Taxation, however, at this once tax-abounding Port, would, to judge from the special table, seem to have fallen into a sad state of prostration. The Hoppo,—who, notwithstanding, is known to remit to Peking, annually, a goodly number of hundreds of thousands of taels, by the Chinese Government supposed to be levied upon foreign trade,—must, for the sake of keeping up appearances, do so out of his own pocket. That is clear. For, at Canton, "the Grower's Tax" both upon Tea and Silk is "*Nil*"; the taxes levied on Silk in the Interior are "*Nil*;" and the information "procurable," manifestly, is well-nigh "Nil" also. At the Port, there are stated to be collected on Tea: "Kwang-fu-shuei" at Tls. 0.0.8.0, and "Kung-hiang" at Tls. 0.1.6.0, together Tls. 0.2.4.0 per picul = 1·0 per cent.; on Silk "Li-kin" at Tls. 4.9.0.0, and "Kwang-fu-shuei" at Tls. 0.7.2.0, together Tls. 5.6.2.0 per picul = 1·3 per cent. The taxes levied inland upon Tea alone are four in number, and, including *le-kin*, four mace, or Tls. 0.4.0.0 per picul = 1·7 per cent. *in all;* making the total inland charges on Tea, shipped at Canton, 2·7 per cent., on Silk 1·3 per cent., *ad valorem.*

Such is the nature of the Special Returns, from which the General Table of "Charges levied on the Principal Exports" is literally made up, and on which, in its turn, Mr. Dick's "Estimate of Chinese Revenue from Foreign Trade, etc.," is literally made to rest. In reference to Tea, Mr. Dick commits the same error which he committed in determining the mean per-centage of his Native Charges on Cotton Goods, in taking the divisor by 97,862 piculs in excess of what he should have done, and confounding the effects of "allowing," and "not allowing, for goods paying commuted Transit-Dues;" whilst he additionally vitiates his result, in the sense of further reducing the amount of Chinese illegal taxation, by omitting from both his Tables the exports of, and charges upon, Tea at Shanghai. Moreover, I have now positively shown, as I was led to conclude from the first, that Mr. Dick's "Native Charges," and consequently his "Excess of Charges at present collected," are, so far as Imports—with the exception of (Opium and) Metals—are concerned, exclusively based on taxes *levied at, or in the immediate proximity of, the Ports;* that, in regard to Exports, they are founded partly on most deficient, curtailed, or unreliable elements, partly on distinct omissions of the most important imposts, viz., the Grower's or Produce Tax and the Inland Le-kin Tax, besides other known taxes, so as to comprehend *less than one-half of the charges actually collected;* and that, inasmuch as Mr. Dick's Table professes to give the total annual Revenue of China from Foreign Trade, and the total amount of Illegal Taxation included in that Revenue, it positively misleads in regard to these two important points.

Indeed, the sole object of the Inspector-General and the Commissioner of Customs at Shanghai, in publishing the Table under consideration, would seem to have been to bring the "Excess of Taxes collected over Treaty Rates," as nearly as could be, down to the "estimated loss to the Chinese revenue by Hongkong being a free port," and to represent the remainder as a paltry sum of half a million pounds sterling, really not worth the attention of Her Britannic Majesty's Government, nor that the body of Foreign Merchants should raise such an outcry about it. As to the "Loss to Chinese revenue by Hongkong being a free port," Mr. Dicke stablishes it in this wise :—"On Opium, the Viceroy, with his large preventive service of steamers, is only able to levy 16 taels a chest in the vicinity of Hongkong. This is apparently the nearest approach he can make to the 30 taels Tariff duty which at the ports farther up the coast is the first charge paid; and the same reason—the ease of evasion—which keeps the first charge low, probably also has the same effect all along the Kwang Tung Coast, on the supplementary charges. The loss on all the charges is probably not over-estimated at 50 taels a chest, and as the quantity of Opium annually sent away from Hongkong without reaching Treaty Ports is about 20,000 chests, the total loss under this head may be set down at Tls. 1,000,000" —about £300,000—"besides which there is some loss on other Imports which I have no means of estimating, and there is the heavy expense of the preventive service. It in no way meets the case to say that the Chinese Government should maintain a still more effective preventive-service than the large one already employed. *The expense of a preventive service is quite as serious a cause for complaint as the loss of revenue.* The most efficient Government would find it impossible to entirely suppress smuggling in such a position, and, like China, could only reduce loss by smuggling, by incurring loss in prevention." It may be considered fortunate for England that the foreign Commissioner at Shanghai is not a native Member of the Chinese Privy Council; or else she might find herself, one of these days, with a second "Alabama Claims" case,—the "*Hongkong Claims*," based on the erection of Hongkong into a free port, with all its possible and impossible consequences, direct and indirect, past, present, and to come, on her hands. I know not what Mr. Dick's ideas of the efficiency of the Home Government may be. Without a foreign colony in the position of Hongkong on the Coast, with a moderate Tariff, and in possession of an extensive and admirably organised Coast-Guard Service, it *fails* in its endeavours "to entirely suppress smuggling." The Chinese Government, to guard a coast extending through nearly 25 degrees of latitude and, excluding Corea, more than 15 degrees of longitude, incurs the "heavy expense" involved in a "preventive service," consisting of about a dozen inefficient gunboats, for the combined purpose of suppressing *piracy* as well as smuggling: and Mr. Dick, blind to everything save the port-freedom of Hongkong, attempts to fasten upon *it* a loss to the Chinese revenue which is solely and entirely owing, *firstly*, to the high taxation to which Opium is subject in China; *secondly*, to the corruption of Chinese officials; *thirdly*, though in a minor degree, to the lawlessness of the maritime population; and *lastly*, to the inefficiency of the Foreign and Native Customs' Service at the ports.

Mr. Dick would seem to have overlooked the fact that Opium-smuggling is not carried on at the free-port of Hongkong,—nor is, as he himself admits, in any way countenanced by the British and Foreign Merchant—, but at the Treaty-ports, and at certain smaller ports on the coast of China, mostly in the vicinity of the Treaty-ports. Thus, *f.i.*, the Commissioner of Customs at Canton reports for 1869:—"Eleven hundred peculs of Opium passed this office last year; this is not eight per cent of the total import, the balance being brought in surreptitiously." And in the special Table, presumably furnished by him also, the "Quantity of Opium imported into Canton in 1868" is stated to be Peculs 807; with the remark:—"Peculs $29\frac{35}{100}$ imported by Bosman & Co., to be prepared and re-exported to California, and Peculs $5\frac{38}{100}$ confiscated Opium, paid no taxes. In addition to the above a large amount is *smuggled into the port* which pays neither taxes nor duties." Now, setting aside the increase of about 300 piculs in the importation of 1869, and taking the quantity which in 1868 passed the Foreign Customs in round numbers at 800 peculs (=8 per cent of the whole imports): the quantity smuggled into the Treaty-port of Canton (=92 per cent) would still amount to 9,200 piculs or nearly 8,500 chests; and since, out of this quantity, "the office," despite of its staff of spies and detectives, managed to seize only $\frac{38}{100}$ peculs,—surely it is quite fair and legitimate to attribute a due share of the wholesale smuggling, which is said to be going on, to what I have just termed the "inefficiency" of the Foreign as well as the Native Customs' Service.

On the lawlessness of the maritime population of China I need not dwell. Under the Government of a country on whose waters piracy is rampant, and alone and not without difficulty is kept in check by the ships-of-war of Foreign Powers; smuggling assumes the character of a comparatively honorable trade; and so it would seem to be regarded by the Chinese Government Officials themselves. To their connivance at it the Commissioner of Customs at Swatow, Mr. Kleinwächter, may testify. "The Opium Statistics," he observes in his Report for 1869, printed in the same volume in which Mr. Dick's "Suggestions" appear, "present the same unsatisfactory features alluded to in the Report for 1868, nor is there much prospect of the strict enforcement of a proclamation, issued last year by the Taotai of Chao-chow-fu at the instance of H. B. M.'s Acting Consul, Mr. Alabaster. This proclamation was intended to do away with the disadvantages under which this port lies by the collection of both Tariff duties and *li-kin*—by this office on the one hand and the local Authorities on the other—against the many small places and ports between this and Hongkong, *where the latter tax only*—if indeed that fully—is || collected; and consequently, as a natural course, the latter places are || resorted to in preference as a channel for supplying the markets of this province and Kiangsi. It was hoped that by equalizing,—*i.e.*, raising the amounts, to be collected in the South, to the same levied here,—would bring about a return of the trade to its legitimate course to this port. *That such would have been the certain result of a sincere legislation, there can be no doubt*, especially as it was accompanied by a regulation which necessitated each ball or parcel of Opium to be stamped before being retailed on pain of confiscation. But when the Deputy, directed by the Vice-Roy to repair to the city of Hwei-chow-foo, some 150 miles distant from Kow-

|| The printed text, instead of "is" and "are," reads in the first place, marked by an asterisk, "used to be," in the second "were"; which is utterly irreconcilable with the plain meaning of the writer, and appears to be an "emendation" *by another hand*. It renders the text simply senseless; and involves its complete misconstruction, by connecting the *le-kin*, which alone "used to be collected" with—Hongkong.

loong opposite to Hongkong—an important station for distributing supplies through Kwantung—arrived, he was told, it is said, by those interested in the traffic, that the proposed collection at that city would simply divert the trade elsewhere, and leave his office a valueless sinecure. *No renewed steps have thereafter been taken by the Vice-Roy*, and unstamped opium is freely current in that neighbourhood, and, as the lower price at which it can be bought not ten miles from Swatow proves, finds its way in quantities throughout the province. . . . No doubt can exist that, *as long as a system prevails by which higher duties are levied at Treaty Ports than at those closed to Foreign Trade*, the former must ultimately sink from the position of forming emporiums for the provinces in which they are situated, to that of the centre of peddling trade in their immediate neighbourhood." This narrative delineates only one phase, and one of the higher phases, of the connivance of Chinese officials at Opium-smuggling. It must, however, here suffice.

Touching the main cause which induces this smuggling trade, I will state it in the words of another Commissioner of Customs,—the late Commissioner at Fu-chow, M. de Méritens. In his Report for 1869, like that of Mr. Klein-wächter published side by side with Mr. Dick's "Sugges-"tions," he expresses himself thus :—" Nos importations d'Opium ont diminué encore cette année. . .de 158 caisses ou 208 peculs sur l'année précédente. Si maintenant nous jetons un coup d'œil en arrière, nous verrons qu'en 1861 plus de huit mille caisses étaient importées à ce port ; en 1862, après l'ouverture de la Douane étrangère, près de 7500 caisses payaient les droits à cette direction. . . .(Dès alors) les importations ont diminué d'année en année dans des proportions considérables. Quel phénomène s'est donc produit ? La consommation aurait-elle baissée subitement dans les mêmes proportions ? Non, pas le moins du monde ; seulement on a cherché les moyens *de se soustraire à des taxes exaggérées*,—et on les a trouvés. . . D'après les calculs les plus indulgents, en accordant des primes et des prix de fantaisie à ceux qui transportent l'Opium dans l'intérieur, il est constant que les importateurs ou les contrebandiers, comme vous voudrez les appeler, peuvent vendre l'Opium à Kieng-ning foo, Yen-ping-foo, ou Changchow, à 60 taels meilleur marché que nos négociants ne peuvent le faire à Amoy ou Foochow. *Cette exaggération d'impôt est donc en fait ruineuse pour le Gouvernement Impérial, et n'a pas été autre chose qu'une prime donnée à la contrebande.* Vous savez, sans doute, qu'il était dit, affiché, et promis que l'Opium qui aurait payé l'impôt du li-kin, soit taels 84 par pecul en sus des 30 taels payés comme droit d'importation à la douane étrangère, serait exempté de toute autre taxe dans l'intérieur; permettez-moi en regard de cette assertion de vous indiquer ici les droits prélevés à chaque cité dans l'intérieur sur tout opium qui arrive, soit qu'il passe en transit ou soit laissé pour la consommation locale. Yen-ping-foo Tls. 5.3.6.0 ; Kien-ning-foo Tls. 5.3.6.0 ; Shing-Tien Tls. 6.6.8.0 ; Ta-an Tls. 10.2.0.0 ; Ching-woo Tls. 5.6.0.0; Show-wa Tls. 5.3.4.0. En tout Tls. 38.50.0, ajoutés aux 84 taels exigés par l'administration du Li-kin (en sus des 30 taels payés comme droits d'importation). Il me semble que ces chiffres sont assez éloquents, et prouvent jusqu'à la dernière évidence non pas la nécessité de poursuivre des gens qui, saisis et frappés sur un point, reparaîtront sur un autre, mais bien *l'urgence qu'il y a à changer de système* et à mettre sous les yeux du Goverment centrale les règles de la vraie economie politique, de même que le relevé de nos recettes douanières Européennes faisant toucher du doigt cette vérité élémentaire, que les recettes s'élèvent et que la contrebande diminue en raison directe de l'abaissement des tarifs."

That, with all these various facts, circumstances, and arguments under his very eyes, any rational person should have attributed opium-smuggling in China to "Hongkong being a free port," appears like an infatuation. But the Commissioner of Customs at Shanghai, supported by the Inspector-General of Chinese Maritime Customs at Peking, goes further. I cannot in this place enter into a full discussion of the question. But what Mr. Dick proposes is: *Firstly*, to raise the import-duty to Tls. 100 per picul, with the view of increasing the Chinese revenue on opium, and to reduce that of India in the same proportion. Again and again he returns to this point, occasionally in something like a threatening tone. "In the case of opium," he thus observes, "the remedy is already in the hands of the Chinese Government and people. By developing the cultivation and increasing the Import duty, a large portion of what is at present the Indian revenue on this article may be gradually transferred to China." I might well ask here: Where do the duties of the British subject, according to Mr. Dick, in his case end, and where do those of the Shanghai Commissioner of Chinese Customs begin? In reference to a discussion on the opium trade which took place in the House of Commons on the 10th May, 1870, he remarks:— "It seems to have consisted in false morality on one side, and loose economy on the other." Mr. Dick's argument obviously partakes of the same character: in regard to his proposal of increasing the import-duty, if the principles of political economy alluded to by M. de Méritens and taught by experience are true; in regard to the threatened development of opium cultivation in China, if the saintly horror with which the Chinese Government view the importation of the drug is more than bare hypocrisy. He appears to overlook that the Treaty of Tientsin will have to be revised, not on the basis of his own moral sense, but on that of the Celestial Government as expressed by the Tsung-li Yamên, which professes to consider opium *almost* as obnoxious as Christianity. And, indeed, had that illustrious Board, instead of listening to the "Suggestions" of its "barbarian" servant, washed its hands of opium-taxation altogether, and, with the view of saving the Chinese people from the "demoralising" influences to which the use of "*the* medicine" is said to expose it, invited our Indian Administration to raise the *export*-duty upon the article by a hundred pounds sterling a chest, or more: we should then have been able to appreciate at least its consistency, honesty of purpose, and strength of conviction.

Secondly, Mr. Dick, not wishing to deal "imperfectly" with the question by merely raising the rate of the Tariff, but to enforce its operation both *at Hongkong* and Macao,—as though the *British Possession* of Victoria, as such, existed not,—and apparently not as yet seeing his way clear to the immediate abolition of its port-freedom, proposes two alternatives, namely: either "the surrounding Hongkong and Macao, at a very large expenditure, with Customs' Cruisers" in order to enable the Foreign Chinese Customs to reach the opium imported,—a sort of blockade which has since been actually enforced;—or else, an arrangement "to the effect *that a branch of the Foreign Customs should be established at Hongkong*, for the purpose of taking an account of, and a bond for, all Opium imported, of passing under cargo certificates all opium re-exported in foreign vessels to Treaty-ports, and of collecting duty only on such opium as was taken over by Chinese purchasers, for shipment in junks, whether to treaty or non-treaty ports; and *that a per-centage* of the revenue gained by the arrangement, calculated with some reference to the proportion lost at present, *should be handed to the Hongkong Government (!)*. To avoid details," Mr. Dick adds, "I speak at present only of opium; and assume that, if it were agreed to let Opium come under the action of the Customs, suitable arrangements could be made for other goods." A proposition of such a purport and nature renders every comment superfluous; but I must freely confess, that, in my judgment, no soberly-thinking man and no loyal subject of England could either have advanced or supported it.

Nor need I dilate on the degree of exaggeration attaching to the estimate at a million of taels, or £300,000, of the alleged annual "Loss to Chinese Revenue by Hongkong being a free port," and the confusion of ideas upon the whole subject betrayed on the part of the Inspector-General in so strongly recommending the "Suggestions" of his subordinate for their thoroughness, as well as on that of the Shanghai Commissioner of Customs himself. To expose the numerous fallacies and erroneous views to which Mr. Dick has given expression, I must reserve for another occasion. My concern here is with the amount in question. The *quantity* of opium smuggled, and for which Hongkong is held responsible, is taken at 20,000 chests, or 22,000 piculs, according to Mr. Dick's remark that "Malwa Opium is 1 picul or (100 catties =) 133⅓ lbs. to the chest; Patna, Benares, etc., 120 catties or 160 lbs., and the Opium sent to China is nearly equally divided between the two kinds."

He, then, gives the number of chests exported from India to China, taking the Indian particulars up to 1866 from an Indian return, and assuming that about nine-tenths of the total exportation come to China, and after deducting from this quantity the imports into China, as returned by the Inspector-General, draws the inference, that the difference in quantity is *smuggled*. His process, apparently, is this :—

	Number of Chests *exported to China.*		Quantity *imported into China.*
1863	75,331	= Piculs 79,097	Piculs 50,087
1864	62,025	= ,, 68,227	,, 52,083
1865	75,128	= ,, 82,641	,, 56,133
1866	76.863	= ,, 84,549	,, 64,516
		Piculs 314,514	Piculs 222,819
Difference for 4 years			Piculs 91,695
Mean annual difference	20,000 Chests	=	,, 22,924;

and calculating the loss of revenue to China upon this quantity at Tls. 50 per chest, he makes his "Hongkong Claims" to amount to the round sum of Tls. 1,000,000.§

I will not insist on what I have reason to believe to be the fact, that the exportation of opium from India for consumption in the Straits, the adjacent archipelago, the Philippine Islands, Hongkong, California, and other parts of the world, not inconsiderably exceeds Mr. Dick's estimate; nor on the circumstance that he makes no allowances for losses at sea. The first glaring error which he commits is, that he assumes the entire quantity of 20,000 chests, by which he takes the Chinese imports, as returned by the

§ The newly-created "Statistical Department," of which Mr. E. C. Taintor has been appointed "Statistical Secretary in the Inspectorate-General, Peking: to reside in Shanghai" (Customs' Gazette, No. xxii, p. 107), raises the above excess to 32,652 piculs in 1869; 36,228 piculs in 1870; 30,074 piculs in 1871; by returning *f.i.* in the latter year the imports into China, which paid duty to the foreign Customs, by upwards of 11,000 piculs short of the truth.—See: "The Returns of Trade at the Treaty-Ports in China, as published by order of the Inspector-General of Customs, critically examined." Shanghai, 1875, 8o.

Foreign Customs, to fall short of the Indian exports to China, to be *smuggled;* and that he not only connects the whole of this alleged smuggling trade with Hongkong, but actually lays it to the charge of that port. Yet the Commissioner of Customs himself observes:—"It would be dealing very imperfectly with the question to raise the rate in the Tariff without taking some measures to enforce the operation of the Tariff at Hongkong *and Macao;* which being—the one actually and the other virtually—foreign ports, are *at present* so circumstanced that *Chinese purchasers* carry their Opium from *both* places, but chiefly from Hongkong, to the amount of about 20,000 chests (a fourth of the whole quantity imported), annually, *free of Tariff duty*, to the neighbouring places on the Canton river, and along the South West Coast, and to those places north of Hongkong, which are not too far distant to make it necessary, for the safety of the article, to have it carried in Foreign vessels." If the writer were asked to explain, how any island on the face of the globe can be (temporarily) "so circumstanced," as to compel native and foreign Customs—officials at ports on the coasts of the opposite mainland,—to allow Chinese traders to evade the payment of Tariff-duties on merchandise purchased at the island: he would find no little difficulty, I opine, in returning a rational answer to such a question. What, however, chiefly calls here for notice is, that of the 20,000 chests of Opium under discussion, Macao imports monthly, as I learn on unquestionable authority, in the mean upwards of 400 chests, or about 5,000 chests per annum, which reduces Mr. Dick's estimate for Hongkong at once to 15,000 chests.

Furthermore, it is stated by those who are believed or known to be well informed, that a considerable quantity of

Opium is yearly imported, without paying the Tariff-duty, into Shanghai, and from thence into other ports, and which Opium has never touched at Hongkong. That smuggling in this tempting article is going on under the very eyes of Mr. Dick, his immediate native superior, the Intendant of Customs, and the Opium office, appears partly from an occasional seizure, recorded in the "Customs Gazette," such as 8 chests of Patna Opium *ex Bertha*, falsely declared as 8 packages, about four piculs of dried prawns being packed on top of Opium; partly from Mr. Dick's own words, in giving *f. i.* the quantity delivered, by his order and as he asserts, "for the purpose of evading the native charges," in 1869, as 1,152·20 piculs and 962 chests, making together more than 2,000 chests. The Inspector-General would hardly thank me for giving publicity to the information furnished to me in connection with this subject. I will, therefore, confine myself to the remark, that a further quantity of Opium of at least 5,000 chests, the alleged smuggling of which cannot possibly be associated with Hongkong, has to be deducted from Mr. Dick's charge against the British Colony. And this agrees very well with the somewhat exaggerated statement of the Commissioner of Customs at Canton, in estimating the quantity, smuggled into that port alone, at about 9,200 piculs or 8,430 chests.

But is even this quantity, at a maximum amounting to 10,000 chests, really smuggled into China? Mr. Dick, strange to say, disregards the fact that the Foreign Customs are but a branch of the Chinese Customs' Service, and *ignores the Native branch of the Service*, levying at the ports of China import- and "transit"-duties upon native and foreign trade, carried on in native bottoms, *altogether*. Yet, he admits at least by implication, as we have seen, that the alleged smuggling trade in Opium purchased by Chinese merchants at Hongkong is in native junks almost exclusively carried on with Canton and certain ports on the neighbouring coast; which ports are, and since the first establishment of foreign commerce at Canton have been, under the fiscal jurisdiction of a special Superintendent of Trade, known to foreigners as *the Hoppo* of Canton. The circumstance, therefore, that out of the ten or eleven thousand chests of Opium, which may annually be imported into those ports, only a thousand chests pass the office of the *Foreign* Commissioner of Customs at Canton, is by no means a proof of the remaining quantity being *smuggled*. Mr. Dick has no right to assume this without positive evidence; and such evidence he has not even alluded to, much less attempted to adduce. The probability, however, is that a certain proportion of the quantity estimated at 10,000 chests really evades the payment of import-duty; and, as we will not suppose the Hoppo and the Commissioner of Customs at Canton to discharge their duties more effectively than do the Intendant, and the Commissioner, of Customs at Shanghai: we may, the total quantities imported being about equal, not unfairly estimate the quantity actually smuggled into the Kuan-tung ports, at about 2,000 chests per annum.

Whether the intermediate quantity of 8,000 chests pays the regular import-duty at the native Custom-houses, or whether it be introduced into China under an arrangement, tacit or otherwise, with the native Customs' authorities, or simply with their positive connivance: in either case it certainly cannot be said to be *smuggled*, since, at the best, no means are taken to *prevent* its introduction "free of Tariff duty." And we have already seen, from the Report of Mr.

Kleinwächter to the Inspector-General, that such is the case, at least to a great extent. But no one acquainted with Chinese officialdom will for one moment delude himself with the idea that Chinese traders are permitted to evade "the Tariff duty," without paying a heavy "squeeze," and the native Authorities levying upon the "smuggled" Opium a tax judged by them more satisfactory to themselves and more beneficial to "the Chinese Revenue" than an import-duty of Tls. 30 per picul, payable to the *Foreign* Inspectorate-General, which, moreover, has no business whatever to interfere in matters appertaining solely to the native branch of the Service. The office of the Hoppo is still a lucrative one, and invariably bestowed on a Member of the Imperial family.* In former years its annual receipts amounted to something like Tls. 3,000,000, about one third of which sum only had to be remitted to Peking for the use of the Court. The present income is greatly reduced; to little more than a million of taels, if I am correctly informed. Out of this sum between Tls. 300,000 and Tls. 400,000 are stated to be derived from Opium. This would give on 8,000 chests, for a mean impost in some form or another, from Tls. 37 to Tls. 50 per chest, which tallies well with the more excessive "Tariff" rate of about Tls. 86, levied, at the port, by the *Foreign* Customs' branch in Canton; and fully confirms my view of the case.

As to the *monetary rate* of Tls. 50 per chest of opium, at which Mr. Dick estimates the alleged loss of revenue, arising to the Chinese Government—or, according to Mr. Wade, to the Provincial Authorities—from Hongkong being a free

---

* The Baron is in error upon this point. The Canton Hoppo is never a member of the Imperial family (*Tsung-shih* 宗室), but is always chosen from the *Nei-wu-fu* (內務府), a Board whose duties correspond very closely to those of the Lord Chamberlain in England. It superintends all the domestic and financial arrangements of the Imperial household.—Ed.

port: it is based on the fourfold assumption, that "it is not possible to levy charges to any great extent on the article after it leaves the port;" that, on the quantity smuggled into the ports, inland duties to the extent of Tls. 10 per chest only are levied at the Chinese Custom-houses and Barriers; that the levying, at the ports, of heavy imposts, in addition to the import-duty of Tls. 30 per picul, stipulated by the Treaty of Tientsin, is *not* contrary to Treaty; and that the entire quantity, imported into China, which pays no Tariff-duty at the *Foreign* Custom-houses, is smuggled. Not one of these assumptions is tenable. It is true that, according to Mr. Dick's table of charges on Opium, previously transcribed, the mean sum levied in the Interior amounts, on the whole quantity imported, to Tls. 11 per picul only, or to nearly Tls. 20 on the quantity affected, but, how little reliance can be placed on this table, is proved by the fact that, whilst Mr. Dick, *f.i.*, returns the "Amount of native charges, levied on the way to the principal market in the Interior" for Fuchow, at Tls. 20.8.6.0 per picul, the late Commissioner of Customs at Fuchow, M. de Méritens, in the same publication, shows that amount, as a matter of fact, to be Tls. 38.5.4.0 per picul, or nearly double of what Mr. Dick sees fit to state. It is, therefore, quite *possible* to levy upon opium, at the inland Custom-houses and barriers, a tax not only of Tls. 20 per picul, as Mr. Dick himself admits, but of Tls. 40 per picul, as M. de Méritens certifies, between the port and the nearest centre of trade; and, since the Ta Ching Dominions, studded over with 卡, extend somewhat farther than from Fuchow to Yen-ping-fu, or from Shanghai to Suchow, it must assuredly be *possible* to levy on opium an additional Tls. 10 or Tls. 12 per chest, *beyond* the principal markets in the vicinity of the ports. But, if this be conceded, it has to be inferred, without positive proofs to the contrary, or to the effect that the consumption of opium in China is confined to the Treaty ports and neighbouring country—which it is not,—that the full inland charges are leviable upon the article, whether it be smuggled into the *ports*, or not; and, if they be not levied, that the fault rest solely with the native Authorities and officials. Nor is it in accordance with Treaty stipulations, that the inland or "Transit"-dues on opium be levied, whether in part or in full, *at the ports*, in addition to the import-duty. The former become payable only in the Interior, and progressively, according to distance and barrier rates. They, being not commuted, should not, and cannot properly, be levied in advance. It is but in *name* that they are collected as transit-dues. Virtually they constitute additional import-duties, and reduce the Tariff import-duty to a mere nominal rate. If their collection at the port be not strictly illegal, it certainly is irreconcileable with Treaty stipulations. Mr. Dick's last assumption has already been disposed of. From all this it is plain, as *à priori* it appears obvious to common-sense, that under no circumstances could Hongkong be held rationally responsible for any loss to the Chinese revenue from smuggling between that port and the Chinese coast, save for a loss on Tariff import-duty, which Mr. Dick himself states to be at the rate of Tls. 14 per picul only. And even the amount of this rate is, to say the least, a very questionable one.

Thus we find "the Hongkong Claims" already reduced to the modest sum of Tls. 28,000,—being Tls. 14 per chest on 2,000 chests,—as a *maximum*. Nor is Hongkong, being a free port, responsible even for this amount of alleged loss to the Chinese Revenue from opium-smuggling. Indeed, having due regard to Mr. Dick's own statement, I am at a loss to understand the very possibility of such smuggling, without our having to lay it to the sole charge of the Native and Foreign Customs' Service, respectively. For, on May 13, 1869, Mr. Dick writes thus to the Inspector-General, Mr. Hart:—"*Hongkong and the Opium revenue.*—The Opium duty should be raised to as high rate as may be found to be possible without encouraging smuggling, and *experience has shown that upwards of 100 taels a chest can be obtained without much risk.*" Now, the mean *total* amount of native imposts, at present raised according to Mr. Dick, is about Tls. 70; the mean amount imposed at the three ports—Amoy, Swatow, and Canton less than Tls. 48; the amount collected at the port of Canton, at, and in the vicinity of, which smuggling is said to be chiefly carried on, Tls. 48.3.4.0; and the import-duty, which can alone be an encouragement to smuggling between Hongkong and the Chinese Coast, is but Tls. 30, per picul. Hence it is plain that, if an import-duty of Tls. 100 per chest can be obtained by the Foreign Customs,—and consequently by the Native Customs as well,—without much risk of inciting to smuggling, that an import-duty of Tls. 30 per picul, (or even an impost of about Tls. 95 per chest, at present raised at the ports), is obtainable without any such risk. And hence it is equally plain that, according to Mr. Dick's own testimony, there exists no external inciting cause for smuggling opium into China; that, consequently, Hongkong can possibly be no cause of loss from smuggling to the Chinese Revenue; and that the only ostensible cause of the loss alleged, which presents itself, is, in combination with the corruption of Chinese officials, *the inefficiency of the Native and Foreign Customs' Service.*

Again, the circumstance that Hongkong is "a free port," on which Mr. Dick lays the whole stress of his argument, has no bearing whatever on the question at issue. If London or Liverpool, with their bonded docks, occupied the same site, the same trade in opium would be carried on with China from either sea-port town. The British Possession of Victoria is no more responsible to China for any smuggling trade going on, in exports from its port, on the coasts of China, than France is responsible to England for any smuggling, that may take place in exports from French ports, on the coasts of the United Kingdom; or than England is responsible to the United States for any smuggling, in exports from English ports, which the American Customs' Service may fail, or be unable, to prevent on the coasts of the North-American Republic.

I fear me, then greatly, that the smuggling-claim of Tls. 1,000,000, preferred by the Inspector-General and the Commissioner of Customs at Shanghai against Hongkong, must, being a baseless fabric, fall to the ground. The character of their own arguments has enabled me to treat the subject somewhat lightly; and I might have laid even less stress on it, had not Mr. Dick, whilst making up a hollow, exaggerated, and disloyal charge against the British Possession of Victoria in mitigation of unlawful and oppressive charges, levied by the Chinese Government upon British and foreign trade, clearly misrepresented the amount of the latter,—thus misleading the British and other Western Governments as well as the public generally in regard to that amount. My proof out of his own mouth is this:—In his table, literally reproduced above, Mr. Dick makes out the total of "excess" of taxation to which Foreign Trade was subject in China in 1858, to be Tls.

2,980,224, that is "if native charges were commuted at Treaty rate of Tariff duty," and not including opium. If we include opium, "not entitled at present to commutation," there have to be added to the above sum Tls. 4,099,426 —(Tls. 1,617,611 + Tls. 808,805 =) Tls. 2,426,416 = Tls. 1,673,010, making the total = Tls. 4,653,234. But in his "Suggestions," addressed to the Inspector-General on January 18, 1869, the Commissioner of Customs states :— "I strongly recommend the views put forward in this despatch to your consideration. In our present position (to sum it up) we collect Import and Export Duties amounting to nearly Tls. 7,000,000 under a Tariff for Foreign Trade, but we fail to influence the extra-Tariff charges amounting (opium included) to *a much larger sum.*" The expression "a much larger sum" than Tls. 7,000,000, certainly partakes of a somewhat vague character. But if, by way of comparison *f.i.* of the prices of two pieces of silk, the price of one of which had been stated to be £7, we were told that the price of the other piece was "much higher:" we would hardly conclude the latter to be less than £11 or £10 *at least.* And a similar language, applied to as many millions, would produce a similar impression. Mr. Dick must, consequently, from his own words be understood to have known, that the "Excess of duties at present collected" over and above the "Amount leviable if native charges were commuted at Treaty rate of half Tariff duty," and including Import and Export duties exceeds by some six or seven million taels the total of Tls. 4,653,234 (opium included), or the total of Tls. 2,980,224 (not including opium), which his table—to a corresponding extent misrepresenting the defective Returns, on which it is based, as the full charges levied,—makes them out to be. But, that he cannot have intended to include in his sum of "nearly Tls. 7,000,000" the uncommuted amount of Tls. 4,099,426, being the *total* of imposts at present collected on opium, is proved by this, that it was impossible for him to take the remainder of at most Tls. 2,900,574, as compared with his tabular total of Tls. 2,980,224,—being a smaller sum,—for "a much larger sum," or the amount of Tls. 7,000,000, as compared with the nearly equal amount of Tls. 7,000,000 for "a much larger amount." Under *any* circumstances, the Commissioner of Customs at Shanghai knew, and the Inspector-General, having convinced himself that Mr. Dick had worked up his subject with much thoroughness," concurred in the knowledge, that, as compared with the amount of Mr. Dick's table, the yearly total of illegal taxation to which British and Foreign Trade is actually subject in China, constitute "a much larger sum."

All this was written before two important documents, fully bearing me out in the view taken of the amount of illegal taxation, levied by the Chinese Government, had come to my knowledge. The first are the new Regulations C, framed by the Inspector-General and proposed by the Tsung-li Ya-mên. In Rule iii. §1, a fine is imposed of "ten times the half-duty (of 1/8) *in order to compensate for the duties and the li-kin*, (the payment of which is supposed to have been avoided) *on the road*, i.e. *in transitu*. Here, then, we have the high and, in a case like this, indisputable authority of the Tsung-li Yamên itself, as well as that of the Inspector-General, Mr. Hart, for the fact that the war and other taxes, levied on foreign trade *in transitu*, amount to about 25 per cent, *i.e.* to about 22½ per cent. *ad valorem* over and above the half-duty of 2½ per cent. stipulated by Treaty. This is probably meant to express the *mean* rate, as resulting from the transit of foreign goods or native produce through two or more provinces.

The second document is a Memorial, presented by the native merchants of Shanghai to the Tao-tai, and a translation of which, as published in the *North China Daily News* of February 9, 1874, I subjoin. It reads as follows :—

In view of the great depression of trade in Shanghai, ascribed to the heavy and multiplied system of taxation existing, the representatives of each trade collectively petitioned the Tautai and other authorities concerned on the 13th of this moon, and fearing the subject should not gain publicity far and near, they therefore publish the petition in the *Shunpau*.

" A General Petition from the Merchants of Shanghai. Whereas the heaviness of Likin dues has led to the stoppage of trade, your petitioners pray for their reduction, that the present deplorable position of merchants may be mitigated and business be thereby revived.

We would humbly advance that the interest of commerce and the welfare of merchants are vitally connected with the subject in question. From the winter of last year to the present time, no less than fifty to sixty merchants have succumbed to the circumstances of the time, the total amount failed for reaching the aggregate of Tls. 2,000,000. Many of these failures have been settled privately, but the suits arising therefrom have been so continual as to form sufficient official proof of the facts set forward. An investigation into the course of this widespread adversity, proves it to be owing to the multiplicity of Tax barriers and to the heaviness of the dues collected. During the time of the Rebellion, Likin barriers, cash shop and house taxes, import and export duties, market dues, boat and timber dues were all successively established. The revenue thus collected was exacted from the life-capital of merchants. The merchants continued to struggle against adversity until, the " creek being drained and the hill removed," they were at length brought to a stand. The authorities were afterwards good enough to abolish cash shop, house and market taxes, including them in the Likin tax ; and subsequently Tseng-kwo-fan further lessened the Likin in order to relieve merchants. But the alleviation thus afforded amounted only to 30 per cent., and has proved inadequate to relieve the heavy weight on trade. Goods coming from the sea are subject to Import dues, merchandise arriving from the interior pays Li-kin at the Barriers en route, and when reaching Shanghai the "Loh-ti-chuan" 捐地落 is further levied. Again, when re-shipped, those sent by sea have to pay Export dues, and those sent to the interior are subject to Barrier dues. In comparing the total of collection with the value of the goods it amounts to 20 to 30 per cent.

In former times, when goods arrived, if there was a market for them, they were sold; if unsaleable they were sent to another market, or from thence perhaps re-imported into Shanghai. The expenses were very small, and merchants therefore gladly repaired to Shanghai. At present, when goods have once entered the town they cannot again leave it, and after they quit the place they cannot return, simply on account of the Loh-ti-chuan.

We beg to represent that at other Ports, although there are Tax Barriers, the "Loh-ti-chuan" impost does not exist, and Shanghai alone is exceptional in the matter. Moreover, in the Province of Chekiang, the law in regard to levying dues is that, if the Li-kin is paid at one Barrier, the receipt then issued carries the goods to all parts of the Province; but in Kiangsoo dues have to be paid at each alternate Barrier; as for instance on the route to Soochow, where dues have to be paid at three stations and to be *viséd* at two alternate ones. Owing to this great difference against Shanghai, merchants—who assemble only where profit is to be gained—view the Port with fear and distrust. In dejection they leave the place to seek a living elsewhere, and it is thus that the outlets to trade become gradually closed and the demand for merchandise extremely limited. These circumstances are much to be deplored. It is not that we shut our eyes to the necessary requisitions of Government; and in support of this, we have merely to revert to the manner in which Shanghai responded recently to the critical call for food and clothes for the North—appearing at the head of the list—but, in our present reduced state we cannot but seek after means to revive from the present distress. We therefore pray for special favour at this crisis.

It has, moreover, to be taken into consideration that with the increased circulation of goods the public exchequer benefits equally with the merchant. If Kiangsoo should be placed on the same footing as Chekiang, duties would thereby be lightened, and there would be every prospect of a revival in the Shanghai trade. In the other alternative it is to be feared that we shall daily sink lower and lower.

With the great results at stake we cannot remain silent, and we have to beg that his Excellency the Taotai will represent the matter to the Governor-General, the Footai, and to Earl Li Hung-chang. Our prayer is that the state of trade at Shanghai having reached a crisis, from which under the existing regime it will be difficult to recover, the "Loh-te-chuan" tax be at once abolished, and the Barrier levies outside be placed on the same footing as in Chekiang.

Here once more the general amount of *li-kin* and other charges, levied by the Chinese Government on (foreign) inland trade, is stated to be from 20 % to 30 % *ad valorem*, or 25 per cent in the *mean*; and if the Chinese merchants had not been certain of the fact, they would most assuredly not have dared to state it to the Tao-tai and Intendant of Customs.

To revert now to my table, the general correctness and results of which have received the fullest confirmation from what has just been said, and can leave no further room for any reasonable doubt. It presents several features, equally interesting and remarkable. The first is, that the Chinese Tariff is, considering the statement of the country and the requirements of the Government, probably the highest in the world. Yet, in regard to it, an able and well-known writer on Chinese matters, though noted for the inconsistency of his political views and the strength of his pro-Chinese bias rather than for the reliability of his information and the soundness of his arguments, Mr. J. Barr Robertson, wrote, at that time under the inspiration of the late Mr. Burlingame, from Shanghai, on January 8, 1868, to the London *Daily News* :—

"We demonstrate to our ministers and governments the advantages of low tariffs, with a logic to which the United States, Canada, the continent of Europe, and Australia have as yet turned a deaf ear. Indeed, I may safely challenge a comparison of the China tariff with that of Canada, the United States, or Australia; but Canada, the United States, and Australia are in no danger of being taught logic at the point of the bayonet; being civilised, they are entitled to indulge their protective and prohibitive tastes. They may be wooed and won, but it must be by pearl necklaces; while China is treated to the fraternal embraces of the West by means of Armstrong guns and Enfield rifles. Yet, in addition to *an almost unequalled low tariff*, the Chinese can point to the immense river steamers which daily glide on the broad bosom of the Yangtsze and steam eight hundred miles into the interior of their empire; they can point to an organised Customs service of foreigners and Chinese under the directorship of Mr. Hart, which has attained a perfection and completeness not to be surpassed in Europe; they can point to a beginning in the purchase of gunboats, and to the establishment of arsenals where, under foreign supervision, Chinamen are taught to cast cannon, and to make every single part pertaining to rifles; they can point to the establishment of a college at Peking for the instruction by foreigners of a select body of their youth in European languages, art, and science; they can point to their adoption of Wheaton's international law, to the building of lighthouses, to the introduction of foreigners to drill their troops, to the survey of their coal-fields and mineral resources by a foreigner; to all this and much more they can point as the evidences of their progress since the treaty of Tientsin."

The most telling and fatal comment on these panegyrics, perhaps, was the Tientsin massacre. It is with all the facts, save one, of which Mr. Robertson informs the West, China "can boast," as it is with her "almost unequalled low tariff." The exception is her progress in *arming herself* against Progress, and paying for her armaments out of the "Excess" of taxation, which she illegally imposes upon Foreign Commerce at large and upon British Commerce in particular.

Mr. Dick gives, in 1869, the following "Comparison of Tariffs," to which I only add the true per-centage for China :—

	United States, 1868.	Great Britain, 1866.	India, 1866.	China, (Tariff and Native Charges), 1868.		Turkey.
				Mr. Dick.	In reality, including "squeezes."	
Import Duties— Luxuries ....per cent.		60 (Tea, Coffee, Spirits and Wines, Tobacco and Sugar).	....	18½ (Opm.)	30	....
Manufactures.. "	....		....	7·86 *a* 10·45	30	....
Metals ...... "	....	....	....	20	30	....
Sundries ..... "	....	....	....	8	30	....
On total value of Imports.. "	44	12·6	1 to 7½	12·3	30	5
Export Duties .. "	free	free	about 8·6	11·8	30	12
Value of Imports........	....	£184,887,802	£ 29,599,228	Tls. 71,121,213		....
" Exports........	....	£136,695,085	£ 56,972,859	Tls. 69,114,733		....
" Both	$642,451,489	£321,582,907	£ 86,573,087	Tls. 140,235,946		....
Duties on whole Commerce.... } p. ct.	25	6·9	8·2	12	30	abt. 8½

Into a discussion of the elements on which this Table is based I need not enter. It matters little whether the mean amount of imposts, levied on commerce in each of the countries chosen by Mr. Dick for comparison, has been quite fairly determined in the case of Great Britain and India, or whether the Tariff of the United States is still as high as it was in 1868. When we consider the condition of the Army and the Police in China, ill paid when paid at all, and worse taken care of; the fearful misery of the prisons; the pittances, with few exceptions, disbursed for the Civil Service; the wretched state of the public roads, wherever such roads exist at all; the neglect of the canals; the ruin and delay of public works; the absence of a Navy possessing any claim to the name, of a Diplomatic Service, of a Postal Service, of a Packet- and Telegraph-Service, of National Collections, and a funded National Debt, etc., etc.: in short, when we compare the Public Administration of China with that of the United States on the one hand, and their tariffs—the present American tariff is for high rates alone comparable with the Chinese tariff—on the other, we cannot but arrive at the conclusion that, even relative to the former, the latter is *exorbitant*.

The next prominent feature of our table is, that the Chinese Government levies, so far as import- and "transit-" duties are concerned, no heavier imposts upon Opium than it levies upon any other class of foreign goods, or native produce. True, the "Stationary Trade Dues" imposed on Opium shops, are high. But it is as certain as is the fact that Opium-smoking prevails nowhere to a greater extent that it does in the Tatar Capital, and in no quarter of Pe-king to a greater extent than on good ground it is believed to do in the Imperial Palace, that the Tsung-li Yamên has, for some years been so strongly urging the "immorality" of the Opium-trade upon the consideration of England and the religionistic sentimentality of the Gladstone Administration, *solely* in the hope of China being, for the excess of her exports, *paid in silver*,—and in precisely the same proportion, in which it may be found practicable to diminish the importation of the *foreign*-grown drug. There lies the whole moral of the Ya-mên's cunningly-worded despatch of July, 1869, to Sir Rutherford Alcock, on the "Opium Trade,"—a despatch betraying itself, by unmistakeable internal evidence, to be, *mainly the composition of a Foreigner*. I am as strongly opposed to the *intemperate* use in China of Opium, as I am opposed to the *intemperate* use of alcoholic liquors and tobacco at home. But I should hold it to be a fatal error on the part of the British Government, were it to entertain the hypocritical appeal of the Tsung-li Ya-mên to England's moral sense and generosity. For the *Chinese* Government to make such an appeal, constitutes of itself a national offence. For the Ya-mên to *threaten* England, unless she consent to the abolition of the cultivation of the poppy in India, with the hatred and anger of the officials and people of China, (i.e. with a repetition of the Tien-tsin Massacre on a larger scale), and the interruption of friendly relations, is, despite of the folly of the thing, a national insult, based so far as the Chinese people is concerned, on a palpable untruth—an insult, which no British Minister save a Rutherford Alcock, no British Cabinet save a Gladstone Cabinet, could have submitted to.

The trade in Opium is no less honorable than is the trade in Wines or in Tobacco. There is no more "sin" in the preparation of opium or morphine, than there is in the preparation of laudanum, from the same plant. The growing of the poppy is as lawful as is the growing of the vine. *Not the manufacture of opium is an evil, but the intemperate use of it.* To foster the extension of the former, as a legitimate and an important branch of Indian agriculture and industry, is the duty of the Government of England; to check the spreading of the latter, as one of the vices to which the Chinese nation is addicted, the duty of the Government of China. It will perform that duty, not by attempting to intimidate or to cajole England, but by setting, in the Palace and in the Ya-mêns of the Empire, the example of temperance, if not of abstinence, to the lower classes; by alleviating the burdens, improving the material condition, and elevating the moral character, of the Chinese people; and, in addition to these essentials, by *wise* measures of public supervision. The abolition of the use of opium in China, even did the Government seriously contemplate it—

which it does not,—would be as idle an undertaking, as would be the attempted abolition of the use of tobacco and alcoholic drinks at home. The people of the West *will* have the one; and the people of the Far East *will* have the other. And they both have a right to each. *Their physical organisation differs essentially.* As a stimulant and a narcotic, opium is remarkably well—nay, admirably—suited to¶ their system, and produces, even when taken habitually and in excess, far less injurious effects upon the Chinese, than do gin and tobacco, when taken habitually and in excess, upon the European and American, physical system.* The *moderate* use of opium I therefore, hold,—and I am speaking upon mature reflection and from personal observation,—to be at least as rational and legitimate a source of enjoyment and solace to the Chinese, as the *moderate* use of tobacco and

¶ I stand by no means singular in this opinion,—the result of personal observation. M. Lamprey, M.B., Surgeon of H.M.'s 67th Regiment, in his Report on the Chinese Hospital at Tientsin. (Shanghai, 1862, 8o., page 14-15) remarks :—"The universal use of the Opium pipe among the Chinese must certainly be owing to some peculiarity of their mental and nervous constitution. . . . It has already been stated that it was very difficult to produce the anasthetic effect of chloroform upon them without prolonged inhalation, and that in the case of a very young child this was also noticed to a marked degree; on the other hand Hyoscyamus and Belladonna produce their action much better on the Chinaman, than on the European. The spirit Sam-shoo the Chinaman drinks, is a powerful agent in producing intoxication in the European...; but it does not appear to be so active on the Chinaman, who, though he imbibes considerable quantities, is very seldom met with in a state of intoxication. There must be some adaptation of the effects of Opium to the Chinaman, which makes the practice of smoking it so universal among his race."

I perceive from a leading article in the *Shanghai Evening Courier* for March 18, 1872, that Consul Dr. Winchester, also, stated in evidence lately given before a Select Committee of the House of Commons, with all the weight of authority conferred by a twenty-six years' residence in China, that, being a medical man, he was "led to the conclusion, that these was a certain aptitude in the stimulant (opium) to the circumstances of the Chinese people;" and that "all stimulants having a beneficial use" (when taken in moderation) "and an injurious use" (when taken in excess), "he considered opium to have both."

* Mr. Lamprey observes :—"I learned that four or five pipes of Opium had little or no effect on the smokers. *A few more pipes stimulated them as wine would:* but it was not till twenty pipes were smoked, that anything like very sensible effects were produced." (Report on the Chinese Hospital, 1862, p. 15).

Dr. George Shearer, in his Report on the Kiukiang Dispensary for Chinese (Medical Reports published by order of the Inspector-General of Customs, Shanghai, 1871, 4o. p. 62) states :—"The number of Opium-smokers, who applied for advice during the year 1871, was 197. Of these 27 used half a mace (or about half a drachm) daily; 54 used one mace; 38 a mace and a half; 41 two mace, (one man smoking the drug for a period of 20, another for

wine is to Western men. The Government of no people possess the right to interdict to them such a use, and to deprive them of such a solace. Against its *abuse* there are no other remedies, whether in England, in China or elsewhere, save those I have indicated.

If the British Government, under such circumstances, were to listen to the Tsung-li Ya-mên's insidious arguments —supported though they be by ill-directed missionary zeal, —and, apparently yielding to the Ya-mên's intimidations, to consent to the prohibition of the poppy culture in India: it would, in my judgment, thereby subvert, in principle, the basis of Free-trade; disown the natural rights of the loyal subject; acknowledge the arbitrary power of semi-barbarous despotism; prostitute the logic of facts; succumb to Tatar cunning and deceit; and, after all, uselessly sacrifice the legitimate interests of British Commerce and Indian Industry:—for, sacrifice them to what end? To the end that the Government of China,—not content, while prohibiting the use of the pure, excellent and cheap salt offered by England, to force upon its subjects, for one of

a period of 30 years); 18 used three mace; 8 used four mace, (one, a subject of asthma and bronchitis for a period of 10 years); 7 used five mace, (one of the number having smoked opium for a period of 17 years at a cost of $80 per annum); 4 used six mace, (one of them a Buddhist priest *used this quantity for 17 years*). The whole of these were supplied with medicine at the Dispensary, and more than a tenth part returned to report themselves cured of the craving and habit. It is possible, that a much greater number were really cured, but on the other hand it is highly probable that many relapsed into their old habit when the state of their finances improved. Poverty, and consequent inability to purchase the drug, was the general excuse pleaded for coming to see me. Some reduced the quantity used from 3 or 4 mace to 1 and there stopped."

Mr. Wingrove Cooke (China, London, 1859, 8o., p. 177-179) relates:—At Ningpo I accepted an invitation from the Rev. Mr. Russell, the Church of England missionary priest, and the Rev. Mr. Edkins, of the London Mission of Shanghai, to visit the opium dens of Ningpo city. Commander Dew, of the *Nimrod*, and several of his officers accompanied us. I had seen the opium-eaters of Constantinople and Smyrna, and the hashish-smokers of Constantine, and I was prepared for emaciated forms and trembing limbs. . . . The Chinese exhibition was sufficiently disgusting, but was otherwise quite a failure. . . . The members of this convivial society were good humoured and communicative. One was a chair-coolie, a second was a petty tradesman, a third was a runner in a mandarin's yamên; they were all of that class of urban population which is just above the lowest. They were, however,

the articles of daily consumption most necessary to health, a product, resembling crystalized mire rather than crystalized sea-water, at an exorbitant price,—might, under the shielding mask of its "impotence," encourage the cultivation of the poppy at home; stealthily and gradually add to its salt-monopoly that of the manufacture and sale of opium; impose upon the people a deleterious drug, while excluding from the country a superior preparation; and cause an annual amount of silver, to the extent of eight million £ sterling, to be withdrawn from circulation in England and to be diverted to China. On the other hand, the Tsung-li Ya-men's threat, recently suggested also by Mr. Dick in the shape of "a temporary measure," to withdraw the prohibition on the home growth of the poppy, need not alarm the Indian farmer. The effect would simply be a demand for the purer and better article, increasing with the increasing *free* production and use of "the deadly poison" in China. Mr. Dick's theory touching this point is a dream. Experience supports my conclusion. Let the experiment be tried.

neither emaciated nor infirm. The chair-coolie was a sturdy fellow, well capable of taking his share in the porterage of a sixteen-stone mandarin; the runner seemed well able to run; and the tradesman, who said that he was thirty-eight years old, was remarked by all of us to be a singularly young-looking man for that age. He had smoked opium for seven years. As we passed from the opium-dens, we went into a Chinese tea-garden—a dirty paved court, with some small trees and flowers in flower-pots,—and a very emaciated and yawning proprietor presented himself. "The man has destroyed himself by opium-smoking," said Mr. Russell. The man, being questioned, declared that he had never smoked an opium-pipe in his life,—a bad shot, at which no one was more amused than the rev. gentleman, who fired it. . . . English physicians, unconnected with the missionary societies, have assured me that the coolie opium-smoker dies, not from opium, but from starvation."

Mr. F. Porter Smith, M.B., in his "First Annual Report of the Hankow Medical Mission Hospital" (Shanghai, 1865, 8o., p. 11) states:—"The number of cases of opium-smoking, applying for assistance in renouncing the vicious habit, has not been large, as no encouragement has been given to such as desire to aggravate the original sum of their guilt, by the addition thereto of the bonus of hypocrisy. The subjects of this habit have exhibited very little, if anything, of the typical symptoms of opium-smoking. . . . It is believed that a small number of cases has been entirely cured. A simple case of opium-eating was the most pitiable instance of the whole number. It is not intended, in these remarks, to justify, in the least degree, this accursed practice, but to show, truthfully, that the vice as practised here cannot be pictured with all the horrors so frequently described as attending it in some other parts of this country."

The last and most important feature of our table, claiming notice, is the boast, that the annual total amount of revenue derived by the Government of China from Foreign Trade, does not fall below four million, as made out by Mr. Dick, but reaches about ten million, £ sterling; and that the amount of ILLEGAL TAXATION, to which that Trade is subject, exceeds *five million*, instead of falling below one million, *£ sterling per annum.* It may be argued, in diminution of this sum: *Firstly*, that the nominal per-centage of inland charges, leviable on foreign goods, is in practice not levied in full, and that a much smaller value than the true value of such goods is permitted to be declared for the purpose of payment of duties. But I have already disposed of this objection, by explaining that the practice in question is restricted to the native inland trade proper, and, though possibly and in certain localities occasional exceptions may occur to the general rule, that *foreign* goods have to pay the full rates,—as is too well ascertained to admit of so much as a doubt. *Secondly*, that not the whole of the percentage, leviable in the importing province, is levied; a portion of the goods passing into the hands of the retail-dealer before they reach the last barrier. True, I have not succeeded in ascertaining whether or not, in such cases, the full duty is collected notwithstanding, either in the shape of a complementary *le-kin*, or in that of a "Stationary Trade" tax. This is more than probable. But what is certain is, that a large portion of the goods are not sold within the importing province, but are sent on to a second and a third province; and thus become subject to double or treble duty.

Thirdly, it may be argued, that the total does not go to the Imperial Government, and that a considerable sum has to be deducted from the gross receipts for expenses of collection. The first point has already been explained. In regard to the second, Mr. Dick also dwells at some length and with much emphasis on the expense of collecting the native charges, more especially those on opium, to which he adds "the expense of evasion," in order, I presume, to impart to the amount a more respectable appearance, and in one sentence estimating "the cost of evasion *equal* to the charges due on the quantity smuggled, less the reduction effected by the smuggling *on the general market price* of the commodity,"—which reduction can, certainly, not benefit the smuggler, so that smuggling opium at Shanghai would appear to be a mere labour of love;—in the following sentence estimating it at "one-half of the amount evaded." Thus, on an "Amount collected" of about £110,500, he very nearly doubles the expenses of the Opium Office, in 1869 about £6,900,—those of "the Defence Tax"—*i.e.* the *chow-fang*-office, engaged in collecting other charges, being in connection with Opium, according to Mr. Dick, too trifling to be taken into account,—and puts them down at about £13,400, "for a piece of work, which could be performed efficiently by the Foreign Customs without inconvenience to the public, and without adding anything at all to the present labour or expense—inclusive of "the cost of evasion" ?—" of that Department." Truly, the Chinese Government must be blind to their own advantage, in not accepting so generous an offer. And might not the Foreign Commissioner of Customs have been equally prepared to add, on similar terms, to the collection of the native charges on opium,—*li-kin*, *chow-fang*, and the like,—free of additional labour to the Customs' employés and of expense to the Chinese Exchequer, the collection of the similar charges on foreign imports at large? Be that as it may: the collection of taxes involves a certain amount of cost, I believe, in all countries; and Mr. Dick appears to me somewhat unreasonable and ultra-zealous in proposing to deprive of their living, and begrudging to a crowd of poor and ill-paid, though, certainly, not over-honest, native officials mostly of inferior degree, their miserable share in a yearly total of *illegal* imposts upon Foreign Trade, which they assist in amassing for the Imperial Government. At any rate, the question here is not:—What is the "net" revenue derived by that Government from illegal taxation? but:—What is the annual burden of illegal taxation, to which Foreign Trade is subject in China?

We shall presently see that this burden has for the year 1870, to be estimated at nearly six million pounds sterling—a sum,† which would form an item even in the budget of the Chancellor of the English Exchequer, and might occasionally save him some little perplexity. Nor does it constitute the whole of the claim, which Foreign Trade can fairly establish against the Celestial Government.

Of the "Tonnage-Dues" which, in 1870, amounted to Tls. 207,815.3.7.5 I will say nothing. The Inspector-General is understood to have written an elaborate Memorandum on the subject, accounting for every cash collected, and to be still occupied in further elaborating it. If the account give the history of the Fund and every phase of its expenditure: it may be expected—speaking from what

† Not quite the whole of this sum is devoted to military purposes. Among the imposts, which the Foreign merchant is illegally made to pay in China, we paid *f.i.*:—"Public Works taxes" of various kinds; "Transport of Tribute Grain tax:" "Detective Office tax;" "Infirmary tax;" "Hangchow Sea-wall tax;" "Sea embankment tax;" "Measure tax;" "District Magistrate's tax;" "Mandarin tax;" "Lawyer's tax;" "Guild taxes;" "Purveyor of Clothing to the Court tax;" etc., etc., etc. All these irregular taxes, however, whose (frequently unintelligible Chinese) name is legion, are chiefly local "squeezes."

I happen to know of the details—to prove an instructive and interesting document.‡ Of course, it will be very different from similar *Chinese* documents. Relative to the latter, Dr. Rennie relates,—in connection with "Hang-ki, who was Hoppo, or collector of Customs, at Canton for five years, out of a salary of about £600, effected an annual saving, it was said, of about £100,000, and just paid, on his arrival in Peking, a few preliminary "squeezes" amounting to about £20,000,—an amusing anecdote, calculated to throw some additional light on *Chinese* Customs matters. I will, therefore, transcribe it. "In the course of a conversation," Dr. Rennie writes, "which Mr. Hart had a few days ago with Hang-ki's headman, some remarks were made about the misappropriation of Custom-house funds by high Chinese officials, and Mr. Hart remarked, "Now, do you mean to say that the sixty-six thousand taels that Hang-ki has had to pay since his return to Peking have been properly exacted? "Yes, it was all right; *the accounts were quite correct and the money regularly accounted for.*" On being asked for an explanation how this possibly could be in the face of such facts as were before them, he proceeded to detail the grounds on which his notions of the correctness of the transactions were based. He said, that *smuggling* at that time was very prevalent on the river, and that good grounds existed to justify a considerable expenditure in the construction and commissioning of Custom-house cutters and cruizers. This expenditure of public public money, which was fully justified, was not, however,

‡ I cannot help thinking, that the conversion of the accumulating Tonnage-dues into a "*Mercantile Marine Fund*," to be administrated by a Mixed Board of Commissioners, as suggested by me, a couple of years ago, in a pamphlet on "The Tonnage-Dues Fund, the Harbour of Shanghai and the Wusung Bar" (Shanghai, 1872, 4o.) is more than ever deserving of the attention of the Foreign Governments in treaty-relations with China.

made, but it was charged in the accounts as having been made, and that consequently the Government were no sufferers, inasmuch as, had the funds not been appropriated by Hang-ki, they would have been much more expensive for the Government; consequently, that it was an actual gainer by this arrangement? There would seem to be little doubt that the Emperor himself must be fully cognizant of and encourage *irregularities in book-keeping*, such as just mentioned,....it being a common occurrence for him to send commissions to the Hoppo of Canton to execute; and it is an understood thing that sums thus expended are not to appear in the public accounts; and it is equally well understood that the Hoppo is not to expect any remittances from the Imperial purse. Sums, which the Hoppo is thus called upon to disburse in the course of the year are stated to be considerable. *From this it would seem that a systematic falsification of his accounts, forms a portion of the recognized duties of a Chinese collector of Customs.*"

Different from the Tonnage Dues are the Coast-Trade Duties. The amount collected from the latter impost, in 1870, by the Foreign Custom-house, reached the sum of about Tls. 1,500,000; in conformity with which Mr. Dick in his *Suggestions* observes:—" On Chinese produce carried from one port of China to another in Foreign vessels, we collect under a misapplication of the Foreign trade Tariff upwards of Tls. 1,500,000,—or about £450,000—a year." It is true that this sum is levied, in the shape of an exorbitant impost, upon native trade proper, but levied upon it only inasmuch as it is carried on in *Foreign* vessels, and, therefore, *placing foreign shipping under a disadvantage out of all proportion, as compared with native shipping.* Thus, Messrs. Jardine, Matheson and Co., in a letter of April 27, 1869, called the attention of the Commissioner of Customs at Shanghai, to the following differential duties, payable on the same quantities of the same identical goods :—

	When shipped in Foreign Vessels at the Foreign Custom-house.		*When shipped in Native Vessels at the Native Custom-house.*	
NANKEENS.—Package of 20 pieces, weighing about 170 lbs.	Foreign Export Duty	Tls. 1.5.0	Chinese Export Duty	Tls. 0.0.4
	Coast Trade Duty	„ 0.7.5	Import Dues	„ 0.0.2
	Defence-Tax	„ 0.7.5		
	(about 18/)	Tls. 3.0.0	(about 4½d.)	Tls. 0.0.6
SILK PIECE GOODS.—Per picul of 133⅓ lbs.	Foreign Export Duty	Tls. 12.0.0	Chinese Export Duty	Tls. 4.0.0
	Coast Trade Duty	„ 6.0.0	Import Dues	„ 1.0.0
	Defence Tax	„ 6.0.0		
	(about £7.2/)	Tls. 24.0.0	(about £1.10/)	Tls. 5.0.0

The imposition of the former duties, (setting the *chow-fung* aside) was *provisionally* granted to the Chinese Government by Sir Frederick Bruce in his frequently cited "Regulations regarding Transit Dues, Exemption Certificates, and Coast-Trade Duties," of which Art. iii. 1. reads :—"Native produce carried coastwise pays full export-duty at the port of shipment ; and at the port of entry, coast-trade duty, the amount of which is declared to be half import-duty." The chief motive of the British Minister, in thus unreasonably burdening British shipping, he explains in his despatch of October 26, 1861, to Earl Russell to have been, that he judged it "of considerable importance at that moment, that the moderate party represented by the Prince of Kung should be able to show that their policy was justified by its results, and that suggestions, made by them, were considered in a reasonable spirit."

I cannot but hold that the view taken of this question by Sir Frederick Bruce, was equally far from being reasonable and politic ; and that the tax itself is irreconcilable both with justice and the spirit of the Treaty of Tientsin. It is true that, in most countries, a participation in the coast carrying-trade is not granted to foreign vessels ; but in most countries also the carrying-service is effectively performed by native enterprize and native craft.‖ Wherever this is not the case, foreign vessels, unless they are altogether excluded from a country, as from Corea, not only are allowed to participate in, but frequently almost to monopolise the coasting traffic between its principal ports. And this simply because the natives find it to *their own advantage* to employ them; so that, inasmuch as they are used by native merchants to carry native goods, being native property and destined for native consumption, they assume the character of native conveyances. In China this is pre-eminently the case; because not only are foreign steaming and sailing-vessels, notwithstanding the excessive duty to which they render the native merchandise subject, largely employed in the coast-trade by Chinese merchants: the latter are also share-holders to a considerable extent in the local Steam-Navigation-Companies, and, themselves, sole owners of foreign vessels and steamers, engaged in that trade. Yet, simply because they are foreign-built or foreign-shaped, the native goods carried in them, become liable to a five- and even a forty-fold duty; than which nothing could place the unreasonable character of Sir Frederick Bruce's arrangement with the Tsung-li Ya-mên on this point in a clearer light.

The question, however, admits of a more positive solution. It is obvious that, if the higher imposts be justly leviable, they must be so leviable either on the foreign

‖ The Inspector-General, Mr. Hart, in his "Memo." on the Wusung Bar of March 5, 1874, prophesies that "the competition coming from the Chinese side will, in ten or twenty years' time, have swept the foreign flag from the coasting trade of China." He also predicts that, within the same space of time, the foreign trade of Shanghai will have been transferred to Chinkiang; but that "the foreign community of Chinkiang will naturally be a smaller one. (Political possibilities aside)."—Would it not have been more prudent of the Confidential Adviser of the Tsung-li Ya-mên, to take warning by prophets, who have, over and over again, predicted "the destruction of the world?"

vessels as such, or else on the native merchandise, conveyed in them, as such. Now, they are not leviable on the foreign vessels, as such; for, ART. XXX. of the Treaty of Tientsin states distinctly:—"The master of any British merchant-vessel may, within forty-eight hours after the arrival of his vessel, but not later, decide to depart without breaking bulk, in which case he will not be subject to pay tonnage-dues. But tonnage-dues shall be held due after the expiration of the said forty-eight hours. No other fees or charges upon entry or departure shall be levied." This is conclusive. Neither however, are the higher imports under consideration justly leviable upon native merchandise as such conveyed from one port to another. For, in the first place, that merchandise has, in its way to the port of shipment, paid or must be supposed to have paid, all inland charges to which it was so far subject; and that, in the second place, it is, in respect of the transit to the port of destination, held by the Chinese Government itself to be subject only to the additional lower imposts, payable at the Native Custom-houses, is proved by the very fact that no higher duties upon the merchandise are there demanded. This is equally conclusive. Hence, native-owned goods, carried from one port to another in foreign vessels are, justly and at the most, liable to no higher charges than those, levied upon similar goods, when conveyed in native vessels, at the Native Custom-houses.

I say: *at the most* are such goods liable to the *Native* charges. For, when the great and substantial advantanges are considered, which the use of foreign steamers and sailing-vessels, more especially the former, insure to the Chinese merchant and to Chinese property,—quickness of despatch, punctuality of transmission, comparative security against loss at sea, complete security against piratical attack and plunder: it appears to me, that an appreciative and enlightened Government, having truly the interests of its subjects at heart, would feel prompted to *subsidise* those foreign coasting-steamers rather than trammel their usefulness by indirect taxation; and that the least, which, in my judgment, the appreciative Members of the Tsung-li Ya-mên who, in their "overpowering distress and anxiety" of mind, give "day and night most earnest thought" to the welfare of the people, can do in this little matter is, to agree to the abolition of the small native transit-dues, alone justly leviable on the Chinese coast-trade, for foreign steamers and vessels altogether.

The Commissioner of Customs at Shanghai, Mr. Dick, also is much of the same opinion. He observes, in part very pertinently:—"The taxes which we collect under this mistaken application of the Foreign Tariff are levied, at the ports of shipment and discharge, on goods which are taxed up to the time of their shipment, and from the time of their discharge, in the interior and also at the ports, by the provincial authorities, under circumstances which cannot be brought within the scope of Treaties." But Mr. Dick proceeds to say:—"I, therefore, advocate the withdrawal of the department [of "Chinese Imperial Maritime Customs"] from its connexion with the Home trade carried on in Foreign vessels, and the limitation of its work to Import and Export Duties, Transit-dues, and Tonnage-dues, (leaving it to Chinese officials to collect the duties, according to Chinese rates, on Chinese produce carried for home consumption in Foreign vessels)." I know not by what right and with what propriety a Foreign subordinate Customs' official of the Chinese, who seems, moreover, to identify himself with the Chinese nation, can speak of, and recommend to another foreign employé in the same service, though *his* superior, the "*withdrawal* of the department § from its connection with the Home trade," or, as a British subject, ignore and of his own authority set aside regulations, agreed upon by the British Representative in Peking with the Tsung-li Ya-mên, and approved by Her Britannic Majesty's Government. The assumption of Imperial airs would seem to have proved infectious in "the department." Are not the Transit-dues,—native inland charges on inland trade, in the payment of which uncertificated, and even certificated, "foreign-owned" goods are privileged to participate on a most liberal scale,—connected with the "Home" trade? Are not the inland taxes on opium so? Are the *le-kin*, *chow-fang*, the Grower's tax, and similar imposts, as levied upon Foreign trade, *lawful* imposts? Mr. Dick's remarks were made *à propos* of "the proper work of the Foreign Customs;" and "believing in regard to Home trade their position"—his remarks are addressed to the Inspector-General, Mr. Hart—"to be the result of accident rather than of special consideration," he is of opinion, that the work in question should be determined by, and restricted to the collection of duties on, *the foreign produce* and *produce intended for foreign consumption*, in which trade is carried on, whether in foreign or native vessels. I am unable to concur in that opinion. In China, possessing no native vessels to transmit even her own produce to Western ports, the distinctive feature of Foreign Trade consists in its being carried on in foreign vessels. At any rate, the idea of con-

§ That not, as might possibly be conceived, the department of the Collection of Coast-trade Dues is meant, and the term "withdrawal" to be taken in a passive sense, the marginal indication shows. It reads:—"Withdrawal of the Department from the collection of duties on native trade, recommended."

signing a foreign coasting-steamer, laden with native and foreign goods, for the collection of differential duties and clearance, to two distinct Custom-houses—a foreign and a *native* one,—appears to me so utterly unpractical, as to utterly condemn itself.¶ The more satisfactory solution of the problem will after all, I incline to think, be the one just proposed by me, and presents the greater a claim, perhaps, to the favourable consideration of the Tsung-li Yamên, as it tends to avert the threatening calamity of "the withdrawal of the department from its connexion with the home trade, carried on in foreign vessels."

Although the foreign coast-trade duties, then, cannot be designated as illegal in the strict sense of the term, and constitute but an *indirect* tax upon foreign shipping: yet, they are not only unjust in themselves, but also at positive variance with existing Treaty-stipulations, and Sir Frederick Bruce had no right or authority to grant such a concession. They may, therefore, not unfairly be added to the charges, which are by the Chinese Government levied upon Foreign Trade contrary to Treaties. The amount of these duties, collected in 1870, is by the Inspector-General returned, *by estimate*, at only Tls. 1,347,642. I have elsewhere shown, that the approximate real amount appears to have been at least Tls. 1,884,188; while in 1871, instead of Tls. 1,138,116, a sum at least of Tls. 1,975,015 should apparently have been returned*. Hence, the item may now be taken at about £600,000 *per annum*, instead of upwards of Tls. 1,500,000, as given some years ago, by Mr. Dick.

¶ Or can the Commissioner of Customs at Shanghai have anticipated the Inspector-General's prophetic enunciation, alluded to in a preceding note, and wished to contribute his mite towards the fulfilment?

* See the pamphlet on the Returns of Trade, quoted in a former page.

The entire annual amount of illegal and undue taxation, to which Foreign Trade is at present subject in China, may consequently be estimated, in round numbers, as follows :—

On a total value of £31,558,600 (representing in 1870, the value of the foreign trade in imports and exports—£39,291,860, less the value of opium—£7,733,260) at about 10·4 per cent., according to the details of the table p. 313 ....£3,283,000
Additional 6 per cent 1,894,000

Together £5,177,000
Coast-trade dues 600,000

Sum total *per annum* ....£5,777,000.

This is independently of a yearly sum of nearly £400,000, which the Chinese Government profits by an excess of duty of about 1 per cent on the whole import- and export-trade, —almost exclusively on the latter—, actually levied over and above the mean rate of 5 per cent. *ad valorem*, contemplated by Treaty.

The "additional 6 per cent" represent the amount of illegal taxes, levied on merchandise transiting into a second or third province, whether from the importing or the producing province, and are arrived at by deducting the mean tariff import- and export-duty of about 6 per cent, the commutation-tax or half-duty of about 3 per cent, and the tabular duty of about 10 per cent, already taken into account, together—19 per cent, from the aggregate of duties levied, viz., 25 per cent, although that aggregate more probably amounts to about 30 per cent, *ad valorem*. The resulting proportion, however, is a not unlikely one and, certainly, the same as the total amount of illegal taxation thus arrived at, keeps *below the truth*,—in all probability *considerably* below the truth.

One might have hesitated in concluding, that on exports also the full mean rate of the *le-kin* charges should have been imposed by the Chinese Government, if we had not, independently of the positive statement of the Chinese merchants, the unimpeachable authority of the Inspector-General, the Tau-tai and Intendant of Customs at Shanghai, and the Tsung-li Ya-mên for the fact,—intimating as they do in distinct reference to the inland charges on Exports, that the duties and the *li-kin*, payable *on the road* from the Interior to the port of shipment, amount to "ten times the half-duty," i.e. to about 30 per cent., independently of export-duty. This leaves, and can leave, no room for reasonable doubt. I may as well, however, take this opportunity to explain once more, that the impression, so general among foreigners, as to the poverty of the Chinese Exchequer and the extreme importance to the Government of the few million sterling, annually collected by the Foreign Branch of Maritime Customs, is utterly devoid of foundation. For obvious reasons, it suits the Tsung-li Ya-mên to plead such a state of matters, and through its agents to spread the fiction abroad. At a time when, as Mr. Wade gave Her Britannic Majesty's Government to understand, the Chinese Imperial Court and Household were almost dependent on the Foreign Inspector-General for their means of subsistence, there were lying in the Palace itself silver bars to the value of a couple of million pounds sterling, *untouched since the days of the Ming*. I have already stated, that the Chinese Government can afford to devote, and almost exclusively devotes, the whole of the revenue derived from foreign trade, to anti-foreign objects.

Now, the whole Foreign Commerce of China, in 1870, was thus repartitioned:—

Country.	Value of Imports.	Value of Exports.	Total.	Per cent of whole Trade.
British Dominions	£ 18,680,000	£ 12,820,000	£ 31,500,000	80
United States	125,000	2,550,000	2,675,000	7
Japan	430,000	828,000	1,258,000	3
Continent of Europe	156,000	924,000	1,080,000	3
Russia	32,000	280,000	312,000	1
Diverse Countries	1,377,000	1,098,000	2,475,000	6
	£ 20,800,000	£ 18,500,000	£ 39,300,000	

Hence, the amount of illegal and undue imposts, now yearly levied by China, contrary to Treaty, upon *British* trade alone, reaches a *minimum* of

£4,500,000:

say, *Four and a half million pounds sterling per annum.*

To an at first moderate extent, but on a rapidly increasing scale, this taxation, or rather this international process of robbery on the part of the Chinese Government, has been systematically carried on ever since the conclusion of the Treaty of Nanking, and more especially so since the ratification of the Treaty of Tientsin. After a careful consideration of the subject, I find that the accumulated sum, exclusive of interest, and *not* taking the Coast-trade dues into account, for which China has thus incurred an indisputable debt to England, may be estimated at

£25,000,000:

say, *Five and twenty million pounds sterling.* There is hardly occasion to calculate what this sum would be, on the coming day of international reckoning between her and China, if England were to claim it with compound interest. Let it meanwhile, however, be borne in mind, that the Western

Powers are now allowing the debt of China to increase, year by year, at the rate of nearly six million pounds sterling; and that the debt is neither an honest debt, nor a debt incurred for honest purposes.

VIII.

CONCLUSION.

Law, Morality, and Expediency.—The principle of "Free Transit through China" shown to rest on both human law and divine.—War a necessary factor of progress, development and civilisation in the economy of nature and human destiny.—The morality of the Opium Trade, and the justice of the stipulations of the Treaty of Tientsin vindicated.—Politico-social state of England.—Conflict between Labor and Capital.—Necessity of finding wider employment for home Labor.—Obstructive policy of the Tsung-li Ya-mên. —Expansibility of the China Trade.—Actual state of affairs.—Warning to the Manchu Government.

Having from the outset taken up my standpoint on the ground of existing International Treaties, it will have been noticed that I have throughout these pages adhered to it, and, simply insisting on the fulfilment of, and judging the commercial policy and action of the Chinese Government by, their clear provisions, excluded every discussion of subjects, not affecting or reaching beyond the actual and indubitable rights of the foreign merchant. My argument, therefore, may be considered as resting on a strictly legal basis. But there are those, both at home and abroad, who would have the Treaties themselves weighed in the scale of morality, or who, like Her Britannic Majesty's Board of Trade, in defiance of the one and in disregard of the other view, place their interpretation and execution on the hollow and dangerous principle of expediency. To enter here into a full consideration of the two antagonistic opinions would be out of place. At the same time I cannot well pass them altogether over in silence.

The moralèstic argument assumes the good old maxim that "an Englishman's house is his castle" to be as applicable to nations as it is to individuals; and contends that the Governments of the Chinese, the Coreans, and other semi-barbarous or barbarous peoples, had and have as much right to shut, if such be their will and pleasure, the doors of their respective States against foreign intrusion, as the Briton has to shut the door of his own private dwelling against whomsoever and whatsoever he may deem fit or proper. This is a fundamental error.

In the first place: according to the doctrine of modern times, the Government of a country is but the executive of the nation, and the sovereign or chief magistrate but the first servant of the people. Hence, if a people desire to hold commercial intercourse with other peoples,—and the Chinese unquestionably do desire this,—its Government cannot lawfully oppose itself to such an intercourse, nor subject it to obstructive regulations and conditions, which shall practically have, or tend to, the same effect. I mean by the term "unlawfully" here: in accordance with a principle of international law involved in the doctrine referred to, whether that principle be as yet recognised or not.

But what is, in the second place, of far greater importance: the Earth was not portioned out by God to such and such races, much less to such and such dynasties, to hold as their own personal property. The Earth, remaining God's, was given to *man*, and in lease only. Few, if any, of the primitive races survive. The more or less civilised nations of the present day, without exception, hold their territorial leases by virtue of conquest and war. War and conquest, indeed, must be accepted as two great and necessary factors of progress, development, and civilisation, in the divine economy of nature and human destiny. There lies, in an *international* sense, a deep moral and religious truth at the bottom of the proverbial saying that "Might is Right."

No savage tribe has ever claimed a larger portion of the Earth's surface than, by right of possession, it actually occupied and deemed necessary for the sustenance, the protection, and the safety of the community: individual possession, within the community and subject to its own particular laws, being invested by those laws and relative to the community, with the character of private property; while mountains and rivers, prairies and forests, highways and byways, in short the soil itself together with its natural productions, continued to be regarded as a leasehold, by the Great Spirit bestowed upon the tribe for the use and benefit of all. Among civilised nations private property has vastly extended its domain. Still, as it includes neither the oceans nor the air, so it includes as yet neither rivers nor mountains, neither highways nor byways; and every civilised people of the present day,—recognising, whether consciously or not, the great principle that "the Earth is the Lord's" and by Him given to *man*—freely throws open that portion of its territorial possessions, to which under its own laws the public rights extend, equally to the foreigner and the native for the purposes of commerce, science, instruction, and all other peaceful, and legitimate pursuits.

It may, therefore, be regarded and laid down as a fundamental maxim of International Law, that, except in times of war, the people of every country have the natural and incontestible right of free access,—for the purposes stated, and subject to the particular laws of each country, provided the latter are based on received principles of justice and humanity, and afford due and efficient protection to the foreigner,—not only to the harbours and frontier-places, but by all public ways of communication available for the native,—lakes, rivers, canals, highroads and byroads,—to the whole Interior of every other country; and furthermore that, in the event of the Government of one people denying this natural right to another people, the Government of the latter is justified to enforce it by war and, if necessary, by conquest.

Touching the bearing of these maxims upon China, I will not urge that the Chinese Government professes to have recently entered the comity of civilized nations, and accepted their principles of International Law. That Government has ever held as a fundamental doctrine, that all the peoples of the Earth constitute but *one single household*, under Heaven and the autocracy of Heaven's Vice-gerent, whom we of "the Outer States" are wont to call "the Emperor of China." It is plain, therefore, that consistently with justice and reason no portion of such a household can be excluded from the enjoyment of its common rights and privileges; and, hence, that the Chinese Government at no time or period had, either according to its own doctrines or to Western principles of International Law, due authority to interdict to the peoples of England and other Outer States, "being members of one family," free access to the ports and, by the public highways, to the Interior of the Central Lands, *i.e.* Chinese, for the peaceful and legitimate purposes of trade and commerce.

The Chinese Government, however, did interdict to British merchants and others all and every access to the Interior of the country, and, aggravating what of itself constituted and should have been insisted on as a *casus belli*, by additional outrages, provoked the first war of 1842 with England. It is called "the first Opium war," because opium entered as an element into it; and this is a further reason, on the ground of which our moralists deprecate or condemn that war, and consequently impugn, moreover, the strict justice of the provisions of the Treaty of Nanking it imposed on the Chinese Government; while they take a similar view of the second war of 1859-60, and the provisions of the Treaty of Tientsin.

The argument in this case is made to rest on "the immorality of the opium trade," and is as devoid of foundation as we have found the argument relative to the presumed right of the territorial exclusion to be. The latter is based on an imagined analogy, which has no existence; the former confounds individual abuse of one of the gifts of God with the gift itself, and characterises it by the effects of that abuse. Sam-shu is prepared from the rice-plant, opium from the poppy. Both preparations, *when taken in excess*, are equally intoxicating and injurious. But so are Guinness's Stout and Bass's Ale. The Tatar Government has, for the reason named, no better right to prohibit even to its own subjects the cultivation of the poppy, than it has to prohibit to them the cultivation of the rice-plant or than the English Government has to prohibit to *its* subjects the growing of hops and the sowing of barley. Besides which, the Chinese Government is as powerless to prevent the people of China from smoking their own opium, as it is to prevent them from drinking their own sam-shu. Nor is it more willing, than it is powerless, to do so. For the Tsung-li Ya-mên, under these circumstances, to demand from the British Government the prohibition of opium-farming in India is hardly less preposterous, than it would be for the British Government to listen to such a demand. For any British subject to support the latter, appears to me scarcely more loyal than it is rational; the true object of the Tsung-li Ya-mên, as previously explained, being transparent. In short: the cultivation of the poppy, undoubtedly, constitutes as moral and legitimate a branch of Indian industry, as the cultivation of the vine, undoubtedly, constitutes a moral and legitimate branch of the industry of Spain, of France, of Germany, and other Christian countries; and the trade in opium is as moral and honorable, as is the trade in wines or any other articles of consumption, by God destined for the use or the solace of man.

In whatever light, however, this question may be regarded by religionistic enthusiasts or dreamers, the essential fact remains that opium became incidentally only, and as a secondary element, mixed up with the great principle of International Law, the breach of which on the part of China led to the first war between her and England, and to vindicate which was its paramount object; the same as it constituted that of the succeeding war, provoked and necessitated by China also. Nor were the conditions, imposed by the victors, in any way onerous or unjust. On the contrary: taking them all in all, they were considerate and lenient to a degree;—the palpable proof of which is, that, as has been already observed, the Chinese Government has since, of its own free will and accord, granted the same conditions to other nations, desirous of entering into diplomatic relations with the Court of Peking. Whether in a divine or in a human sense, therefore, both the Treaties of Nanking and Tientsin and the wars undertaken to secure their provisions, will bear being weighed in the most sensitive balance of morality as well as of justice; and there exist, so far as I can see, no tenable reasons whatsoever why, on this score, either the spirit or the letter of those provisions should be departed from or relaxed in any way.

Such being the case, the plea of *expediency* to this effect falls of itself to the ground. Except from impotence to protest, it can under no circumstances be expedient for a British or any other Government to sacrifice national rights once justly acquired. When, under the Gladstone Administration, the Lords of the Committee of Her Britannic Majesty's Privy Council for Trade, in reference to "the view expressed in some of the Memorials (of China merchants) and even at one time by Sir R. Alcock himself, *viz.*, that the payment of the transit-dues ought to be held to exempt the goods upon which it has been paid from all subsequent internal taxation," deliberately declare, that "there is nothing in the terms of the Treaty (of Tientsin) which appears to their Lordships to justify such a sweeping demand," and that "in view of the internal taxation to which native goods are subject in China, it would be in their opinion both unjust and inexpedient to enforce such a demand, *even if it were warranted by the terms of Treaty stipulations*": their Lordships not only betray a want of sound judgment and a degree of unacquaintance both with the Treaties to which they refer and the state of inland taxation in China on which they rest their argument, truly to be lamented; but they enounce also a new principle of British policy, fatal in itself, and which, if carried out and persisted in, must lead to the ruin of diplomacy and international faith, as well as of Commerce. Their Lordships, under the combined influence of Mr. Wade's strongly biassed opinions and advice, and the unreasonable dread of another war with China, failed to take into consideration, that the surest way to induce and finally bring about such a war is to suffer the foundations, on which peace has been laid, to be broken through; that, without a most faithful observance and the strictest maintenance of Treaty-stipulations, Treaties themselves become a mere farce; that, on their faith in those Treaty-stipulations and in the will and power of the British Government to uphold them, British merchants had invested and invest millions of British money in the China trade, that a British Government who, under the pretext of expediency or any other pretext, decline or evade the responsibility of maintaining Treaty-stipulations, involving large commercial and industrial British interests, break faith with the nation; that a British Board of Trade who, whether in explicit terms or by implication, stigmatise a recent war carried on by England as an unjust war, act, to say the least, with extreme indecorum both towards the nation and the Imperial Government; and that a British Government, who, whether directly or indirectly, repudiate or abandon without cause important stipulations of existing international Treaties, which have been sealed by the blood and the treasure of the British people expended in two wars, betray at once the people and the trust by the people reposed in them. Finally, their Lordships would seem to have entertained not even a suspicion of the vital principle, involved in the wars to which I have just alluded, and, in its practical application, commonly embodied in the sentence: *Free transit through China.*

To carry this principle into effect was, as has been previously shown, the main object of both the Treaties of Nanking and Tientsin; and unless it be in future firmly upheld and strictly enforced, England will have the choice only between two alternatives, *viz., decennial wars with China* or *the gradual abandonment of the China trade.** .

Nor is the question one of trade only. For, what lends to the various matters, discussed in the preceding pages, an importance far beyond the commercial interests involved, is the actual politico-social state of England. That state is not a satisfactory one. Capital and Labour have in our time wonderfully increased; and Competition, stepping in between them, has turned, and is turning, the scale against Labour at home, and, consequent on the resulting discontent and frequent "strikes," somewhat against both home-Labour and home-Capital abroad. Hence, in combination with other causes, the unsatisfactory state referred to. Whilst Capital is looking for new markets and outlets with a view to the remunerative employment of Labour, the worse fractions of Labour are directing their attention to the doctrines of communistic Republicanism; the better and preponderating elements are fixing their thoughts on Emigration. The common tendencies of Labour thus unite in endangering, in presence of the growing strength of Continental competition, the very supremacy of England's manufacturing power, as one of the chief sources of her wealth; and unless, under these circumstances, the private enterprise of Capital be supported in time, by the public policy of the Government, and a due harmony of views and

* The Inspector-General, Mr. Hart, in predicting this gradual abandonment, would seem to have calculated on what appears to be the confirmed sleepiness of the British Lion, and to look upon another war between England and China as a mere parenthetical possibility. (See the note to p. 392 above). But let China not deceive herself. The present unsettled state of Europe, to which alone she has been thus far indebted for immunity, will come to an end.

action be restored between Capital and Labour, between Labour and Capital: who would pretend to foresee the consequences, to which a permanent and widening breach between these two great sinews of national prosperity might ultimately lead? Modern as well as Ancient History furnishes its warnings.

Regarded from this stand-point, "what is called 'opening up' China to foreign trade,"—to use a slightly sarcastic expression of the Lords of the Committee of Her Britannic Majesty's Privy Council for Trade,—appears to me not only to merit in the highest degree, but to imperatively claim, the serious attention of the English Government. And when their Lordships, in alluding to the possible contingency of "a more vigorous policy" resulting in war,—which a weak and yielding policy is *certain* to do,—observe:—"they cannot forget....that the responsibilities and sacrifices, involved in the exercise of force, must fall upon the British nation, and not upon that section of its people, which is engaged in the trade with China": I am unable to concur in a narrow and sectarian view of national constitutionalism and economy, which, denying the very foundation on which a State is built,—the unity of interests,—must, if it were generally adopted, lead to the rapid dissolution and the ruin of any commonwealth. The one thing above all others to be recollected and borne in mind is that, under Providence, England is for her actual prosperity and power mainly indebted to her Commerce and Industry; and that the interests of British Industry and Commerce are, and so long as England's power and prosperity are to endure, ever will be, identical with those of the British nation.

China, it is true, has disappointed the great expectations held out to British manufacturers at the close of the first war, and she has not realized those entertained at the termination of the last one. But the cause remains now a mystery no longer. It has not to be sought in the absence of almost unlimited capabilities and resources of the China trade, but in the persistent obstructiveness and bad faith of the Chinese Government, in opposition to the wishes of the Chinese people. In short: the non-fulfilment of those expectations may be traced to the one single fact, that the indispensable condition of their realisation, *free transit through the Interior*,—established, as the fundamental principle of future intercourse with China, in the Treaty of Nan-king and upheld in the Treaty of Tien-tsin,—has never been honestly carried into effect. The means, employed by the Chinese Government thus to frustrate the main object of both Treaties and of two Wars have been, on the hand, deceit and cunning; on the other, secret prohibition, overburdensome taxation, and vexatious impediment. The special circumstances, which not only have enabled the Tsung-li Yamên to pursue a course at once so dishonest and so fatal to British and Foreign interests, but have facilitated its execution have been:—the sectarian, feeble and unnational policy of the Gladstone Administration; the incapacity, supineness, or subserviency of the Representatives of England at Peking, whom the British Government has seen fit to appoint to that responsible post, and to entrust with the Chief Superintendence of British Trade in China, since the ratification of the Treaty of Tientsin; the swerving, as previously explained, from the principle of free transit, in the practical Trade-Rules of the Supplementary Treaty of Shanghai; the mysterious and underhand consent, given, apparently on the part of England, to the imposition of the *le-kin* tax; the indirect but misdirected aid, which the Tsung-li Yamên has received from the Foreign Customs' Department, notably from the Inspector-General and the Commissioner of Customs at Shanghai, in carrying out its obstructive measures; the state of the Interior of China, which subjects the traveller not only to much privation, hardship, and fatigue, but to a great sacrifice of valuable time; the next to insuperable difficulties of the Chinese language and its numerous dialects, rendering the foreign merchant dependent on his incompetent and untrustworthy native interpreter; and, finally, the extreme unwillingness of *all* Chinamen to give information, more especially correct information, to an "outer barbarian."

It is *notwithstanding* the serious obstacles to trade, thus interposed, and interposing themselves, between the British manufacturer and the Chinese consumer, that the imports from the United Kingdom into China have, since the conclusion of the last war, continued steadily on the increase. The value of the *direct* imports alone, according to the Returns of Trade, published by order of the Inspector-General, was in round numbers:—

1864.	1865.	1866.	1867.	1868.	1869.	1870.	1871.	1872.
£3,495,900	£3,719,000	£4,700,000	£5,647,000	£7,344,000	£8,361,000	£8,087,000	£8,746,000	£8,755,761

This progressive increase, however, satisfactory as it is, affords no indication of the *capabilities* of the China trade for extension, as regards the staple-articles of British manufacture. Some idea of the latter may be derived from a comparison of certain of the principal imports into Chinkiang from 1866 to 1872. They were:—

		1866.	1867.	1868.	1869.	1870.	1871.	1872.
Grey Shirtings............	Pieces	14,384	45,650	174,780	415,094	553,023	760,271	1,028,705
White "	"	1,466	5,069	10,250	15,550	18,544	23,278	24,214
T-Cloths..................	"	1,539	10,847	37,667	147,720	236,801	309,068	382,097
Cottons, assorted..........	"	1,938	15,708	30,602	53,019	100,910	124,399	180,824
Woollen Goods............	"	4,364	9,082	22,440	36,884	65,403	57,736	68,921
Iron—Nail Rod	Piculs	5,014	2,899	8,731	15,545	28,293	44,099	42,751
Foreign Brown Sugar	"	8,976	17,372	27,221	60,503	99,489	169,531	169,386
" White............	"	2,909	8,664	14,719	33,346	61,699	115,618	101,970

That is to say, in the short space of half-a-dozen years the importation into Chinkiang of Grey Shirtings had in 1872 as compared with 1866, increased 71½ times; that of White Shirtings 16½ times; of T-Cloths 248 times; of Cotton goods assorted 93 times; and of Woollen goods 16 times. The importation of Rod and Nail Iron also had, during the same period, augmented 8½ times; that of Foreign Brown Sugar 19 times; and of White Sugar 35 times.

Now, when we inquire into the causes of this remarkable expansion of trade in British manufactures at one of the minor ports of the Yang-tse, which only commands the markets of limited districts within the Provinces of the Two Kiang: they are found to consist in the simple fact, that the merchants at Chinkiang, more and more strictly adhering to the inland charges commutation-clause of Art. xxviii of the Treaty of Tien-tsin as finally determined by Rule vii of the Supplementary Treaty of Shanghai, have to the Chinese trader sold their goods "deliverable" at the various inland marts, paid upon them the commuted transit-dues, and forwarded the merchandise under certificate to its destination. Whilst of foreign imports at large, the proportion of goods, sent into the Interior under certificate, did not, as has been previously shown, in 1870 reach 3 per cent., this proportion is for Chinkiang as follows:—

		1867.	1868.	1869.	1870.
Cotton Piece Goods	per cent.	3·1	32·8	70·2	73·6
Woollen "	"	0·3	12·4	30·2	42·0
Foreign Sugar	"	0·0	24·1	90·0	99·5
Other Foreign Goods	"	4·0	17·1	38·0	40·8
Total Imports per cent.		2·0	25·5	64·5	70·2

Touching the balance of per-centage for the latter two years, it is pretty well accounted for by the quantities remaining in stock, or taken for local consumption and dyeing purposes, for military use free of duty, etc., respectively; so that, at

Chin-kiang, the commutation-principle of RULE vii may be regarded as in full operation, or nearly so. The certificates, therefore, were in those parts, generally at least, respected *in transitu;* while it must needs be inferred from the trade itself, that both to the intermediary native merchant and the inland retail-trader the business is a profitable one; and that the latter either finds means to evade the collection of heavy-stationary trade dues, *or that he can afford to pay them.*

The progressive, and in degree exceptional, development at Chinkiang of the trade in, and the corresponding inland consumption of, British manufactures almost in the direct proportion in which the commutation-principle is applied, leaves no room for doubt as to the nature of the connection between the two phenomena being that of cause and effect. I have had occasion more than once to point out the perfidious object of the Tsung-li Ya-mên and the Chinese Provincial Authorities, assisted by the Foreign Customs-officials, in obstructing by every means at their command the fair execution of the commutation-clause of RULE vii of the Trade Rules attached to the Treaty of Tien-tsin; in leading the mercantile community, misdirected by Sir Frederick Bruce's Notification of October, 1861, to hold to the validity and supposed advantages of the *optional* clause of ART. xxviii of the Treaty itself; and in withholding for years the exercise of his undoubted right to convey under certificate, foreign goods being his own or *Chinese* property generally, from the native trader. The Chinkiang statistics, here adduced, have now placed the object, referred to, in a light, which must exclude every further uncertainty on the subject.

Although unable to complete the preceding statement for the years 1871 and 1872, no corresponding returns having as yet been published, I will subjoin, in reference to the principal articles first enumerated, a comparative table of the quantities imported into Chinkiang and sent inland under transit-passes during the two years in question and the following year 1873 :—

Description of Goods.	1871.			1872.			1873.		
	Quantities.		Per cent.	Quantities.		Per cent.	Quantities.		Per cent.
	Imported.	Sent inland under transit-pass.		Imported.	Sent inland under transit-pass.		Imported.	Sent inland under transit-pass.	
Grey Shirtings..Pcs.	760,271	647,280	85·14	1,[illegible]2[illegible],705	876,660	85·22	704,408	598,499	84·97
White " .. "	23,278	14,160	60·80	24,214	18,953	78·27	23,396	17,755	75·89
T-Cloths ...... "	309,068	232,034	75·07	382,097	307,759	80·55	231,333	192,396	83·17
Cottons, assorted "	50,268	18,991	37·78	73,041	24,949	34·24	68,304	25,260	36·98
Woollen Goods.. "	54,268	30,461	56·13	69,493	36,550	52·60	58,097	27,280	46·96
Iron, Nail, Rod...Pls.	44,323	29,641	66·88	42,750	30,445	71·22	42,685	31,187	73·06
Foreign Sugar.. "	285,150	266,093	93·32	267,832	290,570	108·49	261,998	259,444	99·14

The conclusion to be drawn from this table is, either that the mean of the quantities of each description of goods, imported into Chinkiang during the last three years, constitutes approximately the maximum of trade, for which that port offers at present outlets, or, what appears more probable, that in 1871 the Chinese Authorities had established a sufficient number of *li-kin* barriers along the new line of traffic to check its further growth, and that the trade in that direction is about to decline.

Under any circumstances, we gain from the preceding statistics a full confirmation of the result previously arrived at, namely: that the comparative stagnation of the China trade in British and Foreign manufactures has been *solely owing to the obstructiveness and the bad faith of the Chinese Government;* while they illustrate and prove to evidence the, to England far more important fact, that at least this particular branch of the trade *is capable of a general expansion, corresponding to the expansion which it had undergone at Chin-*

kiang during seven successive years: in other words, that *China presents to the Foreign manufacturer, and more particularly to the manufacturer of England, a field of enterprise, compared with which the similar field of her Indian Possessions sinks into insignificance.* If we take the value of the present consumption of English staple manufactures in China only at £10,000,000, which is considerably below the truth, and apply to it but half the degree, or less, of that expansibility of which the experience of Chinkiang has actually proved it to be susceptible: there presents itself, even under the provisions of existing Treaties, the sober and certainly not exaggerated prospect of the value of that consumption coming to reach, within a decennium, an annual total of from £60,000,000 to £80,000,000 sterling,—provided that the principle of *free transit through China* be honestly carried into effect, and the mineral resources of the country be sufficiently developed to keep the "balance of trade" in a state of due equilibrium. Nor does such an increase of consumption offer anything very surprising, much less incredible, in itself. Let it be remembered that the population of China embraces nearly "one-third of the human race," *i.e.* amounts to between 300,000,000 and 400,000,000, exceeding ten times the population of the United Kingdom; that, *generally* speaking, the bulk of the people are thriving and well to do; that cotton fabrics almost exclusively serve them for the indispensable article of clothing; and that the sum in question, after all, represents yearly wants, in the matter of one of the first necessaries of non-savage life, to the extent of barely 5s. per head, whereas in Great Britain, a larger sum per head is annually expended upon a single article of luxury,—tea.

Considering, then, on the one hand, the actual condition

of England, necessitating the finding of additional employment for Labor at home, and new markets for her staple manufactures abroad; and, on the other hand, the vast consuming power of China for these very manufactures: there are, in my judgment, few objects more deserving of the earnest attention of the British Government, as well as of Parliament, and the various Chambers of Commerce throughout the United Kingdom, than are the Treaty-rights of the Foreign and British Merchant, and the Transit-System, in China, as exposed in the preceeding sections of this essay. Her Britannic Majesty's Government will not only have to take into consideration the large pecuniary debt, accumulating from year to year, which China has surreptitiously contracted, and is going on so to contract, towards England; together with the heavy amount of annual taxation, with and by which the Chinese Government, in open and systematic violation of international Treaty-engagements, continues to burden and obstruct British Trade: but also the perfidious manner in which this unlawful system of taxation has been introduced, extended, and enforced; and the hostile purposes, to which its product has been, and is being, applied. That England should, by mere want of good faith, have been deprived of the fruits of two wars; that her home Labour should have been defrauded of employment for its energies; and that British Commerce in China should have been made, and be made, to contribute six million pounds a year towards effecting its own ruin, because of the incapacity of Sir R. Alcock and Mr. Wade, seems hard; but that the Chinese Government should tax, and thus tax, England, for the main, if not sole purpose of providing military preparations and armaments to be directed against herself appears simply intolerable. No British Ministry could, without betraying the best interests of the country, allow such a state of things to endure; even though Tatar conceit and perverseness render another war unavoidable,—a war, which would, not only on the part of England be a just war, but might be so directed and conducted as to impart to it a character highly popular with the Chinese people; which would involve but a small sacrifice of human life; the cost of which China herself would be able to bear without difficulty; and which would place British relations with the Chinese Empire, both politically and commercially, on an entirely new, and for the first time on a solid, basis, —open up to Western enterprise and industry a field of surpassing vastness, and confer upon the millions of the population of China the benefits and blessings of Prosperity, Freedom, and Civilisation.

But, is not the very prospect of such a war in the highest degree calculated to suggest to *the Government of China* reflections, tending to avert its necessity without the sacrifice of its objects,—reflections of the gravest nature? Let the Tsung-li Ya-mên for once shut its ear to the flattering but deceptive whisperings of an ambitious, selfish, Burlingame Missions- and Hongkong Claims-planning faction, and listen to the clear voice of well-meaning though plain-spoken Reason, of honest though unpalatable Truth. England cannot afford, nor is she willing, to carry on, with a treacherous Government, a distant war every decennium. If a new contest be forced upon her, its aim will involve, and must needs lead to, great and permanent changes in China. They might, and probably would, include—a change of dynasty. There exist elements within the Ta-Ching Dominions which, on such a basis, promise to render easy a satisfactory settlement of pending questions. Let not the Manchu

Government imagine, that it is strong enough to resist the power of England or any other Western State: its armies would be swept away like dust before the hurricane. Let not the Imperial Court indulge in the idle dream that, if Peking afford no safety, safety will be found in Jehol or Moukden: not all the lands "within the Four Seas" would offer a secure refuge from the fate invoked. Let not His Imperial Highness, Prince Kung, and his Colleagues delude themselves with the idea, that it will be time enough to yield when another British Army shall be at the gates of Capital: "Too late!" would then be the only answer vouchsafed. "We come, not to negotiate and to discuss; but *to settle the future of China.*"

A great and long-delayed crisis in the affairs of this ancient Monarchy is at hand. Every well-wisher and true friend of the Reigning Dynasty and the child-Emperor, must counsel them most earnestly, in the interest of peace, to abandon principles belonging to the past and no longer acceptable to the world at large. The Western Powers have no wish for either war or conquest in China. They desire nothing but what will be conducive to the well-being of the Chinese people; nothing but what is consistent with the dignity and the sovereign-rights of the Imperial Government; nothing but what is just and honourable for one independent State to demand, and honourable and just for another independent State to concede. But they will no longer suffer the Sovereign of China to assume, even in name, the Autocracy of the Earth, nor hold diplomatic relations with his Government, save by direct intercourse, and on a footing of equality formally acknowledged. They are—appearances notwithstanding—prepared to enforce the due observance of existing Treaties; to demand material guarantees for that observance, in order to prevent the necessity for future war; and, if necessary, to effect this object, equally desirable for China and the West, by placing a Chinese Dynasty on the Chinese Throne.

Such, if I mistake not, is, essentially, the position of affairs. Let, then, the Emperor and his Government weigh and ponder its contingencies well; and, thereupon, elect—Peace or War. If, bent on their destruction, they should decide upon war: let them at least so conduct it as to secure for themselves some claims to the generosity of the victor. Let them dismiss from their policy and their minds alike, all ideas of a renewal of "the Plot of the Summer-Solstice:" every thought of massacre and poisoning; the last hope of expelling the outer barbarian from "the bayonet-ploughed soil of Cathay." True, they might, and probably would, succeed in momentarily exciting the worst passions of the worst classes of the population against the foreigner, and cause the as yet unavenged international crime of Tientsin to be repeated on an extensive scale. But a fearful retribution would follow quickly upon the deed of blood. The cities and localities of murder and atrocity would be razed to the ground, as was the Yüen-ming-yüen; the guilty, whether coolies of the lowest order, or officials of the highest degree, in any way implicated in the crime, would be blown away from the cannon's mouth;—the hatred of the people of 'Han, ready to burst forth, under the shield of Superior Force, into a consuming fire, would be roused against the Tatar intruder; and few Manchu would, within the once Ta-Ching Dominions, survive to tell the tale of the extinction of their race.

If, guided by wisdom and the true interests of China and their own, the Emperor and his Government decide in favour of peace: let them at once, honestly and unreservedly, enter upon a path of well-considered, moderate, and gradual Progress, cease to waste the public revenue upon useless armaments, and devote it to the improvement of the means of communication, and the development of the internal resources of the country: discharge their foreign confidential advisers,—who, from their ignorance of Western politics and State affairs, if for no other reasons, are wholly incompetent to advise;—and trust for information and counsel to the Representatives of allied States. And, as an earnest of their good faith, let them formally resign into the hands of the Western Sovereigns the hollow title of the Ching Sovereign to Universal Supremacy; accept for "the Central State" the position of one of the Great Powers among the Great Powers of the Earth; and grant to the Ministers, accredited to the Manchu Court, free access to that Court and the Imperial Presence, and to Foreign Commerce,—FREE TRANSIT THROUGH CHINA.

www.ingramcontent.com/pod-product-compliance
Lightning Source LLC
Chambersburg PA
CBHW020536300426
44111CB00008B/687